HEBREW RELIGION

ITS ORIGIN AND DEVELOPMENT

BY

W. O. E. OESTERLEY, D.D., Litt.D. (Camb.)

PROFESSOR OF HEBREW AND OLD TESTAMENT EXEGESIS, KING'S COLLEGE,
UNIVERSITY OF LONDON
EXAMINING CHAPLAIN TO THE BISHOP OF LONDON

AND

THEODORE H. ROBINSON, D.D. (Lond.),
Litt.D. (Camb.)

PROFESSOR OF SEMITIC LANGUAGES, UNIVERSITY COLLEGE, CARDIFF
HON. D.D. (ABERDEEN), HON. D.TH. (HALLE)

LONDON
SOCIETY FOR PROMOTING
CHRISTIAN KNOWLEDGE
LONDON: NORTHUMBERLAND AVENUE, W.C.2

First published . . . 1930
Second Impression . . 1931
Third Impression . . 1933

Printed in Great Britain

HEBREW RELIGION

ITS ORIGIN AND DEVELOPMENT

DEDICATED TO THE MEMORY OF

ARTHUR S. PEAKE

TEACHER, SCHOLAR, FRIEND

CONTENTS

CONTENTS

PART II

ISRAELITE RELIGION

PART III

EARLY JUDAISM

THE PERIOD OF THE EXILE

PREFATORY NOTE

ONE of the important results of the modern study of the Old Testament is the reinterpretation of Israel's religious history. A number of important and valuable works have appeared both in English and in German; our experience, however, in the practical work of teaching has led us to feel that no work hitherto published in English meets the needs of certain types of students; and we believe that there is a large body of general readers who would welcome and profit by a treatment of the subject at once more concise and more extensive than that usually found in English works.

Hebrew Religion, as the study of Semitic Comparative Religion abundantly proves, was very closely related to the religions of all the Semitic nations; indeed, it was made up of elements common to the religion of all early Semites. This being so, a necessary consequence is that for any adequate study of the earlier phases of Hebrew religion this larger area of Semitic belief in general must be taken into consideration.

But as soon as we begin to do this we find that ideas common to early mankind as a whole appear. Therefore we have to go back still earlier and start by considering these, a need soon recognized when, as will be seen, the indubitable marks of them occur in the Old Testament itself.

The first Chapter is devoted to a brief consideration of the earliest stages of religious belief. This is, however, preliminary; we come to grips with our subject in dealing with remnants of animistic conceptions as these appear in the Old Testament : sacred trees, sacred waters, sacred stones, etc. (Chapters II–IV); in each case it seemed advisable for the strengthening of the argument to touch briefly on general Semitic belief concerning the subject under consideration, before coming to the actual Hebrew belief as illustrated in the Old Testament.

b

In Chapter V we deal with Totemism, Taboo, and Ancestor-worship. Chapters VI, VII, and VIII are concerned with the subjects of Demonology, Necromancy, and Magic : these things belong to the background of Hebrew Religion, and their persistence through the subsequent ages shows the hold they had upon many in spite of the general advance in religious thought ; they must therefore be taken into consideration.

The last three Chapters of this Part of our work touch upon the more immediate background of Hebrew Religion. In Chapter IX we draw attention to some of those elements in nomadic belief and practice which continued to play a part after the introduction of Yahweh-worship by Moses ; in Chapter X we consider the subject of the origin of Yahweh-worship among the Hebrews. And, lastly, in Chapter XI we speak of the religious beliefs of the dwellers in Canaan prior to the settlement there of the Israelite tribes ; this, too, had its place in the background of Hebrew Religion, as is amply illustrated in the Old Testament.

The fascinating study of Semitic Religion in its early stages has occupied us for many years ; but the more we learn of it the more do we realize our indebtedness to those who laid the real foundations for its scientific study ; foremost among these are, of course, Baudissin and Robertson Smith, and also, in one particular sphere, Goldziher and Wellhausen. Scholars can never be sufficiently grateful for the brilliant labours of these great investigators. We have made much use in some of our chapters of Robertson Smith's works, and here and there we have quoted him profusely ; but we do not think any apology is needed for this. We should like to express here also our appreciation of the work of Dr. S. A. Cook ; quite apart from other books and articles, his notes in the most recent edition of Robertson Smith's *Religion of the Semites* have been of great value to us. Other scholars to whom we must make our acknowledgements are Buchanan Gray, Frazer, Jastrow, Gressmann, and Nielsen. In the footnotes references to the works of other scholars will be found.

It is against the background dealt with in Part I of our

work that we must study the spiritual history of the
Hebrew people, and in Part II the story is carried down
to the Exile. After a short introduction (Chapter I) we
approach the religion of Israel proper ; this begins with
Moses, and an attempt is made to appraise his work
with special stress on that Covenant which is the *differentia*
of Israel's religion (Chapter II). After a brief sketch of
the religion of Canaan (Chapter III) we note the modifications produced in the religion of Israel by contact with
an agricultural people, and by the consequent change
in the basis of the social and economic order (Chapter IV).
In Chapter V we consider the religion of Israel in the
early monarchy, and in Chapter VI we deal with the
revival of Yahwism in the ninth century. We then
briefly examine the religion of Israel as this appeared
immediately after the time of Jehu (Chapter VII), and this
leads us up to the age of the canonical prophets. Their
general character and teaching are described in Chapter
VIII, while a more detailed study of the eighth-century
prophets is given in Chapter IX, an examination of the
reforms of Josiah in Chapter X, and a study of the seventh-
century prophets in Chapter XI. The way is thus prepared for the further developments which ultimately
resulted in the Judaism which is familiar in New Testament times.

We have to acknowledge the value of work done in
this field by a number of scholars ; references will be
found to their works in the footnotes, but we cannot
refrain from mentioning especially the names of Stade,
Smend, and Marti, to whom all Old Testament scholars
are so deeply indebted.

Then we come to Part III of our work.

The tracing out of religious developments during the
five or six centuries which followed the fall of the kingdom
of Judah is more complicated than in dealing with the
earlier centuries. One of the chief causes of this is the
difficulty in manipulating the material. This difficulty
lies in the fact that while historically there are clearly
defined periods to be taken into consideration—the
Exilic, the Persian, and the Greek—the individual
subjects to be treated cut across the periods. For

example, the Law belongs in a very real sense to the
Exilic and Persian periods, but it goes on developing
through the Greek period and after. Or again, Worship,
with the subject of Pietism, must be treated from the
Exilic period, but the real development runs through
the Persian and Greek periods, and still later, and defies
divided treatment according to periods. The golden
age of Wisdom belongs to the Greek period, but its roots
lie in pre-exilic times ; and, once more, Apocalyptic
belongs properly to *circa* 200 B.C.–A.D. 100 ; this, at any
rate, is when it becomes most prominent ; but it, too,
goes back to pre-exilic times, and its subsequent development was largely due to Persian influence. So that one
cannot deal with all that is embraced within the religion
of the Jews period by period. On the other hand, one
cannot always take an individual religious subject and
trace its development without consideration of the
different periods, because either the subject or its development is bound up with a particular period, which cannot
therefore be ignored.

This difficulty in the manipulation of the subject-
matter is not imaginary, as anybody will find out as
soon as he begins the task of arranging the material
to be dealt with.

The course which we have here adopted is a combination of the two methods indicated : sometimes we deal
with periods, examining religious beliefs as a whole
within a period ; at other times we take a subject and
trace its development irrespective of periods. This may
appear inconsistent and illogical ; we can only assure our
readers that arduous experience has forced upon us the
conclusion that this is the most practical way. True,
it involves here and there a little repetition ; this, however, can hardly be avoided, and it may have the advantage of impressing upon the reader the importance of
certain truths.

We begin with a brief introductory chapter dealing with
Babylonian influence on the Jews. The two chapters
which follow also partake in some sense of an introductory
character. In speaking of " The Early Years of the
Exile " it is important to note that there were two,

possibly three, deportations which took place ; and, as
the sequel shows, there were four different bodies of Jews
whose religious beliefs demand examination : those in
Babylon who were deported in 597 B.C. ; those who were
left in the homeland ; those who settled down in Egypt ;
and those who were deported to Babylon in 586 B.C.
Then, in Chapter III we speak of "The Jewish Community in Exile." A consideration of the communal
life of the Jews in Babylonia shows that in some important
respects this was similar to what it had been in Palestine,
with the result that they were left free in the exercise
of their religion. This leads us on to a discussion of
the Jewish religious observances during the Exile.

Then we deal with the teaching of the two great
religious leaders during the period of the Exile. First,
Ezekiel : the doctrine of God ; superhuman beings ;
individual responsibility ; regeneration ; the ceremonial
law ; apocalyptic thought (Chapter IV). Chapter V deals
with the teaching of Deutero-Isaiah : his conception of
God ; the regeneration of the people ; universalism ; the
"Servant of the Lord."

In the course of these chapters certain other religious
subjects are alluded to, for that is demanded ; but they
are not treated in any detail because they are more fully
dealt with later.

We then come to the Persian Period. Here again an
introductory chapter is called for dealing with "Persian
Influence on Jewish Belief " (Chapter VI) ; but we do not
here touch upon the subject which is the most important
in this connexion, Eschatology, because this is treated as
a whole in a later chapter.

Chapter VII is concerned with the returned exiles
and the teaching of Haggai and Zechariah ; and it is
shown that religious thought and practice become centred
in the Law, the Temple, and the Messianic Hope. It is
here that the need arises for ignoring periods where
circumstances seem to us to make this more convenient.

Chapter VIII treats of the Law ; but here we restrict
ourselves to the particular period in which it began to
come into prominence. It is dealt with again in Chapter

XVI, where we examine it in the more fully developed form which it assumed, especially after the Maccabæan era.

Chapter IX deals, though very briefly, with the subject of Wisdom. Our object in touching upon it here is to show that, while the origins of Hebrew Wisdom go back into pre-exilic times, it exercised the minds of Israel's thinkers during the Persian Period. But the Golden Age of Hebrew Wisdom belongs to the Greek Period, and therefore a fuller treatment of the subject appears in a later chapter.

With Chapter X, "God and the Soul: Worship: Pietism," we come to a subject which, we feel, is best dealt with irrespective of periods. We place it in the Persian period because it is within this period that the various ramifications of the subject develop; but it belongs, of course, both to earlier and later times, which are likewise considered.

We come then to the Greek period. Chapter XI contains a brief consideration of "The Influence of Hellenism upon the Jews." Then follows "The Problem of Suffering," with special attention to the Book of Job (Chapter XII).

After this follows, appropriately enough, "The Doctrine of Immortality" (Chapter XIII). Then, as it is within the Greek Period that the full development of Hebrew Wisdom begins, Chapter XIV is devoted to that. The large subject of Eschatology (Chapter XV) occupies a somewhat lengthy chapter, and even so it has not been possible to touch upon all that is included under the term. We have been chiefly concerned, however, in seeking to show that Jewish apocalyptic ideas were largely influenced by Persian belief; if we appear to have devoted over-much space to this, the reason is that, so far as we have been able to see, it is not sufficiently dealt with in the text-books. It may be thought that this subject would have come more appropriately under the Persian period, but, as we have pointed out, it is from the end of the third century B.C. that the developments in Jewish Apocalyptic begin, so far as the literature is concerned; we thought it best therefore to postpone the subject to this point of time, and to deal with it retrospectively and prospectively.

The last Chapter (XVI), " The Law and its Developments," would, no doubt, have come more appropriately under the Roman Period, because the final development did not take place until after the close of the Maccabæan struggle ; but we did not think it necessary to devote a special division of the volume to the Roman period, for in essentials there were no further developments in the Jewish Religion after the Greek period.

The long period covered, but more especially the variety of material and the various developments, have made our task difficult, and we can hardly hope to have been entirely successful ; many details have perforce had to be omitted ; but we trust that we have passed over nothing that is of fundamental importance, even though in some cases subjects have, owing to the need of brevity, been inadequately treated.

We desire it to be understood that we make no claim to have reached final conclusions, and we would not be interpreted as having intended to be dogmatic. We recognize frankly that there are wide differences of opinion on many parts of our subject ; and we know that there are those for whose scholarship and judgement we have profound respect, who would not endorse all our views ; but among honest thinkers such divergences of view are inevitable, many conclusions are necessarily subjective, and no two investigators can approach any subject from precisely the same angle, or see it in exactly the same perspective. Our attitude towards those with whom we disagree may be seen in the fact that while there are points in the following pages in which we have found that our opinions diverge, yet we have not allowed this to disturb the harmony and unity of our work.

We send this volume out in the hope that it may help many of our readers to understand that long and slow process of divine revelation through the Jewish people which culminated in the life, teaching, and death of our Lord Jesus Christ.

W. O. E. O.

T. H. R.

Part I of this work has been written by Dr. Oesterley, Part II by Dr. Robinson ; Part III is mainly the work of Dr. Oesterley, but Dr. Robinson has contributed the sections on "God and the Soul : Worship : Pietism " (Chapter X), "The Problem of Suffering " (Chapter XII), the section in Chapter XIII which deals with the development of belief in a future life, and Chapter XIV, "The Doctrine of Wisdom."

PREFATORY NOTE TO SECOND IMPRESSION

AMONG the reviews, generally favourable, two justifiable points of criticism demand a few words from us. The first is that there is a want of proportion in the divisions of the book, especially in regard to Part I. We agree with this, and we ought to have mentioned in our Prefatory Note the reason ; it was because we have found that in English books on Hebrew Religion insufficient attention is drawn to the antecedents.

The second has reference to the earliest stages of religious belief, dealt with in the first few pages of the book. Two or three reviewers have denied the truth of certain statements there made. We confess that we ought to have mentioned the existence of differences of opinion here. Had space permitted we should have drawn attention to these and have pointed out that there *is* uncertainty about some things we have said in the first two sections ; but we could not have so discussed the evidence as to give the full reasons for our opinions without considerably lengthening this section of our work ; and this would still further have justified the criticism about the want of proportion.

W. O. E. O.

T. H. R.

PART I

THE BACKGROUND

CHAPTER I

THE EARLIEST STAGES OF RELIGIOUS BELIEF

1. INTRODUCTORY

THE Hebrews were Semites, and their religion, in its origin, did not differ from that of the Semites in general. In order therefore to distinguish clearly those elements which were common to all Semites and those which in course of time came to be specifically Hebrew, it is necessary to have some knowledge of early Semitic religion, so far as this is obtainable.

Now, most authorities hold that the original home of the Semites was the great Arabian peninsula, whence, owing to the pressure of population and scarcity of food, they flowed out in successive waves into the lands north, north-east, and north-west, and formed, in course of time, the various Semitic groups known to us as Babylonians, Assyrians, Aramæans, Phœnicians, Edomites, Moabites, Ammonites, Hebrews, and Abyssinians (Falashas). Thus it is obvious, on the face of it, that the Semites were for many long centuries *nomads* before the various groups in turn became agriculturists and, later, dwellers in cities. And it is important to remember that the religion of nomads cannot be quite the same thing as that of men who have reached the more cultured stages ; nevertheless, owing to the tenacity of religious belief and custom, we must be prepared to see the remnants of the nomadic religious stage in subsequent ages.

We have, however, to go back yet a further step. The Semites formed only a branch of the human family, and there were elements in their religious beliefs and customs which were, in their origin, common to mankind in the earliest stages of which we have knowledge. We have therefore to begin our enquiry by going back to times when man was in a very primitive stage of culture in order to seek the origins of some beliefs and customs which appear both in the religion of the Semites generally as well as in that of the Hebrews.

It is necessary to touch upon this subject, cursorily though it be, because Hebrew religion, at any rate in its earlier stages, cannot be properly understood without some knowledge of primitive [1] beliefs. The roots of religious belief and practice always go very deep, and to cut off the later growth and development from the parent stock would involve frequent misunderstanding of the meaning and significance of the former.

There are three stages of belief through which most, but not all, early races of man have passed, or are passing, as in the case of uncultured peoples of the present day. What kind of religious ideas were held prior to these stages can only be a matter of speculation.[2]

The first of these is the *Animistic stage*. The term *Animism*, first coined by Tylor, is used to express the belief, held by man in a more or less primitive stage of culture, that " every object which had activity enough to affect him in any way was animated by a life and will like his own." But here one must make a distinction.

---

[1] The word is not used literally, but relatively ; of what primitive man, in the literal sense, believed we cannot, from the nature of the case, have any knowledge.

[2] To deal with the difficult subject of *Mana* here would take us too far afield ; it must suffice to quote Codrington's definition : " It is a power or influence, not physical, and in a way supernatural ; but it shows itself in physical force, or in any kind of power or excellence which a man possesses. This *Mana* is not fixed in anything, and can be conveyed in almost anything ; but spirits, whether disembodied souls or supernatural beings, have it and can impart it ; and it essentially belongs to personal beings to originate it, though it may act through the medium of water, or a stone, or a bone " (*The Melanesians*, p. 119 (1891). And see especially Marett, *The Threshold of Religion*, pp. 115–41 [1909]). Marett says in his Preface : " . . . Hence I am ready to assume that, before animism, regarded as an ideal system of religious beliefs, can have come into its kingdom, there must have been numberless dimly lighted impressions of the awful that owned no master in the shape of some one systematizing thought. . . . My theory is not concerned with the mere thought at work in religion, but with religion as a whole, the organic complex of thought, emotion, and behaviour. In regard to religion thus understood I say . . . that it proceeds from indistinct to distinct, from undifferentiated to differentiated, from incoherent to coherent. And that, I claim, is a hypothesis which has the best part of evolutionary science at its back."

There are two theories which can be held regarding, for example, a running stream : it may be argued—for in this early stage of culture man argued on the analogy of himself—that just as a man can move his body at will, so a stream can move itself if it so wishes ; in other words, the stream *itself* is, like a man, a being with a life and a will. On the other hand, it can be argued that the stream moves because some external power causes it to do so. The distinction between the stream being animate itself and being animated by an external power is a great one, and indicates a big advance. There is every reason therefore to postulate two stages within the Animistic stage itself : the earlier is obviously the cruder of the two— that which regards the stream itself as animate ; while the later one shows an advance by its recognition of some external force or power which animates the stream. To distinguish the stages anthropologists apply the term *Animatism* to the former and *Animism* to the latter.

It should be noted, in passing, that Animatism has nothing supernatural about it ; if moving objects were explained on the analogy of man they would come under the category of things natural. Animism, on the other hand, which presupposes the existence of some invisible power, begins to touch upon the supernatural, and therefore our starting-point must be from this stage ; references to the earlier stage will only be incidental.

If it be asked how we are to suppose that man in the Animistic stage represented to himself the power or spirit which animated the stream, it is very doubtful whether any certain answer can be given. Such things are not enquired into by men in a very low stage of culture ; the " primitive " race, like the child, takes many things for granted ; questions are obviously not asked when the mental capacity for framing them is as yet absent.

We use the term *Animism* : this implies the existence of " spirits " ; but it is quite certain that man in this low stage of culture had not the remotest conception of what we understand by spirit. To conceive of an immaterial entity was beyond his power. We doubt therefore whether a definite answer can be given to the question as to how man in this early stage presented to himself that which animated a stream, or tree, or cloud.

2. THE ANIMISTIC STAGE

For purposes which will become clear as we proceed, it is necessary to consider very briefly the more outstanding objects in connexion with which Animism can best be illustrated. These comprise :

1. Trees. 2. Streams, springs, etc. 3. Stones, rocks, and mountains.

1. The movement of a tree when swayed by the wind made it one of the first things to be regarded by man in a very early stage of culture, first, as a living being, and later, as animated by a spirit. Cause and effect, as we understand them, not being recognized, the idea that the branches of a tree moved through the force of the wind did not occur. It was a spirit which occasioned this ; but here it must be remembered that the distinction between matter and spirit which is so obvious to us was unknown to man in undeveloped stages of culture. The primary point of importance suggested by motion in a tree was that it denoted the presence of life ; first, life inherent in the tree itself as a being much in the same sense that a man was ; and then, later, life as manifested by the presence of a " supernatural " being which took up its abode in the tree at certain times. An instructive example of the earlier stage of belief is given in the words of Porphyry : " They say that primitive men led an unhappy life, for their superstition did not stop at animals, but extended even to plants. For why should the slaughter of an ox or a sheep be a greater wrong than the felling of a fir or an oak, seeing that a soul is implanted in these trees also." [1] This we should describe as Animatism ; while as an illustration of animistic belief the

---

[1] *De abstinentia*, i. 6, quoted by Frazer, *Golden Bough*, " The Magic Art," ii. 12 (1911).

following words of Pliny the Elder afford an example :
in writing about trees he says that " these have been (in
the past) temples of gods, and even now with ancient
ritual the simple country folk dedicate a lofty tree to a
god. Not more do we adore images that shine with
gold and ivory than sacred groves and the very silence
in them." [1] A tree is dedicated to a god because it is
believed that a shrine having been thus prepared for him
will be utilized by him as a place of abode ; and at such
times as he sees fit to enter this it is, of course, expected
that he will make his presence known. Pliny's words
imply that the tree did not become a shrine until after it
had been dedicated ; but this would not have taken place
unless there had been some reason for believing that
the god would utilize the abode prepared for him. Trees
must therefore have been looked upon as the abodes of
spirits before some particular tree came to be dedicated
to a god. As an illustration of this we are told, for
example, that " when the missionary Jerome of Prague
was persuading the heathen Lithuanians to fell their
sacred groves, a multitude of women besought the Prince
of Lithuania to stop him, saying that with the woods
he was destroying the house of their god from which they
had been wont to get sunshine and rain." [2] Very
numerous examples of a similar character could be
given.

If, then, a supernatural being takes up its abode
in a tree, which is on that account sacred, it is easy to
understand how in course of time it came to be believed
that oracles were delivered by the indwelling spirit ;
examples of this have been noted in various parts of the
world, both in ancient and later times. In the oracular
shrine of Zeus at Dodona, for example, the oracles were
given by sounds made by the sacred oak.[3] The ancient
Prussians received audible answers from gods which were
believed to inhabit oaks and other trees.[4] The heathen
Lithuanians as late as the fourteenth century A.D. were in

---

[1] Quoted by Baudissin, *Studien zur Semitischen Religionsgeschichte*,
ii. 184 (1878).
[2] Frazer, *op. cit.*, ii. 46.
[3] Farnell, *The Cults of the Greek States*, i. 38 ff. (1896–1909).
[4] Frazer, *op. cit.*, ii. 43.

the habit of receiving oracular responses from oaks.[1] And, to give but one other example, among the natives of Uganda " the trees planted round the ancestral graves were sedulously tended by wise women, whose oracles, like those of the Pythian priestess, were taken as decisive in certain political crises." [2]

These few examples, out of many dozens which could be given, must suffice. Trees were thus regarded by man in an early stage of culture all the world over as temporary or permanent places of abode of spirits, and later of gods. As a consequence they acquired a sacred character. Particular trees, owing to one or more of a variety of causes, would have a special sanctity attaching to them ; such trees, as the evidence shows, became sanctuaries from which oracles were to be obtained.

2. Since running water, rivers, streams, springs, and wells were objects which had activity enough to affect man, these too were believed to be animated by a life and will like his own. And as in the case of trees, the belief concerning these developed from Animatism to Animism. Running water must have appeared to early man, as soon as he became mentally of sufficient development to think about it, as extraordinarily mysterious. Its movement would convince him that it was living ; its force and power were immeasurable ; there would be something terribly awesome in a raging torrent which swept away rocks and trees in its rushing course ; it uttered deafening sounds, as it would seem to man in the dawn of understanding ; it engulfed man and beast like some hungry monster. No wonder that rivers and streams and the sea itself were believed to be living beings like men. And although, in course of time, a spirit animating the water, and not the water itself, came to be thought of as the cause of movement, it is noteworthy that the tendency to the animatistic conception regarding water continued side by side with the animistic much longer than was the case with trees. Thus, the ancient Peruvians who lived on the coast looked upon the ocean

---

[1] Frazer, *op. cit.*, ii. 9.
[2] Keane, in the *Encycl. of Religion and Ethics*, i. 164a. See further Jevons, *Introduction to the History of Religion*, pp. 206–25, 242 f. (1904).

itself as a powerful goddess, whom they called *mamacocha*, " mother-sea " [1] ; to her they were indebted for their food in the shape of fish, one of their staple means of living ; on the other hand, her power must sometimes have been exhibited by engulfing men.

As distinct from this animatistic conception there is, for example, the belief in the water-spirit who inhabited the sacred hot springs of Hierapolis.[2] Other illustrations are to be found in the legend of Heracles and Hesione, and in the better known one of Perseus and Andromeda [3] ; and one has only to think of the Nereids and Nymphs to realize the beliefs in ancient times about rivers and springs. Such ideas, one may confidently assert, have a long history behind them, and have been handed down for untold centuries, since similar ones exist among races in a low stage of culture. For example, " the Tarahumares (Central America) place their houses at a distance from the water and never sleep near it when on a journey lest they should be molested by the indwelling spirit." [4] To go still lower in the scale, Tylor, in writing about savage tribes in Africa, says that " in the east, among the Wanika, every spring has its spirit, to which oblations are made ; in the west, in the Akra district, lakes, ponds, and rivers received worship as local deities. In the south, among the Kafirs, streams are venerated as personal beings, or the abodes of personal deities." [5]

The best illustrations of oracle-giving springs occur in classical writers and ancient historians ; but these must be taken as showing how primitive ideas persist. Thus, to give but one or two examples : from the murmurous flow of the spring which is said to have gushed from the foot of the great oak at Dodona, the priestess drew oracles.[6] The oracle of Daphne, near Antioch, was obtained by dipping a laurel leaf into the water, though

[1] Payne, *History of the New World called America*, i. 451 (1892).
[2] Frazer, *G.B.*, " Adonis, Attis, Osiris," i. 208 (1927).
[3] Hans Schmidt, *Jona, eine Untersuchung zur vergleichenden Religionsgeschichte*, pp. 3 ff., 12 ff. (1907).
[4] E. O. James, in *E.R.E.*, xii. 708a.
[5] *Primitive Culture*, ii. 211 (1873).
[6] Frazer, *G.B.*, " The Magic Art," ii. 172.

" we cannot take seriously the statement that the response appeared written on the leaf." [1] And, once more, " at Delphi the sacred spring may have been either Cassiotis or the more-famed Castaly, which issues from a narrow gorge, shut in by rocky walls of tremendous height, a little to the east of Apollo's temple. The waters of both were thought to be endowed with prophetic power." [2]

It will not be necessary to illustrate this further. Springs, streams, etc., like trees, were conceived of as spirits, or else as the abode of spirits, not only by men in a savage state, but by races which had reached a high stage of culture ; and it would be easy to show that this belief has persisted through the ages, and has probably not entirely disappeared in countries of the most advanced civilization even at the present day.

3. While it is not difficult to understand that man in a primitive stage of culture should have had animistic ideas about trees and rivers on account of their movement, the case is somewhat different when it is seen that similar ideas were held in regard to stones of various kinds. The sight of a rolling stone might well have suggested life ; but sacred stones were not as a rule such as moved or seemed to. And yet stones were regarded both as living themselves, and as being the abode of spirits. The line of thought which suggested this to early man must have been different from that which led him to have the same belief about moving branches of trees and running water. Animistic conceptions about stones were prompted by a variety of things, not by the one guiding thought that movement meant life. " Wherever men have been struck by the appearance or position of a rock or stone, they have regarded it with awe as uncanny, and in innumerable cases they have ultimately erected it into a divinity, brought offerings, and put up prayers before it." [3] But in many cases the appearance of a stone might attract attention without necessarily inspiring awe ; for example, among the

[1] Robertson Smith, *The Religion of the Semites*, p. 178 (1927).
[2] Frazer, *G.B.*, " The Dying God," p. 79 (1911).
[3] Hartland, in *E.R.E.*, xi. 864a.

Melanesians a stone in the shape of breadfruit is believed to effect a good crop of fruit [1]; this would be brought about by burying the stone at the foot of the tree in question. While originally it was, no doubt, believed that the stone itself had this power, in course of time it would come to be imputed to a spirit abiding in the stone ; and one can understand how, by degrees, worship would be accorded to the stone as the embodiment or, later, the symbol of the spirit.

To take another instance, one which points to some development, and one in which the feeling of awe would certainly arise : Hartland refers to rocks and stones having natural depressions somewhat resembling a foot-print, or the impression of what looks like a hand, knee, or head ; this would naïvely but quite naturally be interpreted by savage man as the mark of the spirit whose abode the stone or rock was : " such a mark is looked upon with awe, and, if attributed to a sacred person, usually becomes the object of devout observance, if not of an actual cult." Thus, it is not difficult to understand that a standing stone should have suggested the idea of a man, and be looked upon as such, though of course, a supernatural man ; the modification of regarding it as the abode of the spirit would follow in due course.

Among the Khasis of Assam, we are told, " the sacred upright stones, which resemble the Semitic _mazzēbôth_ (" pillars "), are regarded as males, and the flat table-stones as females. . . . So in Nikunau, one of the Gilbert Islands in the South Pacific, the natives had sandstone slabs or pillars which represented gods and goddesses." [2] The anointing of stones was widespread ; " it appears to have been customary to anoint the sacred cone with olive-oil at a solemn festival, in which people from Lycia and Caria participated—we learn this from an inscription found at Paphos. The custom of anointing a holy stone has been observed in

---

[1] Codrington, _op. cit._, p. 183. Hartland says that " among the Melanesians the shape of a stone rules the idea as to what kind of spirit dwells within it " (_Animism_, p. 78 [1905]).

[2] Frazer, _G.B._, " Adonis, Attis, Osiris," i. 108 (1927).

many parts of the world ; for example, in the sanctuary of Apollo at Delphi." [1]

Examples of holy hills and mountains whose sanctity is due to the presence of an indwelling spirit are very numerous,[2] the particular spot at which the spirit would be supposed to manifest himself would naturally be on the summit. Volcanoes would obviously suggest supernatural activity.[3]

Here again it is not necessary to multiply examples, for these can be found to any extent in books dealing with the beliefs of uncivilized man.

All that was necessary for our present purpose, so far, was to indicate by a few examples the fact that sacred trees, streams, and stones have played a very great part during the two stages of Animatism and Animism, stages through which all races have passed or are passing on their upward path towards higher forms of belief.

Before we come to the next stage it is necessary to touch briefly on the subject of Polydæmonism.

Many authorities make a distinction between Animism and Polydæmonism, but others do not believe that any distinction can be properly made. While it must be admitted that it is not easy to distinguish between a spirit and a demon in the sense in which these words must be understood in the present connexion, we do nevertheless come across some creatures, at any rate in the Semitic area, which compel us to ask whether we must not postulate the existence of a belief in beings which cannot be said to come under the animistic category, and which are certainly not to be classed as gods.[4]

Two illustrations of what we mean may be given : the *Seräphîm*, in the original not in the developed conception, and the *Se'irîm*. What is said of these points to an advance beyond a merely animistic conception, but they are clearly of a very much lower order than gods and goddesses. A spring or a stream or a tree which is believed to move

---

[1] Frazer, *op. cit.*, i. 36.
[2] Baudissin, *op. cit.*, ii. 238 ff., gives many illustrations.
[3] Frazer, *op. cit.*, i. 216–22.
[4] See further T. H. Robinson, *Outline Introduction to the History of Religions*, pp. 65 f. (1926).

because it is animated by a spirit we understand as Animism; but a *saraph* is not a serpent nor is a *sa'ir* a goat indwelt by a spirit or a demon—whatever the later beliefs may have been—but is itself a demon. The ordinary process of development through the three stages is, first the tree itself a spirit (Animatism), then the tree animated by a spirit (Animism), and then the spirit developing into a god or goddess (Polytheism). But in the case of the *Serāphîm* and the *Se'irîm* the process stops short; they do not develop into gods or goddesses, whatever they may have developed from.[1] So that from this point of view it would seem as though Animism in its development diverged in two directions, viz. on the one hand into the Polytheistic stage, and on the other, into a stage in which the beings were of a more " concrete " nature than in the Animistic stage proper, and never developed into anything further; they continued as they were, and ultimately died out—like the arrested development of a species, in another sphere. It cannot be objected that what has been said is an anachronism, because it is dealing with a stage of demonology which belongs to a later age, for we meet with the *Serāphîm*, at any rate, as early as the Mosaic age, and nobody would suppose that they originated at that time; they must be much earlier.

3. The Polytheistic Stage

Polytheism, the belief in many gods and goddesses, has two points in common with the belief in spirits and demons : their multiplicity and the fact that they are unmoral. They may be harmful, or they may be beneficent, but they have no ethical attributes about them.

The first essential difference between a spirit or a demon and a god or goddess, is that the latter has individuality, the former has not. From this it follows that gods and goddesses have each some special attribute, which is not the case with the lower types of supernatural beings. Further, spirits, some harmful and some

---

[1] See further Chapter VI.

not, form a species, which is divided into varieties; therefore they have no names; but gods and goddesses have names. Another difference is that spirits and demons are not tied to any locality, but gods and goddesses are—at any rate in the early stage of belief in them. And lastly, there is this further difference that spirits and demons are sexless—they are represented as hybrids or in the form of animals; but gods and goddesses, at any rate in the Semitic domain, are always conceived of as being in human form.

The existence and character of Polytheism are so well known that it is quite unnecessary to give illustrations.

These, then, are the three stages of belief through which all races pass before they reach a higher form of religion; and the Hebrew race was no exception, as the evidence of the Old Testament shows. Tylor truly remarks that "no religion lies in utter isolation from the rest, and the thoughts and principles of modern Christianity are attached to intellectual clues which run back through far pre-Christian ages to the very origin of human civilization, perhaps even of human existence."[1]

But there are some further subjects to which a very brief reference must be made. While early man was passing through the first two of these stages certain institutions came into being which have been almost world-wide. As remnants of these are found in the Old Testament it is necessary that they should be mentioned; for if we are to study the origin and development of Hebrew religion, we must take all facts and factors into consideration. A few words about each of these three institutions must therefore find a place here.

4. Totemism; Taboo; Ancestor-Worship

The word *Totem* belongs originally to some of the North American Indian tribes. Totemism denotes a form of society in which the members of a clan believe themselves to be united by kinship to some animal or plant from which the clan has descended. The animal or plant, or what-

---

[1] *Op. cit.*, i. 421.

ever else it may be which is thus regarded as the tribal
ancestor, is looked upon with profound veneration by
all the members of the clan or tribe, as the case may be.
It must never be harmed. In the case of an animal it
may never be eaten excepting on very special occasions
when the members of a clan feast on their totem animal ;
and this is a solemn religious rite. Though in its origin
Totemism had nothing to do with religion, in course
of time religion entered into it, and with it, of course,
the supernatural element. Since a man was united by
kinship to his totem he regarded it as his friend ; and
having something supernatural, and therefore powerful,
about it, a man would look to it for help. So that here
was a supernatural power distinguished from all others
by the fact that it was in alliance with him ; it became, as
Jevons says, " a permanently friendly power ; in a word,
it became a god." [1]

In studying the development of the early religious
ideas of the Hebrews on broad lines the subject of
Totemism cannot be ignored. Not that Totemism
existed as an institution among the Hebrews, at any
rate within the historical period ; but the Old Testament
has preserved some distinct traces of its former existence
among the distant ancestors of the Hebrew race ; hence
the mention of it here. [2]

Secondly, there is what is known as *Taboo*, or *Tabu*.
This word is borrowed from Polynesia. It is applied to
the institution, universal among all races in an undeveloped state of culture and even after, in which, for a
large variety of reasons, contact with things and persons
and even names (i.e. their utterance) is forbidden. Things
or persons which are taboo are so because they are
believed to be charged, either temporarily or permanently,
with some supernatural influence. [3] Where it comes from
or how it comes is not enquired into ; it is *there*, that is

---

[1] *Op. cit.*, p. 104 ; and see further, Robertson Smith, *Rel. Sem.*, p. 54
(1927).

[2] On the general subject see McLennan, *Studies in Ancient History*,
pp. 491 ff. (1886), and Frazer, *Totemism and Exogamy* (1910).

[3] Marett remarks that " *Tabu* is the negative mode of the supernatural to which *mana* corresponds as the positive mode " (*op. cit.*,
p. 127).

the practical concern. This is always the underlying cause for the prohibition of contact, whatever other reasons may be added subsequently ; for this supernatural influence is transmissible : " everything which comes in contact with a tabooed person or thing becomes itself as dangerous as the original object, becomes a fresh centre of infection, a fresh source of danger, to the community." [1] And it is just the unknown, the undefined nature of the danger which makes it so formidable and dreaded. Taboo postulates belief in something supernatural and in so far is connected with religious belief.

The other very ancient institution is *Ancestor-worship*. The fundamental idea here is the keeping up of social relations with a dead ancestor. Just as, when living, the head of a family, clan or tribe acted as guardian and protector to his dependents, who in turn honoured and served him as their head, so this mutual relationship was intended to continue after death had removed the former from visible presence among the latter.

We are not concerned here with the various problems connected with the subject of Ancestor-worship, but merely with the fact of its existence.[2] To sum up :

We have thus three stages of belief, the two latter being certainly of a religious character, through which all early races have passed, viz. Animatism, Animism, and Polytheism, and three primitive institutions which have likewise been in vogue among all early races, viz. Totemism, Taboo, and Ancestor-worship. All of these, not even with the exception of Animatism, have left their marks on Hebrew religion, which is the reason why attention has been drawn to them here. With the exception of Polytheism, these marks are relatively faint ; but they are indubitably to be discerned, as will be seen later ; and that this should be the case in spite of the fact that Hebrew religion (even in its earlier polytheistic stages), as preserved in the Old Testament, is a great advance, need occasion no surprise. For new ideas never displace

---

[1] Jevons, *op. cit.*, p. 161.

[2] See further the present writer's *Immortality and the Unseen World*, chaps. viii., ix. (1921), where references to the literature on the subject will be found.

older ones without a struggle, which is often protracted over long periods. This is especially the case in the domain of religious ideas, which are the most tenacious. It is therefore just what is to be expected when it is found that stages of belief overlap one another, when, that is to say, *traits* characteristic of an earlier stage of belief are found to linger on even when a more developed stage has been attained. For ages men will be clinging to the old conceptions even after they have accepted and absorbed much that is new, and both continue side by side, however incompatible with one another.

CHAPTER II

REMNANTS OF ANIMISM IN HEBREW RELIGION : SACRED TREES

1. General Semitic Belief

WE have seen that religious belief in its gradual development among early races passes through the stages of Animism and Polytheism. Since this is recognized as a universal rule among all peoples whose religion develops sufficiently, we may assume that the Hebrews, or their forbears, were no exception. But something more than assumption is needed before this can be accepted as a fact, and therefore the evidence of the records must be examined. As a preliminary to this, however, it is quite necessary to glance, even though cursorily, at Semitic Religion in general so far as the special points to be considered are concerned, for this will be of help in ascertaining, or at least of gaining some insight into, what the beliefs of the forbears of the Hebrews were.

Therefore in studying the various indications of the existence of earlier animistic beliefs afforded in the Old Testament we shall in each case begin with a brief consideration of general Semitic belief on the subject.

While not absent among other races, as we have seen, it was a specifically Semitic belief that trees, and above all evergreen trees, were regarded as the vehicles of the life-producing energy of spirits, and later of gods and goddesses. Animistic conceptions in connexion with them can be shown to have existed until comparatively late times. As Robertson Smith says : " Prayers were addressed to them, particularly for help in sickness, but doubtless also for fertile seasons and the like, and they were hung with votive gifts, especially garments and ornaments, perhaps also anointed with unguents as if

18

they had been real persons."[1] Even at the present day
in Syria there are many trees which are believed to be
possessed by spirits, to whom vows and sacrifices are
made.[2]

In the main, the knowledge we have of the beliefs of
the Babylonians and Assyrians dates from periods of
such a relatively advanced culture that bald animistic
conceptions are hardly to be looked for. Nevertheless,
it is certain that the ancient Babylonians believed that
trees were inhabited by spirits[3]; moreover, the importance attached to sacred trees in their religion
and the reverence with which they were treated necessi-
tates the implication that we have here but the development of animistic conceptions. It is sufficient to point
to the numerous inscriptions in which trees, in the more
or less conventional style, are depicted[4]; worshippers
kneel before these ; in some cases gifts are being offered.
The text on inscriptions of this kind does not suggest
that the tree itself is being worshipped ; it is either the
symbol of a god or goddess, or else it is conceived of
as a sanctuary of the deity or as marking the site of a
sanctuary. But in any case, the existence of a tree in
connexion with worship does not permit of any conclusion
other than that of a development of some earlier
animistic conceptions.[5]

Although the most frequently employed means of
obtaining oracles—large numbers of which occur on
Assyrian texts—was by the examination of an animal's
liver (hepatoscopy), tree oracles were far from being
unknown : the cedar, cypress, and tamarisk are the trees
which are most frequently mentioned in the ritual texts.[6]

As regards the Phœnicians and Canaanites, Robertson
Smith refers to the testimony of Philo Byblius to the effect
that " the plants of the earth were in ancient times

---

[1] Op. cit., p. 195.
[2] Curtiss, Primitive Semitic Religion To-day, p. 91 (1902).
[3] Jastrow, Die Religion Babyloniens und Assyriens, i. 48 (1912).
[4] Monuments of this kind can be seen in the British Museum.
[5] Further details will be found in Baudissin, op. cit., ii. 189–192 ;
Lagrange, Études sur les Religions Sémitiques, pp. 168–171 (1903) ;
Jeremias, Das alte Testament im Lichte des alten Orients, pp. 94 ff. (1904).
[6] Jastrow, op. cit., ii. 200 ff.

esteemed as gods and honoured with libations and sacrifices, because from them the successive generations of men drew the support of their life. To this day the traveller in Palestine frequently meets with holy trees hung like an Arabian *dhāt anwāt* (tree for hanging things on), with rags as tokens of homage." [1]

Among the Phœnicians trees figured prominently in worship, especially in the cult of the goddess Astarte, to whom the cypress was sacred. The myrtle and the palm were also associated with the worship of this goddess. [2]

In describing the festival of the Pyre or Lamp—to give a Syrian illustration—Lucian says : "They cut down tall trees and set them up in the court ; then they bring goats and sheep and cattle and hang them living to the trees ; they add to these birds and garments and gold and silver work. After all is finished, they carry the gods around the trees and set fire under ; in a moment all is in a blaze. To this solemn rite a great multitude flocks from Syria and all the regions around." [3] This is, of course, a greatly developed form of cult, but from the present point of view the main importance is the hanging of offerings on the sacred trees ; for these latter are not merely convenient objects upon which to suspend the offerings, they have a far greater significance than that : being sacred to different deities they represent them ; the offerings are made to the trees as representing the deities. The burning of the trees would not take place unless the gods they represent were present, as is the case here. The ceremony is clearly a development of the earlier practice of presenting offerings to trees, and this, in its turn, points to yet earlier animistic belief.

But the most instructive examples are to be sought among both ancient and modern Arabs. To quote our leading authority on Semitic religion once more, Robertson Smith says in reference to the ancient Arabs, that " while the supernatural associations of groves and thickets

---

[1] *Rel. Sem.*, p. 186.
[2] Baudissin, *op. cit.*, ii. 192–216, where abundant material will be found.
[3] *De Dea Syria*, § xlix.

may appear to be sufficiently explained by the fact that these are the favourite lairs of wild beasts, it appears probable that the association of certain kinds of *jinn* with trees must in many cases be regarded as primary, the trees themselves being conceived as animated demoniac beings "; and again : " Primarily supernatural life and power reside in the trees themselves, which are conceived as animated and even as rational." [1]

Oracles from trees were far from rare : " Sometimes the tree is believed to speak with an articulate voice, as the *gharcad* did in a dream to Moslim ; but except in a dream it is obvious that the voice of the tree can only be some rustling sound, as the wind in the branches." [2]

How these animistic conceptions have persisted up to the present day among the Arabs in Syria could be illustrated to almost any extent ; but to give details, instructive as they are, would take up too much space. For these recourse must be had to such works as Burck-hardt, *Travels in Syria and the Holy Land* ; Doughty, *Travels in Arabia Deserta* ; and Curtiss, *Primitive Semitic Religion To-day*.

2. THE OLD TESTAMENT

Having thus taken a bird's-eye glance at the subject of sacred trees among the Semites generally, we are in a better position to study some of the Biblical passages in which they are referred to. The question of the dates of passages to be quoted need not trouble us here ; later it is one which becomes of importance ; but in the present connexion, since the remnants of the early stages of belief linger on in ages long subsequent to those during which they formed the norm, it is immaterial for our purposes to what period a particular passage may be assigned provided it contains the echo or reflex of some " primitive " belief. At present we are merely concerned to show that the Old Testament itself gives indications that Hebrew religion emerged from the Animistic stage of belief.

---

[1] *Op. cit.*, pp. 132 ff., where illustrations are given ; also in Well-hausen, *Reste arabischen Heidentums*, pp. 104 ff. (1897).

[2] Doughty, *Travels in Arabia Deserta*, ii. 209 (1888).

In Gen. xii. 6–8 mention is made of " the terebinth of Mōreh " [1] (*'ēlōn mōreh*); translated literally this is: " the terebinth of the teacher," i.e. a tree at which divine teaching was given. What is meant is that the oracle was given there, so that it might well be rendered " the oracle-terebinth." This tree [2] stood in Shechem, and it was evidently thought of as extremely ancient, since it was there before Abraham came to Canaan. It was on this spot that Yahweh appeared to the patriarch, in consequence of which he built an altar to Yahweh. One cannot fail to recognize a connexion between the mention of a specific, and obviously well-known, tree and the divine appearance there. The tree was regarded as sacred. Abraham halts at it because he expects a divine manifestation there ; and he is not disappointed. But why should the manifestation take place at the tree ? In the light of what has been said above about sacred trees there is no room for doubt that we have here an instance of the development of the belief that spirits took up their abode in trees. In other words, we have here an indication of the existence of an earlier animistic belief.

The same must be postulated of the terebinth of Mamre, in Hebron (Gen. xiii. 18, xviii. 1 [3]), where Abraham again builds an altar to Yahweh. The spot must have been regarded as a holy one, otherwise it would not have been chosen as a site for this altar ; but it was the presence of the terebinth that made it holy. That the site was a very ancient one is shown by the fact that Mamre is called " the Amorite " in Gen. xiv. 13, 24 ; the Amorites are spoken of as the pre-Israelite inhabitants of Canaan in Amos ii. 9, 10. In later days the personal name became a place-name, and was identified with Hebron (see Gen. xxiii. 19, xxxv. 27, belonging to the P document, where there is no mention of the tree).

In the case of the tamarisk tree in Beersheba which Abraham is said to have planted (Gen. xxi. 33) one might

---

[1] In Deut. xi. 30 it is " the terebinths of M.," but it should be the singular as in the Septuagint.

[2] The terebinth was an evergreen.

[3] In both of these passages the Hebrew has the plural, but as in Deut. xi. 30 we must, following the Septuagint in each case, read the singular ; note also that in Gen. xviii. 4 it is " the tree," not plural.

well ask, What was the point of his doing so ? But this is
in all probability a later tradition to explain the presence
of an ancient tree-sanctuary. The verse must be read
in connexion with Gen. xxvi. 23–25, which describes a
theophany in the same place, but where the tree is not
mentioned. (Cp. Gen. xlvi. 1. On Beersheba, see below,
pp. 35 f.)

In Gen. xxxv. 4 occurs the curious episode of Jacob
burying the " strange gods " together with the ear-rings
of his followers under the Shechem terebinth, which, as we
have seen, was known as the " oracle-terebinth." As
the context speaks of God's appearance to Jacob on the
occasion of his fleeing from Esau, Jacob's action in burying these idols must be understood as meaning that,
since he had accepted *'Elohim* as his God, and thereby
repudiated these other gods, the ill-will of these latter
had to be provided against ; there was no more efficacious
means of achieving this than that of burying them under
the tree-sanctuary of his God, because there they would
be under the control of a more powerful spirit. The
passage is, from our present point of view, a very instructive one, because it clearly implies that the terebinth was
an abode of the deity ; and thus it offers a clear indication
of earlier animistic belief. There is an evident connexion
between this passage and Joshua xxiv. 26, 27, for it is
under this terebinth in Shechem that Joshua sets up a
great stone as a witness lest the people deny God.

An interesting piece of evidence occurs in the isolated
note in Gen. xxxv. 8 : " Deborah, Rebekah's nurse, died,
and she was buried below Bethel under the oak (*'allōn*),
and the name of it was called 'Allōn-bakūth " (i.e. the
oak of weeping). Nothing is known of this Deborah, who
is of course quite a different personality from that of
the prophetess of the same name ; but she must have
played an important *rôle* for the tradition here mentioned
to have been handed down. For the tree to have got
this name must certainly mean that it was a sacred one ;
but we venture to think that it was not because Deborah
was buried under it that it received its name. It is more
likely that the statement that Deborah was buried under
it was made in order to account for the name, the original

reason for which was forgotten. It is not improbable that this tree was a spot where the annual " weeping for Tammuz " took place. Here it need only be said that this ceremony was a widely practised one, very ancient, and derived from the Babylonians ; and as Tammuz was a vegetation god the " weeping " for him, which was always done by women, would appropriately be celebrated by a sacred tree.

The account of the divine appearance at the burning bush (Exod. iii. 2–5) is probably derived from two sources,[1] but in any case it contains two conceptions regarding the deity : fire as indicating the divine presence, and a tree as his abode. With the latter cp. Deut. xxxiii. 16, where it speaks baldly of Yahweh as of " Him that dwelt in the bush " ; a more pointed illustration of an echo of animistic belief could not be given.

Joshua xix. 33 is a late passage—it belongs to the P document ; but for present purposes that does not matter. Mention is there made of " the oak of Beza-'anannim," near Kadesh (cp. Judges iv. 11) ; the meaning of the name is too uncertain to draw any conclusions from it. Evidently it is only mentioned because it was a prominent landmark. But so conspicuous a tree, and above all, one that had a name attached to it, must have had some further significance which has not been recorded. It is also interesting to note that the name still clung to it in late post-exilic times, as its occurrence in the Priestly Code shows.

A highly instructive passage is Judges iv. 4, 5 : " Now Deborah, a prophetess, the wife of Lappidoth, she judged Israel at that time. And she sat [not ' dwelt,' see vi. 11, 1 Sam. xiv. 2, xxii. 6] under the palm tree of Deborah between Ramah and Bethel in the hill country of Ephraim ; and the children of Israel came up to her for judgement." Here we have another example of an oracle-terebinth like the tree in Shechem ; and we can see that the oracle might be given by a woman as well as a man. The word " judgement " must, of course, not be understood in a modern sense : " decision " would far better express what is meant ; and that the people, as we should

---

[1] See, e.g., McNeile, *The Book of Exodus*, p. 16 (1908).

expect, came for the most diverse objects of enquiry can be seen from Exod. xxii. 7, 8. It is a divine oracle which is sought; and the decision is given through a recognized expert. And when it is asked how the divine decision is communicated to the prophetess there can only be one answer: the rustling of the leaves of the sacred tree was believed to indicate the nature of the decision sought; but this could, of course, only be understood and interpreted by one who was expert in such matters. Having then received this message, the prophetess was in a position to give the oracle enquired for. The passage is a striking confirmation of what has already been said as to the indications of earlier animistic belief.

A further indication of the same thing is to be found in the section Judges vi. 11–24. Here we read of the appearance of Yahweh (the "angel of Yahweh" was substituted later for reverential reasons; see vers. 14 ff.) under the terebinth in Ophrah, "that pertained to Joash the Abiezrite," i.e. the terebinth, not Ophrah, belonged to Joash, indicating that it was a private sanctuary. The altar that is built marks the site as a permanent sanctuary, i.e. the tree was one in which it was believed that Yahweh was wont to take up His abode, and at certain times to issue from the tree and sit under it, thus "showing Himself," which is the literal meaning of the Hebrew word rendered "appeared" in ver. 12.

In Judges ix. 6 the Shechem terebinth is mentioned again. The solemn act of making Abimelech king is carried out at this sanctuary, presumably for the purpose of having the deity for witness. The Hebrew text, which says that they made Abimelech king "by the terebinth that was set up," is clearly corrupt, for trees are not set up; on the basis of the Septuagint we must read "by the terebinth of the standing stone" (*mazzēbāh* for *muzzāb*); this is the "great stone" mentioned in Joshua xxiv. 26 (see below, p. 45). The sacred standing stone by the side of the sacred tree is an interesting point, for, as we shall see (p. 124), it was in later times customary for a sacred pole (surrogate for the sacred tree) and the sacred pillar to be set up by the altar.

In the verses which follow we have what is known as Jotham's parable ; we have a similar but much shorter one in 2 Kings xiv. 9 ; as Robertson Smith has pointed out, " the old Hebrew fables of trees that speak and act like human beings have their original source in the savage personification of vegetable species "[1]; and he gives parallels among the ancient Arabs.

In the same chapter (Judges ix.), ver. 37, reference is made to " the terebinth of Mĕ'ōnĕnim," which means " the soothsayers' (or diviners') terebinth " ; it is therefore another instance of an oracle tree mentioned in Gen. xii. 6 (see above, p. 22).

In Judges xx. 33 it is said that " all the men of Israel rose up out of their place, and set themselves in array at Baal-tamar." This is presumably a place-name ; it is never mentioned elsewhere, and its locality is unknown. But in any case it was called after a baal who was believed to take up his abode in a palm-tree. That fact is sufficient for present purposes, as it is a clear instance of a somewhat developed animistic belief.

The terebinth of Tabor, close to Bethel, mentioned in 1 Sam. x. 3, must be identified with the terebinth of Deborah (Gen. xxxv. 8) : the latter stood " below Bethel," and the two names Tabor and Deborah are much alike in Hebrew ; we should undoubtedly read the latter here.

Another tree, the incidental mention of which without explanation shows that it was well known, was the pomegranate tree under which Saul sat (not " abode " as in the R.V., 1 Sam. xiv. 2). As king, Saul dispenses judgement, holding his court under this tree ; the significant point is that this takes place in such a spot. Whether or not the idea was that Saul was supposed to receive inspiration for his decisions from the indwelling deity cannot be said for certain ; but there must have been some reason for this specific mention of the tree. Judging from the many references to sacred trees already dealt with, it can hardly be doubted that this, too, was a sacred tree, and there could only be one reason for its sanctity.

In 1 Sam. xvii. 2 mention is made of " the terebinth

[1] *Op. cit.*, p. 133.

valley " (not " the vale of Elah," as in the R.V. ; the margin gives "terebinth"). Here the point of significance is that a valley should be known by the name of a single tree ; it denotes that there was something specific about the tree, and being a terebinth (i.e. an evergreen) we may conclude that it was a sacred tree.

In 1 Sam. xxii. 6 we read : " Now Saul was sitting in Gibeah, under the tamarisk tree on the height." As is well known, sanctuaries were often situated on elevated spots, and as this tree stood in a sanctuary it was obviously a sacred one. Saul sits under it taking counsel with his followers, because he finds himself in a difficult position. No hint is given, it is true, as to the reason for this spot being chosen ; but it is difficult to resist the conclusion that guidance was sought because of the presence of the deity there.

The burying of Saul's bones under a tamarisk tree (1 Sam. xxxi. 13), or under a terebinth as in 1 Chron. x. 12, in Jabesh, was done with the intention of according them the utmost reverence ; there would be no point in making mention of this unless the tree had been regarded as a sacred one.

One of the most instructive passages is 2 Sam. v. 23, 24 (see also 1 Chron. xiv. 15). After David has enquired of Yahweh regarding his attack upon the Philistines, he is told that when he hears the sound of marching in the tops of the balsam trees it will be the time to bestir himself, " for then is Yahweh gone out before thee to smite the hosts of the Philistines " ; the marching in the tops of the trees, is, of course, the sound of the rustling of the branches. It is quite clear from thi spassage that the belief was held that Yahweh entered the trees, His presence being indicated by the rustling. One could not have a more direct indication of animistic belief.

In 1 Kings xiii. 14 we read of a man of God sitting under a terebinth tree ; as the context shows, this is the spot on which he sought to give answer to enquiries made, but he is lured away by a false prophet. The fact that he is described as sitting under the terebinth would be pointless unless it were implied that this was an oracle-tree. As the scene is in Bethel the tree is in all probability to be identified with the one mentioned in Gen. xxxv. 8, which was also in Bethel.

In later times worship under trees was condemned as heathen, but the passages in which such condemnation occurs show that trees were regarded as sacred in earlier times, and therefore indirectly witness to animistic conceptions ; that this type of worship continued for so long only shows how deeply rooted these conceptions were.

CHAPTER III

REMNANTS OF ANIMISM IN HEBREW RELIGION: SACRED WATERS

1. General Semitic Belief

AMONG the Semites generally animistic conceptions in regard to water were at least as pronounced as in regard to trees. This applies above all to running water, rivers, streams, and springs. Lakes and the sea itself were also the abodes of supernatural beings, but with these we are not so directly concerned.

The ancient Babylonians believed that life was inherent in water; their water deities being, of course, a subsequent development.[1] Thus, the fact that Ea was the god of the deep permits the assumption that in an earlier stage of belief the sea itself was a living thing. In the ancient Babylonian Pantheon there were numerous water-gods, for every river and canal, great or small, had its special tutelary deity.[2] On the great Khammurabi inscription mention is made of the river-god Naru: the name itself probably means "river" (cp. *nahar*, the Hebrew word for "river"). A goddess named Nin-akha-kuddu is often mentioned in connexion with this god, from which fact Jastrow concludes that she was a river-goddess. Evidence of an earlier stage of belief may perhaps be discerned in the mention of water-witches, Jastrow quotes a magical text pronounced against a witch who had enticed a man into the water.[3] Belonging to later times, we are told that in the great temple of Marduk in Babylon there was a spring in which the gods, according to a Babylonian hymn, " bathed their faces."

Jastrow, in concluding his chapter on the remnants of

---

[1] Jastrow, *op. cit.*, i. 48.   [2] *Ibid.*, p. 63.
[3] *Op. cit.*, i. 300, 310.

Animism in Babylonian religion, lays emphasis on the close connexion that is seen to exist between gods and spirits in the popular forms of Babylonian religion. In the magical texts both of these belong to the Pantheon, and the same is the case in other branches of religious literature. Old-world traditional animistic conceptions dominate popular belief down to the latest times, and this in spite of the distinction that had been made between the higher and the lower powers, and in spite of the efforts of the learned classes to systematize and, so far as in them lay, to purify the ancient religious ideas. "Indeed," he says, "it must strike one as a satire on civilization that Animism, in the modified form (*in der abgeschwächten Form*) of Magic, is perhaps to be regarded as the most enduring heritage which Babylon has bequeathed to mankind. Among classical writers the representative of Babylonian culture, the priest, has become synonymous with magician." [1]

Regarding the Syrians, Lucian, in speaking of the sacred lake at Hierapolis, says that in the midst of it there stood "an altar of stone, which was always decked with ribbons ; and many every day swim in the lake with crowns on their heads performing their acts of adoration." [2]

One of the most holy places among the Phœnicians was the pool of Aphaca at the source of the River Adonis. [3] Robertson Smith draws attention to the fact that temples were often erected near springs and rivers, and that while such a position was no doubt chosen partly on account of its convenience—water being required for ablutions and other ritual purposes—yet "the presence of living water in itself gave consecration to the place. The fountain or stream was not a mere adjunct to the temple, but was itself one of the principal *sacra* of the spot, to which special legends and a special ritual were often attached, and to which the temple in many instances owed its celebrity and even its name." [4] He gives various illustrations ; but the most important point for our present purpose is expressed in the words : "The one general principle which runs through all the varieties of the legends, and

[1] *Op. cit.*, i. 200.
[2] *De Dea Syria*, § xlvi.
[3] Baudissin, *op. cit.*, ii. 159 f.
[4] *Rel. Sem.*, p. 170.

which also lies at the basis of the ritual, is that the sacred waters are instinct with divine life and energy. The legends explain this in diverse ways, and bring the divine quality of the waters into connexion with various deities or supernatural powers, but they all agree in this, that their main object is to show how the fountain or stream comes to be impregnated, so to speak, with the vital energy of the deity to which it is sacred." [1]

Regarding the ancient Arabs, the mention of sacred waters is comparatively rare—not to be wondered at in such an arid country as Arabia ; but sufficient evidence exists to show without a shadow of doubt that their belief in this respect was identical with other Semites. In Mecca there was in the times of heathenism the holy well Zamzam into which gifts were cast ; Wellhausen gives other instances of sacred waters at sanctuaries ; he says that as a rule the spring or well lay at the foot of a hill or rock.[2] Robertson Smith says that " as healing springs and sacred springs are everywhere identified, it is noteworthy that the south Arabs regard medicinal waters as inhabited by *jinn*, usually of serpent form, and that the water of the sanctuary at the Palmetum was thought to be health-giving, and was carried home by pilgrims as Zamzam water now is." [3] He also gives instances showing that some holy wells became places of oracles and divination.

Abundant confirmation of the belief that springs and running waters are the abode of spirits is afforded by what can be observed at the present day in Syria, where the beliefs held millenniums ago are still in vogue. For illustrations of this see Curtiss, *op. cit.*, pp. 88 ff., 116 ff.

These few details are sufficient to show the ideas of the Semites in general regarding sacred waters, and will serve as a preliminary to our examination of what the Old Testament says upon the subject ; to this we now turn.

[1] *Rel. Sem.*, p. 173.
[2] *Op. cit.*, pp. 103 f.
[3] *Rel. Sem.*, pp. 168, 178 ; further information is given by Lagrange, *op. cit.*, pp. 158–168. See also the very instructive example given by Frazer, *G.B.*, " Adonis, Attis, Osiris," i. 215 f.

2. THE OLD TESTAMENT

In Gen. xiv. 7 it is said that another name for *Kadesh*
(" sanctuary ") was *'En-mishpat*, " the spring of decision."
This name implies that it was a well to which men came
in order to obtain a decision about some point of dispute ;
it was thus an oracle-well. It must therefore have been
believed to be the abode of a spirit, a holy well, that is ;
and this is borne out by the name of the place in which
it was situated, *Kadesh*, a " sanctuary." Naturally,
the water of such a well was regarded as holy ; and it
was from a similar source that the " holy water " mentioned in Num. v. 17 was brought for use in the ritual for
discovering the innocence or otherwise of a man's wife
accused of adultery. The fact that the water is called
" holy," as well as the belief in its efficacy, means that
it was believed to be impregnated by the nature and
presence of a spirit.

The significance of such a name as *'En-mishpat* justifies
the belief that in the case of other names compounded
with *'En* there was originally a similar significance.
Of course, this does not necessarily follow ; but when it is
realized how often supernatural powers were associated
with springs and wells it will be seen that there is some
justification for believing that place-names connected
with *'En* do point to originally sacred sites. This is
especially borne out by those cases in which the name of a
god is attached to *'En*. Thus, we have *'En-shemesh* in
Joshua xv. 7, xviii. 17, " the spring of the sun " ; if
there were any doubt as to the significance of this name,
it would be removed by the fact that in the latter passage
the Septuagint renders it " the spring of *Beth-Shemesh* " ;
for in place-names compounded with *Beth* the name following it is very frequently of a divine character, so that
Beth in such cases means " temple." *'En-shemesh* was,
therefore, a spring which at one time was connected with
sun-worship.

There is mentioned also in Gen. xiv. 7 the place called
Chăzāzón-tamar,[1] which, according to 2 Chron. xx. 2, is

---

[1] *Tamar* means a " palm-tree " ; it is not known what *Chăzāzón*
means.

the same as *'En-gedi* (" the spring of the Kid ") ; were
it not for the other name by which *'En-gedi* was known,
one would naturally assume that it received its name
because it was situated in a spot where there was pasturage
for flocks ; but as it was marked by the presence of a
sacred palm-tree the spring must have been a holy one.
In the vicinity of *'En-gedi* there was another spring,
called *'En-'eglaim,* " the spring of the two calves " ;
the mention of the *two* calves is interesting—it is not as
though the plural did not often occur—for we naturally
think of the two calves set up by Jeroboam I for worship
(1 Kings xii. 29) ; and from 2 Kings x. 29 it looks as if two
calves were set up both in Bethel and in Dan, not one
calf in each ; in Bethel (1 Kings xii. 32) and in Samaria
also two calves were worshipped (2 Kings xvii. 16, though
in Hos. viii. 5, 6, only one is mentioned). It is therefore
quite possible that *'En-'eglaim* was at one time the sanctuary of a cow-divinity, viz. Astarte (cp. *'Ashtoreth-
Karnaim,* " Astarte of the two horns," Gen. xiv. 5) ;
the large number of images of this goddess with two horns
discovered during excavations in Palestine proves how
prevalent this worship was.

Another spring connected with the name of an animal,
but for an entirely different reason, is *'En-hak-kore* (Judges
xv. 18, 19) ; this has been wrongly interpreted in the
Hebrew text as meaning " the spring of the caller," i.e.
of one who calls upon God. That is folk etymology. What
it means is " the partridge-spring " ; it was the calling-
note of the partridge which gave it the name of " the
caller " (see 1 Sam. xxvi. 20 ; Jer. xvii. 11). The reason
why the spring was thus called is very interesting. There
is another word for " partridge " in Hebrew, *Choglah,* or
more probably *Chaglah* ; this word comes from a root
meaning to "hop," the cognate Arabic root is "to
hobble " or " hop." This second name for a partridge was
given to it because of the way in which it hops along. Now
in Joshua xv. 6, xviii. 19, 21, mention is made of a place
close to Jericho which is called *Beth-Choglah* (*-Chaglah*),
i.e. " the house, or sanctuary, of the hobbler," which must
be in reference to a particular kind of sacred dance
associated with the worship at this sanctuary. That

3

this is not a fantastic idea will be seen by Robertson Smith's reference to Epiphanius : " The Syriac text of Epiphanius (*De pond. et mens.*, § 62), tells us that Atad of Gen. l. 11 was identified with the spring and thorn-bush of Beth-hagla near Jericho, and the explanation offered of the name Beth-hagla seems to be based on a local tradition of a ritual procession round the sacred objects." [1] One can fully understand the identification referred to when reading in Gen. l. 11 of " the mourning (i.e. for Jacob) in the floor of Atad " ; for a ritual dance as a mourning custom was widespread in antiquity.[2]

One other spring connected with the name of an animal may be mentioned, the *'En-ha-tannin*, or " Spring of the dragon," in Neh. ii. 13 : there is good reason for identifying this with *'En-rogel* ; both were in Jerusalem, and the latter was by the " serpent's stone " (" serpent " is used for " dragon " in Amos ix. 3). For a spring to be known by two names was evidently not uncommon, especially when, as in this case, there was a particular reason for it. That *'En-rogel* was a sanctuary is quite obvious, since it was a place of sacrifice (1 Kings i. 9).[3] It is well known that springs were often regarded as places of healing, and according to Num. xxi. 9 a serpent is the emblem of healing. *'En-ha-tannin* may therefore well have been originally a place for healing, the name having been given to it because it was believed that it was the abode of a spirit which appeared at times in the shape of a serpent ; damp spots are a favourite *habitat* for some kinds of serpents. Then arises the question as to what *'En-rogel* means ; it is usually interpreted as meaning " the fuller's spring " ; but this is questionable, and the word never occurs elsewhere in Biblical Hebrew. But the root from which the word comes means not infrequently to " search out " or " enquire " about something (e.g. Judges xviii. 2 ; 2 Sam. x. 3, and elsewhere) ; and there is no reason why this should not be what is meant here, " the well of

---

[1] *Rel. Sem.*, p. 191, note 1. For other references to ritual dances in the Old Testament see the present writer's *The Sacred Dance*, pp. 50 f., 92 f. (1923).

[2] See *The Sacred Dance*, pp. 29 f.

[3] It is also mentioned in ver. 25, and in Joshua xv. 7, xviii. 16 2 Sam. xvii. 17.

enquiring," viz. about what one should do to cure an ailment. In this connexion we are reminded of '*En-harod*, "the well of trembling" (Judges vii. 1), perhaps to be understood in the sense of the troubling of the waters as in the case of the pool of Bethesda.

We have by no means exhausted the references to springs,[1] but sufficient examples will have been given; moreover, there is a further type of sacred waters to be considered.

So far we have been dealing with sacred *springs*, i.e. waters which spring forth spontaneously; but the Hebrews also attached great importance to sacred *wells*, i.e. waters which had to be dug for before they came forth, *Bĕ'ēr*. This distinction is, however, not always observed in the Old Testament. A very instructive passage in this connexion is Num. xxi. 17, 18, one of the oldest fragments of poetry in the Bible, in which the well is addressed as though it were a living being:

> "Spring up, O well"; sing ye to it:
> "O well, which the princes digged,
> Which the nobles of the people delved
> With their sceptre, with their staves."

Such words, sung directly to the well, can only mean that it was believed to be the embodiment of a super-natural being who caused it to spring up. As Robertson Smith says: "In Palestine to this day all springs are viewed as the seats of spirits, and the peasant women, whether Moslem or Christian, ask their permission before drawing water."[2]

The most important site of a sacred well was *Beersheba* (Gen. xxi. 31–33). Opinions differ as to whether we are to understand this name as meaning "the well of seven," i.e. spirits, or "seven wells"; von Gall argues strongly in favour of the former interpretation,[3] so too George

---

[1] See, among others, Joshua xvii. 7, xix. 21, 37; 1 Sam. xxviii. 7; Neh. xi. 29; Gen. xxxviii. 14, 21; Joshua xv. 32, 34, xix. 7; Num. xxxiv. 11.

[2] *Rel. Sem.*, p. 169, note 3. Other parallels, ancient and modern, are given by Dalman, *Palestinischer Diwan*, p. 45 (1901); Gressmann, *Mose und seine Zeit*, pp. 349 f. (1913).

[3] *Altisraelitische Kultstätten*, pp. 44 ff. (1898).

Adam Smith[1]; but most others believe that it means
"Seven Wells." Driver, e.g., says that "the stress laid on
the number ' seven ' in vers. 28–30 seems to show that the
writer intends to explain ' Beersheba ' as meaning ' Well
of seven' (*sheba* being 'seven' in Hebrew); but in ver. 31*b*
it is explained expressly as meaning ' Well of swearing.'
. . . But it is hardly doubtful that the real meaning of
the name is ' Well of seven,' i.e. ' Seven wells,' with
allusion to the number of wells in the locality . . . "[2];
and Robertson Smith points to the fact that " seven is a
sacred number among the Semites, particularly affected
in matters of ritual, and the Hebrew verb ' to swear '
means literally ' to come under the influence of seven
things.' Thus seven ewe lambs figure in the oath between
Abraham and Abimelech at Beersheba . . . the oath
of purgation at seven wells would therefore have a
peculiar force." [3]

However this may be, the main point is that the well, or
wells, of Beersheba was a sanctuary ; and like many
another sanctuary it had also its sacred tree, in this case
a tamarisk (Gen. xxi. 33).[4] The deity which from time
immemorial had been worshipped here was called '*El
'Olam*, the " ancient 'El," or God, who was now identified
with the God of Israel (cp. Gen. xxvi. 24). From Amos
v. 5 we can see that the worship there was reprobated by
the prophet.

Another interesting illustration is that of the well
called *Be'er-lahai-roi*, situated between Kadesh and Bered
(Gen. xvi. 14), for the steps in the development of belief
can be plainly discerned here. There was a very ancient
well sacred to a local god, called 'El-ro'i, a god of seeing,
i.e. one who is seen ; the belief being that the spirit,
whose abode this well was, manifested himself at certain
times ; so that the well was called Be'er-'el-ro'i. This
sanctuary became adapted by the Israelites to Yahweh-
worship, in consequence of which the name underwent a

---

[1] *Encycl. Bibl.*, i. 518*b*.   [2] *The Book of Genesis*, p. 215 (1904).
[3] *Rel. Sem.*, p. 182, where other instances are given. Cp. also the
other form of the Beersheba tradition in Gen. xxvi. 23 ff., where in
ver. 33 the name is interpreted as meaning " the well of the oath."
[4] Cp. also Be'er-'elim, " the well of the terebinths," in Isa. xv. 8,
perhaps the same as that mentioned in Num. xxi. 16.

change ; and because it was believed that no one could see God and live (see Gen. xxxii. 30), the name was altered so as to read " The well of my seeing and (yet) living." [1] Then the final step was that for reverential reasons the "angel of Yahweh " was substituted for Yahweh Himself.

In Joshua xix. 8 a place is mentioned called *Ba'alath-bĕ'ēr*, " the mistress of the well," showing that the belief in a female spirit of a well also existed.

The sanctity of *running water* is well illustrated by the ritual described in Deut. xxi. 4 ; one can therefore well understand that certain rivers were looked upon as sanctuaries of gods ; probably this was the case with *all* rivers originally. The Kishon (Judges v. 21) is a case in point ; in all probability the stream was called after the god Kish, and conceived to be in some direct way connected with him ; so, too, with the rivers Belus and Adonis. That the Gihon was likewise a sanctuary is clear from the fact that Solomon was brought down to it to be anointed king (1 Kings i. 33, 34).

Cases of this kind show that originally the river or stream was regarded as sacred because of the spirit whose abode it was.

We are perhaps apt to overlook the significance of references to well-grown trees standing by waters (e.g. Gen. xlix. 22 ; Isa. xliv. 4 ; Jer. xvii. 8 ; Ezek. xix. 10 ; Ps. i. 3) ; in its origin this was because of the presence of a spirit, primarily in the water.

[1] The Hebrew text of xvi. 14 can hardly be in order ; see Driver's note and his reference to Wellhausen's emendation (slightly different from that here adopted), *op. cit.*, p. 183.

CHAPTER IV

REMNANTS OF ANIMISM IN HEBREW RELIGION : SACRED STONES, ROCKS, AND MOUNTAINS

1. GENERAL SEMITIC BELIEF

THERE are two points of difference between sacred trees, sacred springs, etc., and sacred stones, whether a rock or a boulder or a heap of stones or a pillar. The first difference is that the former have, or were believed to have, independent life, while the latter were inanimate ; and the second difference is that the former were natural sanctuaries, the latter artificial, at any rate as a general rule, among the Semites ; instances of sacred natural rocks occur, but they are not frequent.

Whatever new conceptions, expressed by their ritual or otherwise, the Semites may have developed regarding the nature and meaning of stones as sanctuaries, it is certain that, like sacred trees and sacred springs, they were inherited by the Semites from man in the distant past.

Since a spirit, or later a god, was believed to take up his abode in the stone, it could make no difference, so far as its sanctity was concerned, what its shape or appearance was. Therefore we naturally ask why, among the Semites, the stone sanctuary normally took the form of a standing pillar. Probably more than one answer must be given to this question since, in course of time, new ideas arose. Robertson Smith thinks that "it seems most probable that the choice of a pillar or cairn as the primitive idol was not dictated by any other consideration than convenience for ritual purposes. The stone or stone-heap was a convenient mark of the proper place of sacrifice, and at the same time, if the deity consented to be present at it, provided the means for

carrying out the ritual of the sacrificial blood."[1] But
the pillar or cairn as representing the spirit or the god, or
later as constituting the place of abode of a god, must
have existed long before the developed ritual of the
sacrificial blood. It is therefore possible that originally
there was something more significant about the standing
stone than the mere question of convenience. One
speaks tentatively here because, from the nature of the
case, there can be no certainty ; but the conjecture may
be hazarded that the standing stone was originally chosen
by the Semites as being the nearest approach to the
human form (cp. what was said above, p. 11). This,
however, is merely incidental ; we are more concerned
with the Semites within historic times.

Stone sanctuaries are not to be found among the
Semites of comparatively advanced culture such as the
Babylonians, Assyrians, and Phœnicians ; among these
we should not expect to find sacred stones or pillars in
the primitive sense.[2] But it is possible that a survival
of these is to be discerned in the pillars that stood at
the entrance to temples. Thus, in the representation of
a Babylonian temple dating from the third millennium B.C.
two pillars stand at the entrance.[3] Another example is
that of an Elamite temple which is depicted on a bronze
slab belonging approximately to 1100 B.C. ; this is a particularly interesting illustration, for what are quite
evidently three tree-trunks and a standing stone are
represented. It contains a short Babylonian inscription ;
the Elamites are known to have been influenced by the
Babylonians, and this bronze slab illustrates the fact.[4]

To a later time, third to fourth cent. B.C., belongs a
Punic votive tablet from Sicily on which three standing
pillars are depicted ; the middle one of these stands

[1] *Rel. Sem.*, p. 212. He shows the fallacy of the opinion that sacred
posts and pillars among the Semites were phallic symbols on pp. 456 f.;
not that these latter were wholly absent (see S. A. Cook, *The Religion
of Ancient Palestine*, p. 32).

[2] The anointing of a sacred stone seems, however, to have been
customary among the Assyrians, according to an inscription of Esar-
haddon (Gunkel, *Genesis*, p. 290 [1901]).

[3] Gressmann, *Altorientalische Bilder zum Alten Testament*, p. 138, and
Plate 476 (1927).

[4] Gressmann, *op. cit.*, p. 135, Plate 468.

higher than those on either side of it. As Gressmann
shows, these are supposed to be standing on, or beside,
an altar.[1] Twin pillars stood also at the entrance to the
temples of Paphos and Hierapolis ; and Herodotus tells
us that in Tyre he saw a temple dedicated to Hercules,
" and in it were two pillars, one of fine gold, the other of
emerald stone." [2] These were, of course, originally of
stone. There is also plenty of evidence of single pillars
standing within the precincts of a temple ; " A coin of
the age of Macrinus shows the principal temple at Byblos ;
in the court is a conical stone upon an altar-like basis.
Similar stones appear on many coins of cities in the
Lebanon and on the Syrian coast." [3]

All these represent a great development in the history
of the sacred stone. To get to the earlier phases among
the Semites we must turn first to the ancient pre-Islamic
Arabs. The sacred stone [4] was indispensable, and the
most characteristic mark of the ancient Arab sanctuary.
It represented the deity, not any particular one, but any
god or goddess. Very often there were several of these in
a sanctuary, even when only one god was worshipped
there. Things were hung upon the sacred stone just as
on the sacred tree ; and it was smeared with blood,
doubtless as an act of worship. Beside it a pit was often
dug, called a *ghabghab* ; into this the sacrificial blood was
poured, and votive offerings were also thrown into it.[5]
Sacred cairns, or stone-heaps, were also common.[6]

Still more instructive is the evidence afforded by excavations in Palestine. Thus, on the site of the ancient
Megiddo, a high-place (*bāmāh*) was laid bare with its stone
altar and two standing stone pillars.[7] Similar pillars were
also found on the site of ancient Taanach, among them

---

[1] *Op. cit.*, pp. 126 f., and Plate 437 ; for another example see
Plate 438.

[2] *Herodotus*, ii. 44 ; see also Robertson Smith, *Rel. Sem.*, p. 208.

[3] G. F. Moore, in *Encycl. Bibl.*, iii. 2890. Cp. also the two pillars set
up at the porch of the temple in Jerusalem, 1 Kings vii. 15, 21.

[4] Called *Nuzb*, it served as altar, and corresponds to the Hebrew
mazzebah (" pillar ").

[5] For these and other details see Wellhausen, *op. cit.*, pp. 101 ff.
(1897) ; Kittel, *Studien zur hebräischen Archäologie und Religionsgeschichte*, pp. 118 ff. (1908).

[6] Wellhausen, *op. cit.*, pp. 111 f.   [7] Jeremias, *op. cit.*, p. 209.

two which were scooped out for the purpose of offering
blood or oil on them.[1] The most interesting, however,
are the pillars which were found on the site of ancient
Gezer in the temple there. This " superb megalithic
structure consists of a row of seven monoliths, with an
eighth standing apart, and flanked by stumps of two
others at the northern end." One of these stands in a
socket, and has two cup-marks and grooves, probably
for pouring in oblations "; there is also a long socketed
stone, clearly not an altar, in which in all probability the
Asherah, or wooden pole, was placed. The smallest and
most insignificant was probably the most important ; its
upper end has been worked almost to a point, and its
polished surface, quite absent from all the others, shows
that it must have been kissed, or anointed, or otherwise
handled by the worshippers ; in fact, this little pillar was
clearly the " beth-el " of the temple.[2]

Evidence of this kind is highly instructive, and throws
light on what we read on the subject in the Old Testament.

Finally, a brief reference must be made to holy mountains. After what has been said it needs no further
words to show that holy hills and mountains witness to
the existence of earlier animistic conceptions.

The best evidence regarding the sanctity of certain
mountains among the Semites generally is offered in the
Old Testament ; therefore before giving examples of
ancient Hebrew belief on the subject it will be well to
mention some instances of sacred mountains situated
in non-Israelite territory.

The sanctity of Mount Sinai, in Midianite territory, is too
well known to need further discussion ; it is sufficient
to point to the name " the mount of Yahweh " being
applied to it (Num. x. 33) ; a mountain on which a god
is supposed to reside is obviously regarded as holy.
The idea is extraordinarily *naïve*, but it must be remembered that even this is a development of an earlier
animistic belief. Mount Sinai is an especially interesting

---

[1] Sellin, *Tell Ta'anek*, pp. 103 ff. (1904), where illustrations are given
and many further particulars.

[2] See the *Quarterly Statement of the Palestine Exploration Fund for*
1903, pp. 23–36. For sacred stones in Palestine at the present day, see
Curtiss, *op. cit.*, pp. 84 ff.

instance, because the whole coast-land along the Aelanitic gulf is volcanic, and the mountain was certainly at one time a volcano.[1] A volcanic eruption would necessarily have been regarded by semi-cultured peoples as due to the spirit which made its abode there.

The heights of Nebo, Pe'or, and Pisgah lie in Moabite territory ; the sanctity of the first is seen by the fact that it is the name of a Babylonian deity who must at one time have been worshipped there. According to Num. xxiii. 28–30 sacrifices were offered on Mount Pe'or, which shows it to have been a sanctuary ; its possessor is spoken of in Num. xxv. 3 as the " Ba'al of Pe'or," who was worshipped by the Israelites. Pisgah is also shown to have been a sacred mount, because altars were erected and sacrifices offered on it (Num. xxiii. 14).

We turn now to examine Hebrew belief regarding sacred stones, etc. The presence of holy mountains in Israelite territory will be spoken of at the end of the next section.

2. The Old Testament

In the narrative of Jacob at Bethel (Gen. xxviii. 11–22) there are some instructive points. Jacob takes one of the stones of the place and uses it for his head to rest on while sleeping ; it is owing to his contact with this stone that he dreams, and thus recognizes that it is the abode of a god, a *bethel*. As a result he sets it up as the pillar (*mazzēbāh*), marking a sanctuary, and pours oil on it as an act of worship of the indwelling deity. From the sacred stone as a god's house the place receives the name of Bethel (cp. xxxv. 14, 15).

We have here the adaptation of an extremely ancient local tradition which is made to apply to the God of Israel ; but the remnants of animistic conceptions are as plain as anything could be.

A stone of a different character, but in regard to which

---

[1] The Old Testament, as against the later tradition, locates Mount Sinai in Midianite or Edomite territory. See Exod. iii. 1, xviii. 1 ff. ; Num. x. 29 ff. ; Hab. iii. 7 ; and cp. Jer. xlix. 21 ; 2 Chron. viii. 17 ; and Exod. xxiii. 31 ; Num. xiv. 25, xxi. 4 ; Deut. i. 40, ii. 1. See further Chap. X.

animistic conceptions are also to be discerned, is that
spoken of in Joshua xxiv. 26, 27 ; here it is told how
Joshua " took a great stone (*'eben*), and set it up there
(i.e. in Shechem) under the oak that was in the sanctuary
of Yahweh. And Joshua said unto all the people, Behold
this stone shall be a witness against us ; for it hath heard
all the words of Yahweh which He spake unto us ; it
shall therefore be a witness against you, lest ye deny your
God." The presence of a sacred stone as well as a
sacred tree in a sanctuary was the usual thing, and each
denoted the presence of the deity ; but as a symbol each
was only a development of the more primitive belief of
the actual indwelling of a spirit. The echo of animistic
conceptions is discerned in the naïve belief in the stone,
identified with the indwelling spirit, hearing what is said
and being thought of as a witness.

A somewhat similar illustration occurs in Gen. xxxi.
44–48. The combination of sources in vers. 43–54 makes
the passage a little difficult ; but for the present purpose
it is sufficient to note that in the two accounts of the
covenant between Jacob and Laban, one speaks of a
pillar (*mazzēbāh*) as the witness (ver. 45), the other of a
cairn (*gal*), in the following verse ; and one speaks of the
common meal, following of course a sacrifice, as taking
place by the side of the pillar (ver. 54), the other as
partaken of *on* the cairn (ver. 46)—not " by " as the
R.V. renders (for the covenant feast cp. xxvi. 30).
We have thus another illustration of the way in which a
pillar, or a cairn, is thought of as a witness, being in fact
personified ; and this can only be understood on the
supposition that in more ancient times a spirit was
believed to animate the one and the other (see further
below, pp. 10 ff.).

It is quite possible that some ancient tradition about a
sacred cairn lies behind the narrative in Joshua iv. 1–14,
where it is told of how, when the ark was brought across the
Jordan, twelve stones were taken from the river and
piled up on the bank as a " sign " (ver. 6) and a
" memorial " (ver. 7). Presumably a cairn had stood
here from time immemorial, and its presence was in later
ages explained as in this passage. As this cairn stood in

the middle of the river (ver. 9), it is permissible to suppose
that it was originally set up in honour of the river-god.
On the other hand, according to ver. 20, the stones were
carried to Gilgal (stone-circle, or cromlech) ; so clearly
two traditions have again been combined.

Another indication pointing to originally animistic
conceptions regarding sacred stones is to be discerned
in the fact that certain important stones have names,
though very few of these occur and their meaning is not
always clear. The best known is *'Eben-'ezer*, "stone of
help" ; two such seem to have existed—one near Aphek
in the north of the plain of Sharon (1 Sam. iv. 1, v. 1), and
the other near Mizpah, a little north-east of Jerusalem
(1 Sam. vii. 12). *'Eben-bohan* is mentioned as a boundary-
stone (Joshua xv. 6, xviii. 17) ; *bohan* can hardly be a
proper name, it may possibly mean the "stone of covering," in the sense of protection, and thus somewhat
analogous to 'Eben-'ezer. In 1 Kings i. 9 it is said that
"Adonijah sacrificed sheep and oxen and fatlings by the
stone of Zocheleth which is beside 'En-rogel'" ; the "stone
of Zocheleth" probably means the "Serpent stone" ;
its sanctity is shown by the fact that animals were
sacrificed beside it. Wellhausen suggests a connexion
between this and the Arabic proper name *Zuhal*, the
name for Saturn.[1] That this stone stood in a sanctuary
is seen by its proximity to the sacred spring (see above,
p. 34).

In 1 Sam. xx. 19 the words "the stone 'Ezel" should
be read "by this mound," following the Septuagint ;
the Hebrew text must be emended accordingly [2] ; this
passage therefore does not come into consideration.

An instructive passage occurs in 1 Sam. vi. 14 ; here
we are told that the kine which drew the cart bearing the
ark "came into the field of Joshua the Bethshemite and
stood there ; and there was a great stone there ; and
they clave the wood of the cart and offered up the kine
for a burnt offering unto Yahweh." Laconic as this

---

[1] *Op. cit.*, p. 146. The two pillars that stood in the porch of the
temple (1 Kings vii. 21), called *Jachin* ("He that establisheth") and
Boaz ("In him is strength"), do not come under this category.

[2] The Hebrew word, according to the emended text, means a mound
of soil, not of stones, so it is not a cairn that is meant.

passage is, it must be obvious that the reason why the kine came to this sudden halt was because of the " great stone " ; it is implied that the power residing in the ark had expressly driven them to this spot that they might be sacrificed there. Robertson Smith points to the some-what analogous instance of the ram which presents itself as an offering in lieu of Isaac (Gen. xxii. 13) : " Exactly this principle," he says, " was observed down to late times at the great Astarte temple at Eryx, where the victims were drawn from the sacred herds nourished at the sanctuary, and were believed to offer themselves spontan-eously at the altar. This is quite analogous to the usage at the Diipolia, where a number of cattle were driven round the sacred table, and the bull was selected for slaughter that approached it and ate of the sacred *popana* " [1] (i.e. flat cakes which were sacred offerings). In the verse before us the sacrifice of the kine then takes place on the stone, which thus becomes an altar. But the deity is still thought of as abiding in the stone, because in ver. 18, where the corrupt Hebrew text must be emended on the basis of the Septuagint, it is said : " And a witness is the great stone, whereon they set down the ark of Yahweh, to this day" (cp. Joshua xxiv. 26, 27; Gen. xxxi. 45, dealt with above, p. 43). In 1 Sam. xiv. 33–35 we read also of a great stone being used for an altar, and although nothing is hinted at as to why this particular stone was used, it is extremely probable that it was chosen because it was regarded as a sacred one. See also 2 Sam. xx. 8.

To this ancient belief in the sacred character of certain stones was due the command recorded in Exod. xx. 24, 25 : " An altar of earth shalt thou make unto me . . . and if thou make me an altar of stone, thou shalt not build it of hewn stones ; for if thou lift up thy tool upon it, thou hast polluted it " (cp. Deut. xxvii. 5, 6; Joshua viii. 31). The idea was that if a stone was hammered the indwelling *numen* would be driven out. It is, of course, not to be supposed that this command was given with any thought of the old-world conception ; but it is a good instance of the persistence of a custom long after its original significance has been forgotten.

[1] *Rel. Sem.*, p. 309.

Before concluding, a few examples must be offered of holy hills and mountains which lay in Israelite territory; for these all owed their character, in the first instance, to a spirit who was believed to have his abode in them.

The sanctity of Mount Carmel [1] is sufficiently illustrated by what we read in 1 Kings xviii. ; altars are raised there both to Baal and to Yahweh ; the presence of an altar is enough to prove that a site is holy. Its holy character continued through the ages to very much later times ; it is spoken of by Tacitus as a sanctuary with its altar, but where there was neither temple nor an image of a deity.[2]

Mount Tabor, on the border between the territories of Issachar and Zebulon (Joshua xix. 22; 1 Chron. vi. 77), was a holy mountain, since sacrifices were offered on it ; this may be rightly gathered from Hos. v. 1 : "Hear this, O ye priests, and hearken, ye house of Israel . . . for ye have been a snare at Mizpah, and a net spread upon Tabor." There is an evident reference here to some illicit forms of worship.

Gibeah, which means "hill," lay in the territory of Benjamin ; its sacred character is very clearly seen by its being called "Gibeah of God" (1 Sam. x. 5), and on account of a holy tree there (1 Sam. xxii. 6). Geba, another name for "hill," and a different place from the foregoing, though also in Benjaminite territory, was also a hill sanctuary, as is shown by 2 Kings xxiii. 8 : "And he brought all the priests out of the cities of Judah, and defiled the high places where the priests had burned incense, from Geba to Beersheba."

We have also clear evidence from 2 Sam. xv. 30–32 that the Mount of Olives was a sanctuary in ancient Israel ; and it is evident that this is the mount referred to in 1 Kings xi. 7 : "Then did Solomon build an high place for Chemosh, the abomination of Moab, in the mount that is before Jerusalem. . . ."

The very frequent mention of "high places" (*bāmōth*),

---

[1] Not to be confused with the Carmel in Judah, south of Hebron (see 1 Sam. xxv. 2 ff.).

[2] *Hist.*, ii. 78. See further G. A. Smith, *The Historical Geography of the Holy Land*, pp. 337–41 (1910).

which are always sanctuaries, shows how numerous they were [1] ; their original existence was due to the fact that in course of time hill and mountain sanctuaries were insufficient for the growing population and the increase of settlements ; the " high place " was thus an imitation of the mountain sanctuary. But this belongs, of course, to much later ages. The original sanctity of a mountain or hill was due to the presence of a spirit ; and we must therefore see in the existence of such a thing as a sacred mountain a remnant of very much earlier animistic conceptions.

We have dealt with many of the Old Testament passages which support the contention that the ancestors of the Hebrews passed through the Animistic stage of belief, the marks of which were left even after Hebrew Religion had reached a higher stage. The next step is the Polytheistic stage ; but before we come to this it will be necessary to show that the Old Testament gives indubitable indications that at one time Totemism, Taboo, and Ancestor-worship, as well as some other primitive beliefs, were in vogue among the Semitic forbears of the Hebrews, and that the marks of this having been the case can be pointed to.

[1] On these see below, pp. 124 f.

CHAPTER V

REMNANTS OF TOTEMISM, TABOO, AND ANCESTOR-WORSHIP IN HEBREW RELIGION

1. TOTEMISM

WE have seen that by Totemism is meant a form of society in which the members of a clan or tribe believe themselves to be united by kinship to some animal or plant, mainly the former, from which they are descended. We are not here concerned with the origin of this world-wide and extraordinary institution; various theories are held, but certain knowledge on the subject can hardly be expected, for it clearly goes back to an extreme antiquity, to a time, in fact, when man's reasoning powers were of so primitive a character that it is perhaps not possible for us to get down to his mentality. Even in the case of the most backward races among which the system is still in vogue it probably has a history of many millenniums behind it ; but these more or less primitive institutions have an extraordinary way of leaving their marks for ages and ages after they have lost their meaning, and their remnants are to be discerned not only among the more cultured peoples of antiquity, but even at the present day in Europe. Therefore there is not really anything surprising to find that in the Old Testament and in the religion of the Hebrews remnants of Totemism are discernible. Of course, as Robertson Smith says, " at the stage which even the rudest Semitic peoples had reached when they first become known to us, it would be absurd to expect to find examples of totemism pure and simple. What we may expect to find is the fragmentary survival of totem ideas, in the shape of special associations between certain kinds of animals on the one hand, and certain tribes or religious communities and their gods

on the other.   And of evidence of this kind there is no
lack in Semitic antiquity." [1]

While such evidence is to be found over the whole
Semitic area, we shall, before coming to the Old Testament,
confine ourselves to the ancient Arabs, for in them and
in their stage of culture we find the closest parallel with
the early Hebrews ; moreover, the available *data* are
much greater where they are concerned than among any
other Semitic people.[2]

In his *Kinship and Marriage in Early Arabia*, Robertson Smith writes : " The complete proof of early totemism in any race involves the following points : (1) the
existence of stocks named after plants and animals ; (2)
the prevalence of the conception that the members of the
stock are of the blood of the eponym animal, or are sprung
from a plant of the species chosen as totem ; (3) the
ascription to the totem of a sacred character, which may
result in its being regarded as the god of the stock, but at
any rate makes it to be regarded with veneration, so that,
for example, a totem animal is not used as ordinary food.
If we can find all these things together in the same tribe
the proof of totemism is complete. . . ." [3]

In the pages which follow these words (220–281, and
also 307–312) this proof is furnished ; here it must suffice
to give just a few illustrations.   Under the first head
eleven pages of examples are given ; among them we find
such tribal names as these : lion, ibex, wild cow, steer,
serpent, sheep, wolf, dog, panther, hyæna, etc. ; and it is
shown that these various tribes are named after the
animals.   " To students of primitive society in general,
who have learned what animal stock-names habitually
mean, the mass of such names in Arabia must be highly
significant ; when very primitive races call themselves
dogs, panthers, snakes, sheep, lion cubs, or sons of the
lion, the jerboa, or the lizard, the burden of proof really
lies on those who maintain that such designations do
not mean what they mean in other parts of the

[1] *Rel. Sem.*, p. 444.
[2] For Totemism among the Babylonians see Jastrow, *op. cit.*, ii.
441, 896 f.
[3] *Kinship*, p. 219 (new edition, 1903).

4

world. That the names are mere accidents or mere metaphors is an assumption which can seem plausible only to those who do not know savage ways of thought." [1]

As to the conception that the members of a tribe were of the same blood as the animal whose name they bore, and were thus akin to it, we have such illustrations as that of a whole clan mourning over a dead gazelle ; if a serpent is killed all the members of the serpent clan are bound to avenge it ; the *hyrax Syriacus* was not eaten because he was the brother of man, and " he who eats him will never see his father or mother again." Connected with this conception was also the belief that men could change themselves into animals ; some animals were not eaten because they were believed to be, in reality, men who had transformed themselves into such animals ; an idea of this kind would easily arise if men were convinced that there existed a physical kinship between them and the animal in question. Of a tribe living in Hadramaut, the land in the south-west of Arabia, it is related that in time of drought part of the tribe changed themselves into ravening were-wolves, and that they could change themselves back again into human shape. Others from the same district could change themselves into kites or vultures. In the Sinaitic Peninsula the hyrax and the panther are believed to have been men at one time. Muhammad would not eat lizards because he fancied them to be the offspring of a metamorphosed clan of Israelites. [2]

Thirdly, as to the sacred character of the animal chosen for the totem ; the most significant point here is that the animal may not be eaten as ordinary food, but only when sacrificed on special occasions. Thus, the camel was sacred to a camel clan—it was only eaten when offered in sacrifice [3] ; but to the Arabs in general the camel was common food. [4] Locusts were not eaten by all Arabs ; " in Islam they are lawful, but the copious discussions on the point by the traditionalists . . . show that in the prophet's time there was a doubt as to their lawfulness." [5]

---

[1] Robertson Smith, *Kinship*, p. 237.
[2] For these and other illustrations see *Rel. Sem.*, p. 88 ; *Kinship*, pp. 238 f.
[3] For an interesting example see *Rel. Sem.*, p. 338.
[4] *Rel. Sem.*, p. 218.　　　　　　[5] *Kinship*, p. 228.

That there is not in *each* case evidence forthcoming of the sacred animal being eaten when sacrificed on special occasions is to be expected. Again, to give an illustration from outside the Arab domain, the dove among the Syrians was not eaten ; it was sacred to Ashtoreth, and has all the marks of a totem: "The testimonies to this effect are collected by Bochart, and show that the bird was not merely a symbol, but received divine honour. In Arabia we find a dove-idol in the Ka'ba, and sacred doves around it." [1] Once more, there were several lizard clans among the Arabs, among them the *Dobaib*, ("lizard") ; this lizard was a sacred animal : "its flesh supplied the Arabs with medicines and antidotes to poisons, its bones and skin had magical virtues. Such virtues are generally ascribed by rude nations to animals that are not habitually eaten. . . ." [2]

These few illustrations, out of a large number which could be adduced, show that the animal after which the members of a clan called themselves was regarded as sacred. But when an animal is believed to be the ancestor of a clan all the members of which are his offspring, and, in consequence, all the animals of the same kind as the ancestor are sacrosanct, it is a natural, one might almost say an inevitable, development that the ancestor becomes a god, and all the animals of his kind are thought of as his representatives. That this was the actual course of development among the Arabs has been shown by Robertson Smith in his *Kinship*, pp. 240 ff. "There is abundance of independent evidence," he says, "that not only the Arabs, but all the Semites, often spoke and thought of themselves as children of their gods. . . ." [3] We must therefore hold that it was because Arabic tribes claimed to be the children of their tribal god that they took his name. And when we find among such

---

[1] *Kinship*, p. 229.
[2] *Ibid.*, pp. 231 ff., where further illustrations will be found. Cp. Nielsen, *Handbuch der altarabischen Altertumskunde*, i. 206 (1927).
[3] How ingrained this idea was, and is, may be seen by the fact that a missionary, in teaching a Muhammadan's children that they were descended from Adam and Eve, was corrected by their mother who retorted : "No, the moon is our father, and the sun is our mother" (Nielsen, *Handbuch*, i. 211).

tribes cases like the Banū Hilāl, 'sons of the crescent moon,' or Banū Badr, 'sons of the full moon,' where the divine being is at the same time one of those heavenly beings which primitive peoples everywhere have looked upon as animals, the interval between divine tribal names and animal tribal names is very nearly bridged over, and one is compelled to ask whether both are not reducible to one ultimate principle such as the totem theory supplies." [1]

Now it is in the light of what has been said that we must approach the subject of the remnants of Totemism in the Old Testament.

It should be mentioned here that there are some prominent Old Testament scholars, though their number is very small, who deny altogether that there are any remnants of Totemism to be discerned in the Old Testament; among them notably Lagrange, *Études sur les Religions Sémitiques*, pp. 112–118 (1903), and Ed. König, *Geschichte der alttestamentlichen Religion*, pp. 72–78 (1924); but their objections do not carry conviction; one receives the impression that neither of them approaches the question with an unbiassed mind, and in any case Robertson Smith's arguments are not seriously grappled with by either of them.

In the comparatively advanced stage of culture in which we find even the earliest Hebrews we should not expect to discern anything more in the records of their early beliefs than very faint remnants of such a primitive institution as Totemism; but that certain facts which will be pointed out are such remnants seems to be the most satisfactory and the most natural explanation of them.

We will take the steps of the argument in the order already followed, and begin by pointing out that just as among the early Arabs so the early Hebrews had many animal clan names and tribal names. Thus Simeon means " hyæna "; Leah (= Levi) [2] means " wild cow ";

---

[1] See also *Rel. Sem.*, pp. 125 ff. For other animal names of gods among the heathen Arabs see Nielsen, *op. cit.*, i. 192.

[2] But see further on this Buchanan Gray, *Sacrifice in the Old Testament*, pp. 246 ff. (1925).

Deborah means " bee " ; Rachel means " ewe " ; Caleb means " dog " ; Shobal means " lion " ; Epher means " young antelope " ; Oren means " ibex." Other examples are place-names of animals, which, as Stade shows,[1] received their names from the clans inhabiting them : Aijalon, from Aijal, " stag " ; Shaalbim, " foxes " ; Ophra and Ephron, from Epher, " young antelope " ; Eglon from Egel, " calf " ; Nimra, from Namer, " leopard " ; and many others.[2] All these, it is to be noted, are clan or tribal, not personal, names ; and among the many animal proper names in the Old Testament by far the greater number are those of clans or tribes. The significance of this is that when an animal name is that of a clan it points to an original belief of kinship of all its members with the animal after which they are named ; a *personal* animal name, on the other hand, might be, and is, given for a variety of reasons, but not because the bearer is believed to have kinship with the animal. But even personal animal names, according to Buchanan Gray, are indirectly explained by the totem theory. He explains them thus : " With the break-up of the totem clan system, the clan names became in certain cases personal, instances of which we perhaps find in Eglah, the name of David's wife, the two Deborahs, and other names of early individuals, though we have, it is true, no direct evidence that these were ever tribal. But the strictly personal character of many of the early names classified in the synopsis [3] is open to doubt. . . . It is certainly curious that so many of the early and apparently individual names turn out on closer inspection to be possibly or even probably tribal. . . ." [4]

At any rate, there are a large number of certain cases, of which a few are given above, of clans or stocks named after animals.[5]

Cases among the Hebrews of the conception that the

---

[1] *Geschichte des Volkes Israel*, i. 398, 409 (1886).
[2] See Buchanan Gray, *Hebrew Proper Names*, pp. 86 ff. (1896).
[3] Pp. 88–96 in his book.
[4] *Op. cit.*, pp. 101 f.
[5] The list in Gen. xxxvi. 20–30, containing the names of " the sons of Seir the Horite," has a very considerable proportion of animal names.

members of a stock are of the blood of an eponym animal
are not forthcoming ; that must be frankly acknowledged,
nor is this to be expected [1] ; but of animal cults which
presuppose an earlier totemistic stage there are indications.   Thus, Ezekiel tells of how he saw in the sanctuary
the worship of " every form of creeping things, and
abominable beasts " (viii. 10) ; and in Isa. lxv. 4 reference
is made to those who " sit among the graves, and lodge
in secret places ; which eat swine's flesh, and broth of
unclean meats is in their vessels " ; and again in Isa.
lxvi. 3 there are references to animal cults : " He that
killeth an ox is as he that slayeth a man ; he that
sacrificeth a lamb, as he that breaketh a dog's neck ; he
that offereth an oblation (as he that offereth) swine's
blood ; he that burneth frankincense, as he that blesseth
an idol.   Yea, they have chosen their own ways, and their
soul delighteth in their abominations " ; and also in
Isa. lxvi. 17 : " They that sanctify themselves, and purify
themselves (to go) into the gardens after one in the midst
(i.e. after the leader of the illicit ceremonies), eating
swine's flesh, and swarming creatures, and the mouse."
All the creatures mentioned in these passages and chosen
for the sacrifices were " such as were unclean in the first
degree, and surrounded by strong taboos of the kind which
in heathenism imply that the animal is regarded as
divine. . . . Here we have therefore a clear case of the
re-emergence into the light of day of a cult of the most
primitive totem type, which had been banished for
centuries from public religion, but must have been kept
alive in obscure circles of private or local superstition." [2]
It is not without significance that " the second commandment, the cardinal precept of spiritual worship, is
explicitly directed against the worship of the denizens of
air, earth, and water." [3]

It is further to be noted that although the Old Testament offers little indication of the belief that the members
of a clan with an animal name were the offspring of the

---

[1] It is, however, possible that the conception expressed in Jer. ii. 27
goes back ultimately to totemism : ". . . which say to a stock, thou
art my father ; and to a stone, thou hast begotten us."

[2] *Rel. Sem.*, p. 357.   [3] *Op. cit.*, p. 625.

totem animal, there are hints that worshippers believed themselves to be descended from a god ; and, as we have seen, there are some grounds for holding that this is a development of the earlier belief. Thus, names compounded with a divine name, such as Abijah ("my father is Yah ") or Ahijah ("my brother is Yah "),[1] and others, suggest the question as to whether or not they indicate a transition from the totem conception of kindred with a divine or totem animal to a conception of kinship with a personal God ? To apply a spiritual interpretation to "father " in cases like these might be conceivable, but not so in regard to "brother " ; but to do so even in the case of the former cannot be justified in view of the fact that "the name in question, together with those related to it in form, falls into disuse just when the deeper ideas of the fatherhood of God were developing."[2]

That the *conception* of a physical connexion between a god and his people was not unfamiliar to the Hebrews is evident from Num. xxi. 29 : "Woe to thee, Moab ! Thou art undone, O people of Chemosh ; he hath given his sons as fugitives, and his daughters into captivity, unto Sihon king of the Amorites."[3] It is significant that this downright expression of physical kinship to a god is toned down in later days when Jeremiah, in quoting this passage, says : "Woe unto thee, Moab ! the people of Chemosh is undone ; for thy sons are taken away captive, and thy daughters into captivity " (xlviii. 46) ; and the significance is enhanced when it is seen how familiar Jeremiah was with the conception still in vogue among the idolaters. In the words already quoted he says : "Which say to a stock, thou art my father ; and to a stone, thou hast begotten us " (ii. 27). It must be acknowledged, then, that there are good grounds for believing that some remnants of Totemism are to be discerned in the Old Testament ; the case could be made stronger if it could be more fully dealt with, but that would be out of place here ; for this recourse must be had to the works cited.

[1] For the same thing among the ancient Arabs, see Nielsen, *op. cit.*, i. 192.
[2] Buchanan Gray, *op. cit.*, pp. 253 f.
[3] Cp. also Mal. ii. 11.

2. Taboo

Closely associated with Totemism, indeed indissolubly connected with it in its origin, is *Taboo*. This prohibition to come into contact with certain things on account of their " holiness " is concerned in the first instance with various kinds of animals, the flesh of which may not be eaten because it is either " holy " or " unclean " ; but it applies also to persons, especially those connected in any way with the deity and his worship, and to certain other persons and things with which we are not at present concerned ; it applies also to ground dedicated to the deity. The apparent incongruity that under the term taboo are included both things which are holy and things which are unholy or unclean, is confusing ; but what seems to be a contradiction may perhaps be explained by an analogy : the word " awe " expresses the two emotions of reverence and fear ; reverence attracts, fear repels ; and yet in both there is, if one may so express it, the element of " keep-at-a-distance." One may draw near to a holy thing and yet refrain from touching it just because of its holiness, i.e. out of reverential awe ; and one may keep from an unclean thing for fear of being harmed. The holy thing is awesome ; the unclean thing is awful.[1]

Taboos among the Semites generally existed in plenty ; just one or two instances may be mentioned. For holy animals among the Babylonians and Assyrians details will be found in Jastrow's work.[2] Among the Syrians Lucian tells us that fishes were deemed holy and were never touched ; so too pigeons, while all other birds were eaten.[3] In the great court of the temple at Hierapolis he says that " oxen of great size browsed ; horses too are there, and eagles and bears and lions, who never hurt mankind, but are all sacred and all tame " (§ xli). Elsewhere he says that " they sacrifice bulls and cows alike, and goats and sheep ; pigs alone, which they abominate,

---

[1] See further S. A. Cook's note in his *Notes to the Third Edition* of the *Religion of the Semites*, pp. 548–54.
[2] *Op. cit.*, ii., 874, 896 f., 933 ff., 943 ff.
[3] *De Dea Syria*, §§ xiv., xlv.

are neither sacrificed nor eaten. Others look on swine without disgust, but as holy animals. Of birds the dove seems the most holy to them ; nor do they think it right to harm these birds, and if anyone have harmed them unknowingly they are unholy for that day " (§ liv). What is most significant from the present point of view is the mention of the animals that may not be eaten, specifically said of pigeons and pigs, though it is no doubt implied in the case of the others ; for this prohibition was due to the fact that there was thought to be something divine about them, i.e. it was based on a religious taboo.

Among the Hebrews we find similar ideas. The corresponding term for taboo in the Old Testament is *tāmē*, " unclean," but not in the sense of disgusting or impure ; it is simply a ritual term for something that must not be touched or, in the case of animals, eaten.

In Lev. xi. and Deut. xiv. 7–20 there are lists of animals which may not be eaten. As a large proportion of these are animals which nobody would think of eating, many of the prohibitions would appear utterly pointless were it not that we know from similar prohibitions among other peoples the real reason why they were forbidden. " The most notable feature in the Levitical prohibitions is that they correspond so closely with those of the heathen Semites and yet are expressly set forth as belonging to Israel's peculiar consecration to Jehovah. . . . The unclean creatures therefore are the divine animals of the heathen; such animals as the latter did not ordinarily eat or sacrifice. . . . "[1] Robertson Smith also points out the significant fact that the Hebrew terms for " to have in abomination," and " an abomination," which constantly recur in Lev. xi. in reference to the prohibitions, " are indifferently applied to unclean beasts and to the gods of the heathen, but to nothing else."

There are a number of other taboos which, if broken, require a purificatory ceremony of one kind or another (see, e.g., Lev. vi. 27 ff., xi. 32 ff.; 1 Sam. xxi. 4 ff.; 2 Sam. xi. 4, and others) ; the consideration of these would take us too far afield. It must suffice to have pointed out that the remnants of taboo are to be discerned in the Old

[1] *Kinship* p. 311, and see further, *Rel. Sem.*, pp. 218 ff.

Testament ; and this is a further link in the chain of proof that ancient Hebrew beliefs go back to a great antiquity.

3. ANCESTOR-WORSHIP

It is not difficult to trace the steps whereby it can be seen that there is a connexion between Totemism and Ancestor-worship. Totemism, as already pointed out, explains clan or tribal animal names ; and we have also seen how divine tribal names arise through heavenly beings having been looked upon as animals (see above, p. 52). The two processes of a totem-ancestor gradually developing into a human ancestor, and of a human ancestor gradually becoming divine, are not necessarily successive steps, and may well have often proceeded concurrently ; in that case Ancestor-worship would at a certain stage arise quite naturally.

But however it may have actually come about,[1] of its existence there is no sort of doubt. In the Semitic domain the subject is a highly controversial one, and to enter upon a discussion of it here would take up a disproportionate amount of space. The difficulty does not lie in the *data*, which are abundant, but in their interpretation. Many facts which appear to some scholars to point to Ancestor-worship are held by others to admit of a different explanation. It must therefore suffice if we refer to some writers on the subject, and then give some of the passages in the Old Testament which, in the light of extra-Biblical evidence, must be looked upon, according to the opinion of the present writer, as containing remnants of Ancestor-worship among the Hebrews, or their forbears, of earlier ages. So far as the Semitic area [2] is concerned, and it is with this alone that we are dealing here, the following works contain important material : Goldziher, *Culte des Ancêtres chez les Arabes*,

---

[1] See the present writer's *Immortality and the Unseen World*, pp. 95 ff. (1921).

[2] For Ancestor-worship among the Babylonians, see the relevant chapter in Jastrow, *op. cit.*; Jeremias, *Bab.-Assyr.*, *Vorstellungen vom Leben nach dem Tode* (1887) ; and *Hölle und Paradies bei den Babyloniern*. See also S. A. Cook, *The Religion of Ancient Palestine*, pp. 57 ff. (1921).

passim (1885); Stade, *Geschichte des Volkes Israel,* i. 387 ff. (1886), *Biblische Theologie des alten Testaments,* i. 104 ff. (1905); Wellhausen, *Reste Arabischen Heidentums,* pp. 183 ff. (1897); Hölscher, *Geschichte der Israelitischen und Jüdischen Religion,* pp. 24 ff., 30 ff. (1922); S. A. Cook in Robertson Smith's *Religion of the Semites,* pp. 508 ff., 544 ff. (1927). Representing a rather different standpoint are : Lagrange, *Études sur les Religions sémitiques,* pp. 269 ff. (1903); Vincent, *Canaan d'après l'Exploration Récente,* pp. 288 ff. (1907); Margoliouth in Hastings' *Encycl. of Rel. and Ethics,* i. 444 ff. (1908).

" Even on general principles, the cult of sacred beings who were regarded as ancestors, and of ancestors who were gods or heroic beings, is only to be expected in ancient times and among the Semites. The evidence has no doubt been exaggerated. To Vincent the archæological *data* suggest care for the dead, rather than a cult. But there was evidently a belief in their continued existence, and the denunciation of mourning customs by the Israelite reformers is highly significant." These mourning customs to which Dr. S. A. Cook refers here constitute one of the strongest arguments in favour of Ancestor-worship being in vogue at one time among the ancient Hebrews. We cannot deal with these here in detail,[1] but they may be briefly enumerated : the rending of the garments which was a palliative of the laceration of the body, cutting off the hair, putting on sackcloth, sprinkling ashes on the head, fasting, wailing, baring the feet, and possibly one or two others. To regard these as remnants of Ancestor-worship may be thought by many to be fantastic ; but conclusions must not be drawn before the subject of their origins is investigated in the light of comparative religion ; and even so there are considerable differences of opinion among scholars ; but a strong case can be made out in favour of the contention here represented. This is stated in the present writer's book already referred to.

There are other *data* in the Old Testament which point

---

[1] They are dealt with in *Immortality and the Unseen World,* pp. 141–189.

to the fact that Ancestor-worship was at one time in vogue among the forbears of the Hebrews.

Gad, meaning " fortune," is a divine name ; this is proved not only by such names as Baal-Gad (Joshua xi. 17, xii. 7, xiii. 5), Migdal-Gad (Joshua xv. 37), but by the definite assertion in Isa. lxv. 11," . . . that prepare a table for Gad, and that fill up mingled wine unto Meni." [1] Gad was also the name of one of the Israelite tribes. A tribal name which is known to be a divine name points indubitably to Ancestor-worship at some time, since an ancestor who is believed to be a god obviously receives worship.

Then, once more, the whole subject of the sanctity of the graves, or reputed burying-places, of ancestors is clearly bound up with that of Ancestor-worship. Here again we must content ourselves with a few allusions without going into the subject. Thus, the grave of Sarah, the cave of Machpelah (Gen. xxiii. 1 ff.), is shown by Gen. xiii. 18, xviii. 1, to have been a sanctuary ; this is also true of the graves of Deborah, Rebecca's nurse (Gen. xxxv. 8), of Joseph (Joshua xxiv. 32 ; for Shechem as a sanctuary see Gen. xii. 6, xxxv. 4), of Miriam (Num. xx. 1 ; the name Kadesh, " holy," marks it as a sanctuary), and of Rachel (Gen. xxxv. 20 ; cp. 1 Sam. x. 2). No argument is needed, it may be hoped, to establish the fact that among ancient peoples, if the grave of an ancestor, or reputed ancestor, is a *sanctuary*, it means that that ancestor is worshipped. In the instances referred to the worship had been transferred from an ancestor to that of Yahweh, the God of Israel. [2]

It is held by many modern authorities that the existence of *Tĕrāphîm*, [3] mentioned in certain passages, is an indication of a remnant of Ancestor-worship ; this is denied by other authorities, owing, they maintain, to lack of evidence. It must be conceded that actual proof

[1] Further details are given by Siegfried, in *Jahrb. für protestantische Theol.*, pp. 361 ff. (1875).

[2] For further details see the present writer's *Immortality* . . . pp. 101 ff.

[3] The word is plural in form, but singular in conception, like Elohim ; cp. 1. Sam. xix. 13, where it is spoken of as " it." See also for the view that Elohim means originally the spirits of the dead, 1 Sam. xxviii. 13.

is not forthcoming. The real difficulty lies in the uncertainty regarding the derivation of the word *Tĕrāphîm*. The bulk of opinion inclines to the belief that the word comes from the root meaning "to nourish," or "to maintain," and they point to the cognate Arabic word *táripha* "to have abundance of goods." Others, following Schwally,[1] hold that it is radically connected with *Repha'im*, "Shades" of the departed (cp. the Assyrian word *tarpû*, "spectre"). What the Old Testament says upon the subject is as follows, put very briefly: from Gen. xxxi. 19, 30–35, Judges xvii. 5, 1 Sam. xix. 13, 16, it may be gathered that a household god is meant; it appears to belong especially to the head of the family, it is kept in houses, and it is spoken of as a god. From Judges xviii. 14, 17, 20, 1 Sam. xv. 23, 2 Kings xxiii. 24, Hos. iii. 4, Ezek. xxi. 26 (21 in E.V.), Zech. x. 2, it is quite clear that the *Tĕrāphîm* was used for divination. These are the outstanding facts, and while they offer no proof, they certainly suggest the possibility that the *Tĕrāphîm* was a remnant of Ancestor-worship.

In the light therefore of what has been said in this chapter it must be recognized that the remnants of Totemism, of various Taboos, and of Ancestor-worship, are to be discovered in the Old Testament; and that these old-world institutions therefore played their part in the early background of Hebrew religious belief.

[1] *Das Leben nach dem Tode*, pp. 35 ff. (1892).

CHAPTER VI

SOME FURTHER ELEMENTS IN THE RELIGIOUS BACKGROUND : DEMONOLOGY

BELONGING to the lower *strata* of Semitic belief there are yet two subjects to be considered : *Demonology* and *Necromancy*. This is demanded both because each of these appears in the Old Testament with sufficient frequency, and also because each developed from something that has been already dealt with, and therefore for completeness' sake, apart from other reasons, some notice of them is demanded. We shall deal with the former in this chapter.[1]

In the case of each of these the chief mention of them occurs in the Old Testament in passages which are for the most part late ; but this is no argument against their having existed in the earliest times. The belief in demons and the practice of consulting the departed was widespread among the early Semites, and there is nothing in the nature of things to justify the supposition that the Hebrews formed an exception to the rule. On the analogy of all that has been hitherto said the presumption is that the Hebrews, being Semites, shared with the rest of the race, in the earliest stages of its history, *all* the beliefs which the evidence shows to have been common property. But, further, it must be remembered that even in some of those books of the Old Testament which

[1] It would take us too far afield to deal with Babylonian Demonology ; a good deal of information will be found in Lenormant, *La Magie chez les Chaldéens et les origines Accadiennes* (1874, Engl. trans. 1877); see especially pp. 1–62. The scribes of Ashurbanipal made several copies of a large work of great antiquity in the library of the famous priestly school of Erech ; this work was called *The Evil Spirits*. It is from this to a great extent that our knowledge of Babylonian Demonology is derived ; only part of it has been preserved; it contained a great number of magical formulas used for averting the malignant attacks of evil spirits, etc.

in their present form are demonstrably late, a considerable amount of very early material has been preserved. And when it is realized that the editors of the Old Testament books, from the Exile onwards, had reached a religious development enormously in advance of their distant forbears, the wonder is that they permitted *any* reference to beliefs which must have been abhorrent to them. Indeed, so far as necromancy is concerned, the only reason for its mention was that it might be condemned as incompatible with the worship of Yahweh. Nevertheless, as we shall see, it is not wholly in the later books that references to these subjects occur.

In this chapter we shall restrict ourselves to Demonology. We do not propose, on account of the extensiveness of the subject, to deal with the belief in demons among the Semites generally,[1] but shall restrict ourselves here to the Old Testament, though a few references to the wider sphere will occur. As we study this subject in detail it will soon become apparent that belief in demons is a development of animistic conceptions. And in order to embrace the whole subject as it appears in the Old Testament, it will be necessary to go beyond the stage of primitive belief to which we are otherwise restricting ourselves at present.

In the forms in which demons appear in the Old Testament they may be divided into two classes : (1) Theriomorphic (Animal form) and (2) Anthropomorphic (Human form).

1. THERIOMORPHIC DEMONS

(i) *The Seráphîm*

The word comes from the root meaning " to burn " ; the *Seráphîm* were therefore the " burning ones." This, however, does not refer to the burning of fire, but to the " burning " occasioned by the bites which these demons, who are in serpent-form, gave. Thus, in Num. xxi. 6 it is said : " And Yahweh sent fiery serpents [lit. *seráphîm*-serpents] among the people, and they bit the people ;

---

[1] A good deal of evidence will be found in *Immortality and the Unseen World*, pp. 24–34.

and much people of Israel died." In ver. 8 of the same
chapter it continues : " And Yahweh said to Moses, Make
thee a seraph, and put it on a pole ; and it shall come to
pass, that everyone that is bitten, when he seeth it,
shall live." This is a kind of imitative magic which
shows the antiquity of the belief in this type of demon.
That it was regarded as a true " demon of the waste "
is seen from Deut. viii. 15 : " . . . Who led thee through
the great and terrible wilderness wherein were seraph-
serpents and scorpions " (see also Isa. xiv. 29, xxx. 6).
The generally held Semitic belief that serpents were the
incarnation of demons makes it certain, apart from other
reasons, that the Israelites regarded these *Serāphîm* as
demons of the waste. In one direction they developed
into angelic beings, as we see from the prophet's description of his vision in the well-known passage in Isa. vi. ;
but their original character also persisted, as we can see
from the Deuteronomy passage already cited. This incongruity need not occasion surprise ; there are other
instances of the same kind of thing.

(ii) *The Se'irim*

This word, the " hairy ones," comes from a root meaning " to be hairy," and obviously they must have been
so called on account of their appearance. Let us first
quote the passages in which they are mentioned :
Lev. xvii. 7 : " And they shall no more sacrifice their
sacrifices unto the *Se'irim* (R.V. ' he-goats,' marg.
' satyrs '), after whom they go a-whoring. This shall be a
statute for ever unto them throughout their generations."
2 Kings xxiii. 8 : In the account of Josiah's reforms
occurs this meaningless passage : " . . . And he brake
down the high places of the gates that were at the entering
in of the gate of Joshua the governor of the city . . . " ;
" the high places of the gates " should, it is recognized
on all hands, be " the high place of the *Se'irim* " (reading
ha-se'irim for *ha-she'arim*). This is borne out by 2
Chron. xi. 15, where it is said that Jeroboam had
" appointed him priest for the high places, and for the
Se'irim, and for the calves which he had made."

Isa. xxxiv. 14 tells of the desolation of Edom, and it is said that in the ruins " the *sa‘ir* shall cry to his fellow " (this time the R.V. has " satyr " in the text and " he-goat " in the margin !). We shall return to this passage later. And lastly, we have another passage from Isaiah which will also occupy us again presently, where it says that in the ruins of Babylon the *Se‘irim* shall dance (Isa. xiii. 21) ; in this passage the Septuagint renders the word "demons."

From these passages we learn the following points about the *Se‘irim* : They were worshipped in high places (i.e. they had their own sanctuaries), sacrifices were offered to them there, special priests performed the ritual ; they were quite obviously visible, not only because they were called "hairy ones," but also because the worship of them is paralleled with that of the calves. It is also said that they inhabit ruined sites. To translate the word by " satyrs " is misleading, because the satyr was a purely imaginary creature, a hybrid, partly man, partly goat ; whereas the *Se‘irim* were real. There is no doubt that they were he-goats in the ordinary sense (*sa‘ir* is the usual word for " he-goat "). From the Lev., 2 Kings, and 2 Chron. passages it can hardly be doubted that at one time the Israelites worshipped these animals, either as gods, or as representing gods, just as in the case of the calves. Then, in later days, when, through the work of the prophets, the worship of Yahweh had become such that no other form of worship could be tolerated, these gods were degraded to demons. The *connexion* between demons and goats in Semitic belief has been shown by such writers as Baudissin, Wellhausen, and Robertson Smith, and we need not take up time by enlarging upon the point. It is to be noted that these *Se‘irim* were just as real as *demons* as they had been as *gods* ; that is clear from the Isaiah passages.

Thus, we have in the case of the *Se‘irim* the converse of what happened in the case of the *Seraphim* : the latter developed from demons to angels ; the former were degraded from gods to demons.

Although we are dealing at present with theriomorphic demons, it will be well to discuss here *‘Azazel*, although he began and ended by being a person, but went through an intermediate demonic stage.

(iii) *'Azazel*

The form of this word in Hebrew (*'Azā'zēl*, meaning " complete removal ") has caused difficulty ; its formation is certainly unusual. Cheyne's solution, both on account of its simplicity, as well as on account of its intrinsic probability, is the most acceptable. He believes that its present form was a deliberate corruption, no doubt from reverential feelings, the original form being *'Azāz'ēl*,[1] which means " God strengthens," formed like 'Azaziah in 1 Chron. xv. 21.

The passage about *'Azazel* is Lev. xvi. 7–28 : two he-goats are taken from the congregation of Israel for a sin-offering ; these Aaron sets before Yahweh " at the door of the tent of meeting." Then it is said that " Aaron shall cast lots upon the two goats : one lot for Yahweh, and the other lot for *'Azazel*." Clearly from these words *'Azazel* is regarded as a personal being like Yahweh. Therefore to make *'Azazel* equivalent to the scapegoat is doing violence to the text. It then goes on to say that the goat upon which the lot for *'Azazel* fell was to be sent away for *'Azazel* into the wilderness, clearly meaning that it was an offering to *'Azazel*. From this we also see that *'Azazel* dwelt in the wilderness like the *Se'irim*. Without going into details, for which we have not space, the *data* suggest that *'Azazel* was originally a god of the flocks,—just as Astarte was a cow-deity,— and that this *'Azazel*-ritual was a development and adaptation of what at some early period was an offering to a god of the waste. Then *'Azazel* became degraded to a demon of the waste, possibly being thought of as the head of the *Se'irim*. Finally, he became identified with the author of all evil, i.e. Satan, for in the *Book of Enoch* vi. 7, it is said : " Thou seest what *'Azazel* hath done, who hath taught all unrighteousness on earth . . . " ; see also ix. 6, x. 4–6.

---

[1] It is difficult, in transliteration, to make the difference of the two forms clear ; in Hebrew they are עֲזָאזֵל and עֲזַזְאֵל.

(iv) *Some other Demons*

In Isa. xiii. 21, 22, already referred to, there occur, in addition to the *Se'irim*, some other types of what were also undoubtedly looked upon as demons of the waste. A word or two about these must be said.

First, the *Ziyyim*, translated "wild beasts"; in Jer. l. 39 they are called "the wild beasts of the desert." The word comes from a root meaning "to be dry," and the noun would therefore presumably imply connexion with a dry place, an inhabiter of the waste, as it stands in the same category as *Se'irim*; thus bearing out the Jeremiah reference. While it does not seem possible to identify the animal referred to, it may be taken for granted that it was a real animal of some kind which was believed to be the incarnation of a demon, not an imaginary creature. It is therefore to be reckoned among the demons of the waste.

In the same passage we have what are called *'Ochim*, translated "doleful creatures"; it is parallel with the last type, and, like it, is used in the plural; therefore they, too, congregated in numbers. The word comes apparently from a root meaning "to howl," and according to Delitzsch the cognate Assyrian word *'ahû* means a "jackal"; we are thus justified in assuming that jackals are meant; and they would be regarded as animals in which demons took up their abode.

Then there are mentioned some creatures called *Benôth Ya'anah*, also in the plural, which the Revised Version translates "ostriches"; this is probably right; but the term means "daughters of greed." The Septuagint renders it "Syrens," and makes them parallel with "demons." The Arabs say that demons have the hunger of lions; it is possible that the idea may have something to do with these "daughters of greed," and perhaps it was the voracity of the bird which suggested the connexion with demons. In any case, the Arabs said that demons used ostriches to ride upon; and they also believed that demons appeared in the form of ostriches. At the present day ostriches are not seen in Palestine, but there is historical evidence that they were formerly more widely spread in Asia ; besides, there are quite a number of references to them in the Old Testament. In Job xxxix. 18 it is said that " she scorneth the horse and his rider," so that evidently they were hunted in Palestine in days gone by.

Another type of what were regarded as demons, and which is also mentioned in Isa. xiii. 22, comes under the name of *'Iyyim* ; it comes from a root meaning " to screech," and the word for " hawk " comes from the same root. In view of the fact that many birds were regarded as the incarnations of demons it may be that a bird of prey of some kind was meant. The parallel word in our passage, *Tannim*, another family of demons, and translated " jackals," would favour the R.V. translation " wolves " for *'Iyyim* ; but the meaning of *Tannim* is quite uncertain, and we have already had " jackals " ; a bird of prey therefore seems more likely.

These exhaust the types of theriomorphic demons mentioned in the Old Testament, and, as will have been noticed, they are all demons of the waste, a fact brought out in the context in every case. These animals were really believed to be closely associated with demons, and were, no doubt, often identified with them ; and they were feared just because a harmful supernatural being was believed to take up his abode in them.

Before we come to demons in human form there is one which must be briefly referred to here because it seems to occupy a position, so far as one can judge from the very meagre *data*, between the animal and the human. In Gen. iv. 7 there is a difficult and often misinterpreted passage ; the R.V. translates : " If thou doest well " (it is the Lord speaking to Cain) " shalt thou not be accepted ? and if thou doest not well, sin coucheth at the door ; and unto thee shall be his desire, and thou shalt rule over him." Readers of *Genesis* in Hebrew will know that this is somewhat in the nature of a paraphrase of an ungrammatical and untranslateable passage. Gunkel [1] says that the total corruption of this passage must be explained on the supposition that the text having become illegible—whether through obliteration of the writing

---

[1] *Genesis*, p. 39 (1901).

or mutilation of the manuscript—was reconstructed by a copyist to the best of his ability, on the basis of iii. 16*b* ("And thy desire shall be to thy husband, and he shall rule over thee "). With this most people will agree. But in the R.V. rendering there is one phrase meriting special attention—" sin coucheth at the door." This is an impossible rendering of the Hebrew, because " sin " is feminine, and " coucheth " is masculine. This can, however, be satisfactorily explained, as Duhm [1] points out, by regarding " sin " as a marginal gloss to " coucheth " ; from the margin it was somewhat thoughtlessly put into the text by a later copyist. The words will then run : " . . . But if thou doest not well (there is) one that coucheth at the door." Who coucheth at the door ? Why does he couch there ? And what door does he couch at ? And what has it to do with the context ? It is well known that Assyro-Babylonian demonology had a considerable influence on Jewish belief in demons. Now the Babylonians and Assyrians had a horrible demon called *Rabitzu* ; he is mentioned, e.g., on a magical text translated in Jastrow's *Die Religion Babyloniens und Assyriens*, ii. 765 (1912). He is called the lord of the underworld,[2] and, moreover, a whole class of demons is called after him.[3] The name comes from a root meaning " to lurk " or " couch." *Rabitzu* is thus a proper name, and means the " lurker " or " coucher." In the text which we are considering the Hebrew word for " one coucheth " is *Rōbētz*, the consonants of which correspond with the Assyrian *Rabitzu* ; and therefore *Rōbētz*, like the Assyrian equivalent, should be regarded as a proper name, and the text should read : " . . . But if thou doest not well *Rōbētz* is at the door ! " It is not for a moment suggested that that was the original form of the text, but only that it was the form of some copyist's emendation. The Babylonians believed that *Rōbētz* lurked at the threshold of people's dwellings, and was ready to spring on a man if he came out unwarily ; the Hebrew writer adapted this belief, and spiritualized it by identifying *Rōbētz* with Sin ; so that he interpreted this

---

[1] *Die bösen Geister des AT*, p. 9 (1904). [2] Duhm, *ibid.*
[3] Lenormant. *La magie* . . ., pp. 24, 47.

passage as meaning that God said to Cain, " If thou doest not well, remember, *Rōbētz* is at the door " ; or, in other words, if a man is inclined to do what is wrong there is an evil demon always lurking at hand to aid and further him in his evil intentions.

Rōbētz is thus an animal in that he lurks or couches as animals do, but he approximates to the anthropomorphic form of demon in other respects.

This brings us, then, to anthropomorphic demons proper.

2. ANTHROPOMORPHIC DEMONS

There are not many references to these in the Old Testament, but when considered in the light of Babylonian parallels, they will be found to be significant.

(i) First we have *Lilith*. In Isa. xxxiv. 11–15, where the prophet speaks of the devastation of Edom, he says in ver. 14 : " And the wild beasts of the desert (*Ziyyim*) shall encounter the wolves ('*Iyyim*), and the *saʻir* (" he-goat ") shall meet his fellow ; there, in truth, shall *Lilith* repose, and shall find a resting-place for herself." The R.V. translates *Lilith* by " night-monster," but it is a proper name. The fact that *Lilith*, represented now as a female demon, and now as a male one, was well known among the Assyrians supports the belief that *Lilith* played a part in Hebrew Demonology in pre-Exilic times. The Assyrian beliefs regarding this demon appear in later Babylonian belief in a greatly developed form, for here we have a demon-triad, *Lilu*, *Lilitu*, and *Ardat Lili*—the male, the female, and the handmaid ; the Old Testament *Lilith* would correspond to the second of these, *Lilitu*. They are spoken of as flying, so that they may have been conceived of as having wings, as in later times.

The way in which *Lilith* is mentioned in the Isaiah passage, without explanation, shows that the name was familiar. According to later Jewish teaching, which may well, however, have been handed down for centuries previously, *Lilith* was a night-hag, and got her name from *Lāylah*, " night." The etymology was false, but

Lîlîth was, nevertheless, the night-demon *par excellence*. There is an evident reference to this demon, though her name is not mentioned, in Ps. xci. 5 : " Thou shalt not be afraid because of the night-terror, nor because of the arrow that flieth by day." In the *Midrash* to the Psalms (*Midr. Tehillim*), the comment on this verse says : " There is a harmful spirit that flies like a bird and shoots like an arrow " ; while it is a mistake to suppose, as the Rabbi does, that only one demon is spoken of in this verse, he is no doubt right in picturing *Lîlîth* as one who flies, for the Jewish conception regarding this demon is likely to have corresponded with the Babylonian, which, as we have seen, also described her as flying at nights. In this later Jewish belief, which is, however, largely traditional, *Lîlîth* appears as the head of one of the three great classes into which developed Jewish Demonology divided the demons, viz. the *Lîlîn*, who take their name from her. They are described as of human form, and have wings ; they are all females, and children are their chief victims. *Lîlîth* herself is conceived of as a beautiful woman, with long flowing hair ; it is at nights that she seeks her prey. She is dangerous to men because of her beauty ; but she does not appear to molest women.[1]

(ii) A female demon of a different character is *'Alûqah*, mentioned in Prov. xxx. 15. It is true that, according to many commentators, this is from one of the latest portions of the book of *Proverbs*, belonging to the third century B.C. ; but even if this should be the case, the fact that *'Alûqah* is mentioned without explanation shows that the name was familiar, and therefore traditional ; but more significant is the further fact that *'Alûqah* is only the Hebrew form of the demon *'Alûq*, who figures in

---

[1] It may be of interest to point out, in passing, that this form of the *Lîlîth*-myth was borrowed and adapted (unless all the forms of the myth go back to a common ancestor) in a variety of ways in the Middle Ages. It is conceivably the source of the " Frau Holde " legend, the beautiful woman who dwelt in a great mountain at the entrance to which she appeared on moonlight nights ; and woe to the luckless man who caught sight of her and became fascinated by her beauty for, being lured by her into her mountain home, he was never seen to issue forth again. One form of the Tannhäuser legend, as also that of Peer Gynt, possibly have a similar origin ; and the same may be true of the Loreley story, however much it may have been transformed by Teutonic poetical genius.

ancient heathen Arabian demonology [1]; she was a flesh-devouring ghoul, according to the early Arabs. Her mention here is a good illustration of the fact that the occurrence of the name of a demon in a late passage (if this one is a late passage) does not necessarily mean that the belief in the demon is late. Ingrained ideas often persist through untold numbers of generations, and their non-appearance in earlier writings does not necessarily imply that they were not in existence previously. In this particular case we fortunately have external evidence to show that the demon *'Alûqah* had long been believed in. That this demon is not sexless, and that she has a proper name is, of course, a development ; but that only proves that something corresponding to her existed previously. This may be further illustrated by the mention of some other demons which are referred to in the Old Testament.

(iii) In Ps. xci. 5, 6, it is said to him who trusts in Yahweh that he need not fear the " night-terror," nor the " arrow that flies in the daytime," nor the " pestilence that goes about in the dark," nor the " destruction that wastes at noon-day." Here are four things to which action is imputed ; and on the face of it one might well argue that they are all merely metaphorical expressions. But in the light of comparative demonology this is extremely improbable. Moreover, on general grounds there would be more point in the passage if the writer had in mind certain harmful beings, belief in whose existence was general, but whose power for harm was curtailed when the help of God was sought against them. That this is the case in this passage is very likely.

The first is the " night-terror " ; the very expression suggests a spiritual power, for what human power would be likely to be so described ? Mention has already been made of *Lîlîth*, the night-hag, who would be very appropriately described as the " night-terror," for so she was regarded ; it seems therefore highly probable that *Lîlîth* is referred to here. That her name is not expressed is easily understood ; for according to antique ideas the

---

[1] Wellhausen, *op. cit.*, pp. 149 ff.

mention of the name of a demon was dangerous because it might result in bringing its bearer near.[1]

Then we have the " arrow that flies in the day-time." That this cannot refer to an arrow shot by man is evident, for in that case it would not be spoken of as something of general occurrence, as is here implied. What is meant is the scorching ray of the sun, the result of which, sunstroke, headache, or faintness, was believed to be due to a demon, like all sickness. But what especially compels the conviction that demons are here referred to is the "pestilence that goes about in the dark" and the " destruction that wastes at midday." As to the first of these, we have an instructive parallel in the Babylonian pest-demon, *Namtar* ; he is often spoken of as " violent *Namtar*," and he is said to come among men as the pestbringing envoy from the realms of the dead like a "raging wind." His action is described in a Babylonian magical text in this way : " Wicked *Namtar*, who scorches the land like fire, who approaches a man like Ashakku (another Babylonian demon), who rages through the wilderness like a storm-wind, who pounces upon a man like a robber, who plagues a man like the pestilence, who has no hands, no feet, who goes about at night. . . . "[2]

Regarding the second, the word for " destruction " is *Qeteb* ; if this was not a proper name when this psalm was written, it became so later (see below). But that a demon is referred to may be gathered for several reasons : the word occurs in Deut. xxxii. 24, where the context clearly refers to the activity of demons (see also Isa. xxviii. 2) ; it occurs also in Hos. xiii. 14—an instructive passage because *Qeteb* is brought into connexion with *She'ol*, the underworld ; and in Babylonian demonology there is a parallel to this demon, namely Nergal, who is, on the one hand, " ruler of the great abode of the dead," and, on the other, the blazing midday sun[3] (it is in this latter that he offers a parallel) ; and lastly, the Septuagint rendering of " that wastes at noon-day " is " the midday

---

[1] This would not necessarily apply to *all* demons.

[2] O. Weber, " Dämonenbeschwörung bei den Babyloniern und Assyrern," in *Der Alte Orient*, vii., iv. 16 (1906); Jastrow, *op. cit.*, i. 287, 385.

[3] Jastrow, *op. cit.*, i. 65, 66.

demon." [1] It may be added that in Rabbinical literature *Qeteb* is used as the proper name of a demon. In the Midrash on the Psalms the comment on the word *Qeteb* is : " Our Rabbis said, ' It is a demon (*shēd*).' . . . Rabbi Huna, speaking in the name of Rabbi Jose, said, ' The poisonous *Qeteb* is covered with scales and with hair, and he sees only out of one eye, the other one is in the middle of his heart.' . . . "

It would seem therefore that we have in Ps. xci. 5, 6, four demons referred to, all of which were perfectly familiar to readers ; and though this psalm is an admittedly late one it has preserved traces of early belief in this particular.

(iv) A few other references, indirect or implied, may be added. In Gen. xiv. 3 mention is made of " the vale of Siddim " ; the place is unknown, and the renderings of the Versions show that the translators were mystified ; hence most commentators make the emendation, involving only a change in vowel-points, *Shēdim*, " demons," and read " the demon-valley." If this emendation is correct, which is highly probable, we have here reference to a spot which, for what reason cannot be said, was believed to be the resort of demons.

As is well known, amulets were originally worn in order to ward off the attacks of evil spirits, and there are a number of passages in the Old Testament in which the mention of an amulet implies the belief in demons. Thus, in Gen. xxxv. 4, the ear-rings worn by Jacob's followers are, like the strange gods, hidden away as something unlawful ; this can only have been done because the rings were regarded as superstitious objects. The point of view is a later one, but witnesses to the belief in demons.

Again, the " fringes " spoken of in Num. xv. 38 were knotted cords, and all folklorists know that knots were protective amulets against all kinds of evils [2] ; in the

---

[1] It is also probable that the Hebrew word for " that wasteth " (*yashod*) is intended to be a word-play on *shēd* (" demon ") at the back of the writer's mind.

[2] See Frazer, *G.B.*, " Taboo and the Perils of the Soul," pp. 306 ff. (1911) ; cp. also Deut. xviii. 11, where the expression *chōbēr cheber* means, in all probability, " he who ties a (magic) knot."

first instance these " fringes " were worn as a protection
against evil spirits. For further examples see Gen.
xxxviii. 18, 25 ; Exod. xxviii. 33 ; Deut. xxii. 12 ; Judges
viii. 24 ; Isa. iii. 20 ff.   In course of time these protective
amulets became, probably enough, ornaments pure and
simple.

Most of the passages which have here been referred to
belong to the later periods of Israelite history, but this
only shows how persistent ingrained superstitions are ;
there can be no kind of doubt that belief in demons is an
offshoot from Animism, and belongs to the very early
beginnings of Hebrew belief.

CHAPTER VII

SOME FURTHER ELEMENTS IN THE RELIGIOUS BACKGROUND: NECROMANCY [1]

As will be seen, there is a close connexion between this subject and Demonology on the one hand, and with Ancestor-worship and the Cult of the Dead on the other.

In all that concerns the primitive beliefs of the Hebrews there can be no doubt that material common to the Semites in general is involved ; it will therefore be instructive to begin by taking a glance at the practice of Necromancy among the Babylonians.

"Necromancy," says Margoliouth, "which is an essential part of the cult of the dead, and which must also have been connected with the presentation of offerings to the shades consulted, undoubtedly held a prominent place among the magic arts of the Babylonians." [2]

Among the various categories of Babylonian priests we read of " conjurors of the dead," that is, " priests who bring up the spirits of the dead " ; mention is also made of the " questioner of the dead," [3] the reference being obviously to one who would presumably be what is called a " medium " nowadays, and who was believed to have the faculty of receiving messages from the spirits of the departed. The procedure seems to be referred to in the closing lines of the *Descent of Ishtar* ; it is said there : " In the days of Tammuz, play to me upon the crystal flute, play to me upon the (text mutilated) instrument, his dirge, ye mourning men and mourning women, in order that the dead may ascend and smell the incense." [4]

---

[1] For this subject see also the present writer's *Immortality and the Unseen World*, pp. 125–140, where further details will be found.

[2] In *E.R.E.*, i. 439.

[3] Jeremias, *op. cit.*, p. 288.

[4] Jeremias, " Hölle und Paradies bei den Babyloniern," p. 20, in *Der Alte Orient* (1900).

From this we may gather that the spirits of the departed were believed to be induced to rise up from their abode by the sound of the flute and the smell of the incense.

In the Gilgamesh Epic there is an account of the hero communicating with his dead friend Enkidu ; this he does by the help of Nergal, the god of the underworld, who makes an opening in the earth and causes the spirit of Enkidu to come forth " like a breath of wind." [1] Here it is the god Nergal who acts the part of the " medium."

But although the authorities on the subject are agreed as to the prevalence of Necromancy among the Babylonians, there are otherwise scarcely any examples, which have come down to us, of that particular department of the subject with which we are here specially concerned, viz. the consulting of departed spirits regarding the affairs of men and especially about future events.[2] In the great mass of cases recorded in which mention is made of any relationship between men and departed spirits the main thing is to counteract the harmful activities of the latter. It was believed that for one reason or another many spirits of the departed left their abode in the underworld and roamed about on the earth to the detriment of men ; and it was to combat these untoward activities that the services of the magician were employed ; see further Chapter VIII.

Now, in the Old Testament, while we have next to nothing told us about the spirits of the departed harming men, there is a considerable amount of evidence to show that the departed were consulted either for guidance in the ordinary affairs of life or in regard to future events. The most obvious illustration is, of course, that of the witch of Endor (1 Sam. xxviii. 3-25). The somewhat full account of the *procedure* here given must be regarded, more or less, as that implied in the other references to the consulting of departed spirits where the details are not

---

[1] It is on the twelfth tablet : a translation is given by Ebeling in Gressmann's *Altorientalische Texte zum Alten Testament*, pp. 150–198 (1926).

[2] Jeremias, however, mentions among the different orders of priests the " exorcist of the spirits of the dead," " he who raises the spirit of the dead," and " the enquirer of the dead," called *Sha'ilu* (*Hölle* . . ., p. 28).

given. The following points are to be noted : there is
clearly a firm belief in the literal reality of what is recorded.
The note in ver. 3 about Saul having put away those who
had familiar spirits is, in all probability, a later insertion,
both because it is incongruous in view of Saul himself
going to consult one, and also because they were still
flourishing in the days of the prophets (see below), but
chiefly because the words of ver. 7 show that their
continued presence in the land is taken for granted by
Saul ; when he asks where a woman who has a familiar
spirit is to be found, his servants know at once ; there
is no need to seek for her.   Another point to notice
is that the consulting of the dead is regarded as a last
resort ; the other methods of learning about the future
were by dreams, by *'Urim*,[1] and by prophets. As these
had failed, this last means was employed.

But since the normal methods are spoken of as the way
in which men enquired of Yahweh, to have recourse to
the departed meant an act of disloyalty to the national
God ; it is here that we must see the real reason for the
later prohibitions regarding Necromancy.   It is true, the
prophet (Isa. viii. 19) shows that there is some chicanery
about the business, but it is not that that troubles him ; the
real evil that he sees in it is that it draws people away from
God.   His words are worth quoting : " And when they shall
say unto you, Seek unto them that have familiar spirits and
unto the wizards, that chirp and that mutter ; should
not a people seek unto their God ?   On behalf of the
living should they seek unto the dead ? "   But while he
sees both the folly and the evil of it, his words show that
it was greatly in vogue.   It is similar in Isa. xxix. 4,
where the prophet compares the humbled Mount Zion
(" Ariel," see ver. 8) with one who has a familiar spirit :
" And thou shalt be brought down, and shalt speak out

---

[1] *'Urim* and *Thummim* were the sacred lots used by the priests for
giving oracles ; whether they were of stone or of wood cannot be said
with certainty. The most important passage is 1 Sam. xiv. 41 ; the
Hebrew text is corrupt, but, emended on the basis of the Septuagint,
it should be rendered : " And Saul said : O Yahweh, God of Israel,
wherefore hast thou not answered thy servant this day ? If this
iniquity be in me or in Jonathan my son, then, Yahweh, God of Israel,
give *'Urim* ; but if it be in thy people Israel, then give *Thummim*."

of the ground, and thy speech shall be low out of the
dust ; and thy voice shall be as one that hath a familiar
spirit, out of the ground, and thy speech shall whisper
[marg., " chirp "] out of the dust." Here again it is taken
for granted that the necromancers are busy in the land.
In Isa. xix. 3, although the note of contempt is again
sounded, it is recognized that they are present and
resorted to : " . . . And they shall seek unto the idols
and to the charmers [marg. " whisperers "], and to them
that have familiar spirits, and to the wizards."

Such passages witness to the wide prevalence of Necromancy, and although it is looked upon with contempt by
the prophet, it is only implicitly, not directly, that he condemns it ; and were it not that it became a mark of
disloyalty to Yahweh, it is probable that the prophet
would have regarded it as foolishness rather than as
moral evil. But that it was widely prevalent there can
be no doubt, so that when a little later it is said of the
king Manasseh that he " practised augury, and used
enchantments and dealt with them that had familiar
spirits, and with wizards " (2 Kings xxi. 6), we must see
in this not the resuscitation of practices which had fallen
into desuetude (in spite of earlier reforms), but rather
the official recognition of what had been done by the
people all along.

It is, further, instructive to note how this subject is
dealt with in the various codes of laws preserved in
the Old Testament. The earliest, " The Book of the
Covenant " (Exod. xx. 22–xxiii. 33) [1] contains no prohibition against it, the reason being that at the time Necromancy was regarded as a natural and legitimate practice,
as among the rest of the Semites. The prophets, however,
gradually came to realize that it was incompatible with
the worship of Yahweh ; hence we find that in the Deuteronomic legislation it is prohibited ; in Deut. xviii. 10–12
it is said : " There shall not be found with thee . . . one
that useth divination, one that practiseth augury, or an
enchanter, or a sorcerer, or a charmer, or a consulter
with a familiar spirit, or a wizard, or a necromancer.
For whoso doeth these things is an abomination unto

---

[1] The oldest part of the combined documents J and E.

Yahweh " ; see also 2 Kings xxiii. 24 (the Josianic reformation). The prohibition can have had but little effect, for in the next code (the " Law of Holiness," Lev. xvii.–xxvi.) condemnation is added to prohibition : " The soul that turneth unto them that have familiar spirits, and unto the wizards, to go a whoring after them, I will even set my face against that soul, and will cut him off from among his people " (Lev. xx. 6 ; see also ver. 27).

The subject is not mentioned in the Priestly Code, but the Chronicler accounts for the death of Saul by saying that it was because of " his trespass which he committed against Yahweh, because of the word of Yahweh, which he kept not ; and also for that he asked counsel of one that had a familiar spirit, to enquire thereby, and enquired not of Yahweh ; therefore he slew him . . . " (1 Chron. x. 13, 14). But in spite of prohibitions, and in spite of the death penalty pronounced against those who practised it, we find that long after the Exile Necromancy was still prevalent in Judæa ; for a late writer speaks of a " rebellious people," which " walketh in a way that is not good, after their own thoughts ; a people that provoketh me to my face continually . . . which sit among the graves, and spend the night in vaults " (Isa. lxv. 2–4). The reference here is, in all probability, to what is known as " incubation " : by resorting to a grave or a sepulchral vault and spending the night there, it was believed that the departed spirit would appear to the sleeper in a dream, and that the desired information or guidance would be imparted in this way. That this was one of the ways whereby Yahweh was believed to indicate His will may be seen from such passages as Gen. xx. 3, xxxi. 11 ; Num. xii. 6 ; 1 Sam. xxviii. 6, 15, and others. In the Old Testament three expressions are used in reference to this subject. The first of these is what is called the 'Ôb ; this is translated by " familiar spirit." What is implied by this expression 'Ôb, in other words, what its derivation is, cannot be said with certainty. According to some scholars the root-idea is that of something hollow, on account of the hollow tone of the voice that a spirit may be supposed to utter ; others explain the hollowness in reference to the hole in the earth from which the voice of the departed proceeds ; others, again, hold that it came to be applied to a spirit or ghost because it was believed to appear in bodily form, but was hollow inside. This last seems to be the most probable; but if so, it implies that a real apparition was seen ; nor need one doubt that this was so sometimes ; and it is interesting to note that the cognate word in Arabic means a " revenant."

The word, in connexion with Necromancy,[1] is not always used in quite the same sense. In 1 Sam. xxviii. 7 it is said : " Seek me a woman that doth possess [or, " is mistress of "] an *'Ôb* " : the distinction between the woman and the *'Ôb* is clear here. So, too, in ver. 8 : " Divine unto me, I pray thee, by the *'Ôb*, and bring me up whomsoever I shall name unto thee." So that the woman is the " medium," the *'Ôb* is what spiritualists would call the " control," and the apparition would presumably be called a " materialization." This distinction is also clearly shown in Deut. xviii. 11, where the phrase occurs : " One that consulteth [lit. " asketh "] an *'Ôb* ; so, too, in Lev. xx. 27 : " A man or a woman in whom is an *'Ôb*." In other passages, however, the *'Ôb* is used in reference to the " medium " himself or herself (1 Sam. xxviii. 3, 9 ; 2 Kings. xxi. 6, xxiii. 24 ; 2 Chron. xxxiii. 6 ; cp. also Isa. viii. 19, xix. 3, xxix. 4).

Whatever deductions are to be drawn from this, of one thing there is no doubt, viz. that up to the time of the Deuteronomist the consulting of departed spirits was regarded as something that really took place ; it was not looked upon as a piece of mere chicanery.

Then there is the term *Yidde'oni*, from the root meaning " to know " ; but whether this is in reference to the " medium " who knows how to get into communication with departed spirits, or in reference to the spirit itself who knows, and can therefore give, the information sought, cannot be said with any certainty.

There is also the term *'Ittim*—" whisperers," or " mutterers "—used, however, only in the three Isaiah passages referred to as a parallel to the *'Ôb* and the *Yidde-'oni* ; but whether these formed another class may be

---

[1] In Job xxxii. 19 the same word is used of a " wine-skin."

doubted ; probably it is descriptive of one part of the method of procedure followed by the 'Ôb.

Finally, the possibility must be recognized of the *Tĕrā-phim* belonging to the subject of Necromancy, at any rate in the earlier stage of belief in them ; for if we are to understand by this term a household god (see above, p. 61) which was used for giving oracles, then it must be regarded as at one time having been connected with Necromancy, and as parallel with the *Manes*-oracle, the earliest known form of oracle outside the Semitic domain.[1]

. . . . . .

In all that has been said in this and in the preceding chapters it has not been a question of folk-belief as distinct from the official religion. We have simply taken passages both early and late in which reference is made to the various subjects considered because they afford indications of " remnants " ; for this affords proof that animistic conceptions and the rest were in full vogue among the forbears of the Hebrews, and therefore formed the background of their religion. When we come to consider the later stages of religious development, then of course it becomes necessary always to make a clear distinction between the popular religion and that of the religious leaders.

[1] Stade, *Geschichte des Volkes Israel,* i. 467.

CHAPTER VIII

SOME FURTHER ELEMENTS IN THE RELIGIOUS BACKGROUND: MAGIC

1. TECHNICAL MAGICAL TERMS

SOME consideration of the subject of Magic is also demanded, for it has affinities with the institution of Taboos, as well as with Demonology and Necromancy.[1] Although, strictly speaking, outside the religious sphere, many magical rites verge so closely upon religion that they may justly be called magico-religious. It is quite certain that some forms of magic were not condemned by the official religious leaders of the Hebrews; but even in the case of the particular forms which were forbidden, the religious leaders did not regard them as mere imposture; indeed, it was just for this reason that they were forbidden; the supernatural agencies which by magical rites were supposed to be controlled were really believed to exist.

We will first examine the technical terms used in reference to the magic art, and then turn to some passages in which magical practices are described.

The usual words used in connexion with Magic come from the root *Kashaph*; its original signification is uncertain[2]; the words used in the Old Testament are: *Kesheph*, always used in the plural, "magic arts"; *Kashaph* and *Mĕkashēph*, "magician," of which the feminine is *Mĕkashēphah*; and *Kishēph* "to practise magic."

In Mic. v. 11 (12 in E.V.) it is said in reference to Israel: "I will cut off thy magic arts [R.V. "witch-

---

[1] See further, for Babylonian Magic, Lenormant, *op. cit.*, passim.
[2] Robertson Smith, in the *Journal of Philology*, xiv. 125, 126 (1885), arguing from the cognate Arabic root meaning "to cut," holds that the noun *Resheph* means herbs cut up or shredded into a magic brew.

crafts "] out of thine hand." All that can be gathered
from this passage is that what was done consisted of
manual acts, and that it was abhorrent to Yahweh.
In Exod. xxii. 17 (18 in E.V.) the command is given :
" Thou shalt not suffer a sorceress to live " ; and in
Deut. xviii. 10–14 magic, together with other occult
practices, are forbidden because they are an abomination
to Yahweh. In Jer. xxvii. 9 the prophet merely bids his
people not to give heed to magicians any more than to
the false prophets, diviners, and others. In Mal. iii. 5
magicians together with various other types of evil people
are denounced ; and in 2 Chron. xxxiii. 6 the practice
of magic is mentioned among the other evils introduced
by Manasseh. In the other six places in which the term
in one or other of its forms is used it is not in reference to
Israel, viz. in Exod. vii. 11 to Pharaoh, 2 Kings ix. 22
to Jezebel (figurative use), Isa. xlvii. 9, 12 to Babylon,
Nahum iii. 4 to Nineveh (figurative use), and Dan. ii. 2 to
Nebuchadrezzar.

Wherever this term for magic is used the practice is
either directly or implicitly condemned, but nowhere is
it hinted wherein the evil consisted. We can only
assume, on the analogy of Babylonian magic, that the
term [1] refers to magic in connexion with demons ; this
would account for its condemnation ; for if the supernatural powers supposed to be controlled were believed
to be demons, one can at once understand the condemnation
of a practice whereby reliance was placed upon demons,
and their help sought, instead of on Yahweh. Moreover,
judging again from the analogy of Babylonian magical
texts,[2] this type of magic would appear to have been
practised preponderatingly, if not wholly, for inflicting
harm on people.

When we turn to the other terms used for practising
magic we find that there is not necessarily any word of
condemnation.

The term *lachash* means " to whisper " an incantation

---

[1] The Assyrian word for practising magic is radically the same as
the Hebrew term, viz. *Rashapu* (*Oxf. Hebr. Dict.*).

[2] Jastrow, *op. cit.*, i. pp. 373–92, and Weber " Dämonenbeschwörung bei den Babyloniern und Assyrern," in *Der Alte Orient*,
VII, iv. (1905).

or " to mutter " a spell [1]; this is probably the original meaning, as against Robertson Smith, who regards serpent-charming as the original connotation of the word (see Eccles. x. 11; Jer. viii. 17).[2] The classical passage is Ps. lviii. 3–9 (4–10 in Hebrew) ; this contains an incantation against the machinations of some evil-disposed persons ; it is the innocent victim who has written down the incantation as a protective formula, but which his enemies have tried to counteract, though in vain ; they had tried to make the formula ineffective (like a " deaf " [3] adder which cannot hear the voice of the charmer) by seeking to avoid hearing the incantation. It is the term *lachash* which occurs here of " whispering " the incantation.[4]

In Ps. xli. 7 (8 in Hebrew) the same term is used; but in this case it is the wicked who compose the incantation against a godly man ; and the latter, instead of seeking to protect himself by a counter-incantation, appeals to Yahweh.

In Isa. iii. 3 the R.V. rendering " skilful enchanter " means in Hebrew literally, " experienced (in composing) an incantation," i.e. in writing magical formulas. It is instructive that the prophet here, so far from condemning the practice, mentions the judge and the prophet, with others, in the same list, and regards the taking away of them as a calamity.

In Isa. xxvi. 16, according to most commentators, following the Septuagint, we should read for " they poured out a prayer when the chastening was upon them," the words : " a constraining magical formula (*lachash*) was the chastening to them," i.e. the result of God chastening them was as effective in its compelling

---

[1] On some Babylonian magical texts there is the rubric : " Utter the spell in a whispering voice " (see, e.g., Weber, *op. cit.*, p. 28).

[2] *Journal of Philology*, xiv. 122 (1885).

[3] Baethgen points out that even at the present day in the East when a snake-charmer fails in alluring a serpent away from a house he says it is because the serpent is deaf (*Die Psalmen*, p. 169 [1904]).

[4] For the justification of the interpretation given above one must consult Nicholsky, *Spuren magischer Formeln in den Psalmen*, pp. 29–42 (1927) ; he points to other Psalms (vii., xxxv., lix., lxix., xci., cix., cxli.) as containing remnants of magical formulas, but it would take us too far afield to deal with these (see further *Church Quarterly Review* for April 1928, pp. 204 ff.).

force as an incantation. To translate *lachash* by
" prayer " is entirely without justification ; the other
alteration involves only the change of a dot, which in any
case did not figure in the original, consonantal text. The
word occurs also in Isa. iii. 20 as a woman's ornament ;
obviously an amulet is meant whereby the evil eye was
averted. The only other occurrence of the term is in
2 Sam. xii. 19 [1] ; here it is used of David's servants
whispering together because his child had died. The
conjecture is perhaps hazardous, but when it is remembered that this term is only used in connexion with magic,
and when, as we shall see, the idea of raising the dead by
means of magic was not unknown to the ancient Hebrews,
it is possible that in this passage there is in reality a
reference to an attempt to resuscitate David's child by
means of an incantation.

The next term is that translated " charmer " in the
R.V., it occurs in Ps. lviii. 6 as parallel with *lachash*,
and, translated literally, means " one who ties knots "
(*chōbēr chăbārîm*). The very widespread use of knots
tied or untied for magical purposes is too well known to
need dilating upon.[2] The practice is forbidden, together
with other magical arts, in Deut. xviii. 11 ; and in reference to Babylonian magic it is mentioned in Isa. xlvii.
9, 12 (rendered " enchantments " in the R.V.) ; the act
is referred to in various Babylonian magical texts.[3]

In a passage already referred to, Isa. iii. 3, another
term occurs ; it is rendered " cunning artificer " (marg.
" charmer ") in the R.V. ; what it means is " skilled in
magic arts " (*chăkām chărāshîm*), or perhaps, " in
(making) drugs " ; though in cognate languages the
word means an " incantation." [4] The term does not
occur elsewhere.

Then there is the term *nichēsh* ; in Gen. xliv. 5, 15,
this word is used in reference to Joseph's silver cup

---

[1] Unless in Neh. iii. 12, x. 25, we regard Hallochesh, not as a proper
name, but as " the whisperer (of incantations) " ; the article is certainly
strange in a proper name.

[2] See above, p. 74. For a full treatment of the subject see Frazer's
G.B., " Taboo and the Perils of the Soul," pp. 293–317 (1911).

[3] Jastrow, *op. cit.*, i. 285, 374 f.

[4] Robertson Smith, *Journal of Phil.*, xiv. 125 (1885).

whereby he "divined"—clearly an instance of hydromancy. In a different connexion it occurs in Gen. xxx. 27 in the sense of "observing the omens," but there is no indication of how the omens were observed; this is the case in 1 Kings xx. 33, where no details of the procedure are given. Although in these passages this form of magic is clearly not regarded as harmful, wherever else it is mentioned it is with condemnation, viz. 2 Kings xvii. 17, xxi. 6 (=2 Chron. xxxiii. 6); Lev. xix. 26; Deut. xviii. 10.

Similarly with the term *'anan*, "to practise augury," which is mentioned side by side with the foregoing term. In such an early passage as Judges ix. 37 there is no condemnation of those who practise it, but elsewhere it is always either forbidden or condemned—Isa. ii. 6, lvii. 3; Mic. v. 11 (R.V. 12); Jer. xxvii. 9, and in the other passages above mentioned.

Finally, there is the term *qasam*, rendered "to practise divination," and the noun *qesem* "divination"; but as Wellhausen has clearly shown,[1] this term is the equivalent of the Arabic *Istiqsam* which is used in reference to an oracle by *lot*, and has nothing to do with magic; especially instructive is Ezek. xxi. 26, 27 (21, 22 in E.V.), where we are told of how the king of Babylon stood at the crossways, and in order to be sure which road to take he consults the oracle which is here of a threefold character: the throwing of the arrows, the consulting of the *Tĕrāphîm*, and looking into an animal's liver. The R.V. renders the Hebrew word "to use divination" (*liqĕsam qesem*); it should, however, be "to consult the oracle by lot" (cp. Prov. xvi. 10). Doubtless it came to be connected with magic, otherwise it would not have been condemned (Deut. xviii. 10; 2 Kings xvii. 17), but it cannot, properly speaking, be classed under the terms for magic.

2. MAGICAL ARTS

We cannot conclude this brief consideration of the prevalence of Magic among the Hebrews without making mention of the fairly numerous descriptions of magical acts in connexion with which no technical term is used.

---

[1] *Reste* . . . , pp. 132 f.

However one may seek to explain these things, the fact remains that they are recorded, and the power of certain people to perform them was evidently believed in.

The power of rain-making by magical means has been so widely believed [1] in that it need occasion no surprise to find the belief and practice of it among the Hebrews. Ultimately, it is connected with animistic belief; for, according to old-world ideas,[2] rain was "inspirited" like every other form of water. In the Old Testament, it is true, the remnants of this belief are few, and they offer but a faint reminiscence of what must originally have obtained; but they are sufficiently precise to preclude any doubt as to what is really meant. Thus, in 1 Sam. xii. 16–18 Samuel is represented as bringing rain, by calling unto Yahweh, at harvest time, i.e. during the dry season. Elijah is said to have had the power of keeping back the rain (1 Kings xvii. 1); but he could also bring rain, and in 1 Kings xviii. 42–5, where no mention is made of Yahweh, a kind of ritual is described whereby Elijah obtained rain. Both Elijah and Elisha are credited with power to control flowing water; in 2 Kings ii. 8 Elijah, by smiting the water of Jordan with his rolled-up mantle, is able to keep them parted while he and Elisha pass through on dry land; Elisha, by using this magic mantle, is able to do so too (ver. 14). Of the same prophet it is said that he was able to heal waters which had hitherto caused death and miscarriage; he does it by means of salt put in a new cruse, this he takes to the "spring of the waters" and pours it in (2 Kings ii. 19–22); one would expect some mention of an incantation; but if this was ever part of the text one can well understand its having been deleted by a later editor. There is another case of waters being healed in Exod. xv. 25: this is done by Moses, who throws a piece of wood [3] into the water, which immediately becomes drinkable.

[1] See Frazer, *G.B.*, "The Magic Art," i. pp. 247–319 (1911).
[2] For the ancient Babylonians details are given by Jastrow, *op. cit.*, i. pp. 48 f.
[3] The R.V. has "tree"; but apart from the fact that one does not expect a whole tree to be thrown into the water, the Hebrew word *'ētz* means "wood" as well as "tree."

An interesting instance of imitative magic occurs in 2 Kings vi. 5–7. Here it is related how a man dropped his iron axe-head into the water, Elisha thereupon cuts a piece of stick and throws it into the water at the spot where the axe-head fell ; then it is seen that just as the piece of wood floats, so the iron does the same. Another striking piece of imitative magic is recounted of Elisha in 2 Kings xiii. 14–19 ; he tells Joash the king of Israel to take bow and arrows ; then he lays his hands upon the king's hands (that constitutes a magical act), and bids him open the window eastward, i.e. in the direction of Syria, looking from Samaria, where this takes place. Next, he tells the king to shoot an arrow, which he does, whereupon Elisha utters an incantation : " A victory-arrow *from* Yahweh, a victory-arrow *against* Aram (Syria)." That is the first part of the ritual. Then follows the imitative magic. Elisha bids the king smite the ground with the arrows ; he does so three times, but Elisha upbraids him for doing so only three times ; he ought to have done it five or six times, then he would have wholly defeated the Syrians : since he has only done it three times, he will only gain three victories over them.

Yet another instance of imitative magic occurs in 2 Kings iv. 38–41, again performed by Elisha : a pottage is being brewed by the prophet's followers, and one of them goes out to gather herbs ; among the herbs gathered there happens to be a poisonous one, and this soon becomes apparent when the company begin to partake of the pottage ; but Elisha calls for some meal and casts it into the brew, the immediate effect of which is to make the poison innocuous. The idea is parallel to that of the wood and the iron : because the wood floats the iron will imitate it ; so too, because the meal is harmless so will the poisonous herb become harmless. As in the former case, one expects a magical formula of some sort to be uttered, corresponding to the act of casting in the meal, and it is difficult to believe that something of the kind did not originally stand in the text.[1]

---

[1] It is possible that under the head of imitative magic we should class the looking at a bronze serpent on a pole, which had the effect of curing people bitten by a serpent, Num. xxi. 8, 9.

But Elisha's magical powers were very wide ; in 2 Kings vi. 18–20 he is credited with the power of striking blind and giving sight again ; in the text as it stands it is Yahweh, however, who actually does this, but at Elisha's bidding. Then, once more, Elisha is also represented as being able to raise the dead by means of a somewhat elaborate ritual (2 Kings iv. 32–5). This should perhaps come under the head of imitative magic ; it is, at any rate, suggested by the ritual ; for Elisha, the living, lays himself upon the dead boy, and puts mouth on mouth, eyes on eyes, and hands on hands ; just as Elisha is alive, so the dead boy must become living. A similar story is told of Elijah, though with less detail (1 Kings xvii. 21, 22), and it is possible that the one is only an elaborated version of the other.

The subject of the magic rod offers some interesting points, but only in three cases can the references be regarded as coming strictly under the head of magic. One of these is in Exod. iv. 2 ff., where Moses' rod is turned into a serpent and back again into a rod. Another instance is when Moses, by holding up his rod, ensures success in battle to the Israelites (Exod. xvii. 8 ff.) ; and, once more, when Moses with his magic rod is able to draw water from a rock (Num. xx. 8 ff.). These are clear instances in which the powers of the magic rod are believed in. The thing is, however, of animistic origin, though this origin has been quite lost sight of ; but it is, in reality, a spirit which is supposed to reside in the rod and to effect what is required. An echo of this is to be seen in the fact that the rod is stated to be " the rod of God " (Exod. xvii. 9). The case of the " divining rod " for discovering water (Num. xxi. 18), though doubtless of similar origin so far as the idea is concerned, comes under the head of divination rather than magic ; and this is also true of Aaron's rod that budded (Num. xvii. 2–11 [in Hebrew 17–26]), which is a case of the flourishing or withering of a rod indicating the answer of the oracle.[1]

The remaining passages in which references to Magic occur deal with Egyptian magic and magicians (Gen.

---

[1] For this widespread belief see Frazer, *G.B.*, " Adonis, Attis, Osiris," I., chaps. ix., x., (1927) ; Bötticher, *Baumcultus der Hellenen*, xi. (1856).

xli. 8; Exod. vii. 11, 22 ff., viii. 7, 18, 19 [in Hebrew 3, 14, 15], ix. 11), and in Dan. ii. 2 with Babylonian magic.

A great deal of what has been quoted here from the Old Testament is from passages of admittedly late date; but this in no way indicates that Magic does not belong to the most primitive elements of Semitic, and therefore of Hebrew, beliefs ; very pointedly does Robertson Smith remark that " the savage point of view is constantly found to survive, in connexion with practices of magic, after it has been superseded in religion proper ; and the superstitions of the vulgar in modern civilized countries are not much more advanced than those of the rudest nations. So too among the Semites, magical rites and vulgar superstitions are not so much survivals from the higher official heathenism of the great sanctuaries as from a lower and more primitive stage of belief, which the higher forms of heathen worship overshadowed but did not extinguish." [1] Robertson Smith is referring to the Semites generally, and it applies of course to the Hebrews : we have only to substitute for " higher official heathenism " the " worship of Yahweh," and his words are literally true of the Hebrews. Therefore we are justified, when dealing with primitive forms of Hebrew belief, in illustrating this by practices which were still in vogue among them at a time later by untold centuries, it may be, than that of their origin.

[1] *Rel. Sem.*, p. 441.

CHAPTER IX

NOMADIC RELIGION

Since in the Old Testament there are various beliefs and practices to be observed which were handed down from the time when the forbears of the Hebrews were nomads, it will be necessary to deal shortly with these. It stands to reason that the form of these beliefs and practices will have undergone considerable modification in the course of their history, and that therefore their original form will have been somewhat different from that in which they appear in the Old Testament.

1. New-Moon Festivals

Lunar festivals were common to all the peoples of antiquity, but they were more especially observed among the Semites; so far as these latter are concerned the earliest form of the worship of the Moon is to be sought among the ancient nomadic Arabs. For peoples who had reached an agricultural stage of culture the sun necessarily played the leading *rôle*; but not so for those who were still in the nomadic stage. Owners of flocks and herds, who wandered over the measureless tracts of steppe-land, moved mostly by night because of the heat during the day; to them therefore the moon was of paramount importance [1]; and since all the Semites were at one time nomads, the moon was originally their chief deity. Further, as a god, whenever the moon first appeared in the skies (i.e. at every " new-moon ") its appearance was hailed with joyful shouts; it is significant that the Arabic word *hilâl* means both " new-moon " and " festal

---

[1] Hommel, *Der Gottesdienst der alten Araber und die israelitische Ueberlieferung*, pp. 8, 9 (1901); Weber, " Arabien vor dem Islam," in *Der alte Orient*, dritter Jahrgang, p. 19 (1902). Nielsen, *Die altarabische Mondreligion*, pp. 33, 34 (1904); *Handbuch*, i. 198, 213 ff.

shout." There are numerous indications pointing to the
fact that from the earliest times the appearance of the
new moon was celebrated as a great festival in Arabia,[1]
the reason obviously being the desire to do honour to the
god on his reappearance. But the most important of
all the new-moon festivals was that which fell in the
month *Rajab*, equivalent to the Hebrew month *'Abib*,
for this was the time when the ancient Arabs celebrated
the Spring festival after the casting of their young among
the flocks and herds.[2]

On the analogy of the ancient Arabs, therefore, there
is every reason to believe that the new-moon feasts
among the Hebrews go back to nomadic times. They
are frequently mentioned in the Old Testament, but it is
significant that the object of their celebration is never
hinted at : they are holy days and, like the Sabbath,
days of rest (Amos viii. 4, 5), not because work was
forbidden on them, however, but because they were days
of worship, to which they were devoted. It is noteworthy
that these festivals are not mentioned in the Book of the
Covenant nor in the Deuteronomic law, doubtless on
account of their connexion with lunar worship ; but the
observance of them was too ingrained to be eradicated,
and they continued down to Christian times (see Col.
ii. 16).

2. THE SABBATHS

As a preliminary it is interesting to note the various
reasons why the Sabbath was to be observed ; taking the
several legal codes in the chronological order generally
accepted this is what we find :

In the code of *J*, no reason is given for its
observance, nor is there any command to rest ; it is only
commanded that "thou shalt keep Sabbath," with

---

[1] Meinhold, *Sabbat und Woche im A.T.* (1905) ; Nielsen, *Handbuch*,
pp. 49, 50.
[2] Further details are given by Wellhausen, *op. cit.* ; Nielsen, *Mondreligion*, p. 92. Robertson Smith (*Rel. Sem.*, p. 406) says : " In pastoral
Arabia domestic cattle habitually yean in the brief season of the spring
pasture, and this would serve to fix an annual season of sacrifice."
See also pp. 641 f.

special reference to ploughing and harvest time (Exod. xxxiv. 21).

In the *Book of the Covenant* it is in order that the beasts may rest and that slaves and strangers may be refreshed ; so far as the Israelites in general are concerned it is only said that they are to " keep Sabbath " ; there is no command to them to rest (Exod. xxiii. 12).

In *E* it is because God rested on the Sabbath (Exod. xx. 8 ff.).

In *D* it is because God brought the people out of the land of Egypt, i.e. it was to be observed in memory of that event (Deut. v. 12–15).

In the "Code of Holiness" (Lev. xvii.–xxvi.), belonging to a time soon after *D*, no reason is given ; there is only the command to keep the Sabbath and to refrain from work (Lev. xxiii. 3 ; cp. xix. 30).

In *P* it is because it is a sign between Yahweh and His people (Exod. xxxi. 12–17).

So much for the mention of the Sabbath in the legal codes.

In the earliest passage, that in which the Sabbath is mentioned for the first time, it is seen that the Sabbath, like a new-moon day, was a day on which one could travel on a beast because on that day the beasts rested from their ordinary labour (2 Kings iv. 23).

Three conclusions may be justifiably drawn from these *data* : (1) the real origin of the Sabbath was unknown ; (2) it originated, in any case, before the entry into Canaan ; its unknown origin suggests this ; (3) it was not originally a day of rest from labour.

That the Israelites did not adopt the observance of the Sabbath from the Canaanites seems certain, inasmuch as there is absolutely no trace of its existence among them. Had it ever been an institution among the Canaanites it is hardly likely that it would have died out ; but, as Budde has pointed out, Nehemiah had to take proceedings against the Canaanite tradesmen who brought their wares into Jerusalem on the Sabbath (Neh. xiii. 17–21) ; clearly they knew nothing about Sabbath observance. Though we have, as he says, little information available as to the *ancient* Canaanites, " yet we have abundance from the contemporary Phœnicians, their kinsmen, over the whole of the Mediterranean coastal area as far as Carthage, Gaul, and Spain, but nowhere is there the slightest trace of the Sabbath ; on the contrary, Israel justly feels conscious that no parallel for it is to be found in the whole of her environment." [1]

Further, that the Israelites did *not* get the Sabbath from the Babylonians seems likewise certain for three reasons : (1) the latter observed a five-day, not a seven-day, week ; (2) with them the Sabbaths were evil days, days of ill-omen, on which it was unlucky to do certain things ; and (3) there is good reason for believing that among the Babylonians themselves the word *shapattu* (= Sabbath) was a loan-word borrowed from the ancient Arabs. To deal with these points in any detail would involve a good deal of discussion which would take us too far afield.[2]

Mainly on negative grounds, therefore, it may be concluded that the Sabbath did not originate among the Hebrews, and that they borrowed it neither from the Canaanites nor from the Babylonians. Thus we are forced to the conclusion that they brought it with them from their nomadic life. For our present purpose that is sufficient ; for with the very complicated and still unsettled question as to the real origin of the Sabbath we cannot concern ourselves here beyond saying that, from the nature of the case, it seems highly probable that it originated among the ancient nomadic Arabs [3] ; we say from the nature of the case, because the close connexion between new-moons and Sabbaths, so frequently bracketed together (2 Kings iv. 23 ; Amos viii. 5 ; Hos. ii. 11 [13 in Hebrew] ; Isa. i. 13, lxvi. 23 ; Ezek. xlv. 17, xlvi. i. 3 ; Neh. x. 33 [34 in Hebrew] ; 1 Chron. xxiii. 31 ; 2 Chron. ii. 4 [3 in Hebrew], viii. 13, xxxi. 3 ; cp. Ezra iii. 5), shows that the latter was a lunar feast in its origin ; and this being so, it would originate among nomads ; as we

---

[1] *The Journal of Theological Studies* for Oct. 1928, p. 5.
[2] The subject is dealt with by Budde in his article, already referred to, pp. 6, 7 ; and more especially by Hommel, *Die altorientalischen Denkmäler und das alte Testament*, pp. 18, 19 (1902), and Nielsen, *op. cit.*, pp. 87 ff., 153 ff.
[3] Nielsen, *Handbuch*, i. 244 ff.

have seen, the moon played the leading *rôle* among them.

3. The Passover Festival

The history of the development of this feast, as described in the Old Testament and later Jewish writings, presents us with various features which do not belong to its original form. After tracing this history back and denuding the celebration of the feast of those parts which can be proved to be later developments or modifications,[1] we are able to indicate those elements which, even though they may not all have belonged to the feast as originally celebrated,[2] can with certitude be stated to have been its essential features at the period when it formed one, and probably the most important, of the religious observances of the Hebrews in the nomadic stage. These features are as follows :

(i) *The sacrifice of a victim.* This was taken from the flocks or herds, i.e. either a sheep or a goat or one of the larger animals ; even as late as the time of the Deuteronomic legislation the choice is left open (Deut. xvi. 2). The age of the victim is not mentioned before the time of the Priestly Code (Exod. xii. 5), where it is said that it must be " of the first year " ; this, however, was an extension of the original custom, as we shall see. The victim was eaten at a *sacrificial meal*, which was held in the dwellings of the various worshippers ; it had to be entirely consumed before the morning, since—

(ii) It was a *night celebration*, which took place between sunset and sunrise : the earliest laws do not define the hour closer than this, but it was clearly after darkness had set in.

The night on which the celebration took place was that *of the full moon of the month nearest the Spring Equinox.*[3] It is true, the earliest direct evidence of this is in Deut.

---

[1] The subject is admirably dealt with by Benzinger in the *Encycl. Bibl.*, iii. 3593–3600 ; and especially by Buchanan Gray, *Sacrifice in the Old Testament*, pp. 337–382 (1925) (see also Driver, *Deuteronomy*, pp. 190–193 [1902]).

[2] Its real origin must lie far back in prehistoric times.

[3] Nielsen, *Handbuch*, i. 244.

xvi. 1 : "Observe the month of Abib [the later name is
Nisan, see Neh. ii. 1, equivalent to the month of April],
and keep the Passover unto Yahweh thy God " ; but in
so ancient and important a feast as this it may rightly
be assumed that the Deuteronomic law prescribed
traditional use ; there is nothing in the whole of the Old
Testament that points to any other time.

(iii) The *blood of the victim* was smeared on the outside
of the dwelling-places of the worshippers.

Those are the outstanding features of this feast as it
appears after the demonstrably later accretions have been
eliminated. We have also to remember that the explanations as to the origin and meaning of the Passover given
in the Old Testament are of a late date, when its significance had either been forgotten, or, if known, had to be
reinterpreted for reasons which are fully comprehensible.
Moreover, it must be noted that these explanations, when
examined, are really no explanations ; thus, Deut. xvi. 1
explains it by saying that " in the month Abib Yahweh
thy God brought thee forth out of Egypt by night " ;
but the mention of which night of the month it was on
which this happened is studiously avoided in the whole
section vers. 1–8 ; and in ver. 2 ; "Thou shalt sacrifice
Pesach [there is no article in the Hebrew] [1] . . . of the
flock and the herd," is distinctly ambiguous ; it does not
explain why a sacrifice should be offered ; and when,
further, it is said in reference to the blood on the lintel
that " Yahweh will pass over the door, and will not suffer
the destroyer to come in unto your houses to smite you "
(Exod. xii. 23), it does not explain who the destroyer
was, nor yet why he should want to smite the people.

What the feast originally was, and what its object was,
and what the blood-smearing on the lintel meant are all
obvious to the folklorist and to the student of primitive
Semitic religion, but it may be well to say something in
explanation of them here.

The first thing to note is the time of the year at which
this festival was celebrated : it was in what we call

---

[1] For the contention that the name of the feast " Pesach " (Passover)
was derived from the sacred dance performed during its celebration,
see the present writer's *The Sacred Dance*, pp. 50 f.

7

April, i.e. in the spring ; so that it was a *Spring Festival*.
As is well known, it was a world-wide custom among
uncultured and semi-cultured peoples to offer the firstlings
of the flocks and herds, later the first-fruits of the produce
of the soil, to the deity, in order to ensure the increase
of these during the coming year.[1] In the nomadic stage
it was the increase of the flocks and herds which was of
paramount importance ; but the revival of the vegetation
in the steppe-lands, through which the nomads roamed
with their flocks and herds, was also a matter of real
importance. Their main concern, however, would
naturally be the former ; hence the offering to the fertility-
deity the firstlings of the flocks and herds.[2] In the Old
Testament accounts only one victim is mentioned ; this,
it may safely be affirmed, was not the original custom ;
each head of a family or more probably of a clan, would
have made his offering. And therefore it may be sur-
mised that the offering was made either before each tent
of a nomad encampment, or before the chief tent of a
group belonging to a clan.[3]

Then as to the victim. In Exod. xii. 9 and 46 there
are two prohibitions in regard to it : " Eat not of it raw,
nor sodden at all with water, but roast it with fire " ;
and : " Neither shall ye break a bone thereof." These
prohibitions would have no force unless intended to put
an end to customs still in vogue. They can only mean
therefore that originally the victim was eaten raw,[4]
and the bones pounded up and also consumed ; and this,
indeed, is precisely what one would expect to have been
the case, because, according to early Semitic belief, the
life resided in the blood[5] and in the bones,[6] and the
object of the sacrificial meal at which the victim was eaten
was to absorb the divine life conceived to be present in
the sacred victim, and thus to become united with the

---

[1] For many illustrations see Frazer, *G.B.*, " The Dying God," pp. 246–
285 (1911).
[2] For the Moon as a fertility-god see Nielsen, *Handbuch*, i. 213 ff.
[3] The flocks and herds were the common property of the clan.
[4] This was also done in much later times; see 1 Sam. xiv. 32 ; Ezek.
xxxiii. 25 ; Lev. xix. 26 ; Isa. lxv. 4, lxvi. 3, 17 ; Zech. ix. 7.
[5] See, e.g., Lev. xvii. 11, 14.
[6] See, e.g., Isa. lxvi. 14 ; *Ecclus.* xlvi. 11, 12, xlix. 10.

deity. This in no way detracts from the primary object of the feast. Further, the command in Deut. xvi. 4— "Neither shall any of the flesh, which thou sacrificest the first day at even, remain all night until the morning,"— becomes quite intelligible when the sacred character of the moon, as pointed out above, is remembered ; the sacred feast takes place in the presence of the deity, and must be concluded before he retires.

That the fourteenth day of the month, i.e. full-moon day, was that on which the festival was celebrated was obviously because it was then that the deity showed himself in his full glory.

A more difficult question arises when we seek the meaning of the blood ritual. A variety of explanations have been offered,[1] but it is impossible to deal with these here. We believe the reason of the blood-smearing to have been similar to that for which the Jews in later days fixed on their door-posts what is now called the *Mezuzah*, i.e. a small tube made of wood, metal, or glass, in which is rolled up a piece of parchment containing the *Shema'* (Deut. vi. 4–9 and xi. 13–21) ; the custom is at least pre-Christian : it is referred to by Josephus (*Antiq.* IV, viii. 13) ; the Rabbis in Talmudic times attributed to it a protective power against demons, and this doubtless was the original purpose of it. The Muhammadans have a similar custom of inscribing verses from the *Qu'ran* on their doors and at the entrances to their houses, with a like object. This seems likely to have been the reason for smearing the blood of the sacred victim on the tents of nomads, for not only were the hours of darkness always believed to be the time when evil spirits were particularly active, but on this special occasion there were reasons for more pronounced virulence than usual on their part.[2] With this view Buchanan Gray, among others, agrees. He says : " What the ancient Hebrews endeavoured to repel from their houses were spirits, demons of plague, or

---

[1] Curtiss, *Primitive Semitic Religion To-day*, pp. 226 f. (1902); Trumbull, *The Threshold Covenant*, pp. 203 ff. (1906) ; Frazer, *G.B.*, " The Dying God," pp. 174 ff. (1911).

[2] See Frazer, *G.B.*, " The Scapegoat," esp. chapters ii. and iv. (1913), and " The Dying God," pp. 246–271.

sickness and the like, much as the modern Bedawy or Syrian peasant." [1]

4. The Feast of Sheep-shearing

The term is more strictly " Flock-shearing " ; and the Hebrew word for " flock " (*zôn*) includes goats as well as sheep. Moreover, the Hebrew word for "wool" (*zĕmĕr*) is used of the wool of both sheep and goats. The *shearing* of animals of the flock belongs to agricultural times ; the earlier custom was to pluck off the wool with the hands.

Although this feast is only referred to three times in the Old Testament (Gen. xxxviii. 12, 13 ; 1 Sam. xxv. 2 ff., 36 ; 2 Sam. xiii. 23, 24), it must obviously have been celebrated at regular intervals. There can be no doubt that it went back originally to nomadic times, for the clothing of nomads was made of the wool of sheep and goats as well as from their skins. Like all the ancient feasts it was a joyful time, the technical term *yôm tôb*, " a good day," is applied to it in 1 Sam. xxv. 8, and that much eating and drinking took place is seen from ver. 36. But none the less it was a religious feast. This will be clear when it is remembered that the deity was looked to for the increase of the flocks, so that the wool would also be regarded as his gift ; this was so in later days too (see Hos. ii. 5 [7 in Hebrew]).

The details of this feast which have come down to us are very scanty ; no mention is made of any sacrifice, but it is difficult to believe that any feast among the ancient Semites lacked this. The main thing, however, from our present point of view, is that this feast belonged originally to nomadic times, and was brought from their nomad life by the Hebrews into Canaan.

So far, then, as religion is concerned—and it is only with this that we are dealing—we have seen that the new-moon festivals, the Sabbaths, the feast of *Pesach*, and the feast of Sheep-shearing, belonged to the religion of the Hebrews in their nomadic stage, and that they brought these observances with them when they entered

[1] *Op. cit.*, p. 364.

Canaan, and continued after the Settlement to celebrate them as integral parts of their religion. We have not yet, however, touched upon what was by far the most important element in Hebrew nomadic religion, viz. belief in Yahweh ; but the importance of this demands that it should be treated separately.

There were some other institutions which belonged to the nomadic stage, and which were of a quasi-religious character, at one time wholly religious. With these we do not propose to deal, because they played no real part in the subsequent development of Hebrew religion, though as institutions they continued to be observed long after the settlement in Canaan ; indeed, in one case, even to the present day ; these are : Circumcision, Blood revenge, the Ban, and the prohibition of food before battle. The first of these is claimed as of Hebrew origin, though the accounts are wholly at variance : one describes it as having originated with Abraham (Gen. xvii. 1–14, P) ; another points to Joshua as having introduced it (Josh. v. 5 ff.), while the oldest account connects it with Moses (Exod. iv. 25 ff., J). The rite is, however, common to most Semites, as well as to the Egyptians and many other non-Semitic peoples [1] ; its origin and purpose are unknown, though many theories are held on the latter point.[2]

Blood revenge was prevalent among the Hebrews, as can be seen, e.g. from 2 Sam. xiv. 7, 11 ; Deut. xix. 12 ; in the Priestly Code it undergoes a certain modification, inasmuch as the quarrel has to be judged by the congregation, and there must be witnesses (Num. xxxv. 24, 25, 30). The Ban (*Chĕrĕm* [3]) is vividly illustrated in 1 Sam. xv. ; in one form or another it was practised into late post-exilic times (see e.g. Ezra x. 8). The object of refraining from food before a battle or until the fighting had concluded was that the divine strength gained by means of sanctifying oneself before fighting (cp. Josh.

---

[1] Ploss, *Das Kind in Brauch und Sitte der Völker*, i. 342 ff. (1882).
[2] See L. H. Gray in Hastings' *E.R.E.*, iii. 664–667.
[3] The word means someone or something devoted to Yahweh by being destroyed ; being thus " consecrated " to the deity it would be unlawful for a man to appropriate such a person or thing to his own use (see for a good illustration 1 Sam. xv. 10–31).

iii. 5) might not be hindered from operating through coming into contact with common substance (see 1 Sam. xiv. 24 ; and cp. the expression " to consecrate war " Mic. iii. 5 ; Jer. vi. 4) ; sacrifices were offered before a battle or a campaign (Judges vi. 20, 26 ; xx. 26 ; 1 Sam. vii. 9, xiii. 10).

CHAPTER X

NOMADIC RELIGION : THE BEGINNING OF THE WORSHIP OF YAHWEH

To the nomadic religion of the Hebrews belongs, in its beginnings, the knowledge and acceptation of Yahweh, through Moses, as the God of Israel.

We are not concerned here with the work of Moses as the founder of the religion of Yahweh among the Hebrews ; nor yet with the religious teaching of Moses and his presentation to the people of Him whom they ultimately came to recognize as the one and only God ; this will all be dealt with in subsequent chapters. Our object at present is to point to two outstanding events which, under God, were the immediate causes of the recognition and acceptation of Yahweh by the Hebrew people themselves, after the revelation accorded to Moses. This belongs, therefore, if not to the actual background of Hebrew religion, at least to the threshold of that faith.

The great prophets insisted again and again on the truth that Yahweh was the God of Nature [1] ; they also constantly emphasized the truth that God was " from everlasting." [2] On the very threshold of their entry into the wilderness and of their taking up the nomad life once more, the Hebrews had such a signal illustration of the truth that Yahweh was the God of Nature that it never lost its hold on them, however much other currents of religious belief may have swept them from the main stream of true faith. They also received such a striking illustration of the further truth that in every age Yahweh was revealing Himself to men in accordance with their capacity of apprehension, that through the long years of their history which followed the echo of how this truth was exemplified at this early period resounded again and again in the records of the nation.

[1] See Part II, Chapter VIII, § 2 (b).   [2] See, e.g., Hab. i. 12.

The two outstanding events (we ought more strictly to say two series of events) with which we are about to deal belong closely together, but they can be treated separately. For most of what follows we are indebted to two notable Old Testament scholars. Regarding the first event we make our acknowledgements to the late Prof. Gressmann [1] ; the interpretation which he was the first to offer of what is often called " the passage of the Red Sea," with its accompanying events, may in some respects be open to criticism, since it may not always be possible to reconcile it with the conflicting statements found in the different sources containing the records ; but there is so much in what he says which conforms to the probabilities of the case, and which appeals to common sense, that his interpretation of the events well deserves consideration. In some details we have been led to make modifications, and in some respects we have been able to confirm his view independently ; but for the main thesis we have to express our indebtedness to him.

Regarding the other event, which deals with the existence of the worship of Yahweh before Moses established it as the religion of the Hebrews, we are wholly indebted to Prof. Budde. [2]

1. The Exodus from Egypt, and the Subsequent Events

In Exod. xiii. 17, 18, it is recorded : " And it came to pass, when Pharaoh had let the people go, that God led them not by the way of the land of the Philistines, although that was near ; for God said, Lest peradventure the people repent when they see war, and they return to Egypt ; but God led the people about, by the way of the wilderness by the Red Sea ; and the children of Israel went up armed out of the land of Egypt." The passage is instructive from several points of view. It belongs to the " Elohist " document—that is recognized by all

[1] *Mose und seine Zeit*, pp. 108–121 (1913) ; there is, unfortunately, no English translation of this work.
[2] *Die Religion des Volkes Israel bis zur Verbannung*, pp. 9–31 (1900) ; an English translation, published in New York, forms vol. iv of the *American Lectures on the History of Religions*.

critics ; and this means that a tradition, oral or written, but more probably the latter, was used by a compiler in the middle of the eighth century B.C. in writing the history of his people. That he was really utilizing ancient material will be evident from the following considerations : In going from Goshen to Palestine there are two available routes : one runs north-east along the coast through what in the compiler's time was the land of the Philistines—that was the direct and obvious route to take ; the other led south-east through the desert, via Akaba, and then almost due north—a very round-about way, and quite unnecessary unless there were special reasons for it. Now, in the source used by our compiler (as will be obvious in a moment) it simply stated that the Israelites went by the longer route, without giving the reason for this, which we know, however, from another source. The compiler of this Elohistic document therefore added what he believed must have been the reason, and from his point of view it would have been a sufficiently strong reason, namely, the fear on the part of the Israelites that they would be attacked by the Philistines. But the fact is that at the time of the exodus from Egypt and for a considerable period of time after, the Philistines were not yet in possession of the land which they conquered later, and in which they settled down.[1] The passage under consideration therefore offers a good illustration, many of which are to be found in the Old Testament, of a genuinely ancient historical detail being expanded for the purpose of explanation by a later compiler. The explanation was thoroughly *bona fide*, but nevertheless a mistaken one.

The Israelites, then, took the south-eastern route, not the north-eastern one ; and they did this for the simple reason that Palestine was not their objective. The most reliable sources [2] for the history immediately following

---

[1] The Philistine invasion did not take place until about 1194 B.C. ; for the evidence see H. R. Hall in the *Cambr. Anc. Hist.*, ii, pp. 283 ff. (1924).

[2] JE : Num. xx. 1, xiii. 26; cp. xxxii. 8 ff., xiv. 33 ; cp. also Judges xi. 16.
D : Deut. ii. 4.
P : Num. xx. 1*a*–13, 22, xxvii. 14 ; Deut. xxxii. 51.

the exodus, discrepant though they are in some particulars, make it clear that the objective of the Israelites on
leaving Egypt was not Palestine, but Kadesh ; but for
special reasons they made a stay first at Mount Sinai,
involving a journey still farther south-eastwards. Where
Mount Sinai lay will be considered presently ; it is
necessary first to say a word about the position of the
" Red Sea " (as it is called in the English Version) mentioned in the passage referred to above.

The fact must be recognized that there is no authority
for bringing the Red Sea into the narrative at all if
by the Red Sea is meant what it means nowadays.
The Old Testament speaks of the *Yam-Sūph* as the
waters in which the Egyptians were overwhelmed ; it
means either the " Reed Sea," or perhaps more correctly
the " Sea of Weeds " [1]; and in the Old Testament we
are told quite distinctly where this lay : in 1 Kings ix. 26,
for example, it says : " And king Solomon made a navy
of ships in Ezion-geber, which is beside Elath, on the
shore of the *Yam-Sūph*, in the land of Edom." Elath
lay at the extreme northern part, on the eastern side, of
the Aelanitic Gulf, or the Gulf of Akaba, the long, narrow
arm north of the Red Sea, and running from this sea
to a distance of about 125 miles ; it is on the eastern side
of what is now known as the Sinaitic Peninsula. In
Jer. xlix. 21 it is clearly indicated that the *Yam-Sūph* lay
in Edomite territory, which touched on that of Midian
to the south.[2] When, therefore, the Old Testament
speaks of the *Yam-Sūph* as the waters in which the
Egyptians were overwhelmed, it has no doubt about the
exact spot where this happened.

Coming now to Mount Sinai, it is to be noted first,
that in reading the various forms of the narrative in
whatever sources they are contained, it comes out clearly
enough that Mount Sinai cannot have been very far
distant from the scene of the Egyptian catastrophe.
Mount Sinai has usually been located in the south of
what is now called the " Sinaitic " Peninsula, which takes

---

[1] Cp. Jon. ii. 6 (5) : " The weeds (*sūph*) were wrapped about my head."
[2] Cp. also 2 Chron. viii. 17, and Exod. xxiii. 31 ; Num. xiv. 25,
xxi. 4 ; Deut. i. 40, ii. 1.

its name from the supposed position of Mount Sinai. But the fact is that there is absolutely no evidence for locating Mount Sinai here ; in the Old Testament everything points against it, for it is there asserted quite clearly that it was situated in Midianite territory.[1] It was only in Christian times that the tradition arose about Mount Sinai being situated in the south of the " Sinaitic " Peninsula. Again, we shall see in a moment that there is every reason to believe, from the Old Testament descriptions, that Mount Sinai was a volcano ; but geological experts who have carefully examined the country assure us that the " Sinaitic " Peninsula is not volcanic. On the other hand, the entire eastern coast of the Aelanitic Gulf, right up to where the Old Testament places Mount Sinai, i.e. into Midianite and Edomite territory, *is* volcanic, according to these experts. So that this further supports the Old Testament indications that Mount Sinai was not far distant from the *Yām-Sūph*, or rather that part of it at which the Egyptian catastrophe occurred.

Next, it is interesting to see how very clearly the Old Testament descriptions of Mount Sinai show that it was a volcano. In Exod. xix. 18 we read : " And mount Sinai was altogether on smoke, because Yahweh descended upon it in fire ; and the smoke thereof ascended as the smoke of a furnace, and the whole mount quaked greatly." Again, in Deut. iv. 11, 12, it is said : " And ye came near and stood under the mountain ; and the mountain burned with fire unto the heart of heaven, with darkness, cloud, and thick darkness. And the voice of Yahweh spoke unto you out of the midst of the fire. . . ." Once more, in Judges v. 4, 5, the reminiscence of what happened at Mount Sinai finds expression thus :

> Yahweh, when thou wentest forth out of Seir,
> When thou marchedst out of the field of Edom,
> The earth trembled, the heavens also dropped,
> Yea, the clouds dropped water.
> The mountains quaked at the presence of Yahweh,
> Even yon Sinai at the presence of Yahweh, the God of Israel.

---

[1] Edomite and Midianite territory ran into one another ; there was no clear-cut boundary.

So, too, in Ps. lxviii. 7, 8, similar language is used in referring to the same event : " the earth trembled," " the heavens dropped," " even yon Sinai (trembled) at the presence of Yahweh." Without quoting other passages to the same effect, it is abundantly clear that whatever else may have happened at the time of the escape of the Israelites from the Egyptians, expressions such as " the mountain burned with fire," " the smoke thereof ascended as the smoke of a furnace," " the mountains quaked," " the earth trembled," etc., point to a volcanic eruption of a severe character, accompanied by an earthquake ; this will be further illustrated presently.

Bearing in mind, then, the two facts that the Old Testament places Mount Sinai at the extreme north of the Aelanitic Gulf, and that it clearly represents Mount Sinai as a volcano, which was in eruption just at the time of the Egyptian pursuit of the Israelites, and that an earthquake, as so often during volcanic eruptions, took place at the same time, we can picture to ourselves the course of events somewhat as follows :

The Hebrews, during their flight from Egypt, have reached the coast on the west of what we know as the Gulf of Akaba, the northern extremity of the *Yām-Sūph*. Their way is therefore barred. Evening is not far off, when they suddenly realize that in the far distance the Egyptians are following them. A great expanse of water in front and a powerful enemy behind—what chance of escape is there for the more or less defenceless multitude, with women and children, and encumbered with baggage, to say nothing of flocks and herds which, as nomads, they must have had with them ! Short of a miracle they are doomed. At this moment occurs what must naturally have appeared to the Hebrews as the miraculous intervention of some supernatural being. A volcanic eruption, accompanied by earthquake, shakes the land, and the fire and smoke emitted from the mountain casts a lurid light upon the darkening landscape ; above all, the immense cloud formed by the volumes of smoke rising from the mountain-top, being permeated with incandescent gases, glows with unspeakable majesty ;

and, slowly wafted by the wind, comes towards them. Then occurs one of those terrible cataclysms which have happened again and again in the case of volcanoes situated near the seacoast (two other notable instances will be given presently) : the sea-bottom is raised over a large area by the underlying explosion of pent-up gases, and land appears where a few moments before there was but the dark surface of water. The Hebrews seize their opportunity, and with one accord make for the newly appeared land ; over this they speed and gain the farther side of what had been the sea. But on looking back they perceive that the pursuing enemy has followed their example, and is likewise passing over the land in their wake. But once more there occurs what also has happened time and again since : the sea-bottom, which had been forced upwards, being unable to bear its own weight when the underlying pressure is withdrawn by the gradual dispersal of the gaseous vapours underground, collapses ! The waters which had receded now return with incredible roar and overwhelm the whole body of the pursuing Egyptians.

The picture drawn of what happened at the time of this landmark in the history of Hebrew Religion might well appear fantastic were it not that, so far as the physical cataclysm is concerned, similar occurrences have been recorded at different times since. Two of these may be briefly recounted. On the 29th September, 1538, of our era, Monte Nuovo, close to Naples, came into existence ; immediately prior to its appearance the sea at Puzzuoli suddenly receded ; numberless fish, it is told, lay about on the now dry land, and were carried off in wagon-loads by the inhabitants. After some hours the sea returned as suddenly ; then the earth rose and the mountain was formed ; at the same time, amid terrific thunder, an immense pillar of fire was shot out, together with glowing stones, an enormous cloud of steam, and ashes. As there was no lava-stream very few people perished. The cataclysm lasted altogether two days and two nights. This is an outline of an eye-witness' account, named Simone Porzio, published at Florence in 1551.

The other happened as recently as 1902, when there occurred the appalling eruption of Mont Pelé [1] on the island of Martinique. One of the most remarkable things about it was the moving incandescent cloud which the mountain belched forth. Simultaneously with the eruption there was a fearful gale ; at the same time, too, there was an earthquake which had an extraordinary effect upon the sea ; an eye-witness tells of how it suddenly became rough, it rose higher and higher, and immense waves came sweeping over the city and the surrounding country, and then receded. It has been observed that during volcanic eruptions the sea is often affected in this way, volcanoes being, in very many cases, situated near the seacoast. [2]

In view, then, of what the Old Testament records tell us, and in view of subsequent occurrences of a somewhat similar character, the belief is justified that the account of the " Red Sea Catastrophe " is based on an actual occurrence. More than one account, as already pointed out, has been incorporated in the Old Testament, which easily explains the inconsistencies which are found in the narrative. One must also make allowances for additions and embellishments, as well as for what are intended to be explanatory comments, due to later scribes— an entirely natural proceeding. But in its essence the story tells of an actual historical fact ; and what is of special importance is that it had a most profound effect upon the development of Hebrew Religion.

2. YAHWEH, THE GOD OF THE HEBREWS [3]

Inseparably connected with this providential deliverance of the Hebrews was the founding of what was in effect a new religion ; for the experience at Sinai was what one might call the coping-stone of the edifice of

---

[1] Pelé is the name of the Hawaiian volcano goddess.

[2] For the account given above the writer is indebted to Gressmann, *op. cit.*, pp. 116, 117.

[3] In this section we have to touch upon what belongs properly to Part II ; but we do so only to a small extent in order to show how closely connected with the origin of Yahweh-worship was the Sinai revelation.

which Moses was the builder. That is to say, the beginning of the religion of Yahweh among the Hebrews centred in Moses; and it was the Sinai revelation to which was primarily due the acceptation of Yahweh as their God by the Hebrew people.

We have seen what the religion of the Hebrews was before the time of Moses [1]; we have now to enquire by what means it was that Moses came to the knowledge of Yahweh. Exod. iii. gives us an account of this. Moses was on Mount Horeb, another name for Mount Sinai, in Midian, where he was keeping the flock of Jethro his father-in-law, "the priest of Midian," and where Yahweh revealed Himself to him. Moses had fled to this country, which was situated to the east of the northern extremity of the Gulf of Akaba, to escape the consequences of murdering an Egyptian (Exod. ii. 14, 15). Now, if he was tending the flock of Jethro he was within the district belonging to Jethro's tribe, of which, as priest, he was in all probability the patriarch; and, according to Judges i. 16, this Midianite tribe, or rather clan belonging to the tribe, was that of the Kenites. It is well to bear in mind that there is, and always has been, a strict unwritten law of the desert in regard to the tracts of land belonging to the different tribes among nomads. The division of the land of Canaan in later times among the Israelite tribes was but the adaptation of this tribal law of the wilderness to new conditions. Moses, then, was feeding Jethro's flock in the territory belonging to the Kenite clan. Further, as is well known, among nomadic tribes there were tribal gods; each tribe had its own god, and the god held sway within the limits of the tribal territory; just as in later days there were national gods whose power was restricted to the country of the nation. It follows therefore that Mount Sinai, close to which, according to Exod. iii. 1, Moses was feeding Jethro's flock, was within the Kenite territory of the Midianite land, and that Yahweh, who is described as dwelling on Mount Sinai, was originally the tribal god of the Kenites, and Jethro was His priest. This explains the revered and authoritative position which Jethro

[1] But see further, Chapter XI.

occupies in the sight of Moses. In Exod. xviii. 15 ff.[1] we read of how Jethro instructs Moses in the ways of administering justice ; and in ver. 24 it is said : " So Moses hearkened unto the voice of his father-in-law, and did all that he had said." Again, according to Num. x. 29 ff.[1] Moses says to him : " We are journeying unto the place of which Yahweh said, I will give it to you ; come thou with us, and we will do thee good ; for Yahweh hath spoken good concerning Israel." At first Jethro hesitates, and Moses urges him further : " Leave us not, I pray thee ; forasmuch as thou knowest how we are to encamp in the wilderness, and thou shalt be to us instead of eyes. And it shall be, if thou go with us, yea, it shall be, that what good soever Yahweh shall do unto us, the same will He do unto thee."

It must strike one as somewhat remarkable that Moses, the leader, the law-giver, and the religious head of his people, should pay such deference to his father-in-law, and be guided by his counsel, and be so loth to lose his company. There must have been very special reasons for this. But still more striking is what we find recorded in Exod. xviii. 8 ff. ; after Moses has told Jethro about the deliverance of the Israelites, it continues : " And Jethro rejoiced for all the good which Yahweh had done to Israel, in that he had delivered them out of the hand of the Egyptians. And Jethro said, Blessed be Yahweh, who hath delivered you out of the hand of the Egyptians. . . . Now I know that Yahweh is greater than all gods. . . . And Jethro, Moses' father-in-law, took a burnt-offering and sacrifices for God ; and Aaron came, and all the elders of Israel, to eat bread with Moses' father-in-law before God." This action is incomprehensible except on the supposition that Yahweh was the God of Jethro and his tribe, the Kenites, and that Jethro himself was Yahweh's priest.

There is a good deal in the later history of the Israelites which bears out the contention that Moses adopted

---

[1] The fact that these two passages come from different sources (E and J respectively) is interesting as showing that on this point of the position of superiority ascribed to Moses' father-in-law they are in agreement.

the worship of Yahweh from the religion of the Kenites ;
but with these details we cannot deal here.[1]

Since, then, as we have seen, Mount Sinai was believed
to be the special abode of Yahweh, we can fully understand
that the volcanic eruption, the earthquake, and its effect
upon the waters of the *Yām-Sūph*, resulting in the destruction of the Egyptian pursuers, were all ascribed to
the direct action of Yahweh, the God of Sinai. The
incandescent cloud, blazing, as it seemed, with fire, was
believed to be the manifestation of the deity ; a belief
natural enough to semi-civilized nomads.

It must therefore be recognized that the new religion
which Moses founded was adopted from the Kenite tribe
of the Midianite people. But this statement demands
a little further consideration.

From the account in Exod. iii. 1 ff. we have been
taught to believe that Moses first came to the knowledge
of Yahweh through the divine manifestation at the burning bush. Now, when these verses are carefully examined,
it will be seen that there are two passages in them which
require to be accounted for. The first is in ver. 1,
already quoted, which says : " Now Moses was keeping
the flock of Jethro his father-in-law, the priest of Midian."
One naturally asks, what is the point of prefacing the
account of the burning bush with this reference to Jethro,
the priest of Midian, when it has no connexion with what
follows ? As we have seen, in the light of other passages
we are able to discern the significance of the mention of
the priest of Midian ; but as the text stands there is no
connexion. But this want of connexion with the context
suggests that the passage of which this verse is part is
not in the form in which it appeared originally ; the
assumption is not unjustified that when this verse was
first written down it stood in a different context from
that in which it now appears ; in other words, the passage
is not in the form in which it stood originally. And
this is borne out by the words of vers. 7, 8 : " And
Yahweh said, I have surely seen the affliction of my people
which are in Egypt . . . and I am come down to deliver
them from out of the hand of the Egyptians, and to

---

[1] See further, Budde, *op. cit.*, pp. 41 ff.

bring them up out of that land unto a good land and a large, unto a land flowing with milk and honey. . . ."

Apart from some other points in these verses which might be commented on, it must be asked : How can Yahweh speak of the Hebrews while still in Egypt as " My people " when they have not yet accepted Him as their God, nor even heard of Him ? We must beware of reading into these words modern ideas which they cannot bear ; *we* might say that Yahweh could speak of the Hebrews in Egypt as His people before they had heard of Him because He had accepted them as His people even though they knew nothing about it. But that will not do. That is not the ancient way of thinking, whether of the Hebrews or of any other people of antiquity. In those far distant times a people did not accept a new God unless they knew something about him first. Moses accepted Yahweh because he had learned about Him from His priest Jethro ; the Hebrews accepted Yahweh because, as they believed, He had shown forth His power and delivered them. The fact is that this passage in which Yahweh is made to speak of the Hebrews while still in Egypt as " My people," belongs to a time centuries later than the Mosaic age ; and the whole account is coloured by the point of view of later thought. And therefore, while ancient material lies embodied in the record, we must not look upon the episode of the burning bush as historical in the way that a later writer intended. The revelation of Yahweh to Moses was very real, but it was accorded by means of the instrument which He chose.

Finally, the objection may, quite naturally, be urged that if the religion of the Hebrews was merely borrowed from that of the Kenites, how can the *uniqueness* of the Hebrew Religion be maintained ? The answer is simply : in the use made of opportunity. To both, to the Kenites as well as to the Hebrews, was accorded the light of revelation according to their capacity of apprehension. The Kenites had worshipped Yahweh as their tribal god from time immemorial ; and in course of time the Hebrews came to worship Him too. But what a profound difference there was between the two in the use made of the germ of divine revelation ! In the case of the Kenites no religious development took place because the human response was wanting. In the case of the Hebrews how different ! First through Moses, and later through the prophets, they gradually came to realize more and more fully the Personality and Character of Yahweh, and thus to apprehend, in some measure, the Being of God. All through their history there was, in spite of set-backs, the slow yet continuous increase of this apprehension because of the human response to the divine prompting. True, it was never the nation as a whole that responded ; that is always so. Elect instruments of God first come into touch with Him ; and they are the means of disseminating the knowledge of Him. Moses, with all his limitations—and the Old Testament makes no secret of them— was one of these elect instruments, perhaps the greatest in pre-Christian times ; for his stupendous importance in the history of religion is seen in that he took the first and greatest step towards monotheistic belief that the world had known.

For untold centuries throughout all nations, tribes, and kindreds, religion had flourished, but belief and practice were naïve, crude, crass. Then an insignificant man, belonging to an insignificant people, in an insignificant corner of the world, received through human means the divine spark of revelation ; but he not only received it, he accepted it and responded to it ; and, like St. Paul to the Athenians long after, he said to his people, in effect : "Whom ye ignorantly worship, Him declare I unto you."

CHAPTER XI

" 'Elim " and " Ba'alim " (Polytheism)

We have considered the various elements which together formed the background of Hebrew Religion ; and we have seen how Yahweh was accepted as the God of the people. One other stage must be considered, for this, too, is to be regarded as belonging, in a very real sense, to the threshold of Hebrew religion, namely, the form of the religion in vogue among the more immediate forbears of the Hebrews.

When the Israelites settled down in Canaan they came into contact with a people with whom they were racially closely connected. For the most part these people had for long been agriculturists ; but in the south and south-east of the land were those who were semi-nomads, people who lived on the edge of, or near to, the steppe-land, and who were, nevertheless, not wholly unacquainted with agriculture. As will be seen, the record suggests that the religion of these latter had been the worship of *'Elim*, " gods," which was, however, gradually merging into the religion proper to agriculturists. It is with the belief in these *'Elim* that we shall concern ourselves first.

1. The " 'Elim "

We have seen that the animistic stage of belief gradually develops into the polytheistic stage, and that no clear-cut line marks off one stage from another, but that earlier ideas persist on long after the more primitive stages have been passed. We find this therefore in what was a polytheistic stage, viz., belief in *'Elim*. They are gods, but there are indications of their having developed from beings of a lower order ; indeed, accord-

116

ing to a number of passages containing place-names (see below), it almost looks as though they had not reached the status of gods ; in any case, these place-names seem to point to a time when they were not gods. But before coming to the passages in which the *'Elim* are referred to, there are one or two preliminary remarks to be made.

It is uncertain what the root meaning of *'El* (plural : *'Elim*) is ; that fact would seem to point to the antiquity of the idea expressed by the word, whatever it may have been. Many scholars regard it as connected with a root meaning " to be strong " ; but seeing that the *'Elim* were not always " gods " this is doubtful. In course of time it is likely enough that *'El* came to connote one who was strong, so that from the point of view of later times this derivation would hold good. The words *'elah*, " terebinth," and *'allôn*, " oak " (both from the same root as that from which *'El* comes) contain the idea of " strength," and they were regarded as the abodes of supernatural beings ; but one cannot say for certain whether these trees were regarded as strong from their nature or from the believed connexion of an *'El* with them. It must be confessed that we do not know with any certainty what the root-meaning of the word is.

Secondly, it is to be noted that *'Eloah* and the plural form *'Elohim* are extended formations of *'El* ; but though plural in form *'Elohim* is singular in meaning when used in reference to Yahweh, hence the use of the article with it ; in other cases it has the plural sense, viz. : " other gods," in contradistinction to " the God," i.e. Yahweh ; elsewhere the word means " angels " (Ps. viii. 6). But it is used also of a spirit of the dead (1 Sam. xxviii. 13), and even of a goddess, in 1 Kings xi. 33 ; in these latter cases the form is plural, but the sense singular.

And thirdly, *'El*, when used with the article, denotes, as in the case of *'Elohim*, the (only) God (e.g. Gen. xlvi. 3). Sometimes *'El* has this restricted sense even when written without the article ; but this belongs to much later times (e.g. Isa. xl. 18, and elsewhere).

To come now to consider what we learn about the *'Elim* in the Old Testament.

There are a number of place-names connected with 'El which are very ancient, having evidently been in existence long before the Israelites entered Canaan. Among these are the following (they are mentioned in the book of *Joshua*, excepting when otherwise indicated) : Jabneel, " Let 'El build " (xv. 11) ; Joqtheel, meaning uncertain (2 Kings xiv. 7) ; Jezreel, " Let 'El sow " (xv. 56) ; Jiphtachel, " Let 'El open " (xix. 14) ; Migdalel " the tower of 'El " (xix. 38) ; and the well-known Bethel, " the abode, or sanctuary, of 'El " (Gen. xxviii. 18, 19) ; and Penuel, " the face of 'El " (Gen. xxxii. 31). An example of a different formation is Elteqeh (xix. 44), the meaning of which is uncertain ; and there are others. Now, in regard to place-names like these, the 'El is connected with the place, though for reasons which can now no more be determined ; but the point is that, in a certain sense, in a modified sense, individuality is applied to him ; yet the 'El has no name ; the word is merely used as the title of a supernatural being ; and therefore one cannot say that he has yet reached the status of a god. In other words, these place-names compounded with 'El point to the transition stage of the spirit gradually developing into a god.

But there are other instances in which something approaching a proper name is applied to an 'El ; it will be well to examine these.

When, in Exod. vi. 3, God is represented as saying that by His name Yahweh He was not known to the patriarchs, a fact is stated which all the evidence shows to have been true. It is said in the same context that God was known to them by the name of 'El Shaddai. Whatever the meaning of this word may be (many theories are given by scholars), the R.V. rendering " God Almighty " is, at any rate, quite misleading. But the form of the name, i.e. the combination with 'El, gives an indication of what the religion of the Hebrews in pre-Mosaic times was (cp. also 'El 'Elyon, " the almighty 'El " [Gen. xiv. 18-20 ; Num. xxiv. 16]). The interest centres in the word 'El, " God." We are told of quite a number of these gods in the Old Testament, and doubtless there were many more than those named ; in nearly all cases these gods are

connected with a locality, and even in the one or two
instances in which the name of the locality is not given,
the analogy of the others suggests that in these cases too
the god was connected with a locality. Let us enumerate
some of these.

Very instructive is Gen. xvi. 13, 14. We will give
the R.V. rendering first, which is, however, again misleading : " And she (Hagar) called the name of the Lord
that spake unto her, ' Thou art a God that seeth ' ; for
she said, Have I even here looked after him that seeth
me ? Wherefore the well was called Be'er-lahai-roi ;
behold it is between Kadesh and Bered." The first
part of this verse should run : " She called the name of
Yahweh who spoke unto her, Thou art *'El-roi*." The
idea, and the text which expresses it, are hardly possible ;
the name of Israel's God was Yahweh ; so how could
He get another name ? It would be incompatible with
Yahweh religion ; and as the text stands the name is :
" Thou art *'El-roi*," which as a name-formation is
impossible. It is quite obvious that the original text
has been, unskilfully, worked over in the supposed
interests of later religious belief. What stood there
originally cannot be said with certainty ; but what seems
fairly certain is that there was a holy well here known
as the well of " an *'El* apparition,"—that is, in effect,
what *'El-roi* means,[1]—because the *'El* to whom it belonged
was believed to appear there at certain times.[2] From our
present point of view the main thing is that the passage
witnesses to what must be called the " *'El* religion "
of the immediate forbears of the Hebrews in pre-Mosaic
times.

The next passage is Gen. xxi. 33 ; the R.V. reads : " And
(Abraham) planted a tamarisk tree in Beersheba, and
called there on the name of the Lord, the Everlasting
God." Here we have again a misleading rendering of a
text which has been manipulated in the interests of
Yahweh religion. From Gen. xxi. 30–33, and xxvi. 23 ff.,

[1] G. von Gall, *Altisraelitische Kultstätten*, p. 40 (1898) (the Septuagint has " the well of the vision "). See further Gressmann, *Mose
und seine Zeit*, pp. 290 f. (1913) ; and the *Zeitschrift für die alttesta-
mentliche Wissenschaft*, xxx. 8 (1910).

[2] See also above, p. 36.

it will be seen that there was a holy well here in addition to the holy tree.　In the text before us we should read : " . . . And called there on the name of Yahweh *'El 'Olam*," as though Yahweh *'El 'Olam* were all one name ; but " Yahweh " is a later insertion.　The god, or *'El*, of Beersheba, to whom the tree and the well were holy, was called *'El 'Olam*, " the ancient *'El*."　So here we have again an *'El* of a locality ; upon him Abraham is represented as calling, i.e. he offered him worship.

Further, in Gen. xxxv. 7 we read : " And he [Jacob] built there an altar, and called the place 'El-bethel." With this must be read Gen. xxxi. 13, where the "angel of God " (ver. 11) says to Jacob : " I am the 'El of Bethel, where thou anointedst a pillar," the reference being to xxviii. 10 ff. (esp. 18).　Various points arise here with which we cannot deal now ; what specially concerns us is that another local *'El* is spoken of.　It was clearly a very ancient spot, because the name Beth-el shows that an *'El* had already been worshipped there : that must have been very long ago, for another *'El* to come and take possession—*'El-bethel !*　An interesting sign of developed belief, due to over-working the passage at a later period, is that " *the angel of God* " ('Elohim with the article) says, " I am the 'El of Bethel " ; this must have been done at a time when God could no more be thought of as a local deity, hence the substitution of the *angel* of God.

Another example is probably to be discerned in Gen. xxxi. 42, 53, where the curious expression " the Fear of Isaac " occurs ; as this is mentioned together with " the gods of my father, and the gods of Abraham," it must be the proper name of a god, as the R.V. rightly indicates by printing " fear " with a capital F.　The Hebrew is *Pachad*, a word used in Job iv. 14 of " fear " as the result of a vision.　It is not fanciful to see here the name of an *'El*—*'El-Pachad*—whom Gunkel ingeniously identifies with the *'El* who appeared to save Isaac from being sacrified.[1]　The name " Fear of Isaac " is, in form, parallel to " Mighty One of Jacob " in Gen. xlix. 24.

An interesting instance, again, is the *'El-Berith* of

[1] *Genesis*, p. 219 (1901).

Sichem (Judges ix. 46), presumably an *'El* who presided over covenants (*Berith* means " covenant ") ; in Judges viii. 33, ix. 4, he is called *Ba'al-Berith* ; so that we have here an illustration of the influence of Canaanite religion on the early *'El*-religion of the Hebrews. This is in the post-Mosaic period, which shows the old *'El*-religion still persisting and coalescing with the Canaanite *Ba'al*-religion.

These examples must suffice ; we have but to add such further indications as are afforded by " the company of gods " (Gen. xxxii. 2 [3 in Hebrew]), the " strange gods " spoken of in Gen. xxxv. 2, 4—to mention no others—in order to be convinced of the truth of the tradition that Yahweh was not known by that name by the pre-Mosaic Hebrew dwellers in Southern Palestine. Later religious authorities may have held the theory that *'El Shaddai* was another name for Yahweh, but the old records witness abundantly to the fact that *'El Shaddai* was only one among many *'Elim*. As Gressmann [1] says : " If it be asked what religion the patriarchs had, the answer cannot for a moment be in doubt, since the tradition knows only of the *'El*-religion, but not of a Yahweh-religion, as in the time of Moses, nor of a *Ba'al*-religion, as among the Canaanites." [2]

It is very significant that not a single personal name in *Genesis* contains " Yahweh " in its formation ; the groundwork of the patriarchal narratives must therefore belong to a time when the name of Yahweh was unknown to the Hebrews.

It would be too much to say that in the instances cited the name of the *'El* was a proper name ; but those names certainly seem on the way to becoming proper names. At any rate, they point to certain of the *'Elim* being singled out ; so that the word *'El*, in such cases, is something more than the generic term that it is in the place-names.

The evidence seems, then, to point to the fact that the

---

[1] *Op. cit.*, pp. 426 ff.

[2] It is worth mentioning here that on a cuneiform tablet found by Winckler in Boghaz-keui, the ancient Hittite capital in Asia Minor, mention is made of the *ilani cha-ab-bi-ri*, " the gods of the Chabiri " (= Hebrews).

'Elim form a development of the earlier spirits of the
Animistic stage pure and simple, and that they constitute
a transition from these to gods proper.[1] This was the
type of religion which existed among the more immediate
ancestors of the Israelites.

But side by side with this belief in *'Elim* there existed
among those Canaanites who were purely agricultural the
belief in *Ba'alim*. When an *'El* became sufficiently
individualized to be regarded as the one presiding deity
of a sanctuary, or a place, he came in course of time to
be designated its proprietor or owner (*Ba'al*). While,
speaking generally, the *'Elim* belong to nomadic religion,
and the *Ba'alim* to that of agriculturists, it is possible
that one may discern the transition gradually taking place
in the existence of such names of Jezreel, " let the *'El*
sow," and Jabneel, " let the *'El* build."

2. THE " BA'ALIM "

Ba'al (plural : *Ba'alim*) means " lord " or " owner,"
and Baalism, in its origin, centred in the belief that every
spot of fertile ground owed its fertility to the fact that
a supernatural being dwelt there and made it what it
was. The ground was therefore looked upon as the
property of this supernatural being, who was the owner of
it, the lord or mistress, the *Ba'al* or *Ba'alath*, according
as to whether the owner was a male or a female. How
the owner came to be regarded as the one or the other
cannot, of course, be said ; all kinds of things would
contribute to decide this ; uncultured and semi-cultured
men are very naïve in their reasoning.

According to early Semitic belief, as we have seen,
the water, whether spring, brook, or river, which makes

---

[1] A somewhat hazardous suggestion may be offered here. Among
the place-names compounded with *'El* there is *'Elealeh* (Num. xxxii. 3),
which means " *'El* doth ascend." This cannot refer to ascending
heavenwards, for the *'Elim* were never thus conceived of ; it is, however, possible that originally the ascending was from below. The root
is the same as that used in 1 Sam. xxviii. 13, of the shade of Samuel
ascending from *She'ol*, though there the word used in reference to
him is *'Elohim*. We have no evidence that the *'Elim* were ever believed
to be departed spirits, but the possibility of this having at one time
been the case cannot be wholly excluded.

a spot fertile, is the dwelling-place of a spirit; in course of time the spirit develops into a *Ba'al*; he has made the spot what it is.

The idea that *every* fertile spot or locality owed its fertility to one and the same *Ba'al*, or owner, never entered the mind of people; they would have argued on the analogy of what obtained among men; one human owner to a plot, therefore one *Ba'al* to each plot.

The ownership of the *Ba'al* of a locality was acknowledged and indicated by prefixing this word to the name of the place; as, for example, *Ba'al Mĕ'ôn*, "lord, or owner, of the inhabited place" (Num. xxxii. 38); *Ba'al-Hermôn*, "lord, or owner, of the sacred place" (Judges iii. 3); *Ba'al Pĕ'ôr*, "lord, or owner, of the chasm (or cleft)" (Num. xxv. 3), and others. But in such cases the name of the place is, strictly speaking, an abbreviation; for the word *Beth*, "house of" or "abode of" or "sanctuary of," is understood; so that the full name of the place would be *Beth-Ba'al-Mĕ'ôn*, etc., thus indicating that the place in question was the abode of the *Ba'al*, where he had his sanctuary.

Since the fertility of any locality was the work of its supernatural owner, anything that his land brought forth in consequence of that fertility belonged to him. If seed were sown in it, if vines or fig-trees were planted in it, whatever these brought forth was due to the power of producing fertility possessed by the *Ba'al*, and consequently belonged to him; therefore it would be an unheard-of thing for anyone to partake of the produce of the soil before due payment had been made to the *Ba'al*; hence the offerings of first-fruits. These consisted of a small, but choice, portion of the produce of the soil, which was "thrown down" (this is what the word for "heave-offering" implies) before the altar. It was not enquired how the *Ba'al* partook of the offering, such questions were not asked; that concerned the *Ba'al*, not the worshipper. What concerned the worshipper was that the *Ba'al* should be properly propitiated, otherwise he would be angry, which would mean a bad look-out for the harvest.[1]

[1] See further, Part II, Chapter II, § 3 (*b*).

The place of worship was called a *bāmāh* (plural : *bāmôth*), or " high-place " ; that this means, in general, an elevated spot is proved by the fact that it is used as a parallel with " hill " (e.g. Num. xxi. 28 ; Deut. xxxii. 13, and elsewhere). Why such elevated spots were chosen for sanctuaries was presumably because they were a substitute for mountains [1] ; but there may well have been also the idea that the *Ba'al* liked to be high up, because he was there withdrawn from men. In later times, however, a *bāmāh* was not necessarily on an elevated spot ; the word came to be used of a " sanctuary " (*miqdash*) generally (see Amos vii. 9, Hos. iv. 13) ; and we read of a *bāmāh* situated even in a valley several times (Jer. vii. 31, xix. 5, xxxii. 35 ; Ezek. vi. 3), while in 2 Kings xvii. 9, xxiii. 5, mention is made of a *bāmāh* in the city.

The *bāmāh* was, however, not the only type of sanctuary. Worship was also offered under green trees ; sometimes these stood in the *bāmāh*, though by no means necessarily. Green trees—strictly speaking evergreen trees—were believed to be the abodes of these fertility deities whose presence in them made them sanctuaries ; one sees how near we still are to animistic belief ! In course of time, when sanctuaries were multiplied, and could not always be under green trees, a pole was set up, in place of the green tree, by the altar as a mark of the presence of the deity ; this was called the *'Asherah*.[2]

Besides the wooden pole representing the goddess there was also the stone pillar, called *Mazzēbāh*,[3] which likewise stood beside the altar, and represented the *Ba'al*, i.e. the male deity. This upright stone pillar was the original form of the altar ; and in nomadic times the blood of the sacrificial victim was poured down beside it ; but

---

[1] See above, p. 42.

[2] In the Old Testament this word is used in two senses : as the goddess Asherah (see Judges iii. 7 ; 1 Kings xv. 13, xviii. 19 ; 2 Kings xxi. 7, xxiii. 4, 7), and as the sacred pole representing her (see Deut. vii. 5, xii. 3, the command to burn them, xvi. 21). As the name of a goddess Asherah occurs in the Amarna letters as well as on an inscription found in Tell Taanach (see Sellin, *Tell Ta'anek*, p. 113 [1904], " the finger of Asherah "). Asherah is a different goddess from Astarte (originally Ashtart).

[3] From the root meaning " to set up."

when later, for a more convenient mode of offering the burnt sacrifices, the altar was placed horizontally, the stone pillar continued to be set up beside it. Both the wooden *'Asherah* and the stone *Mazzēbāh* underwent development, becoming in course of time carved idols.

It is essential for the understanding of what we call the religion of *Ba'al* to realize why this presence in every sanctuary of representatives of the male and female elements of the deity should have been regarded as indispensable.

Baalism among the Hebrews originated with the agricultural stage of civilization ; and its great importance lay in the fact that to the people of those times it was inseparably connected with what was, after all, the fundamental condition of life, viz. the obtaining of food : no fertility, no corn ; no corn, no bread ; no bread, no life !

There can be no sort of doubt that at one time or other the question must have presented itself to the minds of the early Semites, when they entered upon the agricultural stage, as to *how* the soil became fruitful and brought forth. In the earlier nomadic stage the question would not have presented itself in quite the same way. That flocks and herds were endowed with fertility was easier to understand than the process whereby the land could be made fruitful. We are not told in the Old Testament how the ancient Hebrews represented to themselves the way in which the fertility of the soil was brought about ; nor is this to be expected ; but certain rites which were practised make it quite clear that they believed that the process whereby the earth brought forth must be in some way similar to that obtaining in other directions.

It is, no doubt, difficult to enter into the mental environment of men in a semi-cultured stage ; but one can understand that with their extraordinarily limited knowledge and *naïve* outlook they would argue on the analogy of themselves, that, just as both men and their flocks increased by means of natural generation, so the crops must somehow be produced in a similar manner. It is well known that " among races which have attained to a certain degree of culture the predominant conception of the gods is anthropomorphic ; that is, they are supposed on the whole to resemble men and act like men." [1] It follows therefore that in the matter of productivity the gods and goddesses were conceived of as acting in the same way as human beings. It is a related conception, and very instructive in the present connexion, that the *Ba'al* is thought of as the husband of the land which he fertilizes ; this appears in Hos. ii., and underlies the figure in Isa. lxii. 4, where the prophet contrasts the married land (*Be'ulah*) with the wilderness : " Thou shalt no more be termed ' Forsaken ' ; neither shall thy land any more be termed ' Desolate ' ; but thou shalt be called ' *Hephzi-bah* ' (= ' my delight is in her '), and thy land ' *Be'ulah* ' (=' married ') ; for Yahweh delighteth in thee, and thy land shall be married." [2]

It is, furthermore, a belief universal among people in a semi-cultured stage, that the gods can, and should, be assisted in their doings by man's co-operation ; and this is what lies at the base of, and is the meaning and purpose of, the widespread institution of sanctuary prostitutes, referred to in the Old Testament under the term *Qĕdēshôth* (Hos. iv. 14, Deut. xxiii. 17, 18 [in Hebrew 18, 19]), meaning " consecrated women," which shows that in its origin there was no thought of immorality.

This religion of *Ba'al*, then, was that which followed upon the belief in *'Elim* ; and it was the religion with which the Israelites first came in contact when they entered Canaan. Since immediately prior to this, through the work of Moses, they had accepted Yahweh as their national God, it was inevitable that among the bulk of the people the worship of Yahweh should have been adapted to Baalism. In passing from the nomadic to an agricultural life, they learned, together with the arts of agriculture, the religion which was inseparably

[1] *Rel. Sem.*, p. 86 ; in his notes S. A. Cook refers to " the union of sky-god and earth-mother," which " can be traced through the Mediterranean area " (p. 537).

[2] S. A. Cook quotes one of the Amarna Letters, in which Rib-Addi, lamenting the famine, says : " My field is like a woman without a husband." In another of these letters the king of Byblos, whose land has been attacked by enemies, says that his fields are like a wife without a husband through lack of sustenance (see also Nielsen, *Handbuch*, i. 207 ff.).

connected therewith. It is probable that at first the
worship of Yahweh continued side by side with that of
the *Ba'als*, but as the settlement proceeded Yahweh
became the *Ba'al* of the land, and, though worshipped in
name, the rites of His worship were those of Canaanite
Baalism.

.   .   .   .   .   .

We have dealt with the background of Hebrew
Religion, the earliest stage from which religion in a truer
sense emerges. This is necessary if Hebrew Religion is
to be scientifically studied. Our next concern is to note
the gradual beginnings of the upward growth whereby,
through slow stages, the Israelites attained to a deeper
apprehension of God.

PART II

ISRAELITE RELIGION

CHAPTER I

PRELIMINARY

THE history of Israel begins with Moses. He was the originator alike of her national unity and of her religion. and it is not surprising that later generations attributed to him the whole fabric of her social and ecclesiastical organization. Before his time we find a group of tribes, possibly recognizing their common kinship, but with little else to hold them together. After him, though we should be wrong if we assumed that the national growth was complete, there is at least a nucleus round which other elements could gather, and a continuity of corporate life which enables us to speak of a real history. No doubt it was centuries before the various sections of which the whole was ultimately composed were fashioned into a single entity, but with Moses begins the process which ends in the appearance of a race which hitherto no hostility or persecution has yet robbed of its sense of nationality or of its faith—the most durable people in human history.

The religion of that type of people from whom Israel ultimately sprang has already been adequately discussed,[1] and it is necessary to make but a few remarks here. Our knowledge of the faith and practice of the ancestors of Israel depends on three sources : (i) archæology ; (ii) comparative religion ; and (iii) the traditions of Israel herself as preserved in the book of *Genesis*, with occasional hints and references in other portions of the Old Testament. The last of the three is that which is best known generally among us, but we are compelled to admit that the record has been coloured and, perhaps, modified by the theology of later days. We have to confess that we do not know for certain whom or what Israel worshipped

---

[1] Part I, Chapters II ff.

131

in pre-Mosaic times, and must depend to some extent on
conjecture based on the statements supplied to us in
the Bible.[1]

The narrative of Gen. xxxv. tells us in ver. 2 that,
as Jacob approached the site of Bethel (whose sanctuary
probably claimed him as its founder) he "said unto
his household, and to all that were with him, Put away
the strange gods that are among you." And in ver. 4
we read that "they gave Jacob all the strange gods . . .
and Jacob hid them under the oak which was by
Shechem." Whether this incident is rightly connected
with Jacob or not, it is clear that the writer believed that
the religion of Israel's ancestors, at one stage and in some
quarters, included a number of deities. Of the various
objects of worship, however, we hear nothing, unless
we are to include the *Tĕrāphim* stolen by Rachel from
her father (Gen. xxxi. 19, 30, 35). We are thus forced
back on conjecture, and must rely on such evidence as
can be supplied from comparative religion and philology.
Now it is an interesting fact that the names of some of
the Israelite tribes appear elsewhere as those of gods.
Gad, as we have seen, is a well-known Semitic deity, a
god of luck, identified in Mesopotamia with the planet
Jupiter. Asher may well be a slight modification of the
name of the great god of northern Mesopotamia, Ashur,
after whom a city and a people are named. Jacob-el
and Joseph-el, forms which imply that the first element
denotes a god, appear as place-names in an Egyptian
record.[2] Further, the common word for "god" in
Hebrew is *'Elohim*, a term which is the plural of a form
'Eloah, not found in the singular except in comparatively
late Hebrew writings. It is commonly explained as a
"plural of majesty," but the only passage where it
seems we may have a reference to its primitive meaning
is 1 Sam. xxviii. 13, where the medium consulted by
Saul says, "I see a god [R.V. margin "Or *gods*," Hebrew,
"*'Elohim* "] coming up out of the earth," and the
apparition is identified as the ghost of Samuel. This
suggests that originally the word was practically equiva-

---

[1] See, however, Part I, Chapter XI.
[2] On an inscription of Thothmes III. *circa* 1500 B.C.

lent to the Latin *Manes*—likewise an animistic plural
with no singular—and was applied to the spirits of the
dead worshipped by so many primitive peoples.[1] Such
evidence as is available, then, suggests that in pre-
Mosaic days some, at least, of the nomad ancestors of
Israel worshipped the individuals from whom the tribes
derived their names. If that be so, then it is clear that,
as a result of the work of Moses, they sank back to the
human level, and resumed their original status as the
eponymous ancestors of the Israelite tribes.

At the same time, many other objects of worship
were recognized, each in his own place, and the records
suggest that such beings as the stone-spirit of Bethel,
the river-spirit of Peniel, the well-spirit of Beer-lahai-
roi, and many another, were venerated at the spots where
they had manifested their presence.[2] The ritual, such
as it was, probably varied, each tribal and local " demon "
demanding a separate formula and ceremonial. At the
same time, it seems likely that there were certain modes
of worship and certain deities which might be regarded
as common to a number of the tribes, though especially
characteristic of none, and among these phenomena of
primitive religion we may perhaps include the Passover,
as a celebration of the sheep deity on whom all pastoral
peoples must depend for their prosperity.[3]

It is, nevertheless, clear that unless and until further
steps are taken, the religion of such tribes cannot develop
to a high stage. The religion of Israel's ancestors
contained no great unifying force, and in itself offered
no prospect of growth. It is, once more, with Moses
that the religious history of Israel begins.

[1] See further, Part I, Chapter V, § 3.
[2] See further, Part I, Chapters III, IV.
[3] On the Passover, see Part I, Chapter IX, § 3.

CHAPTER II

MOSAISM, THE RELIGION OF ISRAEL IN THE WILDERNESS

(i) *The Exodus.*—The historicity of Moses and of his work has never been seriously doubted.[1] Indeed, if we had no record of Moses, it would have been necessary to invent him, for such a work as that ascribed to him demands the genius and inspiration of an individual almost unique. It may well be that as the story has been handed down from generation to generation it has received modifications, and we may feel ourselves disinclined to accept all the details, but a personality and a series of events which have loomed so large in the imagination of a people as Moses, the Exodus, and the Sinai covenant, must have a secure basis in actual fact.[2]

The name of Moses is Egyptian, and forms an element in more than one of the royal names of the eighteenth dynasty, 1600–1350 B.C. Hebrew tradition held that he was of Hebrew blood, adopted by the royal house, and compelled for some crime to flee beyond the borders of civilization. He took refuge with the Midianites, a pastoral tribe whose grazing lands lay to the south of Palestine, married into the family of a Midianite (or Kenite ?) priest, and received a special revelation at a sacred mountain. Here there appeared to him a God named Yahweh [3] ; he was bidden to lead out of Egypt his

---

[1] In view of the statement so frequently made, that the "Higher Critics " deny the historicity of Moses and of his work, it may be as well to insist that only two scholars of repute, Winckler and Cheyne (see especially articles in the *Encycl. Bibl.* signed T. K. C.) have adopted this position, and that it has found no acceptance either among their contemporaries or among their successors. It is utterly untrue to attribute this view to the "Higher Critics " as a body.

[2] See McNeile, *The Book of Exodus*, pp. cix–cxviii (1908).

[3] This, apparently, is the original form of the Hebrew personal name represented in our English Bibles by the word LORD.

kinsmen, the Hebrews, who had been subjected to forced labour by the Egyptian Government. The occasion was to be the celebration of a festival at a spot three days' journey from Egypt in the wilderness—presumably the mountain on which the revelation had been made (Exod. iii. 18). Moses is expressly told, according to one ancient account (Exod. iii. 6), that Yahweh may be identified with the God of Israel's remote ancestors, though it is clear that the name will be strange to the present generation.

Moses carries out his instructions, and finds that the Egyptian king refuses to permit the expedition. Egypt suffers from the wrath of Yahweh ; but the Government is obdurate, and at length, since Israel cannot go to Yahweh's home for the celebration, Yahweh is forced to come to Egypt. The ritual is there observed as well as conditions allow, and Yahweh's presence proves disastrous to the Egyptians. Israel is thus enabled to escape, and an Egyptian force which pursues them is caught by the returning tide as it follows the fugitives across an arm of the sea.[1] Moses then leads the people to the sacred mountain, variously called Sinai and Horeb,[2] and there the union between Yahweh and Israel is brought about.

Unless we accept the conjecture of Josephus (followed, among modern scholars, by Dr. H. R. Hall) that the story of the Exodus is an account of the expulsion of the Hyksos seen from the Semitic side,[3] we have as yet no reference to these events in Egyptian records. To the Pharaoh and to his people it seemed but a small thing. Yet to the world it was the most important occurrence that ever took place on Egyptian soil. It made an ineradicable impression on the Hebrews, and it is not surprising that the whole series of events was interpreted as a miraculous intervention of the God of Sinai, and that this view found expression in many of the details of the story as it now lies before us. Later Israel saw in the

---

[1] Another interpretation of this episode is given by Gressmann, *Mose und seine Zeit*, pp. 108 ff. (1913). See also Part I, Chapter X, § 1.
[2] According to the varying traditions see below.
[3] This is not accepted by most modern scholars.

Exodus an authentication of Yahweh's call of the people, and we can hardly doubt that the same feeling worked still more effectively in the generation which experienced it. When therefore they reached the sacred mountain, they were ready to accept the God who was offered to them.

(ii) *Yahweh.*—Two traditions have survived as to the location of the sacred mountain. That which was current in northern Israel, introduced into the south apparently only at the end of the seventh century, identified it with Horeb, which seems to have been to the north-east of the Gulf of Akaba. The other, that better known in Judah, placed it at Sinai, probably in the neighbourhood of Kadesh-barnea, the modern *'Ain Qadis.* But if there is a divergent tradition as to the locality there is none as to the God who met Israel. In all forms of the story He is Yahweh, and the essential features of His relation to His people are always the same.

It is clear that Yahweh had been recognized and had been worshipped before Israel came into contact with Him.[1] We have, of course, no details as to the earlier cult, and we are entirely dependent on Israelite records for the picture that men formed of Him. We may, however, be fairly sure that Israelite theology in Moses' day did not differ materially from that of other peoples at the same stage of development. The meaning of the name has evoked a good deal of discussion. The ancient Hebrew derivation suggested by Exod. iii. 14—" I AM THAT I AM "—has been suspected, as implying too advanced a metaphysical conception of God for an early nomad people. Other explanations deriving the name from the substantive verb are less open to this objection, and roots suggesting " falling " and " blowing " have been cited as possible derivations.[2] The name does not seem to occur outside Hebrew literature till the ninth century B.C., and we are compelled to admit that we

[1] Cp. Wheeler Robinson, *The Religious Ideas of the Old Testament*, p. 53 (1926).

[2] Stade, *Biblische Theologie des Alten Testaments*, i. 29 (1905); Hastings, *D.B.*, art. " GOD," by A. B. Davidson, ii. 199b.

do not know for certain what its original significance was.

Biblical references give us clearer light on the character assigned to Yahweh. It goes without saying that He is a mountain 'El, and later generations thought of His proper home as being in Sinai or Horeb, even after His dwelling had been established in Jerusalem. Thus, in the early days of the settlement in Palestine, the poet to whom we owe the Song of Deborah can speak of His coming from Edomite territory—from Sinai. And though Amos in the eighth century hears Yahweh roar from Zion, Elijah, a hundred years earlier, goes to Horeb, to the mount of God, in order to get into direct contact with Him.

It would seem that the appearance of Yahweh in His own home was indicated by volcanic phenomena. The descriptions which we find in *Exodus* suggest this very strongly. Palestine proper has no volcanoes, but the Hebrews recognized the presence of Yahweh in the storm. After all, to the primitive mind, an eruption and a storm are not unlike ; volcanic action is, as it were, a subterranean tempest. It was in the storm which swept away Sisera's troops that Israel saw the coming of Yahweh, and the same conception is to be seen in such later passages as Ps. xxix., while His character as a fire-god is attested by the ancient tradition which spoke of His presence in the pillar of cloud and fire. Other references imply that Yahweh was a warrior.[1] Wars, to the ancient Semitic mind, are not merely, not even principally, a question of human armies ; the deities themselves play a leading part.[2] Such accounts as we have of the early battles of Israel suggest that there was little hand-to-hand fighting. The two armies would be drawn up face to face, each would start moving in a charge against its foe, but, before the shock of contact came, one side or the other would, as we should say, lose its nerve, and turn in flight. When our records speak of one or the other being " smitten before their enemies," the stroke is not that of material weapons, it

[1] See, e.g., Judges v. 23.
[2] See, e.g., a passage as late as Zech. ix. 13, 14.

is the panic sent by the more powerful of the two contending deities on the troops of the other.[1] It is only then that men begin to fall; the slaughter takes place in flight and pursuit, and when the two armies stand face to face and fight at close quarters, the fact is thought worthy of special mention. Israel believed that Yahweh was pre-eminent in His power of instilling this panic into the hearts of their enemies. Further, it is clear from the earnestness with which Moses pleads that Yahweh will go with Israel (cp. Exod. xxxiii. 15), that Yahweh is recognized as a guide through the wilderness.[2] He knows the safe trails, the rare wells, the spots where vegetation may be found for the cattle, and can guide His people without danger to themselves. This combination of mountain spirit, storm and volcanic deity, and wilderness guide, clearly goes back to the nomad period of Israel's history. That Yahweh was more, much more, than this, was a lesson which Israel learnt slowly through the centuries.

We do not know who it was that worshipped Yahweh before He became specifically the God of Israel. We may assume that He was in some way connected with the family into which Moses married during his exile, but here we seem to have two different traditions. On the one hand his father-in-law is called either Reuel or Jethro, and is a Midianite priest. If this be the original form of the tradition, we may reasonably suppose that Yahweh also was a Midianite deity. But in Num. x. 29 the father-in-law (or, perhaps, the brother-in-law) of Moses is called Hobab, and in Judges iv. 11 this Hobab is stated to have been a Kenite. Now the Kenites were the smith clan, and seem to have lived a wandering life like that of the curious smith tribes described by Doughty in modern Arabia. The temptation to regard Yahweh as originally a Kenite God is strengthened by the fact that He is so frequently conceived as a God of the celestial fires manifested in the thunderstorm, and of

---

[1] For this the Hebrew uses the word *nāgaph*, while actual blows are described by the root *nākāh*.

[2] It should be remembered that the "wilderness"—Hebrew *midhbār*—is not the absolutely waterless desert, but the region of scanty vegetation and poor rainfall over which the pastoral nomad ranges.

the terrestrial fires appearing in the earthquake and the volcano. But, probable as this last suggestion may be, it still remains a conjecture, and all we know for certain is that Yahweh had an independent existence before His adoption of Israel as His people.[1]

(iii) *The Covenant.*—The task of Moses was to bring together the tribes under his leadership and this God, so welding the former into a single people. As we have seen, the circumstances of the Exodus were likely to help him, but this must not be allowed to detract from the supreme genius of the man who carried into effect the great religious partnership. The story is described in the opening verses of Exod. xxiv., though it would seem that either the tradition or the actual text has received accretions in process of transmission. The main outlines of the original rite, however, seem to be beyond dispute. On the one hand stand the people, on the other the God, the latter represented by an " altar." Victims are slain, and their blood is drained off into bowls. Half of it is then thrown over the altar, the terms on which the covenant is to be made are read before the people, and, on their consenting to observe them, the remainder of the blocd is flung over their heads.

The meaning of this ritual is not far to seek. The blood is the life (Lev. xvii. 11, 14), the vital essence. Two parties, at present independent one of another, are to be united in a single whole, and, to secure the desired union, a third party is introduced. Its life is taken from it and made available for the other two. Both come under it, both are included in it, the same vital essence now covers and embraces the two. They are thus no longer independent entities, they are one, finding their unity with each other in their unity with that third party whose blood now covers them both. Till this point is reached, however near they might have been brought one to another, they are merely contiguous ; now they are continuous, and form parts of a single indivisible whole. We might almost say that now Yahweh is Himself included in the term

[1] Details are given by Budde, *Die Religion des Volkes Israel bis zur Verbannung*, pp. 1–35 (1900).

Israel ; henceforward it will connote not merely a human community, but one of which He is a member.[1]

Thus from the outset the religion of Israel was marked by a unique feature whose importance it is impossible to exaggerate. The principle of one tribe, one tribal god, may have been fairly well accepted among ancient Semitic communities. But elsewhere the god is a natural member of the people to whom he belongs, and is inconceivable apart from it. If through the disappearance of his tribe or from some other cause he loses his people, he ceases to rank as a god, and descends to the level of that intermediate class to whom the Arab theologian gives the name of *Jinn*—a wild god, a masterless and isolated spirit, retaining some of his powers, but practically none of his prestige.[2] As long as his people exists, his position is secure, but he is as dependent on the human members of his clan as they are upon him ; in the nature of the case each is indispensable to the other.

The early Israelite may have thought of Yahweh much as the Moabite thought of Chemosh, but the relationship rested on a different basis. Chemosh always had been a Moabite and never could be anything else ; Yahweh had existed as a God independently of Israel, and, if need be, could so exist again, or could, on the other hand, extend His interests and His influence to others than the original Israel. The connexion between God and people was not " natural " but (if we may use the word without being misunderstood) " artificial." It had a definite beginning at a definite point in time, and might equally well have a definite conclusion. It depended on a " covenant "—a deed of partnership, and if at any time either party violated the terms originally laid down, it was within the right of the other to declare the agreement and the partnership at an end. It is true that we do not meet with the actual formula, " I will become their God and they shall become my people," in so many words till the end of the seventh century, but the essence is implied from the first.[3] This aspect of the religion of Israel was never wholly lost, and while Israel, all through

[1] Cp. Part I, Chapter V, §§ 1, 3.   [2] Part I, Chapter VI, § 1.
[3] But cp. Gen. xxviii. 20–22.

her history, was guilty of repeated breaches of the terms, she was forced to admit that they had never once been broken on the divine side. What Yahweh had said, that He did : His word stood ever sure.

What the terms of the Covenant were we do not know. The passage which precedes the account of the ceremony, Exod. xxi.–xxiii., forms a short code of laws, to which the name " Book of the Covenant " is now frequently applied. But this is simply an Israelite form of the type of code common to practically all the ancient East, known to have existed, with local and national variations, in Babylonia, Assyria, and Anatolia, as well as in Israel. It is essentially the code of an agricultural and commercial people, and has little that can apply at all to a community still on the nomad stage. Even if we could suppose that it was Mosaic in origin, we should have to admit that it was given for a future age, and that it had little practical meaning for the generation which was actually a party to the Covenant itself. This seems so unlikely that it is now widely held that the Code was formulated in a later age, long after Israel had made its home in the promised land. Some have found the basis for the Sinai Covenant in the familiar Decalogue of Exod. xx., not, indeed, in the exact terms in which it has been preserved, but in a more concise form. To this the objections raised against the next three chapters do not apply, but, on the other hand, we can hardly say that the evidence for this view is definite enough to justify a dogmatic conclusion. Another Decalogue—mainly concerned with ritual—appears in Exod. xxxiv., but this, again, is applicable to the settled farmer rather than to the wandering shepherd. Of one thing we may be sure, that the Covenant demanded that the worship of Israel should be paid to Yahweh alone, and that the Israelite should use no other divine name in taking an oath. There may also have been an insistence on the Passover— essentially a pastoral festival [1]—and it is not impossible that a form of the Sabbath in which the use of fire was prohibited on the seventh day was imposed. Beyond these points it is hardly possible even to hazard a conjecture.

[1] Cp. Part I, Chapter IX., § 3.

There were, we may be sure, obligations on the divine side also.[1] These are not clearly stated, but we may assume that Yahweh stood to Israel in the relation normal among such peoples. He was their guide in the desert (cp., e.g., Amos ii. 10) and their inspiration in war (cp., e.g., 1 Sam. iv. 3). Though a member of the community like the men composing it, He had special powers, and was not subject to the laws of decay and death. He was especially the guardian of the blood of the tribe and the supreme judge in cases of dispute between its human members. He had means of making His will known to His people, and could be consulted in times of difficulty, uncertainty, or danger. He would see that vengeance was taken for wrongs inflicted on any member of His community, whether the criminal were an Israelite or a stranger, and would jealously punish any infringement of an oath taken in His name. To His own people He was Lord and King.

(iv) *Sacred Emblems.*—It is possible, though not probable, that through the wilderness period Israel may have had no material object particularly associated with Yahweh round which such cultus as there was might centre. As a matter of fact, all tradition points to the presence of certain things which accompanied the people through their wanderings, and were taken by them into Palestine during their invasion of the country. Three sacred emblems were worshipped in later days, for which it was claimed that their peculiar cult originated in the wilderness. These were the Bull, whose most important sanctuary was at Bethel ; the Snake, which had its home in Jerusalem ; and the Ark, which, after being located in different temples, at last found a home also in Jerusalem.

Of these the first two seem to have been objects of worship in Palestine before the Israelite conquest. Archæological research has revealed numbers of figures both of bulls and of snakes from *strata* which must be earlier than the advent of Israel.[2] It is, however, not

[1] Cp. Gen. xxviii. 20, 21.
[2] Details are given by Sellin, *Tell Ta'anek* (1904) ; Macalister, *Bible Sidelights from the Mound of Gezer* (1906); *Excavations at Gezer* (1912).

quite certain that these represent objects of worship—
a difficulty which frequently attaches to archæological
discoveries. But both were familiar in the cults of the
ancient agricultural world, inasmuch as both were
regarded as symbols of fertility, and the known facts
are against rather than for their claim to be objects of
Israelite cults dating from the nomadic age. Yet each
had traditions surrounding it which took it back to that
early period.

Bull-worship in Israel is first mentioned as an act of
apostasy which took place at Sinai itself. The story, as
recorded in Exod. xxxii., tells how the people grew
anxious at the prolonged absence of Moses on the mountain, whither he had ascended to receive instructions from
Yahweh. They had been brought out of Egypt by
Moses in order to come into contact with Yahweh, and
they had lost their leader without finding their God.
Accordingly they applied to Aaron, who bade them bring
their golden jewels, which he melted down and made into
a calf, telling Israel that this was the God who had
brought them out of Egypt. While the revelry in connexion with its worship was at its height, Moses returned,
investigated the facts, and strongly condemned the action
of Aaron, who defended himself by throwing the blame
on the people, and suggesting that the calf form taken by
the molten metal was not deliberately planned by him,
but was the result of chance.[1] He himself seems to have
escaped punishment, but numbers of Israelites fell by
the hand of the Levites, who took the sword to avenge
the insult put upon Yahweh.

Now we may suspect that at the great bull sanctuaries,
such as Bethel, a story rather like this was told to explain
the origin of the cult. But it would have been Moses,
not Aaron, who was its author, and the pouring of molten
metal into water would be a method whereby men could
ascertain the exact form under which Yahweh preferred
to be worshipped. A later generation, with the prohibition of images in mind, could not endure the slur on

[1] For the justification of this interpretation see the present writer's
article in the *Expositor*, " The Golden Calf," Series VIII, vol. xxiv,
pp. 121 ff.

Moses, and while they could not eliminate the tradition, they transferred the odium of it to Aaron, a man who elsewhere is little more than a lay figure with no independent personality of his own. Possibly we have a relic of a cult connected with Horeb and transferred to northern Israel. It is significant that Elijah, for whom Yahweh's dwelling was in Horeb, made no protest, as far as we know, against the cult of the bull.

The construction of the bronze snake was attributed directly to Moses himself, but the tradition recorded in Num. xxi. 4–9 stated that he made it at the command of Yahweh Himself, in order to cure those who were bitten by snakes on the road between Hor and the Red Sea. It is significant that the species of snake which attacked Israel there is described by the same name as that which is applied to the superhuman attendants of Yahweh seen by Isaiah in his inaugural vision. It will be remembered that it was not till some years after the call of the prophet that the bronze snake was destroyed by Hezekiah. But, apart from the narrative in Num. xxi., we do not hear of the snake till the suppression of its worship.

With the Ark the case is very different. Tradition said that it was carried with Israel through all the wanderings, that it entered the promised land with the people, and that it had a series of resting-places, finding its last home in the Temple of Solomon at Jerusalem. It is true that it received no attention during the reign of Saul, but both Samuel and David are connected with it. Now the Ark was simply a box, and it does not seem likely that such an object would have been revered if it had been supposed to be empty. There was, it is true, a divine power within it, and Israelite history told of its prowess when confronted with Dagon, the god of Ashdod (1 Sam. v. 1–5), and of its power to drive cows ruthlessly away from their calves in spite of their lowing protests (1 Sam. vi. 7 ff.). It seems likely therefore that there was some object within the Ark which represented the deity. Tradition stated that the stones bearing the Law were placed in it, together with a pot of manna and the rod of Aaron. The theory of divine

residence in stones is familiar to every student of ancient
Semitic religion,[1] and it is easy to guess that the stones
were originally taken from the sacred mountain, and
held to contain the very essence of Yahweh Himself.
Again, a later age has so modified the story as to eliminate the suggestion of idolatrous worship, but of the three
objects suggested, the stone (or stones) is by far the most
likely to have dated from the wilderness period.

In further support of this view we may refer to the
traditional Israelite attitude towards the worship of
images. It is sometimes claimed that from the first
the Hebrew cultus was purely spiritual, that it set before
men no material object of reverence. On *a priori* grounds
this appears to be unlikely, and the early stories of the
Ark show that there, at least, was a venerated object
which was held to embody a supremely powerful personality. But we do find a strong feeling against the worship
of *artificial* objects. Two very primitive codes have
come down to us, one of which includes, the other almost
entirely consists of, ritual prescriptions. These are
found in Exod. xx. 2–17, and in Exod. xxxiv. 14–26.
Both seem to have undergone a process of expansion,
especially the latter, but a number of primitive " commandments " may easily be crystallized out from each
passage. The former seems to have been handed down
in northern Israel, while the latter bears the stamp of
Judaic tradition. In Exod. xx. it will be noted that
the "graven image" is straitly prohibited; in Exod.
xxxiv. 17 the "molten image" is forbidden. The bull at
Bethel—if we are right in regarding the narrative of Exod.
xxxii. as a modified form of the tradition of that
sanctuary—was a "molten image," and would not be
excluded by the law of Exod. xx. 4.

No details are given us in Num. xxi. as to the
construction of the bronze snake, but it is quite possible
that this was a carved figure, which would thus avoid
the condemnation of Exod. xxxiv. But the more
primitive feeling, expressed in the altar law of Exod.
xx. 24, 25, is that there must be no human workman-
ship in any object closely associated with Yahweh.

[1] See Part I, Chapter IV.

10

Of course, the receptacle in which any sacred emblem
was placed must be manufactured, but the emblem
itself must be free from human contamination. We
may suspect that it was only after the entry into
Canaan and the adoption of certain forms of cultus
existing there already that in each case the rule was so
modified as to permit the use of an object sanctified by
ages of worship. The primitive feeling is undoubtedly
better represented by the stone than by either of the
other objects.

It remains to mention the Tabernacle. It goes without
saying that the deity must have his home. We need not
accept the elaborate picture of the tabernacle drawn in
Exodus which is clearly a reflection back into an earlier
period of Solomon's Temple. But we may be sure that
there was a special tent, wherein dwelt the very presence
of Yahweh, where men might meet Him, and where,
from time to time, there appeared special manifestations
of the divine glory.

(v) *Sacred Persons.*—The allotment of certain
persons to the special service of the deity is a feature
common to practically all known forms of religion.
Particularly in a more primitive stage of religious
development, men feel that the beings whom they worship
are peculiar people ; there is, as Otto has insisted, an
awful sense of the " numinous." [1] To the undeveloped
mind gods are dangerous, for they are whimsical and
capricious, only to be approached by those who fully
understand their ways and their tastes. Thus in our
Old Testament we have the story of Nadab and Abihu,
who were struck dead for daring to offer " strange fire "
to Yahweh (Lev. x. 1–7), and Uzzah meets with a like
fate for the impulse which leads him to steady the Ark
as the oxen which draw it stumble (2 Sam. vi. 6–8).
Further, the shrine of the deity, with all that belongs to
it, needs special care. In a nomad people, who carry the
divine emblems with them, there must be those whose
duty it is to attend to the movements of the sacred
objects. The will of the god is made known in obscure
ways, and an interpreter is necessary to declare the

[1] Rudolf Otto, *The Idea of the Holy*, pp. 7, etc.

meaning of the signs to the lay world. There is always an intermediary between the object of worship and the great mass of human worshippers.

A priesthood of a kind was, then, a necessity in early Israel as elsewhere. We have, however, a variant tradition as to the actual person or persons who fulfilled this office. The official and generally accepted theory of the writers of the Old Testament was that the priesthood was in the hands of the family of Moses. He himself is, indeed, the first priest, and his successors derive from him their authority. It is true that he exercises ecclesiastical functions only for a short time, and that one of his first acts is to consecrate his brother Aaron, from whom the later Jerusalem priesthood traced its descent. But he always stands even between the priests and their God, for all instructions are conveyed through him, and though he is permitted to delegate to his brother's family the special duties of the sanctuary, he has free access thereto in a fashion denied to all others. For practical purposes it is Aaron and his sons who are the legitimate priests.

We have, however, traces of another tradition which assigned this position not to Aaron but to Joshua. It is said in Exod. xxxiii. 11 that while Moses lived in the camp, i.e. amongst the people, " his minister, Joshua, the son of Nun, a young man, departed not out of the Tent." Here we have a form of the tradition—surely current in Ephraimite northern Israel—according to which the priesthood, while primarily still vested in Moses, is delegated, not to any member of his own family or clan, but to a subordinate member of his own household.

The questions raised by the priesthood in ancient Israel are too numerous and too complicated to be discussed except in an extensive monograph. We do not know whether the name " Levi " applied originally to a clan or to an office—there is evidence for both views.[1] We do not know when the tradition which assigned the first place to Aaron was fully accepted in Israel. We do not know how the priesthoods of the various ancient sanctuaries of Israel were related one to another. But

---

[1] See Buchanan Gray's *Sacrifice in the Old Testament*, pp. 241–255 (1925).

of two facts we may be certain. One is that there must have been a priesthood of some kind from the earliest times, to tend the shrine and its contents, to regulate the human approach to Yahweh, and to interpret the will of Yahweh to men. The second fact is that originally this priesthood was in some way connected with Moses, and that there were thus concentrated in him all the functions of a leader, civil and ecclesiastical. From the start Israel recognized divine leadership in all matters, though it was communicated through a human intermediary.

(vi) *Ritual.*—A large proportion of the books of *Exodus, Leviticus,* and *Numbers* is occupied with prescriptions for the ritual to be employed in the service of Yahweh. This is primarily sacrificial, and every event in the life of the individual or of the community, every special season or occurrence, even every day, had its own appropriate offerings. We find other references in the exilic and post-exilic prophets, especially in *Ezekiel,* and in the historical books, all showing that in its final form the ceremonial of Israelite worship was elaborate and costly. But we may doubt whether we are justified in accepting the tradition which ascribed the establishment of this whole system to Moses. The pre-exilic prophets, who represent rather the older traditions of nomadic Israel, seem without a dissentient voice to deny that sacrifice was enjoined on Israel in the wilderness. It may be, however, that they did not intend to include the Passover [1] (as distinct from the Feast of Unleavened Bread), which was much older than Israel. And when we come to examine the ritual as described for us, we see that it embodies an ecclesiastical year centring round three main festivals. These are even mentioned in one of our oldest ritual codes, that of Exod. xxxiv., and are (1) Unleavened Bread (ver. 18); (2) the Feast of Weeks, the first-fruits of the harvest; (3) the Feast of Ingathering at the " year's end " (ver. 22).[2] These are clearly agricul-

---

[1] See Part I, Chapter IX, § 3.

[2] The Hebrew term is literally "the turn of the year," and other references lead us to think of it rather as the beginning than as the end of the year.

tural festivals, and have little or no relation to the
pastoral life of the wilderness. Apart from any question
as to the date of this passage, it is obvious that it had no
bearing, and could have had no bearing, on the actual life
of Israel till they had settled down in Palestine.

This does not mean, however, that we must necessarily
deny all ritual of every kind to the early days of Israel's
history. At first sight it seems as if the Sabbath also
must have been introduced into Israelite life after the
Conquest, but it has recently been pointed out that
possibly this institution was taken over with the primitive
Yahwism from Kenites, who, as smiths, may well have
observed a *taboo* on fire for one day in every seven.[1] As
we have seen, the celebration of the Passover was older
than Israel, being, indeed, the festival which served as the
occasion for the Exodus. There is nothing in it which
is inconsistent with the nomad life, and its combination
with the days of Unleavened Bread may be due to the
fact that both were, in Palestine, spring festivals. But
it is improbable that there was much more than these,
and we are forced to admit that the observance of even
the Sabbath and the Passover in the wilderness is largely
a matter of conjecture.[2]

It is clear that if there was no sacrifice (except at the
Passover, where, to judge from the narrative in *Exodus*,
various tribes assembled at the sacred mountain),
there was no need of an altar proper. There are instructions for making a primitive altar of earth or of unhewn
stone in Exod. xx. 24, 25, but in view of what we have
already seen, this must relate rather to the worship of the
Palestinian community. But we may, perhaps, include
among forms of ritual the methods adopted for ascertaining the divine will. Here again, while we know a
good deal about the practice of later Israel, we cannot
assert with confidence that the means used in after days
were inherited from the primitive period. Several
methods were in use in the ancient East, particularly those
of the inspection of the entrails of victims and the sacred
lot. The former is clearly out of the question in an

[1] See Part I, Chapter IX, § 2.
[2] See, however, Part I, Chapter IX, §§ 2, 3.

age in which sacrifice was infrequent; we are left
therefore with the latter. In Palestine we hear of two
objects used for this purpose : (1) the *Ephod*, and (2) the
Urim and Thummim. We are not certain what either
was ; the first name seems to have been used both for a
garment and for an image,[1] and may have been a sort of
waistcoat with pockets in it where the other articles were
kept. These, the *Urim and Thummim*, may have been
flat stones, white on one side and black on the other.
If both fell white side upwards the answer was in the
affirmative, if black side upwards then a negative ;
if they differed, no reply was vouchsafed to the question.
This is one of the suggestions made as to their use, but,
once again, we have no certainty either that these objects
can be traced back to the wilderness period or that they
were employed in this manner. We should note also
in this connexion the use of oracular wells and trees.[2]
All we know is that nomadic Israel must have had some
mechanical means of ascertaining the will of Yahweh.

(vii) *Ethic.*—The life of the pastoral nomad is extremely
simple. He has little or no private property, for the
flocks belong to the community as a whole, while his
work demands little apparatus, and leaves small room for
articles of comfort. Even the tent in which he lives may
belong to the whole family, and all he can call his own
will be a few weapons, simple clothes, and cooking
vessels. He is thus free from the countless temptations
which beset people living in a more complicated agricultural and commercial system. Moreover, the conditions
of his life are hard. " In the day the drought consumed
me and the frost by night ; and my sleep fled from mine
eyes," says Jacob in justifying himself to Laban (Gen.
xxxi. 40) ; and he is clearly giving a picture of the normal
shepherd life. There is constant danger from enemies,
animal and human, and the flocks can be preserved only at
the price of relentless vigilance. There is no room for
the leisure and enervating luxury which give so much
occasion for selfishness and vice in other spheres. The

---

[1] Hölscher, *Geschichte der israelitischen und jüdischen Religion*,
pp. 20, 72 (1922).
[2] See further, Part I, Chapters II, III.

nomad thus has commonly a fairly high moral standard, especially in sexual matters. African travellers assure us that nomad peoples such as the Masai maintain an ethical level considerably above that of the agricultural peoples of the continent.

It is significant that a man like Jeremiah could look back on this period of Israel's history as that which attained more nearly than any other to the ideal (cp. Jer. ii. 2, 3). It is equally significant that when, in the time of the monarchy, the corruption of national life reached its height, the first protests made in the name of Yahweh came from two men of the wilderness or semi-wilderness community, Elijah (1 Kings xvii. 1) in the ninth century B.C. and Amos in the eighth (Amos i. 1). All through the history of Israel there persisted the tradition of a high moral standard demanded by Yahweh, and, indeed, it was this influence which in the end proved to be the decisive factor in making Israelite religion unique in the ancient world.

It is sometimes held that the familiar ethical Decalogue of Exod. xx. 3–17, at least in a simpler form, was the work of Moses himself. It is true that the commands have undergone modification, and some of them have been expanded. The second commandment, for instance, probably ran simply : " Thou shalt not make unto thee a graven image " ; the fourth : " Remember the Sabbath day to keep it holy " ; and the fifth : " Honour thy father and thy mother." We may suspect that originally the commandments took some such form, whatever be the date of their formulation, but we cannot say definitely that even thus abbreviated they go back to Moses. While there is nothing in them which prohibits a wilderness origin, the evidence is hardly strong enough to justify us in being dogmatic either for or against their Mosaic authorship.

This much, however, we can say. Whether these commandments are the work of Moses or not, they do represent very fairly the general moral standard which we may ascribe to Israel in the days preceding the Settlement. There are two matters which are vital to the existence of a pastoral clan, that which finds expression in the laws of marriage and that which is covered by the law of murder. The purity of its blood and the sanctity of the life of its members are matters which are fundamental to the tribe, and the most stringent regulations have to be adopted in order to guard them. The practical needs of the community are, no doubt, reinforced by feelings and theories in these matters which come down to us from very early times. The beginning and the end of life are both surrounded with that kind of mystery which arouses the fear and the respect of primitive man, and wherever we go amongst early peoples we find that both are the centre of a number of beliefs and practices. There seems always to be something strange about blood, which is, indeed, not merely a " giver of life " but is endowed with a personality of its own. Thus we hear of the blood of Abel " crying out from the ground," and the primitive law of blood revenge was based not on mere vindictiveness but on the fear that blood unsatisfied might prove an appalling peril to the living.

In addition to the two subjects already mentioned, we must recognize a very strong respect for tradition, for antiquity, and for the standing and authority of the older members of the tribe. Long after they have passed the climax of their physical vigour, the " elders " are of value because of their experience of life, and the leadership of the clan commonly devolves on them as individuals or as a group. It is true that they can no longer protect themselves against violence, but they certainly have a right to be heard in the counsels of their people. Hence the respect paid to a man's parents, a respect which again is strengthened by the facts of birth. We need not doubt that the fifth commandment was recognized and observed from the days when Israel first became a nation, and possibly from still more ancient times.

There is thus no reason to doubt that the ethical standard of primitive Israel stood high. The fact is of the greatest importance in the history of the nation, because in Israel, almost alone of ancient peoples, much of the tradition and outlook of the primitive days was preserved, at least in a section of the community. The time was to come when, amid the breakdown of the social and political

order, there was to be a revival of the old views. The men
who, more than any others, gave to the religion of Israel
that peculiar position which made it of supreme significance in the spiritual history of man were the prophets of
the ninth and eighth centuries, and the moral passion
which inspired them was a direct inheritance from the
days of Moses.

CHAPTER III

THE RELIGION OF CANAAN [1]

In considering the religion of the Hebrews before their entry into the Promised Land, we found ourselves frequently forced back on conjecture. Our sources of information were scanty, and we were compelled to admit that such records and traditions as have been handed down from that age have suffered a certain amount of modification at the hands of the generations through which they have passed. We had some help from the comparative study of religions, but archæology gave us even less than tradition, and the result was a wide margin of possible error. With the period that follows, while there are many points that are far from clear, we are on much firmer ground. There are passages in our Old Testament (e.g. the Song of Deborah in Judges v.) which we all recognize as going back to a very early stage in the history of the settled community, and the light they throw on the faith and practice of Israel even before the establishment of the monarchy is of the highest value. Further, the evidence of archæology is comparatively extensive. Several sites of ancient Canaanite worship have been investigated ; some of them, such as Gezer, dating from a time anterior to the Hebrew occupation of the spot in question ; others, such as Shechem, clearly belonging to the middle monarchy. The combination of our various sources of information gives us a tolerably reliable picture of the conditions and of the course of events.

Our knowledge of Palestine goes back to centuries before the Hebrew conquest of the country. We have, in particular, a series of documents in the Tell-el-Amarna letters,[2] dating from the middle of the fourteenth century

[1] For the archæological aspect see S. A. Cook, *The Religion of Ancient Palestine in the light of Archæology* (1930).

[2] An admirable and popular account of these letters is given by Niebuhr, " Die Amarna-Zeit," in *Der Alte Orient*, i. 37 ff. (1900), and the English reader may be referred to J. Baikie, *The Amarna Age*, 1926.

B.C., which may allude to the Aramæan invaders whom we call Hebrews, and certainly depicts conditions before their occupation. This correspondence reveals to us a country already at a comparatively advanced stage of political and social development, corresponding fairly exactly with that which we glean from the stories of the Conquest preserved in the books of *Joshua* and *Judges*. The land contained many cities, some of them apparently very strong, but most of them independent one of another. Some are ruled by native princes, some by foreign governors, but all are nominally subject to the court of Egypt. The authority of the African state, however, is challenged from several quarters, and is in danger of being overthrown. On the one hand, we have the growing Hittite power in the north, gradually expanding under that master of subtle intrigue, Shubiluliuma. On the other hand, we have a series of invasions from the wilderness by groups of tribes whom modern opinion tends more and more to identify with the Hebrews. The type of civilization is that generally characteristic of the peoples of Western Asia, and it is noteworthy that Mesopotamian culture has so strong a hold on the land that, while the native speech is an early form of Hebrew, the Palestinian chiefs and governors correspond with their overlord neither in that language nor in Egyptian, but in Babylonian, even though there are occasional signs that neither writer nor reader was wholly familiar with it.[1]

In the period which followed that of the Tell-el-Amarna letters, these Aramæan invaders made good their footing in the land and gradually settled down. Probably they never formed a very large proportion of the population, but they were much the strongest element, and the necessities of external pressure, culminating in the Philistine invasions, gave them a position of leadership and authority. They entered the land with the faith and cult (such as it was) of the wilderness, and to appreciate the history of Hebrew religion we must study the reaction on one another of the two types of social order and of

---

[1] See further, *The Cambridge Ancient History*, ii. 260 ff., 330 ff. (1924).

belief. Our first step must be to consider in outline the religion of their predecessors.

(i) *Canaanite objects of worship.*—Canaanite religion shared with that of the Hebrews the general characteristics of a Polydæmonism.[1] That is to say, there were a number of spirits worshipped, many of which were of the same type, though, instead of being merely the " group-spirits " characteristic of a pure animism, they were individualized and isolated. It was not necessary that they should have separate names ; it was enough that they were confined more or less each to his own sphere of influence. But there were several striking differences between the *numina* venerated in Palestine and those which claimed the allegiance of the pastoral tribes.

In the first place, while all classes of animistic spirits probably received attention (and particularly the spirits of the departed), the outstanding deities belonged, not to the *'El* class but to that of the *Ba'als*.[2] That is to say, they were not primarily spirits of the open country, but rather of the arable land, and their chief business was the promotion of agriculture. They were thus essentially fertility spirits, such as are found almost everywhere among early farming peoples. They were local deities rather than tribal spirits, attached to the soil rather than to the clan. Their authority was territorially limited, and one of the most impressive of the exploits of Elijah was his proof of the fact that the writ of a foreign *Ba'al* did not run on Israelite soil.[3]

It goes without saying that the presence of the *Ba'als* was indicated by some material objects. The excavator not infrequently discovers whole or broken snake-heads or bull-heads in stone or bronze. These may have had a special place in the cultus, and the examples of Bethel and of Jerusalem in Israelite days lend probability to the suggestion. But we cannot be certain of the fact, while we have direct evidence as to the presence of two other objects, the *Mazzēbāh*, an upright natural stone, and the *'Asherah*, a wooden pillar. There is some reason to

---

[1] Part I, Chapter I, § 1. [2] Part I, Chapter XI, §§ 1, 2.
[3] This is the real meaning of the trial scene on Mount Carmel, and of the slaughter of the prophets of *Ba'al* which followed it. See 1 Kings xviii., and below, pp. 187 f.

suspect that the latter was connected at times with a goddess, though the reference in Jer. ii. 27 shows that the stone might be feminine and the wood masculine. Specimens of the *'Asherah* have, naturally, not survived, but every pre-exilic sanctuary which has been excavated contained monoliths, sometimes singly, sometimes in variously arranged groups. There can be no doubt that, whatever else the sanctuaries may have contained, these two objects were in practically universal use as emblems of the local deity.

Generally speaking, it may be said that the *Ba'al* took much the same place in the life of the local agricultural community as that filled by the tribal god of the pastoral group. He is the king, the father, the leader in war, the guardian of the locality, and the final judicial authority for his city or village. Apart from his help there is no hope of success in the production of the annual crops ; he controls the rain (an especially important function in Palestine) and causes the seed to germinate. To his bounty are due the products of the soil, especially those three most necessary means of civilized livelihood, corn, wine, and oil. If his worship be not properly carried out, he can and will withhold these things, and in an extreme case he may go yet further and bring on the erring community more positive disasters, foreign enemies, or wild beasts. Israel was not the only people which believed that defeat in the field was the direct result of the anger of the national god. For the rest it seems clear that the *Ba'als* tended more and more to vary among themselves in character and importance, some of them attaining to a wide reputation even outside their own district. An illustration may be seen in the application of Ahaziah to Ba'al-zebub of Ekron (2 Kings i. 2–4).

(ii) *Sanctuaries.*—Just as the dweller on the soil has a more solid and permanent home than the nomad, so the god of the latter is better housed than in a mere tent. It may be taken for granted that the sanctuaries were among the most stable buildings in ancient Palestine, though the materials used were probably the same as those employed in the houses of the wealthier citizens. The foundations and lower courses of the walls were usually constructed of stone or of burnt brick, the upper portions being of sun-dried mud. The latter has, of course, perished, with the result that it is possible to see little more than the ground-plans of the ancient edifices. These, however, make it clear that the whole might have been somewhat elaborate, as it must have been in the greater shrines to meet the complicated demands of the cultus.

The site chosen was not infrequently a hill-top. The city might be at the foot of the hill, and the sanctuary outside its walls above it. This, at least, seems to have been the situation at Ramah, at Gibeah, and at early Jerusalem, and the name *Bāmāh,* " high place," applied to these sanctuaries in the Old Testament suggests some elevation. The site covered a fairly large area, and included places where the victims might be sacrificed, a room or a series of rooms where the worshippers might consume the sacrificial flesh, apartments for the priests, and even spots where the remains of victims wholly offered on the altar might be disposed of. A large part of the space was open to the sky, especially a court where the main altar probably stood in front of the actual shrine itself.[1] This latter was the apartment of the god ; here were placed the symbols most sacred to him ; entry was possible probably to none but priests, and the threshold was carefully guarded by a series of *taboos.* Possibly, as in Mesopotamian and Egyptian palaces and temples, the entrance was flanked by figures representing guardian spirits, and similar objects might be found even inside the shrine. We hear little of images within the inner building, and others beside Israel may have dispensed with artificial figures. But archæological evidence shows that in some sanctuaries, at all events, images existed; thus, in the "high place" at Gezer representations of the nude mother-goddess of Asia Minor were discovered (*Quarterly Statement : Palestine Exploration Fund,* 1903, p. 36 ; and see further, S. A. Cook, *The Religion of Ancient*

[1] For an interesting and very informing account of the altar in Israel see Kittel, *Studien zur hebräischen Archäologie und Religionsgeschichte,* pp. 97–158 (1908); also J. Battersby Harford, *Altars and Sanctuaries in the Old Testament* (1929.)

Palestine, pp. 29 ff. [1921]). The only certain reference, however, in our Old Testament is to the image of Dagon at Ashdod, and this may have been due to ideas imported with the Philistines. At the same time, as we have already seen, the figures of the snake and the bull, worshipped in Israel during the monarchical period, may be relics of a Canaanite cult.[1]

(iii) *The Cultus.*—The whole aim of an agricultural religion is to secure the hearty co-operation of the deity in the production of the various crops. For this reason he needs to be kept in a favourable mood, and he requires the assistance of certain types of ritual which resemble sympathetic magic. All the efforts of the worshippers will be unavailing unless the close bond between the god and his people be constantly maintained and renewed. There are the occasional, often personal, forms of ritual, achieving atonement for ceremonial sins, but the two main items in the cultus were the festivals and sacrifice.

(*a*) The principal festivals were three in number. Over the whole of the nearer East, the greatest agricultural festival in ancient times was that which took place in the autumn, at the end of one year and the beginning of the next. It is true that we have no record of the ceremonial observed on Palestinian soil before the Hebrew conquest, but there seems no reason to doubt that the same kind of ritual was observed there as in other parts of the ancient East. The whole centred round the marriage and death of a vegetation god, and the best account we have comes to us from Theocritus, who describes the rite as performed in Egypt in Ptolemaic times. An element of sympathetic magic is clearly present, and the ceremony is evidently intended to help the fertility spirits to perform their annual tasks.

The next critical point in the farmer's calendar comes with the beginning of the harvest, which takes place in Palestine in spring. Bread was leavened with sour dough, a small piece from each baking being left to ferment and used for the next batch. There is thus a continuity

[1] The model of a cobra in bronze was found on the site of the Gezer temple; an illustration is in the *Quarterly Statement* (*Palestine Exploration Fund*), 1903, p. 222.

in the successive generations of the bread, and it goes without saying that some contamination may be transmitted throughout the year.   The ill-effects of this can be avoided only by breaking the chain, and so for the first days during which the new crop is being used leaven is prohibited, being resumed only when the new dough has begun to ferment of itself.   The cutting of the first sheaf and the eating of unleavened bread are the outstanding features of this ritual.

The third of the three great feasts falls at the end of the wheat harvest, roughly some seven weeks later than the second.   It is less critical than either of the other two, and is mainly a festival of thanksgiving to the god for the crop that he has once more supplied.

(b) Sacrifice [1] is of two kinds, with two fundamentally distinct ideas and aims underlying it.   One type is essentially a gift made to the deity,[2] the other is a common meal in which the god and his worshippers share.[3]   The two types are very widely spread, and it may even be asserted that one or the other, usually both, may be found in the ritual of practically every religion known to us.   The difference of purpose produces differences in the ritual, and the two are very easily to be distinguished.

Gift sacrifices depend on the worshippers' view of the personality and claims of the deity.   He is the lord of the land, and as the king of the community he can claim a certain proportion of the produce of the soil.   We should therefore include under this head the offerings of tithes and first-fruits.   The latter are especially stringent ; the first-born of every animal is sacred, the first year's fruit borne by a tree may not be touched by man.   To bring the fruit into common use is to " profane " it, and the same may be said of the produce of new fields. From time to time land had to lie fallow, and though the

---

[1] We are not dealing here with the origin of sacrifice, which would involve too intricate a discussion. We would only point out that the evidence suggests that in their origin sacrifices were a development of magical rites.

[2] See especially Buchanan Gray, *Sacrifice in the Old Testament*, pp. 1–95.

[3] This is worked out in much detail by Robertson Smith, *Rel. Sem.*, pp. 244–352.

practice was necessitated by the demands of agriculture, the original reasons for it were religious rather than scientific. Even when land had been long worked, the god as the king claimed his tribute, and this took the form of tithe, payable in kind at stated intervals. But the most obvious form of gift, indeed perhaps the commonest, consisted of the bodies of slaughtered animals.

No doubt this practice goes back to an age when the god is supposed to be in need of the same kind of sustenance as men, and to eat and drink as they do. But it was realized at a comparatively early stage that the divine essence was even more attenuated than the human, and that the presentation of food in its simplest form would not be acceptable. The god might, nevertheless, delight in the smell of the victim, and if it could be transformed into a " soothing savour " it would give him both satisfaction and maintenance. So it was burnt on the altar, and the ascending smoke carried the essence of the victim to the god in a condition in which he could readily assimilate it.[1] The gods gather like flies to the scent of the Babylonian sacrifice,[2] and even in Hebrew tradition Yahweh is represented as so delighted with the offering of Noah that He made a solemn promise never again to drown off a race which could afford Him so much pleasure (Gen. viii. 20, 21).

Such a sacrifice might be offered in normal times as a regular gift or tribute, but it had a special place in the elimination of sin. Every religion recognizes and allows for the fact of sin, knowing that there is always something arising from the nature or from the life of man which interrupts the ideal relationship between the worshipper and the object of his worship. The deity will be offended, and something must be done to restore him to a good humour. The obvious method is to make him a gift, and, while other ideas may at times be involved, the conception of a fine or bribe which will restore the divine favour is almost universal.

It goes without saying that the species of animals which

---

[1] The root-meaning of '*ōlah* (" whole burnt-sacrifice ") is " to ascend," i.e. in reference to what goes up on to the altar.
[2] See further Ball, *Light from the East*, p. 40 (1899).

11

might be offered in sacrifice was limited.   There were
always those which were held to be especially suitable,
normally those which man himself used, for food, though
there were notable exceptions.[1]   But the great majority of
sacrifices consisted of the domestic animals, goats, sheep,
and oxen.   Since man enjoyed their flesh, it was natural
to suppose that the deity would take equal pleasure in
eating them, and they must be supplied to him.   The
great exception is human sacrifice.   It seems not unlikely
that in comparatively early days all the first-born of men
as well as of beasts were consecrated in this way.   But
for the general application of the principle of human
sacrifice there is no evidence in historic times in Palestine.
At the same time it certainly existed, though it was
less common than animal-sacrifice.   Among the objects
discovered at the great sanctuary at Gezer were a number
of jars containing the bones of infants, and one skeleton
at least suggested that the rite had been postponed to a
later age of the victim.[2]   We hear of Mesha, king of
Moab, offering up his eldest son on the wall of his city
(2 Kings iii. 27).   He was reduced to the last extremity,
and assumed that his danger was due to the wrath of
Chemosh his god.   His last chance was to recover the
favour of the god, or rather to turn the anger of Chemosh
on Israel by the gift of his choicest possession, his own
son, and the Hebrew record states that in this he was
successful, and that the armies of Israel were compelled
to return to their own land.   It was probably only in
such dire straits that men resorted to the offering of their
own children.

The *communion* sacrifice involved a very different
ritual.   Its aim was to renew or to strengthen the
natural bond between the god and the community.
To this end both partook of the flesh of the same victim ;
in certain instances, especially where Totemism was
prevalent, the worshipper may have felt that he was
actually eating the god, and so absorbing his essence

---

[1] See further, Part I, Chapter V, § 2.
[2] See *Quarterly Statement* (*Palestine Exploration Fund*), 1903, pp.
17–19, where an illustration of the skeleton found *in situ* may be
seen.

in a most practical way ; as its essence entered into both, they were once more united into a single whole. It is to be noted that in early times the flesh of the domestic animals, which belonged to the community and therefore to the god, could be eaten by men only under the auspices of religion. Slaughter involved sacrifice to the ancient mind, and wild game alone was exempt from this rule. The ritual seems to have been much as follows. The worshipper would bring his victim to the sanctuary, present it before the god and slaughter it. Certain parts of it were reserved for the altar fire, and these were first removed and burnt. This was the share especially appropriated to the god. The worshipper, with his family or other group, retired to one of the chambers in the sanctuary, and there began to cook the remainder of the carcass. A portion was necessarily to be given to the priest as the human proxy of the god, and this might be determined by chance or it might be a fixed part of the animal. The latter practice probably grew up when it was found that methods of chance might possibly be controlled by the priest. Thus god, priest, and worshipper all shared in the meal, and the bond between them was renewed and strengthened.[1]

(iv) *Sacred Persons.*—If a priestly order is a necessity to the comparatively simple nomad religion it is still more so to the elaborate cultus of the agricultural community. The essential functions of the priesthood will, of course, be the same at all stages, but a larger establishment will be needed for the many duties which have to be performed. The sanctuary itself needs attention ; the extensive buildings must be kept in a state of comparative cleanliness. The worshippers who come to offer sacrifice have to be guided and instructed in their ritual, for it goes without saying that an offering must be presented in the right way and with appropriate words. The altar must be constantly tended, its fire must be kept alight, and the portions reserved for the exclusive use of the god must be burnt. It is true that the actual slaughter of the victim was carried out by

[1] For the later development of the sacrificial system see Part III, Chapter X, § 3.

the worshipper himself except when the sacrifice was offered on behalf of the community as a whole, but the presentation of the blood and fat was probably to be performed only by duly qualified persons. Moreover, animal sacrifice is a disgusting affair, and it was necessary that something should be done to keep the premises fairly clean, while the ashes of the altar itself had to be removed at frequent intervals if the fire was not to be choked by them. And to the duties about the sanctuary must be added the responsibility for interpreting the sacred lot or whatever means was adopted for ascertaining the divine will.

The priests naturally tended to form close corporations, and the succession was maintained either in the same family or through a process of adoption. The duties were required to be learnt, and involved the knowledge of a store of tradition handed down for generations. But in addition to these " regular " cultic persons, whose functions were professional, there rose from time to time individuals whose relation to their deity was directly personal. Any abnormal state of mind is in the ancient world attributed to direct divine agency, and phenomena like those of second sight, epilepsy, and even insanity, are attributed to possession by some *numen*. There had been a " breathing " which had entered into the subject and transformed him. For the time being he was not himself, and the experiences through which he passed were held to be a direct manifestation of the deity.

The phenomena of this possession have a double aspect. In the first place, there is the experience of the subject to consider ; he becomes conscious of another world than that in which men ordinarily live, and in which he himself normally dwells. He is still aware of the familiar objects of daily life, but in addition to this he is conscious of sights and sounds which those about him cannot appreciate. It is as though a veil had suddenly been withdrawn from a whole universe which is just as real as that so familiar to all men, but which is hidden from them. The man's eyes are " opened," his ears are " uncovered," and the secret world of the gods is available for him also. These phenomena are to be found in many places and under many forms of religious belief, and they are characteristic of the type of person to whom the name " seer " is commonly given.

The outside world, of course, does not share this inner experience, but there are usually signs which show to the observers that the person affected is in an abnormal condition. In Asia Minor and in Palestine these took the form of what is often called *ecstasy*. The muscles might be constricted and the limbs stiffened, the subject remaining motionless and speechless in a trance-like state. On the other hand, there might be the wildest activity, arms and legs being flung about and the movements being apparently quite uncontrolled. The condition was in some measure infectious, and when a group of persons in a state of ecstasy acted together, their movements tended to become rhythmical—formed, in fact, a " dance." Pain was no longer felt, and men in this state might lash themselves or their fellows with whips or gash themselves with knives. We have in the Old Testament a vivid account of the " ecstatic " in the description of the prophets of *Ba'al* on Mount Carmel (1 Kings xviii. 26–29).

These phenomena at a later time were spread over the whole of the Mediterranean world, and one of our best accounts of them comes to us from Apuleius.[1] But they can always be traced back either to Asia Minor or to Palestine ; they do not appear in Egypt till near the fifth century B.C., and there seems to be no trace of them either in early Arabia or in Mesopotamia. Except for Moses himself, who seems to have been possessed of second sight, though probably without the wilder manifestations of the ecstatic proper, the only persons of whom such activities are recorded in the wilderness period are the seventy elders mentioned in Num. xi. 25–29, and this story may well be a reflection back into the nomad age of phenomena belonging to a later time. We certainly have evidence from an early period of the presence of the ecstatic in Syria, and of the recognition of his activities as directly inspired by a *Ba'al*.

---

[1] *The Golden Ass*, xi. 8–17. The date of Apuleius is the second half of the second century A.D. (see also Herodotus, ii. 61 ff.).

(v) *The Ethic of Ba'alism.*—We have seen that the moral standard of a pastoral people is commonly high, and that there is reason to believe that the Aramaean ancestors of Israel were no exception to this rule. But the life of the agriculturist, especially when it is combined with a developed commercial system, is far more complicated and difficult. The institution of private property on a large scale, the presence of a number of different professions side by side, the traditional occupation of a particular piece of territory, the greater stability of society, the gradual raising of the standard of comfort to a point where it becomes luxury—all these facts (and others also) present the more advanced community with problems which are unknown to the more primitive stage, and expose men to temptations previously non-existent or almost negligible. At the same time the demands of the deities become more elaborate in matters of ritual, and it is almost inevitable that religion should develop mainly along this line. The moral requirements of the wilderness stage are not forgotten ; there is still the same insistence on certain types of sexual purity and on the sanctity of human life, but the moral law does not extend the sphere of its application, and a large area of life remains outside its influence. This is not to say that men were unconscious of the ethical demand ; on the contrary, they realized even more clearly than before the difference between right and wrong. But the human conscience grows apart from religion, and it is one of the tragedies of the spiritual life of man that his faith is so often below his private moral standard. The religion of the ancient agricultural world is a signal illustration of this divorce of morality from religion. An act might be universally recognized as a vice or a crime ; it did not follow that it was a sin. Except in so far as religion insisted on the observance of certain primitive *taboos*, it was indifferent to the treatment accorded by a man to his neighbours, and left the vindication of moral and social right either to the individual wronged or to the civil heads of the community.

There is still a graver charge to be brought against the

religion of ancient Palestine. It was not merely indifferent to the claims of simple ethics, it even condoned and authorized direct violations of the moral law. No one would justify murder in ordinary civil life, yet there were times—rare, it is true—when human sacrifice was practised. Sexual irregularity was condemned by the common feeling of the western Semites, but sacramental fornication was a regular feature of the religious life, clearly appearing at other times as well as at the autumn festival. Indeed, it may well have been that this vice was practically confined to the " high places." And the great festivals, especially that of the autumn, seem to have been times of riotous licence, when free rein was given to human passions.

In one way, and in one only, does the ancient religion of Palestine appear to have imposed a moral restraint, and this was due, not so much to any ethical character of the Ba'als, but to their demand for personal respect. If a man bound himself by an oath, he broke his word at his own peril, and was sure to suffer from the vengeance of the god. By its very nature the oath is an attempt to secure a divine sanction. The formula is : " May the god do so " (probably accompanied by a gesture implying ruin) " to me, and so again, if I do . . . " or some similar phrase which invites the deity to take vengeance if the oath is broken. When this has been said the very pride of the god demands that he shall punish perjury, and so strong was the fear of vengeance that a solemn oath taken by one party or the other in the presence of the god was sufficient to settle any dispute. If a man swore that he was not guilty of an offence, it was assumed that he was innocent, for none would dare so to flout the god as to " take his name in vain." But while the oath did undoubtedly have a moral value, its very existence testified to the ethical deficiencies of the religion which required it.

CHAPTER IV

THE EARLY RELIGION OF THE SETTLEMENT:
APOSTASY

WE have seen in Chapter I something of the general character of the religion of the Hebrews in the wilderness, and in Chapter III we have glanced at the religion of Canaan. We have now to see the effect of the impact of a higher civilization, with its more elaborate life and ritual, on the faith of the Hebrew invaders who overran Palestine at some time between the end of the sixteenth century B.C. and the beginning of the eleventh. It was inevitable that contact with the more advanced people, and a change from the social order of the wandering shepherd to that of the settled farmer and trader, should have a profound influence on the whole outlook of the people, and that their religion should be affected as well as other sides of their life. In order to appreciate this we must briefly consider the actual situation of the Hebrews during the centuries which immediately followed the conquest and preceded the establishment of the monarchy.

(i) *Israel in Palestine.*—The conquest of Palestine was neither sudden nor complete, as we learn from the book of *Judges*. The Aramaean invaders at first were able to make good their footing only in the wilder parts of the country, the hills in the centre of the land, and the grazing country to the east of Jordan and to the south. The fertile lands, such as the maritime plain and the plain of Esdraelon, remained in the hands of their former possessors, and there were two belts of unsubdued Canaanites who cut the Israelite settlements into three main divisions. Between those who found a home in the south, with their centre at Hebron, and those who established themselves in the centre, in the Bethel

district, lay Jerusalem, which became Israelite only
when captured by David. Another group in the far
north was again cut off from its fellows by a line of
fortresses stretching from Megiddo on the slopes of the
Carmel range to Bethshean, which guarded the chief
ford across the Jordan, just south of the Sea of Galilee.
Israel brought a new vigour into the country, and as they
gradually spread into the arable districts, largely through
peaceful penetration and intermarriage (Abimelech is
a case in point, Judges ix. 1 ff.), they provided an element
which successfully resisted attacks made from the
outside.   The book of *Judges* is largely a record of these
assaults, and it is significant that Deborah and Barak
are the only " judges " who have to meet a Canaanite foe.
The others fight the battles of the older inhabitants as
much as those of Israel, and the process of welding
together the two elements in the population reaches its
climax in the resistance made to the Philistines.

The Hebrew invaders thus formed but a comparatively
small element in the population, and though their military
prowess enabled them to take and to hold a leading
position, their general culture was below the level of
that of their new neighbours.   It was only gradually
that they took to the operations of agriculture, and they
must have been generally impressed by the superiority
of their predecessors.   It seems, in fact, that they simply
adopted the culture of Palestine *en bloc*.   Their original
language was, presumably, a dialect of Aramaic ; in
Canaan they used Hebrew, the old speech of the people
in the Tell-el-Amarna age.   The civil law which we find
embodied in Israel's earliest codes is a form of that
common to all the peoples of Western Asia, and resembles
the type represented in the law of the Hittites, the
Babylonians, and the Assyrians.   The folk-lore and
mythology, including the cosmology, of Israel, while
presenting us with significant and indeed unique features,
has parallels with Mesopotamian literature, and we gather
from occasional hints in the Old Testament that if the
popular tales, as they were told among the common
folk, had been preserved, we should have found the
resemblance greater still.   We need not doubt that,

just as the Teutonic invaders of the fourth century A.D. adapted themselves in large measure to the culture of imperial Rome, so these new conquerors of Palestine inherited with the land they occupied much, if not all, of the existing mode of life. And to carry the parallel a step farther, just as the northern invaders of the ancient Mediterranean world accepted, in the main, the religion of the land which they entered, so, too, Israel went far in accepting the deities and the cultus which they found already in the country. It is true that no new people can adopt a religion without importing something into it, and that they may in the long run have a profound influence on its nature ; but for some generations we must expect to find little difference, if any, between the faith of the older inhabitants and that of the new-comers.

(ii) *Israel and the Ba'als.*—We have already glanced in brief outline at the religion of Palestine before the entry of Israel into the land. In addition to the natural respect which even a victorious race feels for the higher culture of its defeated enemy, there were strong reasons which predisposed the new-comers to adopt the cultus and belief of their predecessors. The tribal conception of deity which prevailed in the wilderness was exchanged for a theory of territorial dominion. The land belonged to the *Ba'als*, and, while they might differ among themselves in importance and power, the locality in which each made his home owed allegiance to him and to no other. The national gods—and there were *Ba'als* with a wider authority than the village or city—exercised supreme control over their own land, and their worshippers never admitted that they were conquered by other powers. If, in later times, Moab suffers from an invasion of Israel, or Israel is laid waste by a foreign army, the calamity is due to the anger of the national god manifested against his own people ; if and when he can be appeased, the enemy will be expelled as a matter of course. When Naaman the Syrian, in gratitude for his cure, decides that he will worship no god but Yahweh, he can solve the problem of territorial dominion only by taking two mules' burden of earth with him (2 Kings v. 17). It is a piece of Yahweh's land, and on it he can erect an altar to Yahweh and offer Him due service. Even the writer of Ps. xlii.–xliii., though his date can hardly be earlier than 596 B.C., counts it his greatest sorrow that he is leaving his God behind him as he goes into exile.

These illustrations are all derived from a period later than that which we are now considering, but we may safely assume that the ideas which they manifest are survivals from the earlier stage. In the first generations of the settlement men still thought of Yahweh as being no permanent inhabitant of Palestine, but as dwelling in the far south, whence He would come in times of special need to serve His people against their enemies (cp. Judges v. 4). The deities on the spot were the *Ba'als*, and they must be taken into consideration. If they did not receive due reverence and tribute, their anger would be aroused, and they would exhibit their displeasure by bringing calamity on the land. Centuries later Israel suffered from foreign invasion, and a part of her population was deported. The place of the exiles was partially filled by settlers from distant parts of the Assyrian empire, and the new-comers found themselves plagued by lions. Instead of attributing their troubles to the scanty population, which failed to check the increase of wild beasts, they ascribed their difficulties to the anger of the god of the land, i.e. Yahweh, and were not relieved till a priest of Yahweh was sent to teach them how He should be worshipped (2 Kings xvii. 24–28). The narrator of the story fully shares the beliefs which he describes, and here again we need not doubt that we have a survival of a very ancient idea. When they made their home in Palestine, the Israelites must have been in fear lest they should incur disaster by the neglect of the established *Ba'als*, the divine owners of the soil.

Even if they had felt reasonably secure against such disaster—and they may have held that Yahweh could, after all, protect them against the anger of these objects of local worship—there was still another consideration which weighed with Israel. Yahweh was their national God, though He still dwelt in Sinai or Horeb. He had

served them well, led them through the wilderness,
brought them into the land, given them direction when
they needed it, fought their battles for them. But He
was essentially an *'El*, a wilderness god, and they had
no experience of His ability to handle the new problems
with which they were faced. They were now undertaking
gradually the operations of agriculture : could Yahweh
help them ? Did this southern storm and mountain God
know how to grow corn ? Did He understand the culture
of the vine and the olive ? Was He able to supply flax
and other products of the ground so necessary for the
new life on which they were entering ? This is not a
fancy suggestion ; even as late as the time of Hosea
there were men in Israel who did not know that it was
Yahweh who supplied them with the produce of the soil
(Hos. ii. 5, 8). It was almost inevitable that Israel
should turn from Yahweh to the *Ba'als* to secure, not
merely freedom from danger, but also prosperity in the
new venture.

(iii) *The Lesson of the Judges.*—It was through the
bitter experiences of the centuries which elapsed between
the conquest and the establishment of the monarchy
that Israel learned her mistake, and the story of the
lesson is told us in the book of *Judges*. As it stands
that book consists of a series of narratives dealing with
the " Judges " of Israel, compiled in its present form by
a writer or a school of writers who used the incidents
recorded to illustrate a particular philosophy of history.
The whole is a repetition of a regular cycle of events,
and may be stated in a formula : " And the children of
Israel forgot Yahweh their God, and served the *Ba'als*,
and Yahweh sold them into the hand of A (an oppressor),
and they served A so-and-so many years. And they
repented and cried unto Yahweh their God, and Yahweh
raised up for them a Judge, B, who delivered them out
of the hand of A. (Then follows the detailed account of
the exploits of B, taken from much older sources.) And
the land had rest so-and-so many years. And it came
to pass that the children of Israel served Yahweh all the
days of B, but after the death of B they forgot Yahweh
their God . . . " ; and so the cycle is renewed, with its

succession of apostasy, oppression, repentance, and deliverance.

Now this is not a piece of arbitrary punishment, but a very sound interpretation of history. Powerful as a *Ba'al* might possibly be in his own locality, he asked for no allegiance from without, and exercised no authority save in his own limited area. *Ba'alism* was thus necessarily a disintegrating force, separating city from city and village from village. In face of an enemy, be he a Palestinian dynast such as Sisera or a foreign invader such as the other oppressors, there was in *Ba'alism* nothing that would unite the people against him and so create an effective resistance. The hordes that swept in from the desert in search of plunder and the more systematically organized armies of imperially-minded kings alike found an easy prey in the disunited communities into which Palestine was split up, and plundered or destroyed their victims piecemeal.

Before the entry into Canaan Israel was a loose confederacy of tribes, held together by a sense of common blood and the common worship of Yahweh. It was inevitable that the former of these two bonds should be slackened as between the isolated communities in Palestine after the Conquest; and *Ba'alism*, with its village patriotism, offered no cohesive influence. The only unifying force which Israel possessed lay in her worship of Yahweh, and if she once lost her grip on that, she fell an easy prey to the oppressor. It is significant that when the need arose and the appeal went out to the scattered clans, it was sent in the name of Yahweh, and failure to respond brought down a condemnation, based not on national but on religious grounds. The Judges themselves were men and women inspired by Yahweh, and having something of the character of the ecstatic prophet. They were recognized as the means and instruments whereby the national God worked salvation for His people, and it was in Him and in Him alone that the armies of Israel could unite and achieve their triumphs. It was not an accident that apostasy meant oppression, and fidelity brought deliverance; it arose out of the very facts of the situation.

But Israel was slow to grasp the lesson, and some centuries passed before it was fully learned. The country suffered from the domination of Moab and from the invasions of the tribes akin to the Bedawin—Ammonites, Midianites, " Children of the East,"—and was freed each time by the action of a Yahweh-inspired Judge. Finally, the struggle against the Philistines, more severe and lasting than any earlier conflicts, brought matters to a head, and, under Saul and David, produced a genuine unity of the inhabitants of Palestine for the first time in the history of the land. Both men were devotees of Yahweh. Saul was a typical " Nabi'," or prophet of the older type, and was, throughout his life, subject to the onrush of the divine Spirit.[1] David, while less obviously ecstatic, made it his aim to secure the unity of his people in a common faith, and established at Jerusalem a centre not only of the political life of Israel but also of its cultus. Other sanctuaries certainly remained, and received honour, but that which sheltered the Ark (like Shiloh in an earlier generation) had a special pre-eminence, and served as a symbol, both of the royal power, and still more of the oneness of Israel in the worship of her God.

[1] Cp. 1 Sam. x. 10–13 ; xi. 6 ; xviii. 10 ; xix. 23, 24.

CHAPTER V

THE RELIGION OF ISRAEL IN THE EARLY MONARCHY

THE establishment of the monarchy in Israel proved in a certain sense to be the victory of Yahwism. The nation now recognized definitely and finally that for them there was only one God. Others might and did exist, and each must be recognized and duly cultivated in his own sphere. But that sphere lay outside Israel and her land. Any city which was within the community and recognized that it formed a part of the political and national whole, accepted Yahweh as the only being to be worshipped within its own bounds. He had shown by His prowess and by His gifts in Nature that the land did as a matter of fact belong to Him. He was no longer a mountain God with His home in the far south ; He dwelt in Palestine, among His own people, and men could there enter directly into communion with Him.

But this recognition of Yahweh as the true God of Israel—just as Chemosh was god of Moab and Melek of Ammon—did not necessarily mean the triumph of the old religion of nomadic Israel. Forces were at work in the new home which tended profoundly to modify both the theory and practice of Yahwism, and we may suspect that Moses and his immediate successors would have failed to recognize in the popular worship of Israel between Solomon and Ahab the faith which had inspired them in the wilderness. We must glance very briefly, first at the general characteristics of religion in this period, and then at such features as may have been peculiar in different parts of the country.

(i) *Syncretism.*—" Syncretism " is a term used in the historical study of religion to indicate a mixture of two or more religions, especially where the objects of worship

proper to the one are adored with a form of cultus derived
from another.   This type of religious hybridism is very
common where a higher religion has nominally conquered
and ousted a lower type, and instances may be seen in the
history of Buddhism, Christianity, and, to a lesser extent,
in Islam.   In the history of Israel we have, perhaps, the
best illustration of all ; and we shall do well to remember
that even though Yahweh had superseded the *Ba'als*, it
by no means followed that the resultant Yahwism was in
any sense pure.

We have already seen something of the influences and
beliefs which tended to draw the early Israelite settlers
towards the worship of the *Ba'als*.   While Yahweh was
now recognized as the only God of Israel, these forces
had by no means lost their power.   What had happened
was, in effect, that as Israel had taken to the life of the
farmer, her God had done likewise, and must henceforward
be regarded as a fertility deity.   His task with Israel
was no longer that of guidance through the paths of the
wilderness, though He retained the character of rain-giver.
But His function was now less the production of occasional
fodder for the wandering flocks than the regular supply
of the crops.   And the worship of Israel was intended in
no small part to give Him such help as He might require.
For Yahweh the character of a fertility God was new,
but there had been others long in the land.   If He was to
take the place and perform the duties of the old *Ba'als*,
it was only natural that men should assume that they
could best serve Him (and so, indirectly, themselves)
by offering to Him a worship like that which had been
paid to His predecessors.   While, then, the name used
in worship was that of Yahweh, the details of the cultus
were, we may believe, very much what they had been in
Palestine from time immemorial.

It would seem that many of the old sanctuaries, perhaps
all,[1] were devoted to Yahweh instead of to the

---

[1] It should be remarked that recently Dr. A. C. Welch has propounded
a theory of the history of Israelite religion according to which the old
Ba'al sanctuaries retained their original purpose, and a few great
Yahweh sanctuaries were set up.   It is, however, impossible to discuss
the theory in detail here ; it is enough to say that it has not yet commanded
general assent.

local *Ba'al*. In some instances we have narratives which
suggest that an entirely new type of cultus with a fresh
altar was introduced. Such are the stories of Manoah
at Zor'ah,[1] and of the origin of the sanctity of Jerusalem in the time of David. It has been suspected
that the story in Judges xiii. is intended to explain
the sanctity of the rock-altar still to be seen at Zor'ah,
and that the account of the meeting of David and
the angel of pestilence at the threshing-floor of Araunah
gives the reason for the use of the great rock near by as
a holy place. But both rocks, though certainly used as
altars in ancient times, show cup-marks and channels
which are probably far older than Israel,[2] and even if the
theory as to the source of the narratives themselves be
correct (and this is by no means certain), it seems fairly
clear that the places in question were holy long before the
Israelite occupation of Palestine, and that they are to be
classed among the sanctuaries adapted to Yahwism.

It is probable that most of the literature containing the
ritual prescriptions comes to us in its present form from
after the Exile ; but even if that be so it must contain
a very large pre-exilic element, and though we must allow
for the development of the forms, we may suppose that
many primitive features have been preserved. These
belong, not merely to early Israel, but even to the older
Canaanite worship. From this source were derived the
three great agricultural festivals to which allusion has
already been made,[3] the general type of building proper
to the cultus, and, above all, the institution of sacrifice
on a large scale. Equally important with these is the
attitude adopted by His worshippers to Yahweh, and
their altered conception of Him. This may be summed
up by saying that from being an *'El* He had now become a
Ba'al. Indeed, there is reason to believe that the word
"*Ba'al*" was actually applied to Him as a descriptive
title, and that it was not till Hosea's day that the term
fell out of use. If ever there were two men in the history

[1] See further Kittel, *Studien zur Hebr. Arch.*, pp. 104–108.
[2] See Buchanan Gray, *Sacrifice in the Old Testament*, p. 121 (1925);
Kittel, *op. cit.*, pp. 131 ff.
[3] See above, pp. 148 f., 159 f.

12

of Israel who were devoted Yahweh enthusiasts, they were Saul and David. Yet the families of both contained persons whose names were compounded with the word *Ba'al* in such a fashion as to show that he was regarded as a deity.[1] This can mean only that Yahweh Himself was intended and, in fact, He was probably indistinguishable from the older *Ba'als* save by His name.

One other most important feature of the older Canaanite religion must be mentioned. This was the presence of ecstatic prophecy. As we have already seen,[2] there is reason to believe that this was an element in the religious life of Palestine and of Syria before the coming of the Israelites, and that among them it was unknown or hardly known till after the Conquest. But Yahweh enthusiasts appeared as well as *Ba'al* enthusiasts, and they played a prominent part in the politics as well as in the religion of Israel. By the end of the ninth century they had evidently attained some sort of organization, and formed regular communities. The number of them seems to have been large, for we hear of communities outgrowing their homes and being compelled to migrate, while no less than four hundred are said to have been included in the company that attended the court of Ahab (1 Kings xxii. 6). Their social standing seems to have been low, and their methods questionable; but they did at least stand for Yahweh, and were recognized as being the *media* through whom He made His will known. The civil code and ecstatic prophecy existed as regular elements in Palestinian life before the Hebrew Conquest; Israel inherited both the Law and the Prophets from her predecessors in Palestine.

(ii) *Religion in Southern Palestine.*—The comparatively close association of Judah with Israel begins with David. The tribe is not mentioned, either for praise or for blame, in the Song of Deborah, and the belt of unsubdued Canaanites whose centre was at Jerusalem made com-

---

[1] Ishba'al, son of Saul, 1 Chron. viii. 33, and Meriba'al, son of Jonathan, 1 Chron. viii. 34, seem to have been the original forms of the names found in *Samuel* as Ishbosheth and Mephibosheth, while Be'eliada, son of David, is mentioned in 1 Chron. xiv. 7, but appears in *Samuel* as Eliada.

[2] See above, p. 165.

munication between the two sections difficult. It is even possible that the southern settlements were made at a different time and under different sets of leaders from those in the centre and the north of Palestine. And through all the history of the monarchy there was division between the two sections, manifesting itself after the death of Solomon in the great disruption of the kingdom. Yet the kinship between the south and the north was strongly felt, at least in religion, for both parts of the country recognized Yahweh as their God.

The principal difference during the period of the monarchy seems to have been in the form under which Yahweh was worshipped. In pre-monarchic days the chief sacred symbol had always been the Ark—so tradition held—and there seems no reason to doubt it. After the disastrous battle of Aphek (1 Sam. iv.), in which the Ark was captured by the Philistines, and which resulted, as it seems, in the destruction of the old sanctuary of Shiloh, the Ark nearly disappeared, and came into prominence again only with David. After his conquest of Jerusalem, and even before his building operations were complete, David brought the Ark to Jerusalem and set it up for worship there, probably on the hill to the north of the Ophel, where the original Jebusite city had been established. There, on a site close to the great altar of natural rock over which the so-called Mosque of Omar now stands, Solomon built the Temple, as a home in which the Ark should be placed. It is clear that while the king himself held other sanctuaries in reverence (for he sacrificed not only at Jerusalem but also at Gibeon),[1] that of Jerusalem was intended to be the centre of the worship of Yahweh. This meant a definite settlement in the land ; Yahweh dwelt between the Cherubim. A century later it was necessary for Elijah to go to Horeb, the mount of God, to get into close personal touch with Yahweh ; but in the eighth century Amos could speak of Yahweh as " roaring from Zion."[2]

Of the Jerusalem cultus we have few details which can be traced with absolute certainty to the period of the early monarchy. We know practically nothing of the

---

[1] Cf. 1 Kings iii. 4.   [2] Amos i. 2.

worship of the snake, to which reference has already
been made [1]; we do not even know whether this object
found a place in the Temple precincts or whether there
was a separate shrine in another part of the city.   But the
great sanctuary of the Ark continued to be the chief
centre of worship down to the time of the destruction of
Jerusalem in 585 B.C., and sacrifices were offered at the
spot even after that time (cp. Jer. xli. 5).   Though the
northern kingdom far exceeded the southern in extent and
power, there was no other sacred place which challenged
the supremacy of Jerusalem.

(iii) *Religion in Northern Palestine.*—In the south of
Canaan during the monarchical period we hear of several
sanctuaries, e.g. of Beersheba, but none that in any way
approached the importance of the Temple at Jerusalem.
In the north there was none which could claim quite the
same pre-eminence.   It is true that Jeroboam and his
successors gave the old high place at Bethel a special
position, in the hope that it might rival Jerusalem, but
the attempt does not seem to have been wholly successful ;
Gilgal and Dan also claimed the allegiance of northern
Israel, in spite of the prestige afforded to Bethel by the
presence of the royal sanctuary.   Unless we are to suppose
that there are elements in the traditional ritual which
originated in Bethel rather than in Jerusalem, we have
no trace of the type of cultus practised there, but we may
fairly assume that it did not differ greatly from that of
other sacred places in Palestine.   It seems fairly clear
that there were somewhat elaborate buildings, and the
priesthood of Bethel enjoyed the special patronage and
protection of the king.   But our records were all collected
or edited at a period when worship at Bethel was held to
be an act of apostasy, and practically no references remain.

It seems, however, to be clear that Bethel contributed
less, if possible, than Jerusalem to a high moral and
social standard in Israel generally.   In the eighth century
we hear of complaints made by Amos and suggested by
Hosea of iniquities associated with the northern sanctuaries.   Yahweh was worshipped as a fertility God under
the form of a bull, and this in itself would seem to imply

[1] See above, pp. 142 ff.

a sexual element in the cult. Further, northern Israel was comparatively rich and prosperous : her soil was fertile and her opportunities for trade extensive. Social corruption of many kinds flourished, and if we cannot claim that the Temple at Jerusalem exercised a strong influence in favour of the higher morality, we know positively that the tendencies of the northern religion were still more discordant with recognized moral principles. It seems to be clear that here the "*Ba'alization*" of Yahweh was complete, and when Hosea inveighs against the cult of *Ba'al*, he probably means that Yahweh, as interpreted in the northern kingdom, was not the true Yahweh at all, but only *Ba'al* under another name. The type of religion presented at Bethel was a syncretism, in which the later, superimposed religion had no part except in the name of the deity worshipped.

CHAPTER VI

THE YAHWIST REVIVAL

THE conditions depicted in the last chapter were those
of the agricultural and commercial portions of the
community, in other words, those that were settled in
Western Palestine, perhaps to some extent affected by
proximity to Phœnicia. But it must never be forgotten
that there was another Israel, and this fact of the social
and economic division of the people is of the highest
importance for the understanding of Israelite history,
both in politics and in religion. There were certain
tribes which had never made their home on the west of
the Jordan, though they were recognized as forming a part
of the true Israel, owed allegiance to her kings, and were
expected to take their share in fighting her battles.[1]
In Num. xxxii. we are told that the reason for this eastern
settlement was that on the far side of Jordan the land
was a " land for cattle "—grazing country.[2] In the south
of Judah, too, the soil and climate are unsuited for the
production of crops, and we are all familiar with the fact
that David in Bethlehem lived as a shepherd, while
one of the most beautiful stories of his life deals with a
great shepherd chieftain of the southern Carmel, south of
Hebron.[3]

Side by side, then, with the agricultural community
we have groups which still lived on the pastoral, if not
on the nomad, plane of social order, yet recognizing a
common kinship and worshipping a common deity with
their more " advanced " brethren. It was only to be
expected that the tribes of the east and south should thus
preserve far more completely than the rest the ancient
traditions, outlook, and mode of worship which had

[1] Cp. Judges v. 14 (Machir), 15, 16 (Reuben), and 17 (Gilead, i.e. Gad).
[2] Cp. also Amos iv. 1.   [3] See 1 Sam. xxv.

characterized the Aramaean tribes before their entry into Palestine. We shall not greatly err if we ascribe to them a religious and political life not far removed from that of all the tribes in the wilderness period, and, as has already been said, this double standard in Israel is, in a certain sense, the key to the history of the middle and later monarchy. In particular, it was from this element in the population that there came first a protest against that declension from primitive Yahwist principles in Church and State which marked the syncretism of agricultural Palestine.

(i) *Jezebel and Melkart.*—While there were, no doubt, always those who stood for the old ways in Israel and looked back on the wilderness life as the golden age of her history, the opposition to the new order did not come to a head till it was provoked by the introduction of certain foreign influences in the middle of the ninth century B.C. Omri succeeded in raising his kingdom to the position of one of the minor powers of the East, and northern Israel was known after his day to the Assyrians as " Bit Humri "[1] —the " House of Omri." One sign of his position was the alliance with Sidon, and just as the marriage of an Egyptian princess gave prestige to Solomon's court, so the wedding of Jezebel and Ahab attested the high place that Israel now held among the nations.

But the alliance meant the introduction of new and unpalatable ideas and tendencies. Politically Israel, perhaps alone among the nations of the ancient East, preserved much of that democratic spirit which marks the shepherd tribes. It seems that the monarchy was limited, in that a definite " covenant " was made at the accession of each king, laying down the terms on which he held his power. Israel recognized no distinction in status between one freeman and another ; all (including the king) were " brethren." We have no trace of a noble order here, such as we find in Mesopotamia and in Egypt. The king had, it is true, certain prerogatives, but these were restricted, and he dared not transgress the absolute rights of his subjects. Elsewhere the conception of a limited monarchy would have seemed a contradiction in

---

[1] On an inscription of Tiglath-Pileser III, *circa* 734 B.C.

terms, for the very nature of kingship demanded that it should be absolute.

The contrast is well brought out in the familiar story of Naboth's vineyard. When the little freeholder refuses to surrender his ancestral property, it never occurs to Ahab to try to impose his own will on his subject, either by force or by guile. He does not like the situation, but he has to accept it. But his Sidonian wife has been bred in other theories of the royal prerogative, and if the subject will not yield to her, so much the worse for him. Yet even she is compelled to proceed by the recognized forms of justice ; she dare not flout popular opinion utterly.

At the same time the ancient East recognized a great freedom in religious affairs. Conquest, trade, royal alliances, and any other methods of promoting intercourse between two nations were commonly accompanied by religious innovations. The deities worshipped in one place were admitted to another, and, while the supremacy of the older possessor of the land was in some way acknowledged, the new-comers held a recognized place beside him. Solomon had provided ecclesiastical establishments for his wives, and Jezebel brought with her the cult of Melkart, the *Ba'al* of Sidon. This was not in itself objectionable to the great mass of the population, but the national spirit was aroused when she sought to give her own *Ba'al* supremacy over Yahweh, the *Ba'al* of Israel. And there was still an element, strongest in the east, but clearly represented even in Central Palestine, which objected to the worship and even the presence of any imported deity whatsoever.

(ii) *The Yahwist Guilds.*—Among the groups and classes which stood for Yahweh as against all other objects of worship, it is usual to enumerate three, the Prophets, or *Nebi'im*, the Nazirites, and the Rechabites. As we have already seen, the first class consisted of ecstatic devotees, whose wild behaviour testified to their possession by Yahweh, and who stood for Him against all rivals. It is clear that by the middle of the ninth century they had attained to some kind of organized and communal life, and, as we shall have reason to see later, they were in a position to exercise no small political influence. In a very real sense they represented the national God, and made an irresistible appeal to the great mass of the people.

The subject of the Nazirites is obscure. In later times the Nazirite took a temporary vow of abstention from certain practices, notably the cutting of the hair and the drinking of wine. In earlier days, however, the vow seems to have been taken for life, and the Nazirite stood as a permanent protest against certain aspects of the higher social order. The type of the ancient Nazirite is Samson, and as late as the days of Amos the class was closely connected in men's minds with the *Nebi'im*.[1] The ancient Israelite who was devoted especially to Yahweh would use no razor—the opening phrase of the Song of Deborah (Judges v. 2) is best rendered " When the long locks in Israel streamed free "—and would drink no wine. For the vine was one of the typical products of the agricultural life, and was even more closely identified with it than corn. Cereals can be grown by the semi-nomad, who may spend a few months from autumn to spring in a comparatively fertile spot, sowing and reaping his crop. But the vine takes some years of careful cultivation before it yields its fruit at all, and only those who have some prospect of an extended residence in the same spot will undertake its culture. The Nazirite stood for the old ways, and by his existence protested against the un-Israelite character of the settled life.

This feature is even more obvious when we look at the Rechabite. It is true that he first comes into prominence after the days of Ahab, but the story of the prophetic revolution makes it clear that the founder of the order, Jonadab ben Rechab, was a well-known figure in Israel ten years after the death of Ahab. Like the Nazirite he eschewed the use of all products of the vine ; his protest was not so much against drunkenness as against civilization. This is clear from the second outstanding feature of the class—their refusal to live in any house other than a movable tent. Here again we see the protest

[1] Cp. Amos ii. 11.

of the nomad against the farmer. The houses of the Eastern peasantry are often no more than mud and reeds, poor enough and flimsy enough to Western ideas, but they do at least indicate a permanent settlement on the land, for they cannot easily be taken down, transported, and erected elsewhere. To the mind of the Rechabite, the representative of the true Israel, the Aramaean nomad, must have no home on the land. His is essentially a life of movement, and he must be free to pull up his tent pegs and go elsewhere at the behest of his God. To both Nazirite and Rechabite the settlement of an agricultural community was in itself an act of apostasy, a surrender to the *Ba'als*. While it seems probable that both classes were small in numbers, their influence must have been considerable, and their presence and testimony served to form a nucleus of discontent which readily broke into more open and obvious action at the stimulus of the new conditions.

(iii) *Elijah.*—The various tendencies and feelings which made for a reversion to the older conception of Israel's religion found their medium of expression in Elijah. He is one of the most striking characters in the whole of the Old Testament, and his personality made such an impression on his own and subsequent generations that he became the typical prophet to the mind of later Israel. His figure, perhaps owing in part to the striking story of his disappearance, became almost an apocalyptic symbol, and the last of the great prophetic order definitely adopted his style. He stands out before us as a man of intense feeling, a child of his own time in his comparative indifference to the claims of compassion, but possessed by a courage and a fiery enthusiasm able to carry him through difficulties which might well have daunted a lesser man.

With these personal qualities it is important to note his political and religious position. He comes from the east of Jordan, from that part of the country which had never made agriculture its staple occupation, and he carried on in a very real sense the old traditions of early Israel. It is not a mere accident that men associated him in their minds with Moses ; it is possible to assert that there was a gap in the religious history of the people between these two great men. We may well feel that if Moses founded the religion of Israel, it was Elijah who first called the people effectively back to the ideals of his greater predecessor, and thus made possible that further advance which the next two centuries were to witness.

The protest of Elijah was a double one. The first element was moral and political, and manifested itself most strongly in the case of Naboth. The new ideas of the social order which Jezebel championed were inconsistent, not merely with Israelite political tradition, but also with the fundamental ethical principles of the old wilderness Yahwism. The judicial murder of the small farmer was not only a crime, it was a sin, a violation of the well-established laws of Yahweh. The religious authorities of the city community might lay the entire stress on ritual, and in this respect Melkart and the Ba'al-Yahweh of Bethel might be at one, but the true God of Israel, the 'El-Yahweh, held different ideals and made other demands on men. We may, indeed, say that Elijah was a forerunner of the great ethical prophets of the eighth and seventh centuries B.C.

It was with the worship of Melkart that these new and dangerous principles had entered the land, and Elijah fully realized that the real enemy of his people and of their faith was the Sidonian *Ba'al*. It was his task to convince men that Melkart had no standing in the land of Yahweh, and that for Israel the only valid form of worship was that of Israel's own God. The great trial scene on Mount Carmel will stand for all time as one of the most dramatic events in history.[1] There it was shown that, in spite of every advantage, the prophets of the *Ba'al* were unable to summon their god to their help. Elijah did not deny the existence of Melkart, or challenge his claims to adoration in Phœnicia, but he did insist and prove that his power did not extend to Israel. The sequel to the trial makes this yet clearer. The prophets of *Ba'al* were taken and slain—a cruel act, judged by modern standards, but quite

[1] While the narrative in 1 Kings xviii. may have been " embellished in later ages," we cannot doubt that it contains a historic kernel.

in accord with the spirit of the times. We shall make a
serious mistake if we imagine this to have been nothing
more than a piece of brutal vindictiveness. It is the
act which sets the seal on the verdict of the previous
scene. The prophet is sacrosanct, and any act of violence
done to him is bound to be resented and terribly avenged
by the god who is insulted in his person. The slaughter
of the prophets of *Ba'al* is a proclamation to the world,
uttered in compelling and overwhelmingly convincing
language, that *Ba'al* is helpless in the land of Yahweh ;
whatever his power may be in Phœnicia, in Israel his
writ does not run. By no other course of action could
Elijah possibly have brought home to the people the
utter helplessness of Melkart and the futility of offering
him worship. That was Elijah's task, and seldom has
such a duty been performed with more drastic thorough-
ness.

(iv) *The Prophetic Revolution.*—The temptation to a
national apostasy seems to have ceased, at any rate for a
time, with the slaughter of the prophets of *Ba'al*. But it is
most unlikely that Jezebel's own private establishment
suffered further attacks, and within Israel there still
remained the actual sanctuary of Melkart—and would
remain as long as the dynasty of Omri sat on the throne
of Samaria. The danger had been overcome for the
time, but it might recur, and the completion of Elijah's
work was left to other hands. It was finally accomplished
mainly by two men, Elisha, the follower and servant of
Elijah, and Jehu.

We possess a number of stories about Elisha, but they
have little or no bearing on the development of the religious life of Israel, since most of them record miracles
performed by him in one of the prophetic companies and
elsewhere. His importance for our present study lies
in the fact that he stood behind Jehu, and inspired him
to the act of usurpation which ended the rule of the house
of Omri. The new king was simply a tool in the hands
of the prophetic party, and he stood, like them, for the old
isolation of Israel from her nearer neighbours.

The story of the revolution is too familiar to need
extended comment. After the elimination of the royal

house, Jehu proceeded to destroy all traces of the cult of Melkart. The narrative shows that the worshippers of *Ba'al* were few in number, since they could all be crowded into a single building. This is strong testimony to the effectiveness of Elijah's work, for prior to this, and even in his day, it could be said that only seven thousand had not bowed the knee to *Ba'al* (1 Kings xix. 18). But by now the devotees of Melkart seem to have included little more than the official establishment of the Sidonian sanctuary maintained by the house of Omri in Samaria. To them may have been added Phœnician merchants and other temporary residents or visitors, but it is clear that the Israelite element in the group was negligible.

Once more we may, from our own standpoint, condemn in unmeasured terms the savagery and cruelty of the prophetic revolution. It did, indeed, call forth the strongest censure from Hosea a century later. But it did its work, and never again was the supremacy of Yahweh within His own land challenged, as far as we know. He had shown Himself to be supreme ; His rivals had been unable to prove their right to a place in His territory, and had been shown to be utterly powerless to vindicate themselves against the deadliest insult. It is true that Jehu's action meant a break with his immediate neighbours, and compelled him to seek for Assyrian protection. The Assyrians, no doubt, followed their usual practice and insisted on the establishment of some sort of ritual which typified their authority. But there was never any danger that Ashur would oust Yahweh from the affections or in the devotion of Israel ; the danger would naturally come only from her immediate neighbours. In tremendous language the enthusiasts of Yahweh had told the world that Israel must have no other gods before Him.

CHAPTER VII

THE RELIGION OF ISRAEL AFTER JEHU

WHILE the movement which first showed itself under Elijah, and found its completion in the prophetic revolution, settled once and for all the question as to whether any other god than Yahweh should hold sway in Israel, it made, as far as we can tell, comparatively little difference to the syncretistic religion of the country. Elijah raised no protest against the established sanctuaries, sacrifice continued to be offered as of old, and no objection was made to the veneration paid to the sacred bulls at Dan and Bethel. It was necessary first that the absolute devotion of Israel to Yahweh should be secured, before the manifestation of those unique features which distinguished the later Judaism could be made. It is even possible, though unlikely, that subordinate deities were admitted to a place alongside of Yahweh, for as late as the fifth century the Jewish colony at Elephantiné, far up the Nile, accepted other beings as well as Yahweh, though His pre-eminence was recognized.[1] But even if such a practice was admitted, it has been most carefully expunged from our records, and, save in the account of Josiah's purification of the Temple, we find no mention of a foreign cult in an Israelite shrine. Yet the old symbols remained, and the historian qualifies his approval of Jehu's actions with the note that he still continued to permit the existence of the local sanctuaries which the sterner law of later generations strongly condemned (2 Kings x. 29–31). But the way was now prepared, and the eighth century saw the rise of one of the most remarkable and important phenomena that has ever appeared in the history of man's dealings with God.

[1] See Cowley, *Aramaic Papyri of the Fifth Century B.C.* (1923), and *Jewish Documents of the Time of Ezra* (1919).

As we have already seen, we have in reality two Israels. On the one hand, the settled community to the west of Jordan had developed a form of worship and a theology suited to an agricultural life, and similar to those of other agricultural peoples. Their worship was little more than a continuation of the old *Ba'al*-worship, with the substitution of the name of Yahweh for those of the *Ba'als*. On the other hand, the purer, more primitive tradition, with its stress on ethics and its comparative indifference to ritual and especially to sacrifice, maintained itself in the east of Jordan and in the extreme south. There was thus ready to hand a source whence a fresh revival of the older faith might spring. Elijah had been a product of the former district, and, nearly a century after his time, there came from the south the first of the line of the canonical prophets, Amos.

We have very little direct information as to the condition of Israel in the period that elapsed between Jehu and Amos—roughly between 840 and 760 B.C. There are records in the book of *Kings*, but, except for the numerous stories of Elisha, these deal mainly with political events, and record little more than the successive kings of the two realms. But in the protests of the eighth-century prophets we can see what must have been the general character assumed by the religion of Israel during the period. We have an established priesthood, an elaborate ritual meticulously observed, a wealth of sacrifice, and an eschatology which taught that in His own time Yahweh would appear to take vengeance on the enemies of Israel and to set her up as supreme. At the same time religion had little or no moral content. Provided men paid their dues, offered their sacrifices, and observed their *taboos*, Yahweh would not interfere with their treatment one of another. Not only so, but religion was held to override the claims of the ordinary moral life. The common law of Israel, for instance, forbade a moneylender to keep during the night the garment taken in pledge.[1] The borrower must be allowed to have it back, for it was his one covering, and without it he was in danger of suffering severely from the cold. But if the creditor could claim

---

[1] Cp. Exod. xxii. 25–27: Amos ii. 8.

that he needed it for some ceremony in the temple—some form of " incubation," perhaps—he was under no obligation to return it.   Sexual irregularities [1] were at all times abhorrent to the true Hebrew genius, yet there is evidence which shows that ritual fornication was a regular practice at the sanctuaries.   This was the general condition with which men like Amos and Isaiah were faced, and it corresponds so closely with what we know from other sources of the religion of the nearer East that we can hardly doubt that the conditions were those inherited from the old *Ba'alism*, and generally retained throughout the period of the monarchy.

[1] These, of course, do not include polygamy or concubinage, which were regarded as legitimate.

CHAPTER VIII

THE CANONICAL PROPHETS

PROPHETS—*Nebi'im*—were, of course, a familiar feature of the life of Israel. The ecstatics, either in companies or singly, were a well-recognized class, and were accepted as men inspired by Yahweh. It did not follow that what they said was true. Men had not yet learnt to think of Yahweh as moral, and they believed that, in order to entrap to their ruin men whom He would destroy, He might inspire His prophets to utter falsehood. The best known illustration is that of the lying spirit seen in Micaiah's vision, who entered into the prophets of Ahab to induce him to go up against Ramoth Gilead where he would fall (1 Kings xxii. 19–23). Hebrew had even a technical term for such a divine deceit mediated through a prophet, and though the theory underwent certain slight changes, it remained at least till the time of Ezekiel.

(i) *The Nebi'im and the Canonical Prophets.*—The prophets of Ahab were accustomed to deliver a popular message, or at least one which should be satisfactory to their king. But those whose words are recorded for us in the Bible were men of another stamp. They were actuated by a passion for Yahweh no less than their contemporaries, but their thought went deeper, and they conceived of Yahweh in terms very different from those which would have been employed by the earlier *Nebi'im*. Yet to outward appearance there seemed to be no essential difference between the two classes. It is now generally agreed that the canonical prophets were ecstatic, though the extent to which they were subject to this condition is still disputed. There are those who hold that every utterance found its occasion, its form, and its authentication, in an access of the ecstasy, while others believe that while the prophet must have had at least one such

experience at the beginning of his ministry, his later
utterances were consciously composed and delivered in
a normal state of mind.   But, since in abnormal psycho-
logical states it is a man's real nature and opinions that
are expressed, it makes little or no difference whether and
to what extent men like Hosea and Micah were ecstatic;
in any case, they believed profoundly in the truth of what
they said, and they were impelled to speak by their own
intense convictions.[1]

(ii) *The Teaching of the Prophets*.—The result of their
thinking and of their strong convictions was that the
prophets of Israel offered men a new doctrine.   They
varied, of course, among themselves, and each had his
own clearly marked individuality and message.   Yet
the differences depend rather on stress than on any real
variation of opinion as between them.   All were alike
in certain broad outlines of truth, and in these they
differed from their contemporaries, and, indeed, from
practically all other religious teachers.   Outside Israel
the tendency has always been for the man interested in
morals to turn away from religion, believing (and a study
of the world's religions gives him some justification)
that it had no ethical value, and might even be opposed
to the human conscience.   If Israel had had nothing
better to offer the world than the syncretistic worship of
Bethel, then she would have disappeared and her name
would almost have perished—and rightly so.   Any impulse in favour of moral reform would have found
itself opposed to established religion, and the ethical
teachers of Israel would have been compelled, as were
Siddhartha, Euripides, Lucretius, and perhaps Confucius,
to choose between religion and goodness, between God and
righteousness.   The supreme place which must be
ascribed to the Israelite prophets is due to the fact that
they dared to identify God with the good, and asserted
that His character was at least as high as that of man.
It was here that the ancient tradition of nomadic Israel
had its effect.   In early days Yahweh had been the
guardian of the simple ethic of the wandering tribe,
and the prophets insisted that He would retain this

----

[1] See the present writer's *Prophecy and the Prophets*, pp. 44 f.

function, and apply to the far more complicated life of the settled agricultural community those moral and social principles which, on the more elementary plane, had commended themselves alike to the religious instinct and to the conscience of man. The two social orders existed side by side, and, perhaps, men were hardly conscious of the division. Israel was one in religion and possessed a common inheritance, for her traditions traced all the tribes back to a common stock, and though the actual blood of the Palestinians may have been very mixed, the tradition which survived was wholly derived from the Aramaean element. While we must not in any way detract from the moral and religious greatness of the canonical prophets, we cannot blind ourselves to the circumstances which facilitated their unique contribution to human thought about God.

There are certain features in the teaching of the prophets common to them all, of which the most important must be enumerated.

(a) In the first place, the prophets saw *Yahweh as Law*. The normal oriental conception of deity is of beings who are extraordinarily powerful but are almost wholly capricious. The attitude is best represented for us in Islam, and it is impossible to read the *Qur'an* without feeling that in his anxiety to maintain the omnipotence of God, Muhammad was in some danger of depreciating His moral character. We get the impression of a benevolent despot whose will is absolute and above any challenge. There are no standards by which to judge Him, for He recognizes none save His own imperial will. His actions are arbitrary, uncontrolled by any principle, and unchecked by any external power. Such a view is far below that of Amos and his successors. Though they do not use the term, they might have described Yahweh as omnipotent, but they would have said that omnipotence was limited by self-consistency. It was possible to know what Yahweh would do, for He could not be false to Himself. His will might be absolute, but it was reliable ; He did not change, and what was good in His sight to-day would not appear evil to-morrow. He was not a man that He should repent, and His treatment of

His subjects was invariable.   If a man or a nation sow
the wind it must reap the whirlwind, for no other crop
could spring from such a seed except through the violation
of the law of consistency.

It is true that this doctrine is never expressed in so
many words, but we must remember that the ancient
Semite thought in other categories than ours.   Yet it
is always present, and forms a very real basis for all that
these men had to say.   They could predict the divine
action in the sphere of personality because they knew
Yahweh, just as a scientist can predict the behaviour of
the bodies and substances with which he deals if he is
sufficiently acquainted with the principles that govern
their reactions.   The prophets were in this sense spiritual
scientists ; their study was, however, not the structure of
the physical world, but the nature of God and man, and
the principles on which the interaction of the two was
based.   Knowing Yahweh, they knew what He would
do in any given set of circumstances, for they saw Him
as Law.

(b) Further, the prophets saw Yahweh as the *Lord of
Nature*.   Here they were fully in accord with the popular
belief of Israel.   From the first Yahweh had appeared
to men as a deity who had some connexion with the
weather, and was especially a mountain God.   But by
the middle of the eighth century, probably much earlier,
the belief in Yahweh as the Master of the physical
universe had greatly developed.   Over the whole of the
civilization of Western Asia, men told a story, a myth,
of the creation of the earth and the heavens.   It tells of
war between the gods, in which the good gods are
threatened with destruction by the powers of evil,
personified as Chaos.   From this danger they are rescued
by the prowess of one of their number, who defeats
and either slays or imprisons the enemy, then proceeding to form the material universe, including mankind.
In forms of the myth in which Chaos is destroyed, the
world is fashioned from parts of her body ; in other
types of the story it is made in different ways.[1]

One important feature of this creation-myth is that

[1] See Ball, *op. cit.*, pp. 2 ff., and *Myth and Ritual*, ed. S. H. Hooke
(1933).

every race was liable to accept it in outline, and to make its own god the hero.   Thus, in the earliest form known to us, it is the Sumerian god Enlil who destroys Chaos ; in the most familiar form, the Babylonian, it is the god of Babylon, Marduk ; in Assyria the story was told with Ashur playing the chief *rôle*.   We have no reason to doubt that a similar myth was current in Palestine long before the Israelite invasion, and that it was adopted by the new-comers.   It is true that the narrative in Gen. i. (the other creation story, that of Gen. ii., seems to have an independent origin) contains only the faintest hints of connexion with the widespread belief, but there are occasional references, especially in the *Psalms* and in the book of *Job*, which make it clear that such a story was current in Israel, though it was not formally adopted by the theologians, and that the Hebrew form of the myth claimed Yahweh as the Creator-hero.

Along with creation went also control, and the prophets, like all other Israelites, held Yahweh to be the Master of all natural phenomena.   Palestine is a country which is almost entirely dependent on the rain for its fertility, and it is Yahweh alone who can give or withhold it.[1] He also controls the pests of the farmer's life, the swarms of locusts, and the more insignificant parasites which bring destruction on the crops.   Israel is threatened with these as a punishment for her sins, a method which looks arbitrary, but is, nevertheless, subject to rigid moral laws, for the ethical and the physical are not sharply divided from one another.   On the other hand, if Israel is faithful, and obeys the commands of Yahweh, crops will be abundant, for it is He and no other who is the giver of all the products of the cultivated land.   Nothing happens in nature, great or small, except by His will, and that will follow the definite laws of Yahweh's own self-consistent being.

(c) Yahweh is *Lord of History*.—It is not only the world of physical nature but also the world of human relations which is under His complete control.   The polytheist has in all ages represented the struggles of man as bound

[1] For stress on this point, especially in comparison with Egyptian life, cp. Deut. xi. 10–12.

up with the gods' jealousy of one another, and has thought of them as fighting on different sides. Even the monola-trous Semite thought of war as a conflict between national gods as well as between national armies, and it is interesting to find that while Israel was compelled to admit disastrous defeat at the hands of the Philistines, she was careful to add that this did not mean the defeat of her God. On the contrary it gave Him an opportunity of showing His superiority to the gods of the Philistines, insomuch that the people were only too glad to be rid of their divine captive (1 Sam. vi. 1 ff.).

But the peculiar claim of the Hebrew prophet is that Yahweh is concerned to control not merely the fortunes of his own people but the destinies of all nations. The Assyrians may believe that it is by their own military prowess that they have conquered the world ; Isaiah knows better, and sees that Assyria is but the rod of the anger of Yahweh. She is an instrument in His hand, and has been used by Him to vindicate on His own people and elsewhere His own laws and character. As soon as Assyria loses sight of this fact, and claims to have achieved her triumphs purely in her own strength, she in turn will fall. As long as she can be useful to Yahweh she stands, but when her task is done she can be discarded and destroyed (Isa. x. 5–19). Even the great racial migrations are the work of Yahweh : He has brought Israel out of Egypt—that is natural, but He also brought the Philistines from their early home, and the Syrians from Kir (Amos ix. 7).

Within the nation itself, of course, Yahweh's power is absolute. But it is always governed by principles. There are certain types of polity and particular modes of treatment which must inevitably lead to disaster. A social and political order, on the other hand, which gives free play to the rights and privileges of personality will bring safety and prosperity with it. Though the agents of reward and punishment may be foreign powers, they are all controlled by Yahweh, and history is neither the result of the conflict between divine whims nor the outcome of human ambition ; it is the development of a single great purpose.

(d) Yahweh is *Lord of the End of Things*.—It is by no means easy to define the marches between eschatology and prophecy, for the same essential doctrines, the lordship of Yahweh over nature and over history, are involved in both. Perhaps the nearest approach we can make to a distinction is to suggest that in prophecy in the narrower sense Yahweh brings about the end in what we may call normal ways, i.e. through events which are of a familiar type, though their particular manifestation may be abnormally powerful. In eschatology, on the other hand, that which ends the age is not normal, and the events predicted are altogether outside human experience in the past. Eschatology is much older than the canonical prophets, and they found it necessary to correct men's ideas on the subject (Amos v. 18–20), but they insisted with equal stress that Yahweh could and would make an end of things. Indeed, an eschatology is an inevitable corollary of a doctrine of creation, for as soon as men have made up their minds as to how the world began, they will begin to speculate on how it must end.

The great prophets of Israel certainly shared with their predecessors and with their contemporaries the belief that Yahweh would interfere to put an end to the existing order. To some extent their views were eschatological in the strictest sense of the term, and there are passages which suggest that they looked forward to the great day when the heaven should fall and the earth be shattered, that a new world might be born from the ruins of the old. But there was a fundamental difference between the two points of view. The popular eschatology was political and national, while the prophetic was primarily ethical and religious. The people in general held to the doctrine that when matters reached their worst, when Israel was overwhelmed and oppressed by her enemies and was at the very last gasp, the great Day of Yahweh would suddenly dawn, Israel's God would appear in all His splendour and His might, to destroy the old universe of men and things and create a new one in which Israel and Yahweh should have sole pre-eminence. It was a part of the prophetic message to insist on the fundamental mistake of this view. Amos and his successors did not deny the coming of the Day of Yahweh, but for Israel it would be a day of darkness, rayless gloom, not a day of light and glory. For when Yahweh came it would not be to avenge His people on their foes, it would be to vindicate His own moral character by taking a final vengeance on His own people for their apostasy and immorality ; it would mean the ruin of Israel, not her salvation. He who had revealed His Law in Nature and in History, in the beginning of things and in the progress of events, would still more terribly show Himself in the End, when all that neglected or resisted His will should be made to cease from being.

(e) Yahweh is *Lord of Universal Morality.*—The prophetic doctrine was sufficiently novel and significant in that it proclaimed the supreme place given to the moral element in Yahweh's demands on His own people. But it did not cease there. He was concerned to note the behaviour of other nations as well as that of Israel. Wherever wrong, moral wrong, was done, whether it be to Israel or by Israel or by another people to a third, it was a violation of the Law of Yahweh, a contradiction of His glorious will, and must meet with His punishment. It is true that the geographical and political horizon of Israel in the eighth and seventh centuries was limited, and embraced few peoples outside the immediate environs of Palestine, but the principle was of universal application. Wherever cruelty and injustice were found, there Yahweh sat in judgement, and sooner or later His vengeance would fall. Amos condemns Damascus, Philistia, Phœnicia, Edom, and Ammon for injuries inflicted on Israelites (Amos i. 3–15). Any Hebrew patriot would have endorsed the prophet's denunciations. But few would have shared in the indignation Amos expressed at the atrocities perpetrated by Moab on Edom, or have recognized that the God of Israel was interested in the relations between these two peoples (Amos ii. 1–3). Yet such a doctrine is the logical and necessary deduction from the prophetic premises. Yahweh is a moral being, and He is supreme over all races and lands, hence it follows as a matter of course that He must take their general behaviour into consideration and call them to account. It is true that He will not be so strict with those whom He has not " known " (cp. Amos. iii. 1, 2), but they are morally responsible to their own conscience, and since no other deity in the world takes cognizance of their conduct from an ethical standpoint, He will take matters into His own hands and vindicate His claim.

(*f*) *Yahweh makes no ritual demands.*—It is, perhaps, here that we see more clearly than anywhere else the inheritance of the pastoral religion. The syncretistic cultus of the Ba'al-Yahweh was largely based on sacrifice, and its performance was inconceivable apart from the great sanctuaries. It was held that His delight was in the offerings that were made to Him, and that His vengeance would fall most surely on the man who neglected to pay due homage at His shrine. This was fully in line with the accepted beliefs of most religions in the ancient world, and has not altogether faded even in modern times. But the pre-exilic prophets with one voice declare that it is not thus that Israel can win the favour of her God. Some go so far as to deny categorically that sacrifice was ordained at all in the nomadic period, and they seek to revert to the principles and practices of those early days. All are agreed that Yahweh does not want these things, that He is sated with the blood of bulls and goats, that the music of the assemblies is obnoxious to Him, and that He will have no respect to the offerings that people make (cp. Amos v. 21–23). We need not assume that all the prophets thought that animal sacrifice was positively wicked ; probably they might have acquiesced in its practice, if they had not found that men were offering ceremonial worship as a substitute for those spiritual and moral qualities on which the demands of Yahweh really centred. The slaughter of the victims in a religion which requires sacrifice is, as already pointed out, a disgusting business from the æsthetic point of view, but we cannot assume that the ancient prophets were actuated by considerations of this kind. Their objection was rather that it served as a moral opiate, and dulled the consciences of men to the reality of true spiritual values. It has been the practical experience of the noblest spirits in all sacrificial religions that the blood of animals can never take away sin, perhaps because such persons feel that sin is more than a matter of ritual and can therefore never be met by mere ceremonial.

To the ordinary Israelite sin was a neglect of ritual regulations ; to the prophets it was a violation of the moral law. The two were in spheres between which there was no point of contact, and there could be no valid connexion between them. It followed that no ritual within the area of sacrifice could possibly atone for sins committed in the region of morality. A piece of ceremonial might put the worshipper right with a god whose ceremonial demands he had neglected, but it could not possibly affect a relation between man and God which was based on morality. The atonement must be moral, and even the costliest of sacrifices was utterly futile in the effort to recover the favour of Yahweh. The God of Israel, alone among the deities worshipped by men, made no ritual demands ; to Him sacrifice was always a weariness, and, when substituted for morality, an abomination (cp. Isa. i. 11–15).

CHAPTER IX

THE EIGHTH CENTURY PROPHETS

IT was the eighth century which witnessed the last revival of the Assyrian empire, and between 750 and 650 the power of Nineveh reached its zenith. Never before had the authority of the Assyrian king spread so far; his conquests in the west began with the subjugation of Damascus in 734 and did not cease till the end of the century, when his armies had penetrated to the very borders of Egypt. The conquest of that country was the final goal on which the Assyrian kings fixed their eyes, but this was not achieved till well on in the seventh century, and even then was neither complete nor permanent. But the little states, including the two Hebrew kingdoms which lay on or near the route, were thoroughly subdued; Samaria was taken and the northern kingdom brought to an end, while the southern kingdom became a vassal of Nineveh. When Hezekiah, at the very end of the century, allowed himself to be drawn into the general rising of Assyrian subjects which took place with the accession of Sennacherib, the land was overrun and plundered, Jerusalem besieged, though not taken, and the country so thoroughly cowed that it never again revolted against the Assyrian king.

In Palestine itself the social and religious declines which had their origin in the foreign influence of Jezebel had reached the point of maximum danger. In 760 Assyria was still suffering from the temporary eclipse which ended with the accession of Tiglath-pileser III in 745, and under Jeroboam II northern Israel had attained a prosperity which the country had never enjoyed since the days of Solomon. Military victory had restored the old ideal borders to the land, while successful trade poured wealth into the country. But the tendency was for power of all kinds to be concentrated in the hands of the few, and the poor grew poorer yet. In particular a complete social and economic change had passed over the country. The old type of small peasant farmer, the independent crofter, represented by Naboth in the ninth century, had practically disappeared, and the land was now divided up into large estates, worked chiefly by serf or even slave labour. Such a condition is perilous in the extreme, for if the lower classes have not manliness enough to rise against their oppressors they will no longer have the strength to resist the encroachments of foreign enemies. In any case the country is doomed. If we would understand the prophets of the eighth century, we must see them against this double background of rotting social order, and of the advancing Assyrian power.

The prophets whose activity is to be placed in this period are four : Amos (c. 760) ; Hosea, a generation later ; Isaiah, whose ministry covered approximately forty years (740–701), and Micah, who was a contemporary of Isaiah. The work of the first two lay wholly in the northern kingdom, while Isaiah had something to say about Samaria as well as about Jerusalem. Micah had little to contribute to the development of Hebrew religion ; his attitude and teaching were those of Amos, though with a deeper bitterness, since he himself was among those who suffered from the evils he denounced. But each of the other three has his own stress, and merits special attention.

(i) *Amos.*—Like Elijah, Amos was a foreigner to the agricultural community of central and northern Palestine. His home was in the far south, in the neighbourhood of Tekoa, and he was brought up among the shepherd community, adding to his livelihood what he could earn by tending a species of coarse fig. Such a man could enter the community of Samaria and Bethel with a complete detachment. He was in no way implicated in the evils of the social order, and he spoke as one who need not share in the doom he pronounced. An Amos could see with great clearness the sins that were rife about him, and could form an estimate of the moral and religious condition of Israel on the basis of the purer life and faith of the semi-pastoral south.

All that has been said of the teaching of the prophets in general was true of Amos. He saw Yahweh as Law, and so as the God of Nature, of History, of universal morality, while he insisted that Yahweh had never demanded sacrifice and did not want it. Among other evils he denounced the utter lack of any real moral quality in the worship of Bethel, and condemned the immoralities and illegalities not merely overlooked but actively countenanced in the Israelite cultus. He proclaimed a " Day of Yahweh," which should mean the ruin of the evil-doers in Israel, and deplored the failure of the people to take warning by the calamities which had befallen them, and should have recalled them to a sense of the real demands of Yahweh.

The point, however, on which Amos fastened with clearest insight was the unfair dealing of man with man. He found the trader, while meticulously observing the regulation abstention from business on the Sabbath, planning how he could on the morrow cheat his customers in every possible way. Still more terrible was the mal-administration of justice. This is a standing social evil in the East, but it seems to have reached its height in eighth century Israel. The smallest bribe offered by an influential person was sufficient to win a case, and it seems probable that the economic change already mentioned had been brought about in part by the illicit use of the processes of law. The precedent set by Jezebel had been only too freely followed, and men had lost their freedom through the decisions given against them by corrupt judges. It was enough, says Amos with bitter scorn, to give the judge a pair of shoes, and the defendant would be handed over as a slave—they sell the poor for a pair of shoes (ii. 6).

Hence the supreme demand of Amos is for fair dealing as between man and man. Justice, equity, honesty (v. 24) —these are the qualities which Yahweh demands of Israel. There is hope, but not much, of a reform which will lead to safety. But, if Israel will not seek Yahweh, abandoning the vain quest at the sanctuaries, and will not look for Him in righteous act, her doom is certain. There are those who hold that Amos could already see

the Assyrian threat in the distance, though he does not
expressly mention it, but whether he realized the means
that would be used or not is a matter of small importance.
He knew Yahweh, and he knew the state of Israel ; he
knew, then, that destruction was the only possible issue
(cp., e.g., vii. 9).

(ii) *Hosea*.—Hosea offers in many ways a strong
contrast to Amos. His work is probably to be dated some
twenty years after the time of his predecessor, for there
are signs of the collapse of the monarchy through frequent
revolution (cp., e.g., viii. 4, xiii. 10, 11). He is a native of
the north, and cannot contemplate the sins of his people
with any abstraction or detachment. He is that truest
of patriots, the man who identifies himself with his
country, feels her calamities as though they were his own,
and repents with bitter tears for her sins as if he had
himself committed them. He is a man of intense passions,
feeling strongly, yet thinking clearly, and his very style
breathes his whole fervent nature.

We cannot think of Hosea apart from the tragedy of
his marriage, told to us by the historian in the first
chapter of the book that bears his name, and by himself
in chapter three. It was from the agony of his own
experience that he learnt his lesson and received his
message. If he could so love a woman who was probably
from the first unworthy, and certainly showed herself
faithless, how much greater would be the love of Yahweh
for His people !

The sexual metaphor as an expression of the relation
between the worshipper and the object of his worship
was only too common in the ancient East. In Hosea
it was purified and ennobled, being delivered from
the grosser elements which have thrown so black a
shadow on much of the religious life of the agricultural
world. It seemed to him that Yahweh's attitude to
Israel was that of a loving husband to his wife. Sin was
the rejection of that love, the surrender to another of
something most precious which belonged to the great
Lover alone. On Israel Yahweh had lavished every sign
of His tender affection, yet when she had given thanks for
the benefits she had received, her gratitude had been paid,

not to Yahweh but to the *Ba'als*. It may be that they were still freely worshipped in Israel, but it seems more likely, in view of the history of Israel's religion, that Hosea penetrated the thin disguise of the name, and saw that the syncretistic cult of Yahweh was in reality only *Ba'al* worship, realizing that men must get away from the ritual and from the official sanctuary if they would truly win the favour of Yahweh. This view is supported by the fact that Hosea is the first to condemn explicitly the bull-cult of Bethel.

Of course, Hosea had much more to say than this. He felt the iniquities of Israel much as Amos had felt them, and would equally have demanded fair dealing. The marriage metaphor is not the only one he uses to express the ideal relation between Yahweh and His people ; and the picture of the father teaching the infant feet to walk is one of the most touching and most tender in our Bibles (xi. 1–4). He condemns the politics of Israel as Amos does not, and denounces the appeal to Assyria (does this point to the reign of Menahem ?) as an act of apostasy (viii. 9–11). Israel is Yahweh's and Yahweh is Israel's ; let that be enough. She has nothing to do with any foreign power, whether of gods or of men. And Yahweh's supreme demand to his mind is for a quality expressed in the Hebrew word *chesed*, quite untranslateable in English. It means love, but more than love, for it is not merely an attitude adopted by one person to another, but that essential quality of the soul from which love, sympathy, pity, devotion, all spring. It may produce an attitude of the inferior to the superior, of man to God. It may imply the attitude of the superior to the inferior, of God to man. Or, again, it may be the attitude of equals to one another, of man to man. In any case it implies a full appreciation of and a complete devotion to a personality.

Hosea thus goes deeper than Amos. Where the latter lays the stress on the external conduct, the former searches the inner springs of action. It is not enough to demand of men that they should behave themselves : they must have that deep within them which will compel them to upright and loving conduct. It is this which Yahweh

Himself has exhibited in His dealings with Israel, and she can fulfil His demands only by giving Him her answering love. But, as things were, there was little or no hope. It was better for Israel to perish than to continue as she was, and Hosea attributed to Yahweh a love which could even destroy, though at appalling cost to Himself.

(iii) *Isaiah.*—Isaiah stands in a position different both from that of Amos and from that of Hosea. Whilst Samaria was included in the range of his prophecies, until the fall of the northern kingdom, Isaiah lived and did his main work in Jerusalem. He seems, according to tradition, to have played a more prominent part in the political life of his time than did either of his predecessors. We hear of his facing Ahaz directly, and giving advice and comfort to Hezekiah, while he constantly maintained the inviolability of Jerusalem against the Assyrians. He has been classed among the great statesmen of the ancient East, but though his conclusions and policy were thoroughly statesmanlike, the grounds on which he based them were religious rather than political. It is impossible here to give even an outline of the chief elements in his teaching ; we must be content to call attention to the aspect of religion which is most prominent of all in him.

The great contribution of Isaiah to the developing picture of Yahweh and Yahwism was his insistence on the *holiness* of Yahweh. This was by no means a new idea, for the conception of holiness in one form or another is necessarily almost as old as religion itself. As applied to human affairs it indicates a separation from the ordinary and the secular, a thing set apart for the sole use and enjoyment of the deity. But with Isaiah this conception had gained a moral content too often wanting elsewhere. Since Yahweh was supremely good, it followed that any thing or person set apart for Him must also be good, and the nation especially consecrated to Him must justify its position by a high moral standard. Isaiah addressed himself to much the same evils in Judah as Amos found it necessary to denounce in the north, but his stress was rather different.

It is characteristic of the teaching of Isaiah that he not only thought of Israel as being holy to Yahweh, but conceived of Yahweh as being holy to Israel. That is to say, the consecration and concentration were mutual. Israel could not dispense with Yahweh, but it was equally true that Yahweh needed Israel for His self-expression. Israel was His people, therefore He could not suffer her to be destroyed ; Jerusalem was the spot in which He had chosen to set His name, therefore the city could not be entered by a foreign enemy.

Yet the sin of Israel must meet with punishment, and Isaiah saw clearly enough that foreign invasion must come. But this did not mean, as it meant to Hosea, a destruction practically complete. However much Judah suffered for her sins, there must always be a remnant, who should be ready to start a new life in a better community and a more perfect order. At its head would be a king who should be the ideal of human monarchy, the perfect ruler. It is with Isaiah that we find the beginning of that conception which later ripened into a full Messianic doctrine, and we shall not greatly err if we trace it back to the prophet's conception of the mutual holiness of Yahweh and Israel.

(iv) *Hezekiah's Reforms.*—In 2 Kings xviii. 4–6 we have an appreciation of Hezekiah, largely from the pen of the editor of the book, which speaks of him as the most perfect king who ever sat on the throne of Judah, with the one exception of David. This is based, as it seems, on a reform which he carried through, destroying the local sanctuaries or "high places," those old seats of Ba'al-cults but imperfectly turned to the service of Yahweh, and breaking in pieces the bronze serpent which tradition carried back to the days of Moses.

We know also that on the death of Sargon in 705, Hezekiah and the other western princes joined in the general revolt against Sennacherib engineered by Marduk-apal-iddina (the Biblical Merodach-baladan), king of Babylon. One element in the revolt was almost certainly the elimination of the Assyrian cult imposed by Tiglath-pileser on Ahaz in 734, and the removal of the "pillars" and "asherim" probably included the destruction of a symbol of the supremacy of Assyria. Further, in the few details which are given to us, we seem to have an

14

adumbration of the reforms carried out nearly a century later by Josiah. Is it possible that the account is in some measure a reflexion back into the eighth century of events which were properly confined to the seventh ? The historian or compiler of the books of *Kings* wrote under the stress of the influence of Josiah's reform and the principle of the centralization of sacrifice which was its outstanding feature. Hezekiah's interest in the national worship, and his undoubted attempt to introduce a purer form of it than had been current, may well have led this writer or school to believe that he must have gone farther than he actually did, and to ascribe to him a measure which was not taken, as a matter of fact, for three-quarters of a century after his time. In any case, even if the record in 2 Kings xviii. be historically accurate, no permanent effect was produced by the reforms, for Hezekiah's son and successor, Manasseh, reverted to the old ways, and re-established the local sanctuaries. That there was some purification of the worship of Israel we need not doubt, and we may be sure that it had its influence in preparing the way for yet more complete reformation.

CHAPTER X

THE REFORMS OF JOSIAH

THE long reign of Manasseh, extending, according to 2 Kings xxi. 1 for fifty-five years, i.e. from 696 to 641 B.C., was held by later Israel to be the worst period in the religious life of Judah. All that which Hezekiah had achieved was undone, the successors of Isaiah, if they attempted any public work, were suppressed—tradition even tells us that in this reign Isaiah himself was put to death by being sawn asunder [1]—and Jerusalem was deluged with innocent blood ; human sacrifice was offered, and various forms of necromancy were resorted to—an act of apostasy, since the spirits of the dead were illegitimate objects of worship. At the same time, Manasseh remained a faithful vassal of the court of Nineveh ; and, save for a late tradition in *Chronicles* (2 Chron. xxxiii. 11), we hear no more of Assyrian invasion. The period was one of comparative prosperity, which remained undisturbed until the break-up of the Assyrian empire and the brief recrudescence of Egypt at the end of the seventh century. It seemed as if the work of the prophets, especially of Isaiah, had been undone, and his threats remained unfulfilled except in the ravaging of the land by Sennacherib in 701.

(i) *The Reform.*—In the reign of the grandson of Manasseh, Josiah, there came a change. The old Assyrian empire was crumbling, the last of her great kings, Ashurbanipal, died in 626, and the shock of the Scythian invasions prevented her from recovering herself in time to resist the combined forces of the Babylonians and Medes. In 621 Josiah undertook repairs to the

---

[1] In the apocalyptic book, called *The Ascension of Isaiah*, v ; the earliest portion of this composite work belongs to the first half of the first century A.D.

Temple, which, presumably, had been neglected during his minority. In the course of the work a book was found claiming to be the law of Moses, laying down prescriptions for the establishment of a single sanctuary where sacrifice and tithes might be offered. On the basis of this law a thorough reform was undertaken throughout the whole land. First the Temple itself was purified, and the motley collection of strange cults, gathered from almost every known people, was flung out and destroyed. Then the king and his emissaries toured the whole country, destroying the local sanctuaries, and paying particular attention to that which still existed at Bethel. Henceforward the great altar at Jerusalem was the one spot on which sacrifice could be legitimately offered to Yahweh.

We may suspect that, as in the case of Hezekiah, the reform had a political aspect, and was to be regarded as a gesture of independence. Certainly thirteen years later Josiah lost his life at the hands of the supporter and friend of the falling Assyrian power, Necho, king of Egypt. Yet we need not suspect Josiah's motives, and we shall find it difficult to overestimate the importance of the step which he took. On the one hand, it may be regarded as the completion in a practical way of the work begun by Elijah. Whatever the Ba'alistic associations of the local sanctuaries may have been, Jerusalem was now, at least, free from them, and there was no other place where they could be revived. Moreover, the concentration of sacrifice in one place made it essential that the piety of Israel should find some other means of expression. It is true that it was not till after the Exile that this result manifested itself, but in the end it led to the establishment and growth of the worship of the synagogue, a cultus which required neither priest nor altar nor temple, and which has therefore survived to the present day in spite of all the vicissitudes that the people of Israel have suffered, and in spite of the fact that they have had no place of sacrifice for eighteen hundred and fifty years, and no independent native government in a land of their own for twenty-five centuries.

(ii) *Deuteronomy*.—It is usual to identify the Book of the Law found by Hilkiah in the Temple with *Deuteronomy* or with an original draft of that book. The position has been challenged in recent years, one or two scholars seeking to place it later than the exile, others carrying it back to the early monarchy. Neither position, however, has yet found general support, and what Dr. Welch calls the " regnant hypothesis " still holds the field for practical purposes.

Deuteronomy is an expanded edition of the so-called " Book of the Covenant " (Exod. xxi.–xxiii.), rewritten from a nobler and more humane standpoint, and containing a great deal of material not found in the earlier code. It has been provided, possibly by later hands, with hortatory introduction and conclusion, and it is possible that in its pre-exilic form it was a good deal shorter than it is to-day. But its outstanding characteristic is its tone, which is strongly reminiscent of the outlook of the eighth century prophets. It is generally held to be a compromise between the ideals of Hosea and Isaiah and the priestly establishment, an attempt to attain the moral aims of the prophets without abandoning the institution of sacrifice and all that it implied. If this be so, then it holds a very important place in the religious history of Israel, as an effort to translate into terms of practical life the ideals which the eighth century prophets held before their people, and it has made the civil and ecclesiastical law of Israel unique. Nowhere else do we find the humanitarian atmosphere, the care for the weak and the helpless, the consideration shown to those who are unable to defend themselves—aliens, women and slaves, the constant demand for love with and behind the ritual, the stress on motive and character rather than on actual deeds ; and it is not surprising that men have believed it to have been compiled by the prophetic school, driven underground by persecution, and preserved till a better day should dawn.

But there is another aspect of the case. Whether or not *Deuteronomy* was the book found by Hilkiah, some book was found, and that book was immediately accepted as having divine authority. Hitherto the will of Yahweh had been made known through His chosen instruments, priests or prophets ; now Israel began to feel that this was unnecessary. Jeremiah attests the reverence that was paid to this or some other code, and insists that, in the form in which it was made known among the people, it was largely the work of the priests. He was faced with disbelief and rejection. Men said that they now had the will of Yahweh before them in black and white, and had no more need of prophet and priest to interpret it.[1]

In this feeling there was much truth. For neither priest nor prophet was to endure indefinitely, and it was well for Israel in later days that she had some spiritual support so concrete and indestructible as a book. The influence of the idea of revelation through literature has been incalculable, and, as far as we know, the eighteenth year of the reign of Josiah was the first occasion on which the conception emerged in human religion. For the first time we have *Scripture*, and though there is much in the Old Testament which is certainly earlier than the end of the seventh century, it was only after the acceptance of *Deuteronomy* that the rest took similar rank. It is with Josiah's book that the history of the Bible begins.

Finally, the importance of *Deuteronomy*—or at least of the book which was responsible for the centralization of worship—is to be seen in its effect on other portions of the Old Testament. There grew up a school, which seems to have been most active during and after the Exile, which collected, transcribed, and " edited " the traditions, laws, and history of Israel. The men who were chiefly responsible for this work wrote in the spirit of *Deuteronomy*. Their judgement was framed on its provisions, and they saw all history in its light. In the book of *Kings*, for instance, which is one of their compilations, every monarch of Israel and Judah is either commended or condemned, and the ground on which sentence is recorded is his adherence to or his neglect of the law of the central sanctuary. It is sometimes a little difficult for

[1] Jer. viii. 8.

us to allow for the Deuteronomic element in reading our Old Testament, but the fact is unmistakeable. The reforms of Josiah had an effect reaching far beyond their own day, and one of the most fruitful results of the teaching of the eighth century prophets was the construction and appearance of this great Book of the Law.

CHAPTER XI

THE SEVENTH CENTURY PROPHETS

THE last forty years during which the kingdom of Judah existed form one of the great critical epochs in history. The ancient kingdom of Assyria came to a violent end, not merely losing its imperial authority, but ceasing for ever to exist as an independent entity. Its capital, the great and famous Nineveh, was left a heap of blackened ruins, whose very site was forgotten for two and a half millennia. For nine centuries the supremacy of the civilized world had lain between the great empire on the Tigris and that which lay along the Nile. The power of the latter had steadily weakened, but there was always the hope of a revival until the final defeat of Necho at Carchemish in 605. Egypt never again stood in a position to make a bid for the hegemony of the world. Babylon, for many a century a nominal vassal of Assyria, achieved under the new Chaldean dynasty both freedom and empire, and the ninety years which followed the accession of Nabo-polassar were the most brilliant in her whole history. Judah, crushed between the two great world-powers, saw her Temple destroyed, her capital laid in ruins, the best elements in her population deported, and her independence so completely eclipsed that it has never since been restored.

Excluding Ezekiel, whose work lay entirely in Babylonia,[1] though he was born in Jerusalem and may have performed the functions of the priesthood at the old Temple, there are four of our canonical prophets whose activity is to be placed in the last forty years of the kingdom of Judah. The work of Jeremiah covers the whole period : his ministry began in 626, and did not cease with the fall of Jerusalem in 585. Contemporary with his earlier utterances are those of Zephaniah, who seems

[1] There are, however, scholars who hold that some of Ezekiel's prophecies were uttered in Jerusalem.

216

to have been roused to prophecy by the same series of events with which Jeremiah first dealt. Nahum must be assigned to the years immediately preceding the fall of Nineveh ; and while the exact date of Habakkuk's work is less certain, it probably lay between 608 and 600. Of the four, Nahum is negligible for our present purpose, since he deals solely with the ruin of Nineveh from the standpoint of an Israelite patriot. The book which bears his name is unique in the prophetic literature, and its chief value—apart from its magnificent style—lies in the illustration it affords of the popular prophecy of Judah in this period. But the other three are important, Jeremiah and Habakkuk pivotal.

(i) *Zephaniah.*—One of the world-shaking events of the latter part of the seventh century was a series of invasions or raids by peoples inhabiting the unknown north and north-east. Throughout ancient history the civilized world that bordered on the Mediterranean was subject to such invasions, and in the end it was the irruption of " barbarians " which brought the Roman world to destruction. The tribes who made themselves felt during our period were known to the Greeks by the collective names of Scythian and Cimmerian. Herodotus tells us that they dominated Western Asia for twenty-seven years, which must be taken as indicating the time over which their raids extended, for they do not seem to have made any permanent settlements in the south. They overran the whole of the fertile crescent, being checked only on the borders of Egypt, and their interference contributed materially to the downfall of the Assyrian empire and the destruction of Nineveh. It would seem that in 626 (though the facts are disputed in some quarters) hordes of these people poured into Palestine, ravaging and destroying where they could. They even, it seems, besieged Jerusalem ; but they were ill-equipped for operations against strong fortifications, and the city itself remained unhurt.

Whether we are right or not in maintaining the historicity of this series of raids, it was in the year 626 that both Zephaniah and Jeremiah began their ministry. The former was probably of the royal house, for his genealogy is traced farther back than that of any other prophet, and the highest name is that of Hezekiah. Zephaniah is fully in line with his predecessors of the eighth century in his denunciation of Israel's sin, but he brings out an element in the prophetic teaching which was little stressed by them. That is eschatology. His picture of the Day of Yahweh is thoroughly apocalyptic, and in the third chapter we have set before us a great gathering of the nations which ends in the triumph and final supremacy of Judah. We cannot suppose that he was alone in his expectation, and certainly among those who came after him, especially in times of distress, there were many to take up and complete the picture which he sketched in outline.

(ii) *Jeremiah.*—We know more of Jeremiah than of any other Old Testament character. We have a larger amount of prophetic utterances from him than from any other prophet except Ezekiel ; we have a number of records describing events in his life written by some sympathetic associate, possibly Baruch ; and he has also left us detailed accounts of some of his own experiences, particularly in his direct dealings with Yahweh. The figure revealed by this material is singularly attractive, and never fails to call forth the sympathy and admiration of every serious student. Except Hosea, whom in temperament and outlook Jeremiah somewhat closely resembled, no other Hebrew prophet suffered so terribly in the course of his service, and it was this very pain and struggle which gave him his supreme value and unique place in the history of religion.

In theology Jeremiah had little to add to the work of his predecessors. All that was said about the prophetic message in general applies to him, and, save for one idea which we must notice later, he did not go beyond the doctrines of the eighth century prophets. But his relations with Yahweh were very different from theirs. Though he was shy and retiring, yet he loved human society, and would have sought nothing better than a quiet home in his native village of Anathoth. Yet all his life he had to stand alone, never knowing the responsibilities of family life, and excluded even from the simple festivals of the home. He was filled with a double passion, a patriotism like that of Hosea which meant an overwhelming love for his people, and an equally overwhelming devotion to his God. The consuming desire of his soul was to see the two united in a valid and permanent bond which no human sin could break, and all his life, save perhaps for two short intervals under Josiah and Gedaliah, he was doomed to disappointment. He knew only too well that the only hope of salvation for Judah lay in this close association ; for while Yahweh did not need Israel, the nation was lost unless it could find its safety in a firm association with its God. For forty years he saw and proclaimed the coming doom. Many times it seemed as if his threats were on the verge of fulfilment, but always the danger passed, and those who placed a superstitious trust in the mere physical presence of the Temple and of the Ark seemed to be justified.

This experience had its reaction on his own soul. It was always difficult to distinguish between the prophet who spoke the truth and the prophet whom Yahweh was using to entrap some poor victim to his ruin. In Jeremiah's day the authenticity of the prophet was attested mainly by the fulfilment of his predictions, and if they remained inoperative it was assumed that the speaker was one whom Yahweh had sought to destroy. Jeremiah, conscious of the reality of his own call and experience, saw his words returning void, and had to endure the mockery of those about him as a man seduced by Yahweh. Indeed, he shared the belief himself, and human literature holds few more awful expressions of poignant agony than Jeremiah's remonstrance with Yahweh in chap. xx. 7 ff.

But it was just this bitter pain of spirit that gave to Jeremiah his importance in the history of religion. The old conception of religion, in Israel and elsewhere, made it a matter of the community, the tribe, or the state. The human unit in the combination of God and man was not the individual but the group, and the individual found his religion only through the group. As far as we know, Jeremiah was the first, whether in Israel or elsewhere, to stand face to face with his God, apart from and even opposed to the people to whom he belonged. Shut out as he seems to have been from the general worship of the people in the Temple, he was forced back on his own personal relations with Yahweh, and discovered his God for himself. Fully to appreciate the heroism of the man, we must remember that he had no thought of a doctrine of religion after death. The whole drama of his relations with Yahweh must be played out on the stage of this life, and it was a drama of two characters only in the last resort. First of all men, as far as we know, Jeremiah lived alone with his God, the world shut out, and he is in a very real sense the father of all individualism in religion, the founder of personal faith.

One actual doctrine remains to be noted. It was during Jeremiah's early ministry that the reforms of Josiah were carried through, based on the Book of the Covenant. The prophet seems to have accepted the situation, but as time passed he realized that a religion dependent merely on a book was as futile as a religion dependent merely on sacrifice. Yet, from the start the relation between Yahweh and Israel had been of the nature of a covenant, a voluntary agreement resting on the deliberate choice of the people by the God and the equally deliberate acceptance of the God by the people. Again and again had the terms of the agreement been broken on the human side, though never on the other, and again and again had it been restored. What was needed was some form of covenant which would enter so deeply into the heart and mind of man as to make a breach as impossible for man as for God. Jeremiah saw that even a written covenant, as long as it was that and nothing more, was practically worthless, even though it were graven on the solid stone. To be valid it must be set in men's inward parts and written on their hearts, and nowhere is the grand optimism of the prophet more completely illustrated than in his prophecy of the *New Covenant*.[1] Yet there was one feature of the ideal agreement which even Jeremiah did not see. A covenant, as the writer of the Epistle to the Hebrews so well knew,

[1] Jer. xxxi. 31–34.

was valid to the ancient mind only when it was made through the life-blood of a third party, when the two contracting sides had found their common unity by absorption in the vital essence freely available in the very life of a third.   So, for the fulfilment of the greatest word ever spoken by a prophet the world had to wait six hundred years, till that night when Jesus, gathered with His disciples in an upper room, took a cup, and when He had given thanks, gave it to them and said : *This is my blood of the Covenant, which is shed for many.*

(iii) *Habakkuk.*—Amos and his successors had proclaimed that Yahweh was both omnipotent and righteous, that He punished sin and rewarded goodness.   It was inevitable that men should look on the world about them in order to test the theory of the prophet.   And it must be admitted that the facts do not at first sight endorse the doctrine.   It does not follow that the unjust man meets with calamity and perishes in shame and despair ; nor does it always happen that the righteous has a prosperous life and a happy death.   And the clash between the hypothesis and the fact necessarily produced a problem.   It could not have been raised as a problem till the righteousness of God was a recognized element in men's creed ; but when that was once accepted, the question was bound to arise and demand at least some attempt at a solution.

A century and a half had passed since Amos delivered his message at Bethel ; that, however, is but a short period in which men may see something of the implications of their own theories and beliefs.   Jeremiah felt the urgency of the question, but it did not take the place in his thinking that it did in that of Habakkuk, and when he propounded it he was told not to trouble himself about a theoretical question, since more difficult practical problems were awaiting him.   It is the centre of the thought of Habakkuk.   The death of the honest, democratic king Josiah had roused doubts in his mind, and he was smarting, along with others in Israel, under the despotic rule of Jehoiakim, a prince who sought to revive the glories and the monarchic absolutism which had not been known in Israel since the days of Solomon, and rested his power on the support of Egypt. It was not enough to Habakkuk to know that the Chaldean armies would take vengeance on the oppressor ; the mere fact that the righteous could suffer any undeserved pain was problem enough for him. " Thou that art of purer eyes than to behold evil, and that canst not look on perverseness, wherefore lookest thou upon them that deal treacherously, and holdest thy peace when the wicked man swalloweth up the man that is more righteous than he ? " (i. 13.)

There was the problem. The only answer Habakkuk received was that the righteous should live by his fidelity, a reply which may form a contribution to the solution, but can hardly be taken as a solution itself. It is, indeed, not too much to say that this question has agitated the minds of thoughtful men ever since, and that no complete answer has ever been found. It may well be that the answer is finally beyond the grasp of human finite intelligence, and that its communication or discovery would raise further questions that would yet more bewilder the mind of man. It has exercised already the most profound influence on human thinking, and may in the long run prove to be the most important question that man has ever asked. Various attempts were made at a solution in ancient Israel, but these belong to the exilic and post-exilic periods, and cannot be discussed here.[1] It is enough to note that it was Habakkuk who asked it, and left the age to close with the great problem propounded but unsolved.

(iv) *The Fall of Jerusalem.*—We have traced in severest outline the story of Israel's religious life. We have seen how through Moses she was first led into communion with that deity whom she came to know as her own peculiar possession and privilege. We have noted the comparative simplicity of Israel's religion in her national childhood, and observed the syncretistic corruptions into which her adolescence fell. We have watched the growth of a nobler standard, due to the contact between the two widely sundered elements in her population,

[1] See Part III, Chapter XII.

and have heard the voice of the prophet thundering his essential principles, the moral nature and demands of Yahweh, and we have glanced at the way in which successive prophets each in turn threw a characteristic of the religion of Yahweh into prominence until the picture grew more and more complete.

There was yet much that Israel had to learn. There is nothing in the pre-exilic prophets and writers which we can call unmistakeable monotheism, though we shall agree that their doctrines must lead logically to the conviction that there is but one living and true God. There is as yet no valid doctrine of a future life. Men did not believe, it is true, that the dead ceased to be, but they either lay crumbling in the grave or else passed to the joyless gloom of *She'ol*. In either case they were cut off, not only from man but also from God, for Yahweh had no place or part with those beneath. Philosophy, even such philosophy as that of which the Semitic mind was capable, was not yet born, and centuries were to pass before the Jew, in contact with the Greek, ventured on the ocean of metaphysical speculation.

Yet the prophets had taught her enough for her own immediate safety, and none can say what might have been the issue had their precepts been accepted and followed by the nation at large. But the nation did not follow. Except for sporadic movements, such as the reform of Josiah, the great mass of the people went on their old, evil, and dangerous ways. It was not by mere preaching, however completely inspired, that the great lessons of the Kingdom of God could be brought home to them, and they could grasp the truth set before them only when it was presented with the super-logic of facts. So Israel refused to accept the hope offered to her, and went on the way that led to destruction. The monarchy, an isolated phenomenon in the long history of Palestine, had served its turn ; in no other *milieu* could the doctrines of the great prophets have been adequately proclaimed or illustrated. But Israelite independence was no longer necessary ; it had become indeed a snare, and the nation must be taught by sterner methods. So when the Chaldean armies surrounded Jerusalem, broke down its walls, laid its houses in ruins, and burnt its temple, they were but fulfilling unconsciously the purpose of the God of Israel, who had to inflict upon His people this last of human calamities that they might learn as a whole the essential principles of the Kingdom of God.

PART III

EARLY JUDAISM

THE PERIOD OF THE EXILE

CHAPTER I

BABYLONIAN INFLUENCE ON THE JEWS

It is a necessary preliminary to the study of the condition, religious or otherwise, of the Jews in exile, to consider very briefly the question as to whether, and if so how far, they were affected by Babylonian influences. We are thinking here, of course, primarily, of religious influences ; but since, to the Hebrew, every department of life had from time immemorial been connected with religion, even the purely secular and cultural spheres of Babylonian life may have indirectly contributed in affecting the Jews religiously, as they must certainly have done in other respects. To take but one example : it is no exaggeration to say that contact with the mercantile life of Babylon (see Ezek. xvi. 29, xvii. 4 ; cp. Nahum iii. 16) originated the trading habits of the Jews which became later characteristic of them [1]; that this had a detrimental effect upon their religious life seems to be clear from Ezek. xvi. 29.

But it is with religious beliefs and practices that we are specially concerned now. There are plenty of

[1] During the excavations undertaken by the Pennsylvania University in Nippur, which was situated on the river (properly canal) Chebar (Ezek. i. 3), a great number of tablets containing business transactions were unearthed, showing that Nippur was a great mercantile centre. On many of these tablets the names of Jews occur, such as Hananiah, Gedaliah, Pedaiah, Benjamin, and others, who appear to have carried on business transactions with the leading mercantile house of the city, Murashu Sons. The tablets, it is true, all belong to the reigns of Artaxerxes I and Darius II (465–405 B.C.), which is, of course, rather later than the period under consideration ; but the Jews mentioned on these business documents are not likely to have been the first among their people to conduct mercantile pursuits. See, on this subject, Hilprecht, *The Babylonian Expedition of the University of Pennsylvania,* vol. ix., pp. 28, 76 ff. (1898).

indications showing that before the Exile Assyrian religion, which was largely identical with that of Babylonia, greatly influenced the Hebrews (see, e.g., 2 Kings xxiii. 11, 12 ; Zeph. i. 5 ; Jer. vii. 17, 18, cp. xliv. 17–19, 25 (Ishtar) ; Ezek. viii. 14–17 [Tammuz]) ; but the Jews were now to come into direct contact with these and other forms of Eastern religion ; and we know from such a passage, e.g., as Ezek. xiv. 1 ff., that many of the exiles were deeply influenced by them. We are not without definite knowledge regarding the details of Babylonian religion at this time.

In Babylon itself was the great temple E-Sagila of Marduk, " Lord of Heaven and earth " ; this temple had been built on a grandiose style by Nebuchadrezzar. The most imposing ritual in connexion with his worship took place on Nisan 10, New Year's Day. On this occasion a great procession, in which the king took the leading part, was formed, and the god Marduk was taken from his temple and placed on his ship ; this was then drawn to his sanctuary outside the city, where prayer was offered to him ; on the following day the procession returned to the temple of the god.[1] Great multitudes thronged the whole way along which the procession passed, and there can scarcely be a doubt that many of the Jewish exiles witnessed this imposing ceremony. They could hardly fail to contrast it with the humble and comparatively simple worship to which they had been accustomed in their own land. It is well within the bounds of possibility that the prophet had this great annual procession in mind when he wrote : " They have no knowledge that carry the wood of their graven image, and pray unto a god that cannot save " (Isa. xlv. 20) ; the very fact that he utters a polemic against the Babylonian god suggests that among his people there were those who were in danger of being drawn into worshipping him. A still more pointed passage is where the prophet claims for Yahweh, the God of Israel, the victory in the combat with the primeval monster Tiamat, which, according to Babylonian mythology, had been achieved by Marduk :

---

[1] See Zimmern, " Das babylonische Neujahrsfest," in *Der alte Orient*, xxv., Heft 3 (1926).

" Awake, awake, put on strength, O arm of Yahweh ; awake as in days of old, as in ages long since past. Art not thou that which clave in twain Rahab, that pierced the Dragon ? Art not thou that which dried up the sea, the waters of Tehom Rabbah ? " (Isa. li. 9–10.) It is impossible not to see what the prophet's object is here, viz. to set against the Babylonian deity the superiority of Yahweh ; but he is writing for his own people, and therefore there would be but little point in his words unless he saw that many of the exiles were being attracted by Babylonian worship.

Again, Nippur, near which was situated Tel-abib on the great canal Kabari (Chebar), was the centre of the worship of Bel (=Enlil), called the " lord of lands," who dwelt on the " great mountain," the summit of which reached to heaven. We know from Ezek. iii. 15, viii. 1, that a colony of the exiles was settled in Tel-abib ; they were therefore in close proximity to the temple of Bel, and must often have been witnesses of his worship, judging by the prophet's words in Isa. xlvi. 1 : " Bel boweth down, Nebo stoopeth . . . " ; his contemptuous irony may well have been intended to counteract a tendency on the part of some of the exiles to partake of the worship of these gods.[1] It is very necessary to remember what is pointed out elsewhere that, according to the ideas of the times, the gods of Babylonia had proved themselves stronger than the God of Israel ; this afforded an additional inducement to offer them allegiance.

A further mark of the influence of Babylonian religion is to be discerned in Isa. lxv. 11 : " But ye that forsake Yahweh, that forget my holy mountain, that prepare a table for Gad, and that fill up mingled wine unto Meni." Gad, the god of Fortune, occurs on Assyrian tablets [2] ; Meni is not mentioned elsewhere : both were evidently worshipped by the Babylonians, but Gad was widely venerated in Syria too. It is quite possible that these were astral deities, as the destinies of men were believed

---

[1] The centre of the worship of Nebo was Borsippa, the sister-city of Babylon.

[2] Zimmern's edition (third) of Schrader's *Keilinschriften und das alte Testament*, pp. 479 f. (1889). Gad has been identified with the planet Jupiter (see *Encycl. Bibl.*, ii. [1557]).

to be influenced by the stars ; if so, the passage is an illustration of what is said in Isa. xlvii. 13, where in reference to Babylon the prophet says : " Let now the astrologers, the star-gazers, the monthly prognosticators, stand up, and save thee from the things that shall come upon thee."

How strong Babylonian influence is likely to have been upon the exiles may be gathered from various passages in the book of *Ezekiel*, in which we find a great familiarity with Babylonian mythology and religion. A brief reference to these will be of interest.

In i. 4 the prophet tells of how in his vision Yahweh appeared to him in a great cloud driven by a stormy wind " out of the north " : according to Babylonian belief the abode of the gods was in the north ; here in the north lay the " holy mountain " of the gods (xxviii. 14, 16 ; and see Isa. xiv. 13 ; Job xxxvii. 22), as well as " the garden " of the gods (xxxi. 8, 9). Again, a very pronounced Babylonian trait occurs in the description of the " four living creatures " (i. 5 ff., especially ver. 10) ; the " face of a man " refers to Nebo, the " face of a lion " to Nergal, the " face of an ox " (i.e. bull) to Marduk, and the " face of an eagle " to Ninib ; these are the astral gods of the four corners of the earth, who, according to the prophet, are the ministers of Yahweh. Once more, in ix. 2–11 we read of the seven avengers who take vengeance on the idolaters in Jerusalem ; they come from the north, and are messengers of Yahweh : " And behold, six men came from the way of the upper gate, which lieth toward the north . . . and one man in the midst of them, clothed in linen, with a writer's inkhorn by his side. . . ." The prototype of these seven were the seven planets, gods of the Babylonian pantheon ; the man with the inkhorn by his side clearly represents the god Nebo, who was the writer of the Book of Fate. In each case the prophet adapts Babylonian beliefs to the religion of Yahweh. Finally, in chapter xl., where the plan of the new temple is described in a vision to the prophet by a man " whose appearance was like the appearance of brass," we have a procedure which is paralleled in Babylonian literature ; one of the inscriptions of Gudea, for example, tells of how

Gudea in a vision sees a divine figure who bids him build a house ; heavenly beings appear with stylus and tablet who show him the plan. The idea, common to the ancient East, is that everything on earth has its corresponding pattern in heaven.[1]

The prophet himself was not affected by these things so far as his belief in fundamentals was concerned ; but the allusions he makes without a word of explanation show that he spoke of things which his hearers knew all about. The exiles were living in surroundings in which they constantly witnessed the celebration of Babylonian religious rites ; they were thus familiar with these as belonging to a people far more highly cultured than themselves ; it is therefore difficult to believe that such things were without effect upon them. The probability is that an appreciable number of the exiles gave up the religion of their fathers and became worshippers of the Babylonian gods.[2] But while in some respects Babylonian culture influenced the Jews, it seems certain that Babylonian religion did not permanently affect them ; it would be difficult to point to any essential doctrine or religious practice of Judaism of which it could be said that it was the result of Babylonian religious influence.

It is true that in some respects affinities between the religions of the Babylonians and the Hebrews are to be discerned, such as the *She'ol* belief, the sense of sin which appears in both Babylonian and Hebrew psalms, and others ; but in none of these can it be proved that Babylonian influence affected Hebrew religion ; it is far more likely that both can be ultimately traced back to a common origin. The name of Yahweh (though not in this form), it is well known, appears [3] on some Babylonian inscriptions ; but there is nothing to show that, apart from the name, there was anything in common between the Babylonian deity and the God of Israel.

---

[1] Jeremias, *Das alte Testament im Lichte des alten Orients*, pp. 361 f. (1904).

[2] Cp. also such Babylonian theophoric names as Sheshbazzar and Zerubbabel.

[3] But not before the ninth century B.C. (see G. R. Driver, in *Old Testament Essays*, p. 20 [1927]).

Again, some of the *Genesis* narratives were in all probability indebted to a Babylonian prototype, but so far as religious ideas are concerned the far more spiritual tone of the Hebrew forms proves that in this respect Babylonian influence was non-existent.

It has been claimed that the monotheistic belief of the Hebrews is to some extent indebted to Babylonian religion ; a true comparison between the two shows the complete untenability of the claim.

It is granted that Babylonian demonology [1] left permanent marks on Jewish demonology ; but this hardly comes under the head of religion.

The conclusion is that while during the Exile Babylonian influences in many directions strongly affected many of the Jews, and in a certain number of cases fatally where religion was concerned, yet the Jewish religious leaders saw to it that the essence of Judaism was untouched by those influences.

See further, Part I, Chap. VI, § 2.

CHAPTER II

THE EARLY YEARS OF THE EXILE

1. THE RECORDS OF THE DEPORTATIONS

ALTHOUGH we are dealing exclusively with the religion of the Hebrews, it is essential that at times the historical background should be taken into consideration in so far as this tended to affect religious conditions. We must therefore begin by quoting the records which tell of the leading away of the people from Palestine to Babylon. There were two, possibly three, occasions on which this happened ; the first was in 597 B.C.

"And he [i.e. Nebuchadrezzar] carried away all Jerusalem, and all the princes, and all the mighty men of valour, even ten thousand captives, and all the craftsmen and the smiths ; none remained, save the poorest sort of the people of the land. And he carried away Jehoiachin to Babylon, and the king's mother, and the king's wives, and his officers, and the chief men of the land carried he into captivity from Jerusalem to Babylon. And all the men of might, even seven thousand, and the craftsmen and the smiths a thousand, all of them strong and apt for war, even them the king of Babylon brought captive to Babylon " (2 Kings xxiv. 14–16 ; in 2 Chron. xxxvi. 9, 10, the account is extremely meagre).

The repetition in this passage, with the variation in the number of the exiles, is perhaps due to a combination of excerpts from two different sources. But in any case, the number was comparatively small ; and this is borne out, moreover, by the further variations in numbers given as three thousand and twenty-three in Jer. lii. 28.

It should be noted that the renderings " captives," " carried into captivity," and " brought captive " of the Revised Version are somewhat misleading. In the

233

original the idea is that of leading away,[1] not captivity.
The point is not unimportant, as will be seen later.

Another thing to note is that the statement that only
the poorest sort of the people of the land were left is not
quite accurate in view of what is said about the second
deportation, eleven years later : "And the captain of
the guard took Seraiah the chief priest, and Zephaniah
the second priest, and the three keepers of the door ;
and out of the city he took an officer that was set over
the men of war ; and five men of them that saw the king's
face, which were found in the city ; and the scribe, the
captain of the host, which mustered the people of the land ;
and three score men of the people of the land, that were
found in the city " (2 Kings xxv. 18, 19). It is difficult
to believe that the poorest sort of the people could have
been found capable of bearing the load and responsibility
of the important posts here mentioned. The passages
2 Kings xxv. 23–26, Jer. xl. 7–12, should also be consulted
in this connexion.

The second deportation took place in 586 B.C. ; it is
recorded in 2 Kings xxv. 1–22, especially vers. 11, 12 :
" And the residue of the people that were left in the
city . . . did Nebuzaradan the captain of the guard
carry away captive. But the captain of the guard left
of the poorest of the land to be vine-dressers and
husbandmen " (cp. 2 Chron. xxxvi. 17–20) ; the number
of the exiles in this case is not given ; but according
to Jer. lii. 29 it was eight hundred and thirty-two.

Yet a third deportation is referred to in Jer. lii. 30, in
the year 581 B.C. (i.e. the twenty-third year of Nebuchadrezzar), when seven hundred and forty-five more
exiles were led away. Possibly it is to this that Josephus
refers when he says that in this year, the twenty-third
year of Nebuchadrezzar, the king " took those Jews that
were there (i.e. in Egypt) captives, and led them away to
Babylon " (Antiq., x. ix. 7) ; but it must be granted that
if the same event is referred to one would expect some
mention of Egypt in Jer. lii. 30.

One other episode must be noted. A body of Jews

---

[1] The technical terms for the " leading away," and therefore of the
Exile, are golah, galuth.

under the leadership of Johanan the son of Kareah, fearing the wrath of the king of Babylon on account of the murder of Gedaliah, fled to Egypt, compelling Jeremiah to go with them, and settled down in Migdol, Tahpanhes, Noph, and in the country of Pathros (i.e. Upper Egypt) (see 2 Kings xxv. 25–26 ; Jer. xli.–xliv.).

So much, then, for the records which tell of the deportations from the homeland.

2. The Religious Beliefs of the People

From what has been said it will be seen that we must consider the religious condition of four different bodies of Jews during this early period of the Exile :

(i) Those in Babylon who were deported in 597 B.C.

(ii) Those who were left in the homeland.

(iii) Those who had settled down in Egypt.

(iv) Those in Babylon after the 586 B.C. deportation.

(i) The exiles who were led away in 597 B.C. could take comfort in the knowledge that Jerusalem still stood intact, and, even more important, in the thought that the Temple, the dwelling-place of the God of Israel, though despoiled (2 Kings xxiv. 13), was still in existence. Their belief was strong in the inviolability of the city of God, proclaimed by Isaiah long since (2 Kings xix. 34), as well as in that of the Temple (Jer. vii. 4).   This meant for them that Yahweh was still in the midst of His people, mighty to save.   The downfall of the great Assyrian empire, of but recent date, had signally proved that Yahweh's will must prevail (cp. Nahum i. 1 ff.).   There was, indeed, much reason for the exiles to believe that an instrument was being raised up to smite Babylon (Jer. xxviii. 1–4).   What their God had done before He would do again, before long ; such was their belief, though falsely inspired : there would be a return to the homeland.

The faith in Yahweh of these first exiles, then, was undiminished in spite of His having permitted them to be carried away into a heathen land ; so that Jeremiah could liken them to the good figs in his vision of the two baskets of figs (Jer. xxiv. 5). True, their inability to worship God as they had been accustomed to would be bitter to them ; but they could comfort themselves with the thought that this was only a temporary hardship. Though their hopes were founded on the misguided teaching of false prophets (Jer. xxix. 8, 9, etc.), yet for the time, at any rate, their belief was real and their trust genuine.

(ii) If our knowledge of the religious condition of the first exiles is to some extent based on inference, we have abundance of detail regarding those, the great bulk of the nation, who had been left in the homeland. Both morally and religiously things could hardly have been worse ; religion was practically the same as it had been in earlier times among the mass of the people ; the Josianic reform might never have been instituted, the prophets with their teaching might never have existed. The ancient Canaanite *Ba'al* cult was still practised (Jer. vii. 9 ; Ezek. vi. 13) ; the centralization of worship, with its primary object of doing away with the false worship in local sanctuaries, was a dead letter (Jer. ii. 28, vii. 17–19 ; cp. Ezek. xxxiii. 25) ; alien cults of all kinds were shamelessly observed : the worship of Ishtar, " the queen of Heaven " (Jer. vii. 18) ; Sun-worship (Ezek vi. 4–6) ; Tammuz-worship, and other Babylonian cults (Ezek. viii. 9–18) ; still other forms of worship are also referred to in Ezek. v. 11.

Frequent stress is laid on the ominous part played by the leaders of the people, both priests and prophets ; a few years before the first deportation Jeremiah says in reference to the former : " Woe unto the shepherds that destroy and scatter the sheep of my pasture! saith Yahweh. Therefore thus saith Yahweh, the God of Israel, against the shepherds that feed my people : Ye have scattered my flock, and driven them away, and have not visited them ; behold I will visit upon you the evil of your doings, saith Yahweh " (Jer. xxiii. 1, 2). Of the prophets he says : " Both prophet and priest are profane ; yea, in my house have I found their wickedness, saith Yahweh." Here in Judah things are just as bad as they had been in the northern kingdom : " And I have seen folly in the prophets of Samaria ; they prophesied by Baal, and caused my people Israel to err. In the prophets of Jerusalem also I have seen a horrible thing ; they commit adultery, and walk in lies, and they strengthen the hands of evil-doers, that none doth return from his wickedness ; they are all of them become unto me as Sodom, and the inhabitants thereof as Gomorrah " (Jer. xxiii. 11–14 ; see also the rest of this chapter).

A picture of hopeless immorality is drawn by Ezekiel in reference to Jerusalem, the " bloody city," the details of which must have been described to him by those who had come from there (Ezek. xxii. ; see, too, Ezek. xxxiii. 21–29, and v. 5–10). And Jeremiah draws attention to the melancholy fact that the people seem to have no sense of their sinfulness ; they are quoted as saying : " Wherefore hath Yahweh pronounced all this great evil against us ? or what is our iniquity ? or what is our sin that we have committed against Yahweh our God ? " (Jer. xvi. 10).

In contemplating this picture of religious and moral depravity of priests, prophets, and people, one realizes the superb individuality and strength of character of such men as Jeremiah and Ezekiel, who in face of over-whelming odds not only stood firm, but by their pre-dominating influence and exalted teaching preserved the knowledge of God among men and handed on the torch of revelation. Though clearly in a small minority, they must have had their followers ; true, nothing is said of these, but *somebody* must have preserved the records of the teaching of these inspired teachers.

(iii) The little that we are told about the Jews who went to Egypt at this time is but a further illustration of the falling-away from the worship of Yahweh which was so pronounced in Judah. We read of Jeremiah rebuking the people in Pathros, and especially the women, for their worship of the " queen of heaven " ; they refuse to give up this form of worship : " We will certainly perform every word that is gone forth out of our mouth, to burn incense unto the queen of heaven, and to pour out drink offerings unto her, as we have done, we and

our fathers, our kings and our princes, in the cities of
Judah, and in the streets of Jerusalem ; for then we had
plenty of food, and were well, and saw no evil. But
since we left off to burn incense to the queen of heaven,
and to pour out drink offerings unto her, we have wanted
all things, and have been consumed by the sword and by
the famine . . ." (Jer. xliv. 15–19). That other cults
were also practised is clear from the words " burning
incense unto other gods in the land of Egypt, whither ye
be gone to sojourn " (Jer. xliv. 8 ; cp. ii. 16–19). As
a result, the destruction of all the men of Judah in the land
of Egypt is prophesied (ver. 27), as well as the downfall of
Hophra king of Egypt (ver. 30). It is interesting to note
that Ezekiel, in making a similar prophecy, mentions
Seveneh, i.e. Syene or Assouan, in Upper Egypt, where, as
we have learned from the Elephantiné papyri, there was
also a Jewish colony. As the Jewish Temple belonging
to this colony was standing in 525 B.C., when Cambyses
conquered Egypt, it is quite possible that Jews were
already settled there in Jeremiah's time. They worshipped Yahweh (which they pronounced Yahu). The
fact that Jeremiah makes no reference to these Jews
(on the assumption that this colony was already in existence in his day) need not cause surprise, for Pathros
was a district which covered a very large area.

(iv) Lastly, we turn to the exiles again, reinforced
now by those of the 586 B.C. deportation.

As long as the monarchy existed, i.e. as long as the
nation, as such, was in being, even though subject to
a suzerain power, as long as the Holy City stood firm in
her glory, and, above all, as long as the Temple remained
inviolate, belief in Yahweh, the God of the people, was
justified ; hope and the eager expectancy of deliverance
from exile would animate the hearts of the people. But
this was now all past. Yahweh had forsaken His land
(Ezek. viii. 12, ix. 9), and therefore His people ; so it was
interpreted both by those in the homeland and by those
in exile. The God of Israel had succumbed before the
gods of Babylon ; Marduk and Ishtar had proved themselves stronger than Yahweh ! They would not wholly
forget Him ; but they were now in a land belonging to

other gods to whom they believed worship was due. This is all graphically described by Ezekiel : " Then came certain of the elders of Israel unto me, and sat before me. And the word of Yahweh came unto me saying, Son of man, these men have taken their idols into their hearts, and put the stumbling-block of their iniquity before their face ; should I be enquired of them at all ? Therefore speak unto them, and say unto them, thus saith Yahweh : Every man of the house of Israel that taketh his idols into his heart, and putteth the stumbling-block of his iniquity before his face, and cometh to the prophet, I, Yahweh, will answer him therein according to the multitude of his idols, that I may take the house of Israel in their own heart, because they are all estranged from me through their idols . . . " (xiv. 1–11). It was a kind of syncretistic worship such as had been practised in connexion with *Ba'al* worship in Canaan.[1] Nevertheless, among many of these there was yet the possibility of their being kept from the allurements of the Babylonian temples, hence both the prophet's warning as well as his words of encouragement in ver. 11, " that the house of Israel may go no more astray from me, neither defile themselves any more with all their transgressions ; but that they may be my people, and I may be their God, saith Yahweh." And, doubtless, among these waverers many remained true to their God, but there will have been many others who believed the gods of their conquerors to be more powerful than Yahweh, and who transferred their allegiance altogether, thus losing their religious identity, and becoming absorbed by the people of their new surroundings.[2]

But we know that there were yet others who had come wholly under the influence of the teaching of Jeremiah and Ezekiel, and whose faith had never wavered. To these exile was a bitter experience ; they longed for the land of their fathers, and the sad memory of

---

[1] See Part II, Chapter IV, § 2.
[2] *Tobit* i. 10 may well be an echo of actual fact, the memory of which had been handed down ; it is said there : " And when I was carried away captive to Nineveh, all my brethren and those that were of my kindred did eat of the bread of the Gentiles."

days gone by would be reflected in their psalmist's words :

How shall we sing the Lord's song in a strange land ?
If I forget thee, O Jerusalem, may my right hand forget (her cunning)[1] ;
May my tongue cleave to the roof of my mouth if I remember thee not.
(Ps. cxxxvii. 5, 6; R.V. 4. 5.)

This clinging in affectionate remembrance to their God and to the homeland marked the true servants of God, and their loyalty to their ancestral religion was only intensified in face of surrounding opposition.

We have been concerned so far with the state of religion among the Jews during the first ten years or so of the Exile. We shall have to consider next the course of religious development during the succeeding years of exile.

---

[1] The reference is to the use of the right hand in playing the harp as an accompaniment to the singing ; the verbs in vers. 1–3 of the psalm are in the perfect, so that this psalm does not belong to the Exile, but echoes the frame of mind of the faithful among the exiles.

CHAPTER III

THE JEWISH COMMUNITY IN EXILE

1. COMMUNAL LIFE IN THE EXILE

THERE are some clear indications in the Old Testament records that the communal life of the Jewish exiles in Babylon was similar to that to which they had been accustomed in their own land. This, as we shall see, had a direct bearing on the continuity of religious belief.

Our first indication as to the conditions of life of the exiles is to be sought in Jeremiah's letter sent " to the residue of the elders of the *golah*, and to the priests, and to the prophets, and to all the people." As this letter was sent from Jerusalem, it must have been sent before the destruction of the city, and therefore before the second deportation. It runs as follows : " Build ye houses, and dwell in them ; and plant gardens, and eat the fruit of them ; take ye wives and beget sons and daughters ; and take wives for your sons, and give your daughters husbands, that they may bear sons and daughters ; and multiply ye there, and be not diminished. And seek the peace of the land [so the Septuagint instead of " city " in the Hebrew text] whither I have caused you to be carried away, and pray unto Yahweh for it, for in the peace thereof ye shall have peace " (Jer. xxix. 1–7).

The mention of the building of houses and the planting of gardens implies liberty to move about within areas of settlement ; so that there were *colonies* of Jewish exiles. But this implies, further, that the exiles had complete freedom in the exercise of their religion ; indeed, there is nowhere any hint that they suffered any disabilities in this respect. Jeremiah clearly takes this for granted ; for when he bids the exiles marry and beget children he knows that Jewish fathers bring up their children in their ancestral faith.

16   241

Again, in Ezek. viii. 1, the prophet says : " As I sat
in my house and the elders of Judah sat before me, the
hand of the Lord God fell there upon me " ; see also
xiv. 1, and xx. 1 ff. That gatherings of this kind could
take place in the prophet's own house shows that a good
deal of freedom of action was permitted to the exiles.
It is also of interest to note that the ancient position of
the elders as leaders of the community reappears. It
was the disappearance of the monarchy that brought this
organization, originally characteristic of nomadic times,
into being once more. But it meant, and this is the
important point, that families and clans were permitted
to dwell together. What a boon this was to the exiles
will at once be realized when it is remembered that there
were very large and widely separated tracts of country
over which they might have been indiscriminately scattered. In this connexion we find that in the lists of the
returned exiles (Ezra ii. 3 ff., 20 ff., 33 f., viii. 1 ff., 16 ff.)
these are enumerated not only according to heads of
families, but also according to the districts in which their
families had lived *before* the Exile ; thus, there are
mentioned the children of Pahath-moab, of Bethlehem,
of Anathoth, of Kiriath-jearim, of Beeroth, of Ramah, of
Geba, of Bethel, of Ai, of Nebo, and of Jericho—to
mention the best known place-names ; and clearly, if
they are enumerated in this way as returned exiles it
must have been under such designations that the various
communities were known in the land of exile, otherwise
such an enumeration would be entirely pointless.[1] And
thus the conclusion is obvious that in Babylonia the Jews
were allowed to live together just as they had done in
Palestine. From this there follows the important fact
that in this community-life not only was the sense of
nationality upheld, but, more important, the Jews in exile
were able to practise their religion with the traditional
customs and usages in connexion therewith, as far as it
was possible.

---

[1] Kittel, *op. cit.*, iii, pp. 113 f. It is, of course, possible that in
these *Ezra* passages the chronicler is transferring the conditions of his
own time to earlier times ; but, upon the whole, the view given above
seems the more likely one.

2. Religious Observances among the Exiles

In Ezek. xi. 16 it is said : " Thus saith the Lord God,
whereas I have removed them (i.e. the exiles) far off
among the nations, and whereas I have scattered them
among the countries, yet have I become unto them a
sanctuary only to a small extent in the countries where
they are come." [1] The meaning of this last sentence is
that the important externals of the worship of Yahweh,
as it had been in the past, were now wanting, and therefore the form of worship was insignificant as compared
with what they had been accustomed to in the Temple.
This raises therefore the important question as to what
kind of substitute for the Temple services was adopted
by those among the exiles who were loyal to their ancestral
religion, and intended to remain so.

Jeremiah, and other spiritually-minded prophets, had
already contemplated the possibility of a non-sacrificial
worship [2] ; this was now to become a reality. But it was
only the compelling force of circumstances that could have
induced the people to remain content with a form of
worship alien to tradition and practice. For the relationship hitherto conceived to exist between them and their
God had been exhibited in such numberless ways ; no
animal was killed for food but that part of it was dedicated
to Yahweh as His due ; no bread was eaten of which in
some form the first-fruits had not been offered to Him ;
no feast was inaugurated without bringing to Him the
gifts due. The sacrificial system had touched the people
in endless ways in everyday life, as well as in their worship
proper.[3] And now this had all ceased. To substitute
a new form of worship must at first have presented real
difficulties. Kittel suggests,[4] with much probability,
that since the regular feasts could not be observed as in the
past, the seasons at which they had been kept were
celebrated as *memorials*. At such gatherings what more

[1] The Revised Version rendering : " . . . Yet will I be to them a
sanctuary for a little while . . .," does not represent the Hebrew ; it
also obscures the meaning of the passage.
[2] See, e.g., Jer. vi. 16, 20, vii. 21, 22 ; Mic. vi. 6, 7.
[3] Stade, *Geschichte des Volkes Israel*, ii. 9 (1888).
[4] *Op. cit.*, iii. 125.

likely than that the mercies accorded in the past by the God of Israel to His people should be the subject of commemoration ? The exodus from Egypt, the deliverance from the pursuing Egyptians, the revelation at Sinai, the entry into the promised land and its final possession. Such commemorations would keep the thought of divine mercies before their minds, and kindle hopes for the future ; for what God had done in the past He could do again. True, we have no proof that such commemorative substitutes actually took the place of the earlier festal celebrations ; but there is much in Deutero-Isaiah's outlook and prophecies [1] somewhat later that suggests the probability of this. We have direct evidence, moreover, of the institution of annual fast-days, which were, however, abrogated after the Return (Zech. vii. 3, 5, viii. 19) ; if, therefore, fasts were observed it is impossible to believe that this should not also have been the case in some form with feasts. Further, the Sabbath, though now without its prescribed sacrifices, became the chief and regular day of worship. This may be seen, for example, by the stress laid on the Sabbaths, and the denunciation against their non-observance, in Ezek. xx. 12–24. As a day set apart for congregational worship every week the Sabbath became supremely important during the Exile ; and it is not difficult to indicate, in the light of later evidence, what the main elements at these weekly assemblies for worship were. Not infrequently mention is made of both priests and prophets among the exiles—obviously they would have been the leaders in worship ; the reading of the prophetical books and of such a book as *Deuteronomy* will have been an important element ; the presence of prophets would make the spoken word a notable part of the service ; sacred songs, sung during the Temple worship, and therefore very familiar, would be sung ; and doubtless other psalms would have been composed and used. Nor can it be doubted that public prayer soon became a prominent feature. These are all among the earliest elements of the Synagogue liturgy ; and all authorities are agreed that the origins of the synagogal worship must be sought in the period of the Exile.

[1] E.g. li. 1–3, 7.

Together with the Sabbath great stress came to be laid upon the rite of Circumcision ; though, of course, familiar in pre-exilic times, it had not been emphasized before as it was during this period ; the uncircumcized were, it is true, spoken of with contempt, but, with the exception of the Philistines, few such existed among the nations in the surroundings of Canaan ; so that it could not have been the special mark of a true son of Israel.[1] But conditions in exilic times were different. The Jews now came into contact with peoples of another kind who knew nothing of such a custom ; and thus Circumcision became one of the *distinctive* marks of a Jew. It was during the Exile that there arose among the Jews, as never before, the consciousness of being different from other peoples ; the conviction of superiority over others began to assert itself, and not without reason ; for their grasp of the truth of the ethical righteousness of God, together with the corresponding demands made upon them as the people of God, marked them out as standing, in a religious sense, on a much higher plane than any other people. They felt the need therefore of adopting an attitude of aloofness towards all who stood on a lower religious plane.[2] One special means, as Kittel has shown,[3] of emphasizing the separation between themselves and others was in the more strenuous observance of the ancient laws regarding purification and forbidden food. As in the case of the Sabbath and Circumcision so with these ; they had all been known and to a greater or less extent observed in pre-exilic days ; but they had not been, as they now became, of fundamental importance, for they now assumed a new significance. It is for this reason that in the Priestly Code [4] much emphasis is laid upon these laws, as on certain others ; though quite out of harmony with the spirit of the time and the advance of religious thought, they were nevertheless taken up as

---

[1] The oldest legal code makes no mention of it.

[2] Jewish exclusiveness had, it is true, already been emphasized in *Deuteronomy*, but it was during the Exile that this became accentuated (see Lev. xix. 2, xx. 22–6, xxii. 31–2).

[3] *Op. cit.*, iii. 127.

[4] It is not intended to imply that the Priestly Code *as we now have it* was a product of the Exile.

part of the Law, not for what they had originally meant—for the original meaning was for the most part quite forgotten—but simply with the object of making the separation of the Jews as obvious and ostentatious as possible. As an illustration of this we may instance the laws regarding clean and unclean animals in Lev. xi.; this is an expansion of the Law of Holiness (Lev. xvii.–xxvi.), which itself embodies some things of immemorial antiquity. That the compilers of the laws which ultimately took the form of the Priestly Code had any knowledge of the original reason why certain animals were *taboo* is extremely unlikely; nor was this knowledge necessary, for the fact that some foods were prohibited and therefore not eaten by Jews differentiated them from their Gentile neighbours; that was the main point.

One important consequence of this elaboration of the Law was a great increase of priestly activity, though of a kind very different from that of earlier days. The Temple, with its sacrificial system and cultural rites, was for the present non-existent; but the priesthood now found scope for its energies in framing multifarious precepts for the regulation of the everyday life of the people in accordance with an elaborated legal code; new cases were constantly arising as to the bearing of the Law on particular acts. For example, in view of the prominence given to the observance of the Sabbath on which all work must cease, it became necessary to define with exactitude what constituted work; this raised many nice points, the settling of which called forth the exercise of much ingenuity. Then there arose, too, the question of what work on the Sabbath might be regarded as permissible because necessary, and since every act of labour was prohibited much casuistry came into play, which, judging from the records of later times, did more honour to mental acumen than to honesty.[1] In short, the priests had plenty to occupy them.

The development of all this took time; but it was during the Exile that the elaboration of the Law began; and however much, in process of time, it tended into

---

[1] The Mishnah tractate *Shabbath* contains later developments, but it will not be questioned that it has preserved much traditional material.

directions detrimental to true religion, it must in fairness be recognized that in its origin the motive was entirely good. The priesthood was actuated by the desire to make their flock realize at every step that as the people of God they must by act as well as by word prove to themselves, as well as to the world of their surroundings, that they were different from others, different in religion, different in morals, different in manner of life.

What has so far been said has been mainly concerned with the externals of religion ; we have to deal next with the more important subject of religious teaching.

CHAPTER IV

RELIGIOUS TEACHERS : THE PRIEST-PROPHET EZEKIEL

THE externals of religious belief which, as we have seen, were prominent during the exilic period, were the outcome of the teaching of the religious leaders. Important and indispensable as such externals must always be, they are nevertheless of value only in so far as they represent the outward expression, necessarily inadequate, of underlying religious truths. To discern and to grasp these religious truths we must go to the teaching of the religious leaders who expounded them. Just as in the earlier history of Israel the prophetical teachers were men whose ideals soared far above the thoughts of the mass of their contemporaries, so during the exilic period the teachers put forth truths which few of their followers could assimilate. In dealing therefore with the religion of the Hebrews during this, as during any other period, it must necessarily be the teaching at its best. And this is as it should be ; only it must be realized that the people in general did not (nor were they capable of doing so) grasp to the full or assimilate the truths which their religious teachers put before them.

The first of these teachers, so far as we know, was Ezekiel ; and it is to his writings that we must go first to see what Hebrew religion at its best was at this time.

1. EZEKIEL'S DOCTRINE OF GOD

In one respect Ezekiel's experience of God differed from that of any prophet before him. He had known Yahweh as the God of Israel in the land of Israel ; he had also come to know Him as the God of Israel in a foreign land. True, other prophets, such as Amos, Isaiah, and

Jeremiah, had taught that Yahweh was more than a national God, and that His power was equally manifested in other lands ; but Ezekiel was the first to have the proof of this by actual experience.[1] It cannot be doubted that this fact had a real influence upon his conception of God. Further, it seems certain from some of the mental pictures which he presents that he was not unfamiliar with the elaborate ritual wherewith the Babylonians worshipped their gods ; if heathen conceptions of their gods were such as to necessitate the worship of them on so grand a scale, how infinitely greater must be the one and only God, who, unlike those gods, was a reality. To this must also be added the remarkably vivid powers of imagination possessed by Ezekiel ; these worked upon his mental vision when his thoughts were occupied with the greatest and most sublime theme of the Personality of God. And, finally, the contrast between the mighty and merciful and pure God, with the age-long ingratitude and unfaithfulness of His chosen people, placed in vivid and terrible relief the immeasurable distance between the divine Creator and the pitiable insignificance of created mortals.

Thus it came about that Ezekiel's outstanding conception of God was that of the *divine transcendence*. How this is illustrated by his frequent endeavour to express his sense of the divine majesty will be seen from the following words : " . . . And above the firmament that was over their heads was the likeness of a throne, as the appearance of a sapphire stone ; and upon the likeness of the throne was a likeness as the appearance of a man upon it above. And I saw as the colour of amber, as the appearance of fire within it, round about, from the appearance of his loins and upwards ; and from the appearance of his loins and downward I saw as it were the appearance of fire, and there was brightness round about him. As the appearance of the bow that is in the cloud in the day of rain, so was the appearance of the brightness round about. This was the appearance of the likeness of the glory of

---

[1] Jeremiah, it is true, had this personal experience when he had been carried off to Egypt (Jer. xliii. 6, 7), but this happened late in his life.

Yahweh. And when I saw it, I fell upon my face "
(Ezek. i. 26–28). Very significant here is the way in
which the prophet shrinks from a direct mention of the
Almighty—" the likeness as the appearance of a man " ;
to Ezekiel the holiness of God is such that He is enveloped
in light and fire, unapproachable, and very far distant
from man ; and the utmost that man can do at the thought
of His presence is that he should fall upon his face.
And even when, in the spirit, Ezekiel receives a divine
communication, his first act is to fall down and hide his
face in the presence of the glory which indicates the
divine presence.

This teaching of Ezekiel on divine transcendence is
one aspect of the conception of God which is balanced
by that other aspect, so characteristic of Jeremiah, of
His condescension. Jeremiah, in his doctrine of God,
lays emphasis on His nearness ; but Ezekiel is overwhelmed by His transcendent holiness and greatness,
and therefore in a real sense His far-offness from man.
These two aspects of the conception of God were held in
wonderful balance, as we shall see, by another exilic
prophet. The twofold truth has rarely been more
exquisitely expressed than in Dryden's words :

> Thy throne is darkness in excess of light,
> A blaze of glory which forbids the sight.
> O teach me to believe Thee thus concealed,
> And search no farther than Thyself revealed.

But in the further history of Jewish religion this " proportion of faith " seems, with the one exception to be
referred to, to have been incapable of achievement.

2. Superhuman Beings

Of angelology in the strict sense of the term Ezekiel
has but little to say ; but he refers to other superhuman
beings, and this demands a little attention in view of
later developments. It can hardly admit of doubt that
what Ezekiel has to say of these intermediate beings
between God and man was an outcome of his doctrine
of divine transcendence.

While normally Yahweh speaks directly to the prophet,

there are quite a number of passages in which intermediate supernatural beings are mentioned. Thus, in xl. 3 f., it is not Yahweh but " a man, whose appearance was like the appearance of brass," who speaks to the prophet. In xi. 1–6 it is a spirit that speaks to him ; in ii. 2 the spirit sets him on his feet (see also iii. 14, viii. 3). This may be a development of the idea of the spirit mentioned in such passages as Judges xiv. 19 ; 1 Kings xxii. 21 ; 2 Kings ii. 16 ; but it is clear from the way in which Ezekiel speaks of this being that in his thought it is of a much higher order than in the earlier conception.

But another type of supernatural being mentioned in various passages points to Babylonian influence. The ancient conception of the Cherubim—in all probability of non-Israelite origin—meets us here ; and again, there is a development, and their hybrid forms, lion, bull, eagle, with four wings and hands beneath, but all having the faces of a man, point very clearly to Babylonian influence (i. 5–10, and cp. x. 1 ff.). Due to the same influence is the reference to the seven destroying angels, of human appearance, in ix. 1–11. These are probably seven planets, who were Babylonian deities, but the prophet subordinates them to Yahweh—a clear indication of his monotheistic belief—and they act as His instruments in carrying out His purpose.

3. INDIVIDUAL RESPONSIBILITY

Perhaps nowhere in the book of *Ezekiel* is the teaching on this subject set forth more tersely than in the words : " The soul that sinneth it shall die ; the son shall not bear the iniquity of the father, neither shall the father bear the iniquity of the son ; the righteousness of the righteous shall be upon him, and the wickedness of the wicked shall be upon him " (xviii. 20 ; the whole of this chapter deals with the subject). Most striking here is the contrast between this teaching and the authoritative words put forth not much more than a generation before of " visiting the sins of the fathers upon the children, and upon the third and upon the fourth generation of

them that hate me " (Deut. v. 9). The difference between these two points of view was a result of the Exile.
Previous to this the belief in the solidarity of the nation,
and in earlier days the solidarity of the tribe, carried
with it the conviction that individuals necessarily
shared in the prosperity of the nation as a whole ; so
that if the ancestors did what was right, or, on the contrary, what was wrong, every member of the nation partook of the resulting prosperity or misfortune. The
individual was considered only in so far as he was one
of the items that went to make up the nation. But when
the nation, as such, ceased to exist, and Israel consisted
merely of scattered individuals far from their homeland,
it followed in a very natural course that the importance
and significance of the individual came to the fore.
Each individual, Ezekiel teaches, is responsible for his
own acts ; for the evil that he suffers if he has sinned, he
has nobody but himself to blame ; while, on the other
hand, he cannot rely on the good deeds of his ancestors
to stand him in stead if he himself is lacking in these.

It is instructive to compare again Ezekiel's teaching
on this subject with that of Jeremiah. The earlier
prophet, as we know, was the first to teach that man,
the individual, not the nation, was the unit,[1] and it is
very remarkable that even before the Exile he should
have taught what in effect constituted a fundamental
change in the conception of religion. The difference in
the teaching on Individualism between these prophets
is briefly this : Jeremiah's individualism centres in man's
close relationship with God, and he is thus the earliest
exponent of *personal religion* ; Ezekiel's individualism
emphasizes man's own responsibility for his deeds, and
he is thus the first to teach *personal responsibility*. One
can easily see how from these respective points of view
two differing ideas regarding the individual in the sight
of God arose ; for, according to Jeremiah's teaching, man
feels that he is precious in the sight of God ; while,
according to Ezekiel's teaching, man feels his insignificance
and unworthiness in the sight of God ; for the sense of
responsibility, whatever else it may do, reveals his short-

[1] See Part II, Chapter XI, § 2.

comings to man.   Thus the teaching of these two prophets on Individualism touches closely upon their respective teaching on the divine Personality ; for it follows naturally that Jeremiah's conception of God envisages pre-eminently His nearness to the creature ; but Ezekiel, with his conception of the divine transcendence, feels how great is the distance between the Holy One and sinful mortals.

4. REGENERATION

Whatever specifically characteristic points in his teaching a prophet may have, it will always be found that they are dependent upon, or the outcome of, his concep-tion of God.   In chapter xxxvi. 16 ff. the word of Yahweh comes to Ezekiel, reminding him of the past ingratitude and unfaithfulness of his people ; but in spite of this, it goes on to say : " I had pity for mine holy name, which the house of Israel had profaned among the nations whither they went.   Therefore say unto the house of Israel, Thus saith the Lord God : I do not this for your sake, O house of Israel, but for mine holy name, which ye have profaned among the nations, whither ye went. And I will sanctify my great name. . . . And I will sprinkle clean water upon you, and ye shall be clean ; from all your filthiness, and from all your idols will I cleanse you.   A new heart also will I give you, and a new spirit will I put within you . . ." (vers. 16–30).   The prophet here teaches—and it is a necessary outcome of his belief in the holy all-power of God—that the divine purpose, however thwarted by a renegade people, will ultimately prevail.   For the honour of His holy name, He will see to it that the people, in spite of themselves, will accomplish their destiny as pre-ordained by God. The first step in the process of their regeneration is the divine cleansing, followed by the creation of a new spirit within them.   This, as the words of ver. 31 show, brings about the true condition of repentance—self-loathing because of past sin : " Then shall ye remember your evil ways, and your doings that were not good ; and ye shall loathe yourselves in your own sight for your iniquities and for your abominations." Ezekiel follows Jeremiah here to some extent; but he goes his own inimitable way in the remarkable picture contained in chapter xxxvii., in which he sees the valley full of dry bones, representing Israel dead in sin, and through the action of the divine spirit the dead bones become clothed with flesh, and live, quickened to a regenerate life.

Ezekiel's teaching on divine forgiveness, cleansing, and consequent regeneration of His people, reaches a religious stage which transcends anything hitherto existent in the religion of the Hebrews.

5. THE CEREMONIAL LAW

The teaching of Ezekiel about the ceremonial law and the importance he attaches to its observance, and further, his idealization of the Temple and its services—all these are the logical outcome of his conception of the majesty and holiness of God. As a priest he sometimes over-emphasizes the priestly point of view; that, perhaps, was inevitable; but zeal for the glory of God in things external as well as spiritual was the real motive-power in all his teaching.

As an illustration of the importance he attaches to the ceremonial law we have his words in iv. 14 : " Then said I, Ah, Lord God! behold, my soul hath not been polluted; for from my youth up even until now have I not eaten of that which dieth of itself, or is torn of beasts ; neither came there abominable flesh into my mouth." In chapters viii.–x. he makes it clear that the most abominable sin of the people is the way in which they have desecrated the Temple by the introduction of alien cults. It is noteworthy that in these chapters there is placed in contrast to these debasing rites some of those passages in which the transcendent glory of God is described (viii. 2, x. 1, 4 ff.), showing that it is his conception of the divine transcendence which calls forth his abhorrence of everything that is not in accordance with what the worship of God should be.

Then, to turn to another side of Ezekiel's teaching on the ceremonial law, the directions which he gives regarding the dress of the priests, and the need of the priests keeping separate from the people, may well strike us as *naïve*, for the primitive idea of *taboo* comes to the fore again (xliv. 17–19) ; and it is not to be denied that old-world ideas do assert themselves here ; but it must be remembered that this is not peculiar to Hebrew religion—it is a phenomenon which appears again and again in the history of every religion ; human nature is thus constituted. The fact must, however, be registered here because Ezekiel's insistence on ceremonial observances was not without its effect on succeeding ages. It is fully in accord with Ezekiel's priestly point of view that he regards the sons of Zadok as the representatives of the true priesthood, before which the idea of a temporal ruler recedes into the background, and the Levites as a subordinate order (xliv. 10–27 ; cp. xlii. 13, xliii. 19) ; in *Deuteronomy* all the Levites were priests.[1]

Thus to the prophetic activity of Ezekiel, already referred to, we must add the priestly point of view ; so that in spite of a somewhat narrow view in some directions a broader outlook is to be discerned in others.

6. ESCHATOLOGICAL-APOCALYPTIC IDEAS

What Ezekiel says about this subject is in the main the current material of which the earlier prophets had made use [2] ; but he adds some apocalyptic *traits* which occur in his book for the first time, though there can be no doubt that here, too, traditional material has been utilized.[3]

The ideas regarding the final catastrophe which will overtake the sinners in the last day are briefly as follows : the day itself is spoken of in vii. 7 ff. : " . . . The time is come, the day is near ; a day of tumult, and not of joyful shouting, upon the mountains. Now will I shortly pour

[1] In the Priestly Code, however, priests and Levites appear as distinct orders ; this is what one would expect after what Ezekiel had taught.

[2] See Part II, Chapter VIII, § 2, ii (*d*) ; and below, Chapter XV, § 1.

[3] Chapters xxxvii.–xxxix. are those especially, though by no means exclusively, concerned ; but the traditional authorship of xxxviii. and xxxix. is denied by a number of scholars.

my fury upon thee, and accomplish my anger against thee, and will judge thee according to thy ways . . ." (see also xiv. 19, xxii. 22). The terrors of that day are mentioned again and again : they will be seen in the natural world, darkness, and cloud (xxxiv. 12), storm and tempest (xiii. 11), drought (xxx. 12), and fire (xx. 47, 48 [in Hebrew xxi. 3, 4]), etc. ; further, famine and evil beasts, pestilence and blood, and the sword (v. 15–17) ; and the most terrible of all, the sword of Yahweh (xxi. 3–5 [in Hebrew 8–10]), and the cup of destruction from Yahweh (xxiii. 31–4). In that day Yahweh will be king, but He will reign in fury (xx. 33, 34). This last point illustrates the variety and not always consistent character of eschatological thought in the prophetical books—a mark of the different traditions current. It is said in this last passage that Yahweh Himself will be king ; but elsewhere when the future is spoken of it is one of the house of David who will be king : " And I will set up one shepherd over them, and he shall feed them, even my servant David ; he shall feed them, and he shall be their shepherd. And I Yahweh will be their God, and my servant David prince among them. And I will make with them a covenant of peace . . ." (xxxiv. 23 ff. ; see also xxxvii. 24–6). The term " shepherd," applied to the Messianic ruler, becomes from now onwards a constant trait in eschatological thought.

The blessedness of the Messianic times finds frequent mention : the cleansing of the people from sin is, of course, a necessary preliminary (xxxvi. 33) ; the ingathering of Israel, from all the lands in which they are dispersed, will then follow (xi. 17 ; cp. xx. 34) ; and the remarkable thought that even those will be gathered who are in their graves occurs in xxxvii. 12–14. In that day, further, the land will be very fruitful (xxxvi. 34, 35), and there will be peace and plenty (xxxiv. 25–7). A large amount of space is taken up with the account of the destruction of Israel's foes ; this, of course, was one of the oldest popular traditional ideas regarding the Day of Yahweh (xxv.–xxxii., xxxv.).

Especially characteristic of Ezekiel's thought regarding the Messianic era is his emphasis on the cult (xx. 40, 41) ;

in xxxvii. 26–8 he says : " . . . And I will multiply them, and will place my sanctuary in the midst of them for evermore. My tabernacle shall also be over them ; and I will be their God, and they shall be my people. And the nations shall know that I, Yahweh, am he that sanctifieth Israel, when my sanctuary shall be in the midst of them for evermore." The very great importance attached to worship in the Messianic times is seen by this prophet's description of the Temple (xl.–xlviii.).

A marked inconsistency is that long after the Messianic time has been inaugurated and the people are dwelling securely, the great foe Gog, at the head of Israel's enemies, will come to destroy the land of Palestine. Gog seems to have been the name of a legendary people living in the far north, and it is evident that the prophet, whether Ezekiel or another, was utilizing some traditional material in writing about them in xxxviii., xxxix. ; but he is doubtless applying the mythical names of Gog and Magog to some actual enemies whom he has in mind.[1] Some, at least, of the apocalyptic pictures presented point to the utilization of extraneous ideas ; thus, in xxxviii. 18–23, we have a curious mixture of Hebrew and non-Hebraic thought ; the passage is a remarkable one, and therefore worth quoting in full : " And it shall come to pass in that day, when Gog shall come against the land of Israel, saith the Lord God, that my fury shall come up into my nostrils. For in my jealousy and in the fire of my wrath have I spoken ; surely in that day there shall be a great shaking in the land of Israel ; so that the fishes of the sea, and the fowls of the heaven, and the beasts of the field, and all creeping things that creep upon the earth, and all the men that are upon the face of the earth, shall shake at my presence, and the mountains shall be thrown down, and the steep places shall fall, and every wall shall fall to the ground. And I will call for a sword against him unto all my mountains, saith the Lord God ; every man's sword shall be against his brother. And I will plead against him with pestilence

---

[1] Hölscher favours the theory that Gog represents Gyges king of Lydia who reigned about 660 B.C. (*Hesekiel, der Dichter und das Buch*, p. 189 [1924]).

17

and with blood ; and I will rain upon him, and upon his
hordes, and upon the many peoples that are with him,
an overflowing shower, and great hailstones, fire and
brimstone.   And I will magnify myself, and I will make
myself known in the eyes of many nations ; and they
shall know that I am Yahweh."

This is not the place to deal with the many points of
interest arising out of this passage ; one has but to read
it to realize that it contains diverse elements.   It offers
one of the best illustrations of the fact that the eschatological and apocalyptic ideas in the prophetical books
are largely drawn from extraneous sources.   This will
be further dealt with in Chapter XV.

CHAPTER V

RELIGIOUS TEACHERS: DEUTERO-ISAIAH

THE latest record that we have of Ezekiel belongs to the year 571 B.C. ; whether he lived and taught after this we have no means of knowing.

From the writings which have been preserved of the great prophet whom we designate Deutero-Isaiah,[1] it is evident that his ministry began at a time when the menace to the Babylonian empire had become serious. In a passage from another part of *Isaiah* which clearly belongs to this period the coming doom is foreseen : " Behold, I will stir up the Medes against them, which shall not regard silver, and as for gold, they shall not delight in it. And their bows shall dash the young men in pieces ; and they shall have no pity on the fruit of the womb ; their eye shall not spare children. And Babylon, the glory of kingdoms, the beauty of the Chaldeans' pride, shall be as when God overthrew Sodom and Gomorrah " (Isa. xiii. 17–19). This points, in all probability, to the time when Cyrus, after his conquest of the Lydian kingdom, 546 B.C., was in a position to begin his campaign against the Babylonian empire of Nabonidus. Thus the Deutero-Isaianic writings may be assigned to the period between 546 B.C. and 538 B.C., the year of the first return of Jewish exiles to Palestine.

1. THE CONCEPTION OF GOD

With the teaching of this prophet on the nature and personality of God we reach the zenith of Hebrew religious belief. Monotheism had, indeed, been implicit in the teaching of earlier prophets ; but never before had it been explicit, never before had there been the reiterated

[1] Isa. xl.–lv.

insistence upon the truth as expressed by this prophet.
God is the Creator from everlasting, the eternal and only
One : " Before me there was no God formed, neither
shall there be after me. I, even I, am Yahweh ; and
beside me there is no saviour " (xliii. 10) ; " I am Yahweh,
and there is none else ; beside me there is no God . . .
I am Yahweh, and there is none else. I form the light
and create darkness ; I make peace, and bring calamity ;
I am Yahweh that doeth all these things " (xlv. 5–7).
" For thus saith Yahweh that created the heavens ; he
is God, that formed the earth and made it ; he established
it, he created it not in vain, he formed it to be inhabited ;
I am Yahweh, and there is none else " (xlv. 18). As
the Creator of all, the cosmic forces are to Him but small
and insignificant : " Who hath measured the waters
in the hollow of his hand, and meted out the heavens
with a span, and comprehended the dust of the earth in a
measure, and weighed the mountains in scales, and the
hills in a balance ? . . . Behold, the nations are as a
drop of a bucket, and are counted as the small dust of
the balance ; behold, the isles are as the fine dust that is
lifted up " (xl. 12–15). And, once more : " Hast thou
not known ? Hast thou not heard ? Yahweh is the
everlasting God, the Creator of the ends of the earth ;
he fainteth not, neither is he weary ; there is no searching
of his understanding " (xl. 28 ; cp. also ver. 8.)

Passages like these show to what a sublime height of
conception this prophet had attained ; no doubt there
were things happening in the world which may have
contributed to this—the fall of nations and the impotence
of Babylonian and other gods ; but there was something
more and something deeper than this that gave to this
prophet such an insight into and apprehension of the
nature and personality of God. The natural evolution
of ideas does much to deepen and enlarge men's thought
of God ; but there come moments when to such development there is needed the self-revelation of God Himself
(we may not know how or by what means) and without
which development alone merely disperses itself and
becomes thin air, or else degeneration supervenes, of
which the history of religion has offered many illustrations

Here was one of the men to whom God vouchsafed to reveal Himself in a very special way, and there are not many to whom such revelation has been accorded, but when there is response, as in the case of Deutero-Isaiah, they become landmarks in the history of religion. This prophet could say with truth in the name of God, " My thoughts are not your thoughts, neither are your ways my ways "; but at times he himself was the mouthpiece whereby the thoughts of God were proclaimed.

It is instructive to see how this prophet, with all his insight into the greatness and omnipotence of God, was not unmindful of that other aspect of the divine character, of which he speaks, for example, in such words as these : " He shall feed his flock like a shepherd, he shall gather the lambs in his arm, and carry them in his bosom, and shall gently lead those that give suck " (xl. 11), thus combining the characteristic teaching of Jeremiah on the divine condescension with that of Ezekiel on the transcendental character of God.

2. The Regeneration of the People

The deeply religious character of this prophet was such that in whatever direction his teaching tended, his Godward thought always predominated. This is well illustrated in the words of comfort and encouragement to his people, in which he tells them of how God will deal with them in the time that is to come. In the restoration of the nation which he portrays and which is about to take place in the near future, the first condition must be a people purified from sin, and therefore he cries in the name of the Lord : " I have blotted out, as a thick cloud, thy transgressions, and, as a cloud, thy sins ; return unto me, for I have redeemed thee " (Isa. xliv. 22). It is the first act of divine mercy ; a regenerated people, ready therefore and fit, as God's chosen servants, to welcome the divine presence in their midst : " But thou, Israel, my servant, Jacob whom I have chosen, the seed of Abraham my friend ; thou whom I have taken hold of from the ends of the earth, and called thee from the corners thereof, and said unto thee, Thou art my servant, I have chosen

thee and not cast thee away ; fear thou not, for I am
with thee ; be not dismayed, for I am thy God ; I will
strengthen thee ; yea, I will help thee ; yea, I will uphold thee with the right hand of my righteousness "
(Isa. xli. 8–10). There are many other words to the same
effect ; and what is very noteworthy is the fact that the
prophet fully realizes that nothing which the people
have done has called forth these marks of divine pardon
and loving protection ; the nature of God as love impels
Him to be true to Himself, and therefore for His name's
sake His mercy is shown forth : " For mine own sake, for
mine own sake, will I do it ; for how should my name be
profaned ? and my glory will I not give to another "
(Isa. xlviii. 11). Both Jeremiah and Ezekiel had uttered
a similar thought. And the sequel, the prophet teaches,
shall be a worthy response on the part of the people :
" All thy children shall be taught of Yahweh, and great
shall be the peace of thy children. In righteousness shalt
thou be established " (Isa. liv. 13, 14). Regeneration is
thus prominent in this prophet's thought ; and while in
this he follows Ezekiel (cp. Ezek. xxxvii.), he handles the
subject quite independently, and develops it in his own
way with a warmth of feeling and a depth of apprehension
of the love of God which is unrivalled elsewhere in Hebrew
religious teaching.

3. Universalism

With his exalted conception of the unity and all-power
of God it followed that Deutero-Isaiah could not be
content with the restrictive idea of Yahweh as a national
God. He speaks therefore in the name of God, saying :
" Look unto me, and be ye saved, all the ends of the
earth ; for I am God, and there is none else. By myself
have I sworn, the word is gone forth from my mouth,
and shall not return, that unto me every knee shall bow,
every tongue shall swear " (xlv. 22, 23). " The God of
the whole earth shall he be called " (liv. 5).

And it is in accordance with this universalistic idea
that the prophet points to Cyrus as God's anointed,
called forth to do His will : " Thus saith Yahweh to his

anointed, to Cyrus, whose right hand I have holden, to subdue nations before him " (xlv. 1); " My counsel shall stand, and I will do all my pleasure, calling a ravenous bird from the east, the man of my counsel from a far country " (xlvi. 10, 11).

As the instrument for the conversion of the Gentiles it is but natural that Israel should be regarded as preeminent ; hence those passages which, on the one hand, speak of the nations as joining themselves to Israel, and, on the other hand, those which describe them as subservient to Israel : " Thus saith Yahweh, The labour of Egypt, and the merchandise of Ethiopia, and the Sabeans, men of stature, shall come over unto thee, and they shall be thine ; they shall go after thee ; in chains they shall come over ; and they shall fall down unto thee, they shall make supplication unto thee, saying, Surely God is in thee, and there is none else, there is no other God " (xlv. 14). And again, in the well-known passage, xlix. 22, 23 : " Behold, I will lift up mine hand to the nations, and set up mine ensign to the peoples, and they shall bring thy sons in their bosom, and thy daughters shall be carried upon their shoulders. And kings shall be thy nursing fathers, and their queens thy nursing mothers ; they shall bow down to thee with their faces to the earth, and lick the dust of thy feet ; and thou shalt know that I am Yahweh, and they that wait for me shall not be ashamed." [1]

The final conception, however, is that of the leadership of Israel among the Gentiles, without any thought of subserviency on the part of the latter : " Behold, I have given him for a witness to the peoples, a leader and a commander to the peoples. Behold, thou shalt call a nation that thou knowest not, and a nation that knew not thee shall run unto thee, because of Yahweh thy God, and for the Holy one of Israel ; for he hath glorified thee " (lv. 4, 5). In this passage it is noteworthy that the thought of God again predominates ; it is because Yahweh is their God that this nation will join itself to Israel.

[1] This passage and the next are regarded by some commentators as of different authorship, but this is not necessarily the case.

It is impossible to over-emphasize the importance of this universalistic teaching, and of Israel being designated the instrument whereby the conversion of the Gentiles was to be brought about, for quite evidently in the mind of Deutero-Isaiah there was the thought of the religion of the Hebrews becoming a world-religion. Doubtless there was in the teaching of some of the earlier prophets that which logically tended in the same direction ; but it is in Deutero-Isaiah that this becomes a concrete expectation. Two things were primarily responsible for this : the Exile, with the wider outlook upon the world which it offered ; but still more Deutero-Isaiah's conception of God. With his apprehension of Yahweh as the God of the whole world, there followed of necessity that He should be thought of as the God of all men, and that the worship of Him should become world-wide.

4. The " Servant of the Lord " Songs

Though there are some notable exceptions, the majority of modern scholars regard these four songs (Isa. xlii. 1–4, xlix. 1–6, l. 4–9, lii. 13–liii. 12) [1] as not belonging to Deutero-Isaiah. The difficult problem need not trouble us, as we are dealing with religious teaching ; who gave the teaching is of less importance than the fact that it *was* given. One thing, however, seems certain : the spirit and style of these songs are so reminiscent of Deutero-Isaiah, and some of their outstanding thoughts are so similar to his, that if this prophet was not the author it must have been somebody very much under his influence and wholly imbued with his spirit who wrote them. [2] But there is justification in either case for treating them separately, because there can be no doubt that they were originally independent pieces, and did not stand in the text as they do now.

Nor are we, for the moment, concerned with the question as to who the " Servant of the Lord " was (see below) ; one thing only we would wish to state with

---

[1] According to some scholars the first three songs should respectively comprise xlii. 1–9, xlix. 1–13, l. 4–11.

[2] The present writer finds it difficult to resist the conclusion that they were written by Deutero-Isaiah (see below, pp. 269 f.).

emphasis : the contention that Israel as a nation is meant seems to us quite out of the question ; only a forced and unnatural exegesis can give such an interpretation to passages like xlix. 1, 5, 6 ; and if Israel is the " Servant," how are we to understand liii. 4–6 ? Who is the " he " and who the " we " in such words as : " Surely *he* hath borne *our* griefs and carried *our* sorrows ; yet *we* did esteem *him* stricken of God and afflicted. But *he* was wounded for *our* transgressions . . . " ? In xlix. 3, it is true, Israel is definitely mentioned as the servant ; but it must be obvious that in face of vers. 5, 6, " Israel " is a gloss ; for if Israel is the servant, how can it be said that he is " to bring Jacob again to him, and that Israel be gathered unto him (Yahweh) " ? How is Israel " to raise up the tribes of Jacob, and to restore the preserved of Israel " ? [1]

Who the " Servant " was we are not prepared to say, other than that he was a real, not an idealized, man (see below).

What is of greater importance than these controversial questions is the teaching contained in these songs. This is of the deepest significance, as will be seen.

First, as to the vocation of the " Servant." The words, " I have put my spirit upon him " (xlii. 1) can be interpreted as marking him out as the Messiah,[2] or as in reference to the divine gift to enable him to fulfil his calling as prophet. For the present let us leave it open as to which is meant. Then there is the universalistic teaching which we have seen to be so characteristic of Deutero-Isaiah. In xlii. 1 it is said : " He shall bring forth judgement to the Gentiles " : judgement here means the righteousness and justice of divine principles ; this, together with ver. 4 and xlix. 6, " I will also give thee for a light to the Gentiles, that my salvation may be unto the end of the earth," shows that, as Deutero-Isaiah

---

[1] It is also worth pointing out that the rhythm (three strokes to each half-verse) is broken if " Israel " is inserted. For a very sane presentation of the " Servant " representing the collective nation (though the present writer finds himself unable to accept this interpretation) see Wheeler Robinson, *The Religious Ideas of the Old Testament*, pp. 202 ff. (1926).

[2] See further below, p. 267.

teaches elsewhere, the religion of the Jews was to become a world-religion.

One other subject the teaching of which is the same as that found elsewhere in this book is the conception of God ; this will become clear as we proceed.

But now we come to deal with teaching which belongs specifically to these songs. The " Servant," in spite of his high calling, is subdued, humble, and of extreme gentleness : " He shall not cry nor lift up, nor cause his voice to be heard in the street. A bruised reed shall he not break, and the smoking flax shall he not quench " (xlii. 2, 3). It is difficult to see how or why the " Servant " should be thus depicted unless it portrayed an actual person. But what was to be gained by describing the Messiah [1] or a prophet in this way ? It was not such a figure that would appeal to the people. Had the writer intended to present an *ideal* man, he would, one feels, have constructed a different picture. But he could not help himself, because his hero was one whom he saw as he was ; it was, in any case, going to be a difficult thing to account for the facts of the life and sufferings and death of this chosen instrument of God ; but the writer was dealing with things as they were, not as he would have wished them to be.

He sees, further, that this " Servant " was in personal appearance unattractive ; he was the victim of some scourge, so that men turned from him as from some unclean person (lii. 14, liii. 2, 3). Here, if anywhere, according to the belief of the times, was the case of one suffering calamity and disease because he had sinned : " We did esteem him stricken, smitten of God and afflicted " (liii. 4). Yet it is perfectly clear to the writer that this " Servant " was a righteous man : " He had done no violence, neither was any deceit in his mouth " (liii. 9). So that here was the problem of a righteous man suffering. How was it to be accounted for ? The writer of these songs teaches—and he was the first to put forth the doctrine—that since sin must be atoned for, and since the " Servant," as a righteous man, cannot be

---

[1] The portraiture would be still more difficult to account for if the idealized nation were meant.

atoning for his own sins, therefore he is atoning for the sins of others : " He was wounded for our transgressions, he was bruised for our iniquities ; the chastisement of our peace was upon him, and with his stripes we are healed " (liii. 5 ; cp. ver. 8).

Now there are some reasons, in spite of what was said just now, for holding that the writer of these songs believed the " Servant " to be the expected Messiah ; this is denied by many modern scholars ; but there are the following points to be considered :

There is no doubt that one of the functions of the Messiah was to lead back the people from captivity and rule over them in their own land, if not as king, at least as prince ; this is clearly seen in the case of Zerubbabel, whom these prophets regard as the Messiah (Zech. iv. 11, 14, vi. 12 ; Hag. ii. 1–9 and 23). Similarly in xlix. 5, 6, the " Servant " is described as one who is to bring back the people and restore them to their own land. This is further emphasized if vers. 7–9 of this chapter be regarded, as they may well be, as belonging to the second song.

Then again, the way in which the spirit of God is said to rest upon Zerubbabel (Zech. iv. 6, 14 ; Hag. ii. 4, 5) is paralleled by xlii. 1 ; and further, Zerubbabel is spoken of as " my servant " (Hag. ii. 23 ; cp. Isa. xlii. 1, xlix. 3, 6, lii. 13, where the hero of these songs receives a similar title).

Leader of the captives to their native land, one on whom the spirit of God rests, one who receives the title of " my servant "—to Zerubbabel, who is admittedly regarded as the Messiah, these things apply ; so that if they are also all applied to the " Servant " of these songs, the fact is a strong argument in favour of the contention that the " Servant " was thought of as the Messiah.

There is a further consideration which points in the same direction : in xlix. 7 it is said in reference to the " Servant " : " Kings shall see and arise ; princes, and they shall do homage," and in lii. 15 : " So shall he startle [1] many nations ; kings shall shut their mouths

---

[1] The text can hardly be in order ; the Septuagint has : " So shall many nations marvel at him."

because of him." There would not be much point in these words if the "Servant" were thought of as an ordinary ruler ; but they are very significant if he was intended to be thought of as the Messiah. And if the idealized nation were meant there would be a mixing-up of the ideal and the real ; but this is not the way of the writer of these songs.

But if this is so we are confronted with the difficulty of the death of the Messiah under conditions which are wholly inappropriate (liii. 9) ; the "Servant" witnesses for Yahweh and His truth, he suffers for this, and bears the sins of others ; ultimately he dies a martyr's death.

This is not the kind of Messianic picture that is to be expected ; nor, as we shall see, was the writer of the songs satisfied with it, extremely beautiful as his whole conception is. There is, however, another and supremely important matter in connexion with the "Servant" which must be referred to, and it is concerned with what is, after all, the fundamental teaching of the whole of this book—the conception of God, a conception which, as we have seen, reaches the summit of Hebrew religion. Nothing is more significant in all these songs than the intimate and close relationship of the "Servant" with God—incidentally this might well be urged as a further indication of the Messiahship of the "Servant" ;— thus in xlii. 1 : "Behold ; my servant, whom I uphold ; my chosen in whom my soul delighteth ; I have put my spirit upon him " ; in xlix. 1–3 : "Yahweh hath called me from the womb . . . and he said unto me, Thou art my servant in whom I will be glorified " ; in l. 4 ff. : "The Lord God hath given me the tongue of them that are taught . . . the Lord God hath opened mine ear . . . the Lord God will help me . . . " ; in liii. 6 : "Yahweh hath laid on him the iniquity of us all." This intimate relationship between the "Servant" and God must be thought of in connexion with the enlarged and exalted conception of God which is peculiar to this book. In particular, it must be recognized that in this book there is a constant emphasis laid upon God as the Everlasting : "The Everlasting God, Yahweh, the Creator of the ends of the earth, fainteth not, neither is weary ; there is no

searching of his understanding " (xl. 28) ; in one form or
another this thought of God as eternal finds expression
again and again (see xl. 8, xli. 4, xliii. 10, xliv. 6, xlviii.
12, li. 6, 8, lv. 13). Is it too much to believe that to a
man like Deutero-Isaiah, with his deep apprehension of
the spiritual nature and majesty of God, this conception
of the eternity of God should have suggested the possibility of His being concerned with the spirits of men after
death ? The current *She'ol* belief did, at any rate,
recognize the continued existence of the shades of men
in the Hereafter ; it was a nebulous and unsatisfying
belief ; and in the mind of Deutero-Isaiah, who believed
in the divine eternity, may there not have been an
incongruity in the thought that the interest of God, the
Creator, in man, created in His own image, should be
restricted to the short span of this life ? It can hardly
be denied that with a developed conception of the
Personality of God, with a deeper apprehension of His
spiritual nature, and with a fuller realization of His
creative power, there must necessarily, sooner or later,
have arisen a doubt as to the correctness of a belief that
God was only concerned with men in this world. With
his sublime conception of God, to Deutero-Isaiah the
traditional belief that God was concerned only with men
in this life must have been agonizing when he had before
him the picture of the righteous chosen " Servant "
ending in death that intimate relationship with God
which had been so marked all through his life. So the
conviction came upon him that death was not the end ;
for what else can the words mean : " Therefore will I
divide him a portion with the great, and he shall divide
the spoil with the strong, because he poured out his
soul unto death, and was numbered with the transgressors " (liii. 12) ? How, after being dead, can it be
said that he shall have a portion with the great, unless
he was to rise from the dead to take the part assigned him
by God ? Ezekiel had already formulated the conception
of the nation dead in sin rising to righteousness through
the action of the divine spirit. Deutero-Isaiah's adaptation of this conception in a higher sense was made easier,
seeing that he had the figure of the *righteous* " Servant "

before him. Thus, there is some justification for believing that Deutero-Isaiah was the first to adumbrate, if nothing more, a doctrine of the resurrection among the Jews.[1] Such a conception would naturally, at first, be only of a tentative character ; many years too would pass before it could become a generally accepted belief. But such a thought, however inspired, could only arise in the minds of the people's most advanced thinkers ; and among these Deutero-Isaiah stood out pre-eminent.

Our conclusion, therefore, is that the " Servant " was an actual person who, on account of his pre-eminent righteousness, was believed by the prophet to be the Messiah. He suffered in a " naughty " world because of his righteousness ; but his suffering was to the prophet of comparatively small moment, because he was convinced that the " Servant " would rise from death to complete his work ; and it was the " Servant's " close relationship with God, and the prophet's profound belief in the righteousness and eternity of God, that compelled this conviction.[2]

5. OTHER TEACHERS OF THE EXILIC PERIOD

In addition to the great outstanding teachers already mentioned there were many others, fragments of whose teaching have come down to us, e.g. Lamentations ; Isa. xiii. 1–xiv. 23 ; Obad. 1–14 ; Lev. xvii.–xxvi., and some of the Psalms. As compared with Ezekiel and Deutero-Isaiah, however, there is nothing of sufficiently outstanding importance to demand separate treatment.

Then, further, there was the Deuteronomic circle of teachers whose interpretation of the past history of the people is indelibly impressed on the historical books. These were men of deep piety and religious feeling, and their influence is to be seen in all the writings of this period ; but their contribution to the development of Hebrew religion was not equal to that of the two great prophets mentioned.

Finally, there was the very important priestly school

---

[1] Persian influences regarding the doctrine of Immortality may well have been exerted as early as this time (see further below, Chapter XV, § 2 (iv).

[2] On the subject of vicarious suffering, see below, Chapter XII, § 2.

whose influence upon the formulation of the Law was profound and very far-reaching ; but while we know that their activity was already exercised during the exilic period, it is not until we study the post-exilic literature that we come to the details of their teaching. To this we shall devote our attention in Chapter XVI.

6. Summary of the Development of Hebrew Religion during the Exilic Period

The profound and far-reaching developments in Hebrew Religion during the Exile may now be summarized. At the base of the teaching of the exilic prophets lay that of the great prophets of the preceding centuries, so that a great deal of the religious teaching of this period was not new ; as this has already been dealt with [1] we are not now concerned with it ; the developments from this earlier teaching is what we must keep before our minds.

The external religious observances which during the Exile assumed a prominence and importance never previously accorded to them were the rite of Circumcision and the Sabbath. Owing to the inevitable absence of the sacrificial services worship took the form of assemblies of the faithful, primarily on Sabbaths, at which there are reasons for believing that the main elements consisted of the reading of the prophetical writings and *Deuteronomy*, preaching, the singing of psalms, and the offering of prayer.

Both at such assemblies and in all probability at other times the great religious truths connected with belief in Yahweh were put forth.

The chief inspirers here were Ezekiel and the prophet we speak of as Deutero-Isaiah. The former's teaching on divine transcendence surpassed all that had hitherto been taught. His doctrine of man centred in individual responsibility. Further, as an outcome of his conception of God he looked for the regeneration of his people ; this culminated in his picture of the resuscitation of the people from death in sin to a new life through the action of the divine spirit ; a thought which contained the germ of belief in resurrection. As a priest, Ezekiel insisted

[1] See Part II, Chapter VIII, §§ 2, 3.

upon the need of the observance of the ceremonial law ; and his ideal picture of the renovation of the Temple and its services preserved among the exiles the hope of its realization in a happy future in their own land.

In Deutero-Isaiah the conception of God reached its highest and final development in Hebrew Religion. He conceives of Yahweh as the God of the universe, and therefore the God of all peoples ; with him the truth of the unity of God is reiterated, and becomes explicit as never before. He teaches, too, that God is from everlasting to everlasting. The religion of the Jews was to become a world-religion. While thus fully in accord with Ezekiel's conception of the divine transcendence, he balances this truth with what he teaches on the divine condescension, comparing God's love and care for men with a shepherd's solicitude for his flock. Ezekiel's teaching on regeneration is continued by Deutero-Isaiah, but he emphasizes more fully the divine mercy in blotting out the sins of the people.

A special importance attaches to the religious teaching contained in the " Servant of the Lord " songs ; whether Deutero-Isaiah was the author of these, as we hold, or another, is a matter of less importance than the teaching contained in them. The writer's universalistic teaching is in entire agreement with what is taught on this subject in the rest of the book.

There are reasons for believing that the " Servant " was, in the mind of the writer, the Messiah. As the chosen of God and a righteous man his suffering cannot have been for sins which he had committed, according to the traditional belief ; therefore, the writer teaches, his suffering is for the sins of his people ; it is the first time that the doctrine of vicarious suffering is put forth. The suffering " Servant " ultimately dies a martyr's death ; but to the writer, with his sublime conception of the eternal and righteous God, this cannot be the end ; and he therefore teaches, implicitly it is true, that God will raise up His " Servant " from death to complete the work He gave him to do.

Teaching of another kind was given during the Exile, but as the details of this occur only in post-exilic writings, they are not dealt with here.

CHAPTER VI

PERSIAN INFLUENCE ON JEWISH BELIEF

WHILE the antecedents of the religion of Persia (Zoroastrianism) [1] go back to the fifteenth century B.C., when Iranian influence can be traced in Syria and Palestine, it was not until the time of Cyrus, probably a little earlier, that the Jews, coming into contact with the Persians, had an opportunity of learning about their religion.

The question as to how far the religion of the Jews was influenced by that of Persia is a very controversial one ; some scholars deny any Persian influence, others see a good deal of it. Both extreme positions are probably exaggerated. In one direction it seems quite impossible not to see that strong Persian influences had been at work, viz. in the domain of Eschatology and Apocalyptic ; but as we are dealing with this in Chapter XV we shall not refer to it further here.

But in other directions it is recognized that there is a great difficulty in deciding whether or not Persian influences are to be discerned. What cannot but strike even a superficial observer in comparing Zoroastrianism with Judaism is the existence of some remarkable parallels ; not that these necessarily denote the influence of either on the other ; but even assuming that there was *no* influence (apart from Eschatology) it is impossible not to recognize that the Jewish religious leaders must have felt considerable sympathy with much that they saw in Zoroastrian belief and practice.

We will enumerate the more prominent parallels

---

[1] Zoroaster is the Græcized form of the Persian Zarathustra. There is uncertainty as to when he lived ; that it was before 600 B.C. may be taken for granted ; probably, however, not very much before that date.

between the two religions in order to show that there was much similarity of thought between them.

Zoroaster appeared as a reformer and spiritualizer of a religion which had been in existence long before his time. His rejection of the gods of this earlier religion, and his teaching that there was only one God, must have appealed to the monotheistic belief of the Jews.

Ahura Mazda (" Wise Lord "), he taught, was the one God and All-Father of the world, who dwells in light, Creator of the sun, moon, and stars, of light and darkness, of the earth and all on it. This teaching suffered deterioration afterwards ; but so far as Zoroaster himself was concerned he was a monotheist.

Nobody, of course, would for a moment suppose that the monotheistic belief of the Jews owed anything to Persian religion here ; but the parallel is worth mention if for no other reason than that it must have commended Zoroastrianism to them ; and this would make it easier to understand Persian influence in other directions. But even here it is possible that in a small but interesting particular, Persian influence may be discerned. Ahura Mazda, as we have just seen, was said to dwell in light and to have created light and darkness ; an act of praise in which this belief is expressed was said daily at dawn. One of the oldest pre-Christian Benedictions in the Jewish Liturgy, which was also said at dawn, begins with the words : " Blessed art thou, O Lord our God, King of the Universe, who formest light and createst darkness." It may be merely a coincidence, but if so it is certainly a very striking one. The Jewish Benediction was, no doubt, based directly on Isa. xlv. 7 ; but that Deutero-Isaiah may have adapted extraneous beliefs to the religion of Yahweh, as Ezekiel had done, is not an unreasonable supposition.[1]

Again, apart from Judaism, no religion laid such emphasis on moral living as Zoroastrianism did. The great reformer declared his task to be the setting-up of a kingdom of God on earth ; his adherents must be pure in body as in mind. Many of the Zoroastrian laws are

[1] Gen. i. 1–5 belongs to the Priestly Code, and therefore does not come into consideration here.

puerile, and sometimes repulsive ; but the high ethical ideal which was set must have appealed to the Jewish religious leaders as entirely in accordance with their Law.

Arising out of this there is the further point of parallelism that Zoroastrianism was a book-religion just as Judaism had come to be. Each had its Law ; and what may conceivably have influenced the Jews was the fact that the Persians believed in the pre-existence of the divine Law which they personified. The Jews identified their Law with Wisdom, which they personified ; and, as we see from Prov. viii., they believed in the existence of Wisdom before the creation of the world.[1] And finally, it is probable that the Angelology and Demonology of the Persians directly influenced Judaism ; in these things the earlier form of Iranian religion persisted in spite of Zoroaster's teaching. This is true also of the Dualism of the Persians, which, however, was never accepted by the Jews.

Our main conclusion therefore is that while there was much in Persian religion which would have been regarded with sympathy by the Jews, they were influenced but little directly thereby. The great exception to this was in the domain of Eschatology ; but as this requires more detailed examination, a separate chapter must be devoted to the subject (see Chapter XV).

---

[1] Prov. viii. belongs to the latest portion of the book of *Proverbs*, probably the third century B.C. ; but this is not to say that it may not in some respects reflect earlier thought.

CHAPTER VII

THE RETURN FROM EXILE

1. PARTICULARISM AND UNIVERSALISM

THE difference in mental outlook between priest and prophet was age-long. Fundamentally, it is engendered by tendencies which are inborn in man ; but it is fostered by the difference of calling and function as between priest and prophet. The two points of view were already in evidence long before the Exile, and although they did not necessarily cause a cleavage between the priesthood and the prophetical office, yet signs were not wanting which pointed to the fact that difference in aim and method made a fusion of the two mental attitudes characteristic of them respectively difficult, at times impossible. That the priestly and the prophetical points of view were in evidence during the exilic period is certain, though the actual proof of this only emerges fully later. Nevertheless, the diverging tendencies are already clearly discernible in the mental attitudes of Ezekiel the priest and Deutero-Isaiah the prophet respectively.

These tendencies we express, in one main direction respectively at any rate, by the terms Particularism and Universalism. In the present connexion the former term connotes, in general, a somewhat restricted nationalistic point of view, while the latter denotes a wider mental outlook. The particularistic attitude conceives of God as the God of Israel, the universalistic attitude would express itself in such words as : " Look unto me, and be ye saved, all the ends of the earth " (Isa. xlv. 22). The former would regard Israel as alone worthy of divine consideration, the latter would include the Gentiles within God's scheme of salvation.

We draw attention to these tendencies here because

they are discernible in this period ; they come to grips in subsequent periods, and the conflict becomes a death-struggle.[1]

2. THE RETURNED EXILES

It was not until the period of the Exile was drawing to a close that, as we have seen, Deutero-Isaiah arose as a teacher of his people. During most of the exilic period, therefore, the dominant influence had been exercised by the circle of priestly teachers whose interest centred in the study and elaboration of the Law and its observances. Thus it is that we are confronted by the ironical fact that to Deutero-Isaiah the misinterpretation of his own words which we find in vogue in the time of John the Baptist became applicable : " The voice of one crying in the wilderness " ; instead of : " The voice of one crying : In the wilderness . . ." For the voice of Deutero-Isaiah, as the sequel shows, proclaiming the most sublime teaching the world had ever heard, made little appeal. The earlier priestly influence and teaching had taken root too deeply. Concentration on the *minutiæ* of legal observances was having a narrowing effect upon the mind ; to the priestly teachers the Jews were the people of the Law, and therefore they had no interest in Gentiles. As it was Yahweh who had given the Law His pre-eminent demand must be the observance of His Law. As the Jews were His chosen people they must be His chief concern. And thus the universalistic teaching of Deutero-Isaiah did not bear fruit ; some there were who followed in his steps, and later the spirit of his teaching emerged ; but for the present their influence, with one exception to be referred to in the next chapter, so far as we can gather from the records, was negligible. From now on belief and practice narrowed down, in the main, into nationalistic grooves ; and the religion which the greater prophets, and especially Deutero-Isaiah, would have made a world-religion,

---

[1] As outstanding illustrations of the particularistic and universalistic attitudes respectively, we may point to Joel iii. 9–14, and the book of *Jonah* ; both belong to the Greek period.

assumed of set purpose a form which excluded non-Jews.

Before we come to deal with the great thought-movements the seeds of which, though taking root during the Exile, did not come to full fruition until rather later during the post-exilic period, we must take a brief glance at the more prominent points of teaching of which we have records during the few years immediately following upon the Return. This is advisable because, so far as our present knowledge goes, there is a gap in the history after the time of Haggai and Zechariah—perhaps Malachi should also be included ; so that the few years from the Return to the building of the Temple, 538–516 B.C., are cut off, as it were, from the subsequent history, which is not taken up again until more than half a century had passed.

In 520 B.C. we find a considerable community of returned exiles settled in Jerusalem and the vicinity ; their chief leaders and teachers are Haggai and Zechariah, though there are indications that priestly influence was dominant.[1]

The exiles had returned with the ostensible purpose of rebuilding the Temple ; but they were in no hurry to undertake the task. Material conditions were dispiriting : most of the people depended upon agriculture for gaining a living ; but the seasons were bad, crops were poor, harvests were delayed ; there was a dire struggle for existence. Haggai taught that this was all due to God's anger because they had not built the Temple—a not very inspiring conception. Zechariah joined with Haggai in urging the people to build the Temple, for this was an indispensable condition for the coming of the Messiah. Indeed, Messianic expectation forms the central point of Zechariah's teaching. His "Night visions" are all concerned with the preparation of the people and the land for the coming Messiah and the Messianic era. Both Haggai and Zechariah point to Zerubbabel as the coming Messiah, who is for them, therefore, a purely temporal ruler. These points must be considered a little further. There is no need to insist here upon the close connexion,

[1] See, e.g., Hag. ii. 11 ff.

from post-exilic times onwards, between Messianic teaching and the " Day of the Lord "[1]; it is brought out clearly by Haggai and Zechariah.[2] The former gives utterance to the traditional ideas regarding the "Day of the Lord " in ii. 6, 7, of his book : " Yet once, it is a little while, and I will shake the heavens, and the earth, and the sea, and the dry land ; and I will shake all nations, and the desirable things of all nations shall come, and I will fill this house with glory, saith Yahweh of hosts." This world-cataclysm is to herald the coming of the Messianic era ; for this prophet's main concern is the rebuilding of the Temple in view of the advent of the Messiah, i.e. Zerubbabel, according to Haggai (see ii. 20–23)—it is to be made glorious through the offerings which are most prized by the nations, i.e. silver and gold, which, however, in reality belong to Yahweh (ver. 8). Zechariah's teaching is entirely in accordance with this ; for him, too, a world-cataclysm, with the destruction of the nations, is to herald the opening of the Messianic Era with the advent of the Messiah (Zerubbabel, see Zech. iii. 8, 9, iv. 10, vi. 9–15[3]) ; this is not stated in the definite terms by Haggai, but is clearly implied in i. 11–15. Zechariah, however, though also anxious for the building of the Temple, is far more concerned with the preparation of Jerusalem (ii. 1–13 [in Hebrew ii. 5–17]), the purification of the people (v. 1–4), and the removal of wickedness from the land (v. 5, 11) ; all of which are preparatory to the Messiah's advent (cp. Mal. iii. 1–6).

The main points to be noted here are that the Messiah is thought of as a purely human ruler, that his advent is to be marked by a world-cataclysm, the " Day of the Lord " ; and that the Gentiles are either to become subservient to Israel, or to be destroyed. The last two points are important to bear in mind in view of later apocalyptic teaching.

[1] For the earlier eschatological teaching see Part II, Chapter VIII, § 2 (d). It will be dealt with more fully below, Chapter XV.

[2] Only chapters i.–viii. come into consideration here.

[3] In vi. 11 we must read " crown " for " crowns," and the name of Joshua was inserted in place of Zerubbabel at a later time when the Priest was at the head of the theocratic government. The Hebrew text of vi. 9–15 is in considerable disorder, and shows clear marks of having been tampered with.

Then, prominent in the very meagre literature belonging to these years is the reference to angels. Noticeable in the book of *Zechariah* is the frequent mention of an angel as intermediary between God and the prophet. It must be evident from the way in which this is represented as the normal way of divine communication that belief in these intermediate beings had become a fixed element in the religion not only of the leaders but also of the people themselves. In all his visions the prophet tells of an angel who is the mouthpiece by means of which God speaks (i. 19 [in Hebrew ii. 2], and often) ; this is very different from the direct intercourse which is invariably found among the earlier prophets ; but we must doubtless see here the outcome of Ezekiel's teaching on divine transcendence. A somewhat different conception regarding the superhuman being is observable as between Ezekiel and Zechariah ; the former, who speaks of this intermediate being as a " spirit," seems to think of it as more closely associated with the personality of God than is the case with Zechariah ; for this latter always speaks of a " messenger," usually translated " angel," and this gives the impression of being intended to express more pronouncedly the distinction, or separation, between God and His supernatural instrument. If we are correct in this, it points to a further step in the teaching of the wide distance between God and man.

In *Zechariah* we meet for the first time with the word " Satan " as applied to a superhuman person ; he is represented as " *the* adversary," [1] the word occurring with the definite article. Satan appears here as one of the angels ; he is not yet an evil spirit, but a superhuman being whose special function is that of accusing men before God (Zech. iii. 1–2).

During those few years, then, which followed immediately upon the return of the exiles to the homeland, the thought of the building of the Temple, together with the Messianic Hope with which it is so intimately connected, fills the foreground ; and the messages regarding the coming of the Messiah which the prophet receives are

[1] As a proper name " Satan " occurs for the first time in 1 Chron. xxi. 1.

all given through the intermediary of an angel. So that Messianism and Angelology are really the only two subjects which occupy the mind of the one true successor of the prophets, at this time, namely, Zechariah. That the seeds of thought-movements which were to reach great developments were already beginning to germinate we know from the subsequent literature and history ; and faint signs of them are to be discerned in the books of *Haggai* and *Zechariah* ; and, doubtless, during the seventy years of silence which followed the completion of the Temple these movements were proceeding apace ; for when the curtain rises again we find that considerable development has taken place. But this leads us to subjects which demand, each of them, special and individual attention.

CHAPTER VIII

THE LAW [1]

WE have seen that during the period of the Exile and immediately following upon the Return, the interest of the Jewish religious leaders was centred, first on the written Law, mainly the book of *Deuteronomy* ; but it is highly probable that the Oral Law had already begun to take shape ; secondly, on the Temple ; and thirdly, on the Messianic Hope. These three—the Law, the Temple, and the Messianic Hope—are the foundations upon which the religious superstructure of post-exilic Judaism was built.

The clearest way in which to discern the steps in the development which now takes place will be to study the four following subjects, dealing with each separately, though, as is only to be expected, each will to some extent encroach upon the others. These subjects are : the Law, Wisdom, and Worship ; and Apocalypse, to be considered later. Why Wisdom is assigned the second place will be explained when we come to deal with it. Worship will naturally include the subject of Pietism, and out of this there arises inevitably the problem of suffering ; and the connexion between the Messianic Hope and all that is included under the term Apocalypse will become sufficiently clear when the latter is studied. For reasons which will be explained later, the Law and Wisdom are each dealt with under two periods.

The dating of the literature which comes into consideration offers considerable difficulties, for opinions differ regarding the dates of the books ; for our purpose, however, precise dating is not a *sine qua non* ; what is demanded is that the Biblical books, or parts of them, to be utilized shall belong to the period to be studied ; and in regard to this there is a fairly general consensus of opinion.

·　　·　　·　　·　　·　　·　　·

[1] This subject is also dealt with in Chapter XVI, where its further development will be considered.

We start with the Law. The first beginnings of what came to be the religion of the Law of post-exilic Judaism are to be sought in the time of the Josianic reform, when the book of *Deuteronomy* was adopted as that which gave the norm of religious observances and practice. From this time the religion of the Hebrews began to become the religion of a book.

The combination of the prophetic and priestly ideals characteristic of *Deuteronomy* is to be found in the teaching of Ezekiel ; but the tendency for the priestly ideals to predominate began already during the Exile ; and this, as we have seen, is emphasized by Haggai and Malachi, and to a somewhat less extent by Zechariah. The tendency becomes more pronounced in some parts of chapters lvi.–lxvi. of the book of *Isaiah*.

Very instructive are the two phrases with which these chapters begin : " Keep judgement," and " Do righteousness." The former means : Observe the Law ; and it is interesting to note that in *Deutero-Isaiah* the corresponding phrase is : " Seek judgement " : the Hebrew word for " judgement " (*mishpat*) would be better rendered " justice " or " equity." When used with the verb " to keep " the meaning of *mishpat* undergoes a change, and connotes legal ordinances. The second term means : Do the righteousness of the Law. Thus the two terms are parallel, and they show that emphasis was laid on the observance of legal precepts. This is borne out and illustrated by much that is written in these chapters (Isa. lvi.–lxvi.) as well as elsewhere in the literature of this period. Thus, much stress is laid on observing the Sabbath, and this primarily in a negative direction, i.e. by not doing anything that might profane it : " Blessed is the man . . . that keepeth the Sabbath from profaning it " (Isa. lvi. 2 ; cp. ver. 6) ; this is more fully illustrated in Neh. xiii. 15–22, where Nehemiah takes drastic measures to prevent the Sabbath from being desecrated. The prominent place which Sabbath observance had now come to occupy may be seen further from, e.g., Isa. lviii. 13, lxvi. 23 ; Neh. ix. 14, x. 33 ; and another indication of the importance of the Sabbath is to be gathered from the fact that a proper name, *Shabbethai*, is formed from it (Neh. viii.

7, xi. 16 ; Ezra x. 15). But it is in the Priestly Code, which belongs to this period, that the development of Sabbath observance is seen most clearly ; in Exod. xxxi. 12–17, for example, it is to be observed as a "solemn rest," and "everyone that profaneth it shall be put to death."

Besides the stringent law regarding the Sabbath, a new importance is attached to the festivals and especially the new-moon festival, because all the other feasts were regulated by it ; they are dealt with especially in Num. xxviii. 11–31.[1]

The law regarding sacrifices also underwent development during this period, and what is most important here is the prominence of the element of atonement, owing to the deeper sense of sin, a result of prophetical teaching, and the experiences of the Exile.

One other matter, so far as the law regarding sacred observances was concerned, was the importance attached to the sacred dues ; nowhere does this come out more clearly than in Mal. iii. 8–10 : " Will a man rob God ? Yet ye rob me. But ye say, Wherein have we robbed thee ? In tithes and offerings. Ye are cursed with a curse ; for ye rob me, even this whole nation. Bring ye the whole tithe into the storehouse, that there may be meat in mine house . . . " (cp. Neh. x. 37, 38).

The development of the priesthood is seen primarily in two directions, the distinction between the Levites and the priests (Num. xvi. 10, 18–23), and the position of the High-priest, who tends to become a civil ruler as much as the holder of the chief sacred office.

All that has been said refers to specifically sacred matters ; but the many ordinances in the Law dealing with other things shows that it affected the people in multifarious ways in ordinary life.

It will be well now to consider quite briefly some of the effects which Legalism had on the religious life of the people.

That its observance was a source of joy to many a

---

[1] Fasting came into prominence during this period ; but with the exception of the Day of Atonement (Lev. xvi. 29–31), it is not dealt with in the Law.

devout soul goes without saying ; but a subtle danger lay in the fact that the diligent carrying out of legal precepts might have the effect of engendering self-righteousness, and of making a man think that because he kept the divine law, therefore God was, as it were, placed under the obligation of rewarding him for this. There is a passage, for example, in Ps. xix. 7–11 (8–12 in Hebrew), which, while showing how a godly man rejoiced in the Law, contains some thoughts which might easily suggest self-righteousness in the heart of one less spiritually-minded :

The Law of Yahweh is perfect, restoring the soul :
The testimony of Yahweh is sure, making wise the simple.
The precepts of Yahweh are right, rejoicing the heart ;
The commandment of Yahweh is pure, enlightening the eyes.
The fear of Yahweh is clean, enduring for ever ;
The judgements of Yahweh are true, and righteous altogether.
More to be desired are they than gold, yea, than much fine gold ;
Sweeter also than honey and the honeycomb.
Moreover by them is thy servant warned,
In keeping of them there is great reward.

The psalmist is speaking of his personal experience in saying that the Law makes wise and enlightens the eyes, and though there is nothing to suggest that in his case this conviction engendered a sense of superiority, it cannot be denied that the danger of this was present, and might well manifest itself in the case of others, as indeed we know happened in course of time. So, too, in the matter of reward for keeping the ordinances of the Law ; with the psalmist it is likely enough that all that was meant was delight in doing what was right, which is its own reward ; but there are passages elsewhere which certainly express the feeling that he who keeps the Law has a claim on God to receive reward (see, e.g., Ps. cxix. 17, 22, 94, 121, 173) ; and there is plenty of evidence in later times to show that he who kept the Law felt that he had a right to expect reward from God.

The importance of this subject, in view of later develop-ments of Judaism, justifies a further illustration, which may be seen in the contrasted points of view between Deutero-Isaiah and the later chapters of the book of Isaiah (lvi. ff.), i.e. between the prophetic and the priestly

ideals. Both these writers describe the means whereby
the coming deliverance and salvation, upon which they
both lay stress, is to be attained. In the former we
have, for example in lv. 1, these words : " Ho, every one
that thirsteth, come ye to the waters ; and he that hath
no money, come ye, buy and eat ; yea, come ; buy wine
and milk without money and without price." Here, in
figurative language, the people are bidden to take what
is *freely* offered them, i.e. the blessings of the Messianic
time. Simple acceptation is all that is required. In
lvi. 1, on the other hand, the coming salvation must be
acquired by the fulfilment of legal ordinances : " Observe
(or, Keep) the Law," i.e. do what you ought to do in
obeying legal ordinances, and thereby acquire, as of
right, reward. It is not fanciful to see here the beginnings
of what in later Judaism developed into the doctrine of
works, i.e. that the works of the Law are meritorious and
demand reward *per se*. The efficacy of works and the
claim of reward for doing them is a doctrine which appeals
to men as being no more than what bare justice demands ;
and because that is true between man and man, it is also
assumed to be true as between God and man. In later
Judaism, where the doctrine of divine grace plays a relatively subordinate part, this doctrine of the merit of
works and therefore the right to claim reward is naturally
somewhat prominent. It is not contended that during
the period with which we are dealing there was any formulated doctrine on this subject ; but there are indications
of the existence of the new trend of thought ; they are
but the beginnings from which, in course of time, large
developments grew. It is for this reason that attention
to the subject is drawn here ; it will be more fully dealt
with in Chapter XVI.

CHAPTER IX

WISDOM

THE golden age of Hebrew Wisdom belongs to a later period (see below, Chapter XIV) ; but inasmuch as the roots of the Wisdom literature proper are to be discerned in much earlier days, it is well that something should be said on the subject here, especially as there are strong reasons for believing that the pursuit of Wisdom, in the Hebrew sense, occupied the minds of some of Israel's thinkers during the Persian period, the material of still earlier times being the basis of this. It is worthy of note that as early as the time of Jeremiah the " wise man," or *Chakam*, occupies a recognized position side by side with priest and prophet : " For the law shall not perish from the priest, nor counsel from the wise, nor the word from the prophet " (Jer. xviii. 18). Equally pointed is a passage in *Isaiah* where, because of the people's insincerity of worship, the prophet says : " The wisdom of their wise men shall perish, and the understanding of the prudent men shall be hid " (Isa. xxix. 14). So that it is evident that already in the eighth century B.C. the wise men were known as a class ; and since they were also scribes,[1] there can be no doubt that they wrote down their wise sayings ; in a word, Wisdom as part of Hebrew literature was in existence in the eighth century B.C., and therefore the supposition is a reasonable one that both during the Exile and the Persian period collections of wise sayings were being composed as well as collected, thus forming the basis for the future development of Wisdom writings to be discussed later.

The earlier Hebrew Wisdom literature was largely

---

[1] For the proof of this, as well as for the pre-exilic Wisdom literature, see the present writer's *The Book of Proverbs*, pp. 20–26, 68–73 (1929).

influenced by Egyptian and Babylonian thought ; but, however great their indebtedness to external influences, the Hebrew Wisdom writers had an individuality of their own, and created a type of Wisdom literature distinct from that of any other nation. What is specifically Hebrew here is the religious connotation of Wisdom ; not that this is absent from Egyptian and Babylonian Wisdom writings,[1] but among the Hebrews it is the wholly predominating element.

In the Hebrew literature Wisdom is not used in the sense of pure knowledge ; at first it meant the faculty of distinguishing between what was useful or the reverse, and between what was beneficent or harmful ; but an ethical element soon entered in, and then it came to mean the faculty of distinguishing between what was good and what was bad. This faculty was, however, believed to be a divine gift ; and to use this gift in the right way was to establish a true relationship between a man and his God. And since the faculty to distinguish between what was good and what was evil was a divine endowment, it followed that *every* form of Wisdom was from God. And, further, as in its widest sense Wisdom can be exhibited in a variety of ways—forethought, foresight, discernment, carefulness, skill, etc.—all of these were the gifts of God ; and thus Wisdom in a religious sense was brought into the everyday affairs of men. But while there were many forms of Wisdom, the highest form, the zenith, was the fear of the Lord ; hence the frequent phrase : " The fear of the Lord is the beginning (or zenith) of wisdom."

During the Exile the Jews were brought into close touch with Babylonian thought and culture, and the result of this is to be seen in the later literature. One example of this may be given as appropriate in the present connexion. According to the Babylonian cosmology, Wisdom dwelt in the depths of the sea with Ea, the creative deity. Apsu, " The Deep," is called the " house of Wisdom," because out of it came forth the wisdom of Ea and the word of Ea ; one of the epithets applied to

---

[1] In the Egyptian Wisdom book, *The Teaching of Amen-em-ope*, for example, the religious element is very prominent.

the god Ea is : " Lord of Wisdom." [1] The thought of
Wisdom having been in existence before the Creation
evidently influenced the later Jewish sage who wrote
Prov. viii. 22, 23 :

Yahweh begat me at the beginning of his ways [i.e. his acts of Creation],
The first of his works, of old [he begat me] [2] ;
I was set up from everlasting, from the beginning,
Or ever the earth was.

And the idea of the deep being the original *habitat* of
Wisdom seems to be reflected in Ps. xxxvi. 6 (7 in
Hebrew) :

Thy judgements are (like) the great deep,[3]

where the Hebrew has for " the great deep " *Tehom
Rabbah*, the ancient proper name for the ocean. Thus
the Hebrew belief regarding the origin of Wisdom is,
in all probability, from Babylonian thought.

It can be shown that of the various collections of wise
sayings which have been incorporated in the book of
Proverbs, some are pre-exilic, others are late post-exilic [4] ;
this being so, it is difficult to believe that between the
dates, say 700 and 300 B.C., there should have been an
entire suspension of the work of the Sages [5] ; and therefore although one cannot definitely assert that any
particular collection or collections in the book of *Proverbs*
belongs to the exilic or Persian period, yet the probabilities
of the case point to this having been so. That the
Sages, in their oral teaching as well as in their writings,
did a great work in bringing religion into the everyday
life of the people is certain ; and this is the justification
for the brief mention of the subject here.

[1] Jeremias, *Das alte Testament im Lichte des alten Orients*, pp. 29,
80 (1904).
[2] For this rendering of the verse, see the writer's *Proverbs, in loc.*
[3] The content of this psalm, viz. the problem of the wicked in prosperity, shows that it is post-exilic.
[4] See the writer's *Proverbs*, pp. 20–26.
[5] The interest in Wisdom literature is illustrated by the fact that the
Babylonian " Wisdom of Achikar " circulated in an Aramaic translation
among the Jewish colonists in Elephantiné (middle of the fifth century
B.C.).

CHAPTER X

GOD AND THE SOUL: WORSHIP: PIETISM

In dealing with this subject, which covers the whole area of devotional and practical religion, it is impossible to observe the bounds of any period ; we shall therefore treat it as it is presented in the whole post-exilic period, referring also to earlier times where the consideration of a particular thought or practice is made clearer by referring to its earlier history. Some incursion into subjects already dealt with or which will come before us again later is inevitable ; but it will be readily understood that the slight repetitions involved cannot well be avoided.

1. The Universality of Yahweh

No nation has ever undergone so striking a spiritual experience as that which befell Israel during the Exile. She had been brought up on the old territorial conception of religion, which confined a deity and his worship to a limited area, save and in so far as it might be formally transplanted with all the paraphernalia of the *cultus* to some other spot. She was steeped in the same kind of theology which made Naaman take with him two mule-loads of Yahweh's land in order that he might be able to worship Him ; and though at different times and in different circles the home of Yahweh was assigned to various sites, it was generally felt that His dwelling was not far from the land of Israel, even though it might be in Sinai. Even that saint to whom we owe Ps. xlii.–xliii.[1] was not free from this idea. It is true that he feels terribly the disaster which has befallen his country, and the jeers of his captors, but the thought

---

[1] The definite dating of psalms is always a matter of uncertainty, but this psalm (for the two are surely two parts of one whole) seems to have as its author one of the exiles carried away with Jehoiachin in 596.

that overwhelms him is the conviction that in the land
to which he is journeying through affliction and peril
he will be separated from his God [1]; we may fairly assume
that he did not stand alone. The testimony of Jeremiah
may be cited to prove that some at least of the exiles of
the 596 deportation were men of deep religious faith,
who sympathized with the prophetic ideals (cp. Jer. xxiv.).
But these men of faithful souls went into Mesopotamia
believing that they had left Yahweh behind them. Their
great discovery was to be that they were mistaken.
They had not left Yahweh behind them ; He was with
them in Babylonia.

There may have been several causes which contributed
to this conclusion, and probably it did not come home to
exiled Israel at once. We may conjecture that the most
powerful influence was the continuance of prophecy
among the deported Judeans. The belief of Israel,
however, went farther than this. It is quite possible
to hold that a god may manifest himself in more than
one spot, even though the sites of his revelation may be
as distant as Palestine and Mesopotamia, and still to
admit the existence of other deities valid enough for
other nations and races.

But this new discovery, that Yahweh had not been left
behind, was reinforced by much of the teaching of the
pre-exilic prophets. They had held that Yahweh was
the Lord of the physical universe, the Lord of all human
history, the Lord of universal morality.[2] The final
conclusion of such doctrines could be nothing but an
absolute monotheism. Yet men are very slow to realize
the implications of their own beliefs, and but for the
experience of the Exile, Israel might have postponed the
final step for some centuries. The speed with which
great souls among them attained a monotheistic conclusion (and a couple of centuries is a very short time in
which to develop a wholly new idea such as this) was in

---

[1] Ver. 6 (7 in Hebrew) shows that he has reached the northern part of
the land, Mount Hermon, where the Jordan rises, hence " the land of
Jordan." That the psalm cannot belong to the Exile itself is clear
from xliii. 3, 4, i.e. the Temple is still standing ; it was not destroyed
until 586.
[2] See Part II, Chapter VIII.

part due to the circumstances of the fall of the Chaldæan
empire. The gods and goddesses of Babylonia were
powerless to control or to foresee events ; the God of
Israel could predict them because He ordained them.
We must not suppose that ancient Mesopotamia actually
worshipped objects of wood, stone, or metal, in the sense
that they attributed to the material things a personal
divinity ; such a belief would be pure animism. They
did believe, however, that these things had some special
connexion with the great deities, and truly represented
their presence. Men believed that the image was, in a
certain sense, the portable home of Ishtar or of Marduk
or of Nebo. What the Israelite prophet realized by the
end of the Exile was that there was no personal, spiritual
reality behind these objects. The great gods simply
did not exist, they were nothing beyond the images
(cp. Isa. xliv. 9, 18) ; there was only one living and true
God, Maker of heaven and earth, and Lord of all things
—Yahweh, the God of Israel.

2. THE WORSHIP OF ISRAEL

In pre-exilic Israel worship was limited to certain
spots. The old patriarchal stories spoke of Abraham as
" calling upon the name of Yahweh," and made special
mention of the place where this was done. Thus, we have
in Gen. xiii. 4 one account of the origin of the sanctuary
at Bethel ; at other spots also Yahweh appeared to him,
in consequence of which he built an altar and offered
sacrifice. But it would seem that even the patriarchs
could enter into communion with their God only where
He chose to meet with them ; and throughout the earlier
history of Israel, that is, until the recognition of the great
sanctuaries such as Jerusalem and Bethel, we have
occasional theophanies which testified to the fact that
worship might be offered in the place where they occurred.
Originally, no doubt, these places had been consecrated
to different *numina* ; probably early tradition located
different " '*Els* " at Bethel, Peniel, 'El-lahai-Roi,[1] etc.,

---

[1] See Part I, Chapter X, § 1.

but in process of time Yahweh alone was accepted, and all local objects of worship were absorbed into His own *cultus*.

This still left a large number of sanctuaries, and it is unlikely that any Israelite in the cultivated portions of the country had very far to go to find a place of sacrifice.

But the reform of Josiah concentrated sacrifice in Jerusalem, and made its temple the one spot where worship could be duly paid. For it must be remembered that, to the ancient world, worship always meant sacrifice. Prayer was, of course, employed, but it was normally an accompaniment of sacrifice. We hear, it is true, in the patriarchal traditions and elsewhere of prayer being offered where sacrifice is not mentioned ; but it was generally before the altar that men made their requests to God. Had Israel been confined to the older methods and ideas of communion with God, even the evidence of His presence in Babylonia would have helped them little unless they had been free to do as the Egyptian Jews of the fifth century did, and build a temple where they could offer sacrifice with their prayer.

It was but a single generation that could have lived under the *régime* inaugurated by Josiah, yet the time seems to have been long enough at least to suggest the possibility of worship apart from the Temple. For it was obviously impossible for people living in distant parts of the country to appear as regularly at Jerusalem as they had done at the old local shrines. Indeed, in the Deuteronomic law itself provision was made for this in more than one way ; for its promoters clearly recognized that a fundamental change in outlook was involved in the centralization of sacrifice. In particular the ritual provisions of *Deuteronomy* permitted the eating of domestic animals apart from sacrifice. Hitherto every meal of meat had been, as it were, a " communion service " ; it was now transferred from the sphere of religion to that of secular life (Deut. xii. 20–28).

Here, then, we have a significant illustration of the great change which necessarily took place with the reforms of Josiah, though it is but one symptom of a modification which must have made itself felt in every

department of life. In the old days the line between
secular and sacred was closely drawn, it is true, but almost
every act of man's life had its cultural affiliations. Now,
with the sanctuary far away, the religious aspect but
seldom obtruded itself on men's consciousness. Attend-
ance at the three great festivals was still enjoined, but
even if this prescription were rigorously enforced, many
Israelites would necessarily spend months together
without any religious exercise apart from the weekly
abstention from labour on the Sabbath.

No religion can live on a negation, and those to whom
active observances of some kind were a necessity of the
religious life were compelled to find their exercise in new
ways. Here the experience of the Exile was of profound
value. Even if sacrifice could not be offered, prayer was
possible to a God who was really everywhere. The sense
of the universality of Yahweh alone made it possible for
any Jewish religion to continue in Mesopotamia ; and,
comparatively scanty as it was, the exiles clung to it with
determination.

It must be at once admitted that evidence for the
growth of details in the new form of worship which
Israel developed is greatly lacking. It is not till the
beginning of the fourth century that we find anything
like an organized *cultus* accepted ; but then, in Ezra,
we have the traditional founder of synagogue-worship.
Yet it must surely be clear that he, in so far as he may
have organized the worship of the community, was
relying on tendencies and practices which came into
being before his time. Of these the most important
was the Law ; in its general aspect this has already been
dealt with (Chapter VIII) ; but it is necessary to call
attention to it here in order to emphasize the unique
place which it took in the worship of Israel.

The Law lay at the heart of all the thinking of the later
Judaism, and in a very real sense the worship of the
synagogue was, and is, the cult of the Law. There
were, of course, other elements ; prayers were recited
and hymns were sung, and instruction of various kinds
was given both to children and to adults ; but the centre
of the whole was the reading of the Law, followed by

exposition and comments from those best able to expound and apply it. There grew up thus a class of men whose whole time was given to its study, those to whom the name of " Scribes " is especially applied in New Testament times. While the official religion of Israel centred in the Temple with its sacrificial system (see next section), it was the Law which formed the basis of worship for the average Israelite, and constituted his weekly, even his daily, study.

The practical value of this element in worship is too obvious to need special emphasis. The time was to come when Israel was to lose all the external paraphernalia of worship, when her Temple was to be destroyed, and sacrifice was to cease. But for the Law her faith and her nationality would have perished ; but for the Synagogue her religion would have ceased to be. These were things which she had already carried wherever she had gone. In every place where the Jew was established there was at least a " place of prayer " ; and the larger cities contained synagogues. In Palestine itself there were many such institutions which survived the destruction of the Temple, and such a form of worship as this could be destroyed only with the extermination of the Jewish race.

As compared and contrasted with all religions in which the element of ritual is strong, Judaism offered, and offers, a standing protest against materialism in religion. There is room, no doubt, for that form of misguided worship which we call bibliolatry, but its temptations are less subtle and pressing, less general in their application, than those of any other form of the cult of a material thing. The worship of the Synagogue, followed in this respect by that of the Christian Church, stands as a testimony to the pure spirituality of true religion, and echoes that greatest of all sayings on the subject of the human approach to God : " God is Spirit, and they that worship Him must worship Him in spirit and in truth " (John iv. 24).

3. The Development of the Sacrificial System

But side by side with this gradually developing spiritual worship there was the official religion which centred in the Temple with its sacrificial system. It is therefore necessary that something should be said about the development of this which took place after the Exile.

That the reason for this development was the growth of a deeper sense of sin is evident from the type of sacrifices, as will be seen presently. If it be asked why the realization of sin should have been one of the results of the Exile, the answer is that it was due to several factors ; thus, the teaching of both Ezekiel and Deutero-Isaiah on the transcendental character of God, with the inevitable recognition of the insignificance of man in His sight must have generated the sense of unworthiness. Then, again, it is not unnatural to believe that the exaltation of the divine Law with its ever-increasing demands tended to make many feel their inability to fulfil its requirements adequately ; in later times, it is true, the observance of legal precepts had just the contrary effect and occasioned spiritual pride ; but at first this was not so ; the spirit engendered was rather that illustrated by Neh. viii. 9, where it is said that " the people wept when they heard the words of the Law."

But, above all, it was the fact of the Exile itself which contributed to a deepened sense of sin ; for the spectacle of the exiles, representing the whole nation, banished from the centre of their worship, was the most signal mark of divine disfavour, which could only be explained by the recognition of national sin ; and this, we can well understand, would be retrospective.

In any case, whatever the causes, the fact is quite obvious that during the post-exilic period a deeper sense of sin prevailed. And nothing witnesses to this so clearly as the development of the sacrificial system. Thus, we have, to begin with, two types of sacrifice, the " guilt-offering," called 'āshām, and the " sin-offering," called chattāth ; both terms are pre-exilic, and their earlier connotation is that of compensation for injury (e.g.

2 Kings xii. 17, in E.V. 16) ; but as applied to animal victims presented on the altar they occur only in exilic and post-exilic literature.[1] It is not always easy to see what the difference between the two offerings was ; but regarding the guilt- or trespass-offering (*'āshām*) the idea seems to have been that the guilt incurred through a trespass was atoned for by it, and it was offered concurrently with the restoration of something to a fellow-man ; while the " sin-offering " (*chattāth*) was thought of as a means of the removal of sin. In both the idea of expiation is suggested.

Then we have the Incense-offering spoken of in the Priestly Code (Exod. xxx. 34–8) ; this is never referred to by Ezekiel, and though there is a reference to it in Jer. vi. 20, xli. 5, he evidently regards it as a foreign custom ; otherwise it is not mentioned in pre-exilic literature ; it must therefore be regarded as specifically post-exilic. Whatever symbolic significance this may have come to have (see Ps. cxli. 2 ; Rev. v. 8, viii. 3, 4), its original intention is perhaps to be sought in the parallel of the ascending smoke of the burnt-offering, though the sweet smell would, no doubt, have been thought of as in some sense pleasing to the deity.

Of special importance was the *Tamîd* ; this was the daily morning and evening burnt-offering (Num. xxviii. 3–8 ; Exod. xxix. 38–42), which was a development of the pre-exilic morning burnt-offering and evening meal-offering (2 Kings xvi. 15).   In its developed form its importance was emphasized by having the meal-offering and a wine-offering as its adjuncts (Num. xv. 4, 5).   The continuous burning of the altar-fire was a result of this twofold daily burnt-offering, and it is not improbable that the idea of the fire being never quenched was due to Persian influence. The term *Tamîd* means " continuous " here [2] (cp. Num. xxviii. 3, " a continual burnt-offering ") ; the abbreviated form, " the *Tamîd*," in reference to this sacrifice belongs to later usage, and occurs first in Dan. viii. 11–14,

---

[1] That in Hos. iv. 8 *Chattāth* does not mean " sin-offering," but simply " sin," is clear from the parallel word " iniquity," which occurs in the second strophe of the verse.

[2] The adverbial use is earlier and more frequent.

xi. 31, xii. 11.[1] It came to occupy the central position of the Temple *cultus* ; the feelings aroused by its cessation in the reign of Antiochus Epiphanes can be seen from the *Daniel* passages referred to.

Of less importance, but worth a passing mention, were the libations ; wine has taken the place of water in the Priestly Code (Exod. xxix. 40), and both wine and oil offerings have lost their independent character, and are only used as accompaniments to the more important sacrifices.

In regard to all the sacrifices the ritual tends to become more elaborate (as an example see Lev. iv. 15–21 in connexion with the *chattāth*) ; and their main object centres in their atoning efficacy, thus they were means of becoming reconciled to God. *All* sacrifices, whether bloodless or bloody, effect reconciliation (cp. Ezek. xlv. 15, 17); i.e. they are the means of obtaining divine forgiveness. The term *le-kappēr*,[2] " to effect atonement," expresses the basic idea, and the sin-cleansing power of blood becomes very marked (see, e.g., Lev. iv. 5, 7, 16–18). It is nowhere explained why blood should atone for sin ; it was a divine ordinance, and that sufficed. When, in Lev. xvii. 11, the expiatory efficacy of blood is ascribed to the " life " that is in it, this is no explanation, but only the expression of an accepted fact. To discuss the reason or reasons why blood should have been thought of as of atoning efficacy would take us too far afield ; it must suffice to say that, like so many religious ideas, there is a long history behind it.

The idea reached the zenith of its expression in the institution of the Day of Atonement (Lev. xvi.)[3] ; its object is stated clearly enough in Lev. xvi. 33, where it is said that the priest shall " make atonement for the holy sanctuary, and he shall make atonement for the tent of meeting and for the altar ; and he shall make atonement for the priests and for all the people of the assembly."

---

[1] The R.V. renders " the continual burnt-offering," but in the original it is a proper name, " the *Tamid*."

[2] The noun *kappara* is post-biblical.

[3] For an admirable and convincing presentation of the reasons why the Day of Atonement must have been instituted in post-exilic times see Kennett, *Old Testament Essays*, pp. 105–118 (1928).

It was thus an annual complete atonement for all sin ; whatever sin had been unatoned for during the past year, or whatever sin had been unconsciously committed, or forgotten, all were atoned for on this great day ; it gave assurance of reconciliation with God, and of a renewed right relationship with Him.

A word must here be added regarding the thought of some of those deeply spiritual minds which contemplated the entire absence of sacrifices in worship. It is possible, however, that in regard to some of the earlier pre-exilic passages which have been sometimes held to advocate the abolition of sacrifices, there has been something of an overstatement of the case. For example, the passage Amos v. 21–5 is sometimes interpreted in the sense that the prophet was advocating the abrogation of the whole sacrificial system as it existed in his day ; this passage runs : " I hate, I despise your feasts, I will take no delight in your solemn assemblies ; for though ye bring me burnt-offerings —[1], and your meal-offerings, I will not accept, neither will I regard the peace-offerings of your fat beasts. . . . Did ye bring unto me sacrifices and offerings in the wilderness forty years, O house of Israel ? "

These words were a rebuke against a developed form of sacrificial worship which had become debased through contact with Canaanite religion ; but that Amos contemplated the entire abrogation of the sacrificial system at the time at which he lived, i.e. before, as yet, prophetical teaching had had time to make itself widely felt, is difficult to believe ; for one thing, he must have known that during the nomadic period of the wanderings in the wilderness sacrifices were offered (see above, Part I, Chapter IX, § 3), though not of the agricultural type to which he refers ; moreover, what would he, as one who faced realities and knew that the people were not yet capable of offering purely spiritual worship, have suggested as a substitute if *all* sacrifices were to be abolished ? Or again, when it is said in Isa. i. 10–17, " To what purpose is the multitude of your sacrifices unto me ? saith Yahweh . . .," the denunciation is

---

[1] Something has fallen out of the Hebrew text here.

not against the sacrificial system, as such, but against the particular sacrifices of those to whom the words were addressed ; evil living made insincere worship. Had the lives of the worshippers been in accordance with the teaching of the prophets, his words would not have been necessary.

Not until there was some definite form of worship to take the place of the sacrificial system would its needlessness, and therefore its entire abolition, be contemplated ; and this was not the case until the Exile had taught the possibility of a purely spiritual worship. Then the thoughts expressed in such passages as Mic. vi. 6–8, generally acknowledged to be a late passage, and Ps. l. 8–15, became very significant, and show the exalted trend of thought among Israel's most spiritual teachers. But this by the way.

The impression gained that there *was* a certain element of mechanical religion in connexion with the sacrificial system is rectified by reading the psalms of the post-exilic period. It is not to be expected that in what is somewhat of the nature of a legal code, i.e. the P document, a true insight into the mind and emotions of the worshippers is to be gained ; for this, in addition to the psalms mentioned, one must look to the best religious instincts of the people as handed down and embodied in the writings of the later Rabbis. No greater wrong has been done to the religion of the later Judaism than the ignoring of their teaching on sin and atonement, as it appears in the earliest years of the Christian era, but which reflects earlier teaching. The difficulty here has been that this teaching is largely obscured by a mass of other material in Rabbinical writings. This has, however, now been remedied, and in a recently published volume, *Studies in Sin and Atonement in the Rabbinic Literature of the First Century* (1928), Dr. A. Büchler has provided us with all that can be desired to gain a clear and unbiassed estimate of what Judaism teaches on these important subjects. We cannot do better than close this section with some words from the Introduction to this work : " The extent to which the relation of the Jew to his fellow-man and the social duties generally expressed themselves in obedience to the Torah or in sin, and how far they influenced Rabbinic ethical legislation and determined its standard, can be learned from the relevant statements and the decrees of the Rabbinic authorities of the first century . . . The actual practice of sacrificial atonement for social sins as recorded in the Rabbinic literature, and the religious conception of atoning sacrifices, the preliminary essential acts of repentance, restitution, conciliation, and confession preceding the sin offering, and their religious and moral values, give insight into the Rabbinic concepts of sin and sacrificial atonement."

4. God and the Individual

The religion of the ancient world was primarily concerned with communities rather than with individuals ; and this is true of the religion of Israel. But with Jeremiah, as we have already seen, the individual human being begins to take on a new importance. The community as a whole is still, of course, the more prominent ; but one man may reach God apart from his fellows ; he is no longer dependent on or wholly linked up with the community in his dealings with Him whom he worships. This has a double aspect. In the first place, Yahweh may come into contact with and control the religious experience of a man by himself. In Jeremiah's struggles there is no thought of Israel as a whole ; the rest of the world seems shut out, and the man stands alone with his God. But on the other side we have the doctrine of individual responsibility. It is this latter which is especially emphasized by Ezekiel. Indeed, Ezek. xviii. might almost be a commentary on Jer. xxxi. 29, 30. And to Ezekiel this teaching was fundamental. He held to a rigid theory of divine retribution, and while we may feel that the picture he draws of Yahweh is harsh, inhuman, and mechanical, we must admit that he fully realized the truth that " whatsoever a man soweth, that shall he also reap."

On the old " communal " view of religion, insisting as it did on the absolute solidarity of the race, the sins of the generation which preceded the Exile could be met only by the complete destruction of the whole nation; but Ezekiel, following Isaiah here, could not believe that Yahweh would destroy the people who represented Him to the world, and thus believed profoundly in their ultimate restoration. A new start was possible, and was possible only because with the destruction of the actual sinners the sin was wiped out. Each generation, each individual, could begin life afresh, and could lay the foundations of a new order, in which Israel could achieve the great purpose for which she had been chosen and maintained in the world : the proclamation of Yahweh as the Lord of all mankind.

The old view did not die ; there was too much truth in it. It has always lived on, although some forms of Judaism, and of its daughter faith, Christianity, have tended to obscure or even to lose sight of it. Yet it maintains itself in such great utterances as the Pauline : " No man liveth unto himself " ; " Ye are members one of another " ; and the more complicated human society grows, the more obvious does the truth become. But the other aspect, the importance of the individual in religion and in human life, received, and must continue to receive, due attention, and is unmistakeably in evidence in the history of post-exilic Jewish thought.

It is, above all, in the psalms that we naturally look for at least one element in this new doctrine. Opinions as to the dating of the *Psalms* have undergone considerable changes in the twentieth century, and most scholars to-day would attribute a much larger number of the psalms to the pre-exilic period than did their predecessors. Many of these have the appearance of being the utterance of individual souls, the plea of the oppressed righteous against the wicked oppressor, the cry of the victim for vengeance on the tyrant. Yet the view is rapidly gaining ground that where such " individualistic " psalms are to be assigned to the pre-exilic age, they either present the community under the guise of an individual, or they form part of the regular ritual carried out in certain forms of legal process whereby Yahweh was invoked.

In other psalms, however, we may assert without

possibility of error that we have the cry of a single person. Some of these are among the richest literary fruits of men's spiritual experience, and are as valid for us to-day as when they were first penned. One feature of these expressions of the inner life of men is that they are dateless, meeting the needs of saints and sinners in all ages and of all races. Among such psalms we may instance xi., xxiii., xxv., li., and many others.

THE GREEK PERIOD

CHAPTER XI

THE INFLUENCE OF HELLENISM ON THE JEWS

THE Greek period may be reckoned as beginning about 300 B.C. and lasting to the time when the power of Rome began to extend its influence eastwards, i.e. until about 100 B.C.[1]

After the death of Alexander in 323 B.C. a period of great turmoil followed, during which his leading generals fought among themselves, each trying to secure some portion of the dismembered empire for himself. The battle of Ipsus, 301 B.C., was, for the time being, decisive ; a settlement was reached, the empire of Alexander being divided as follows : Lysimachus ruled in Asia Minor, Demetrius Poliorketes in Greece, Seleucus in Syria and farther eastward, and Ptolemy in Egypt ; to the kingdom of the latter belonged also Jerusalem and the southern part of Palestine. We are concerned here with the last two only.

Alexander's ideal had been to create a world-empire which should be not only a political unity but the component parts of which should be welded together by the unifying influence of Greek culture.

One of the most potent means whereby this was achieved was by founding cities on the Greek model and peopling them with Greeks, and in the case of already existing cities by forcing them to adopt the pattern of the Greek city-state, i.e. the city was governed by a council (*Boulé*), elected annually by the people, instead of the earlier senate (*Gerousia*), which consisted of representatives of the aristocracy.

---

[1] Not that Greek influence ceased at this date ; but at its best it was during the period indicated that Hellenic influence was exercised.

The successors of Alexander were his zealous imitators in this, and a great part of the East was soon dotted with numerous centres from which Hellenic culture, language, and customs radiated. Palestine was included in this ; among the Hellenized cities here may be mentioned Joppa, Gaza, Askelon, Dora, Apollonia, Ptolemais, and Scythopolis, on the west of Jordan ; and Hippus, Gadara, Pella, Dium, and Philadelphia, on the east of Jordan, and others.

Judæa, being thus surrounded by a network of Greek cities, could not fail to be influenced by the Greek spirit, and it must have been at work for some time previously when we find that early in the second century B.C. both the leaders and a large section of the people were eager to welcome Greek customs ; thus, in 1 Macc. i. 11–15 it is said : " In those days came there forth out of Israel transgressors of the law, and persuaded many, saying, Let us go and make a covenant with the Gentiles that are round about us ; for since we were parted from them many evils have befallen us. And the saying was good in their eyes. And certain of the people were forward herein, and went to the king, and he gave them licence to do after the ordinances of the Gentiles. And they built a place of exercise in Jerusalem according to the laws of the Gentiles ; and they made themselves uncircumcized, and forsook the holy covenant, and joined themselves to the Gentiles, and sold themselves to do evil." It should be noted here that the words, " since we were parted from them," whatever it may be to which reference is made, point to the fact of still earlier contact with and influence of Hellenism on the part of one section of the Jews of Jerusalem.

It is important, further, to note that in this passage, which is a crucial one, there is, with the exception of the mention of the Abrahamic rite, no reference to religion. These words were written at the very least fifty to sixty years later than the beginning of the reign of Antiochus Epiphanes, when the champions of orthodoxy and the Law had won the day, and when everything contrary to the Law, or what was considered as contrary to the Law, would have been emphasized ; but in spite of this, with the

20

exception mentioned, there is no question of Hellenic influences having affected the religion of the Jews. This point needs emphasis.

By the end of the fourth century B.C. Greek thought was not what it had been a century earlier ; it was not the spirit of the culture of Athens of the fifth century that influenced the oriental world of the third and following century ; by this time the enlightenment of those earlier days had resulted in the decay of the popular religion and the sovereignty of Individualism and Intellectualism of which the ultimate outcome was Scepticism and Positivism. "There remained a civilization dominated by art and science ; this alone, and not the spirit of ancient Greek culture, is what permeated the East from the time of Alexander . . . the Forum, the theatre, the gymnasium, the public baths, were built in the Greek architectural style ; the cities received their democratic constitution ; commerce and the army, bibliography and art, brought various loan-words into the oriental languages. At the most all this affected merely the surface of things. Of a deeper spiritual Hellenic influence during the third and second centuries on the educated classes there can be no question, let alone the bulk of the people."[1]

This being so, we must realize that that considerable section of the Jews which was attracted by Hellenism, such as it now was, did not become renegades to their own religion because they were offered what they conceived to be a more enlightened religion, but, firstly, because the external allurements of Greek civilization fascinated them, and secondly, because political considerations made it worth their while. They did not accept a new religion ; they merely became atheists. This explains the fact that in spite of Greek environment, in spite of their being the subjects of an alien Greek sovereign, in spite of the influence of the Greek language, Greek ways of thought, Greek customs, etc., the *religion* of the Jews remained quite unaffected by Greek ideas or Greek philosophy.[2]

[1] Hölscher, *Geschichte der israelitischen und jüdischen Religion*, p. 163 (1922).

[2] The conception of Wisdom personified is no doubt in part due to the influence of Greek thought, but that approximates to philosophy rather than to religion ; see further below, p. 340 ; and, in any case, such a

Upon the Jews themselves there is no doubt that Hellenism had effects in a large variety of ways, especially upon the Jews of the Dispersion, as witness, e.g., the existence of the Greek Old Testament, necessitated by the fact that the Jews outside Palestine could understand their Scriptures in no other language ; but in whatever directions this influence manifested itself, orthodox Judaism as it existed during the Greek period, and as it has existed ever since, was unaffected.

Schürer believes that the influence of the Greek spirit was so strong among the Jews of Judæa by the beginning of the second century B.C. that had the process of Hellenization been allowed to continue, without the drastic intervention of Antiochus Epiphanes, the Judaism of Palestine would presumably, in course of time, have assumed a form in which it would have been no more recognizable, a form much more syncretistic than that of a Philo.[1] We believe this estimate to be erroneous ; for even the Jews of the Dispersion, living in the midst of Greek influences of every conceivable kind, without the hold that Jerusalem and the Temple would naturally have upon those within their sphere—even those Jews of the Dispersion as a whole remained loyal to the religion of their fathers.

book as *The Wisdom of Solomon*, like *Ecclesiastes*, only represents individual thought, not that of any large section of the Jews. Doubtless, one can point to Philo, on whom Greek philosophy, methods of thought, and general world-outlook exercised a profound influence ; but Philo was very exceptional. It is difficult to believe that many Jews, even of the Dispersion, were similarly influenced ; for had that been the case would not some more manifest signs of it have been preserved ? Philo's guiding principle, the essence of his intellectual and religious thought, was the contrast between the spiritual and the material ; but could this be said to be characteristic of orthodox Judaism of the last century B.C. and the first century A.D. ?

[1] *Geschichte des jüdischen Volkes*, i. 189 f.

CHAPTER XII

THE PROBLEM OF SUFFERING

LIKE every new truth, the doctrine of individualism brought new problems with it. Chief of these was the problem of suffering, which, though not created by the teaching of Jeremiah and Ezekiel, was yet terribly reinforced thereby ; and it has troubled the mind of man without intermission from the last days of the kingdom of Judah. We are forced to admit that, though we may have light on the problem, and though for many its pressure is no longer crushing, we have as yet found no answer which we can regard as finally valid and satisfying to the human mind. Nevertheless, even if a conclusive answer to the great question has not been suggested, by grappling with it much light has been thrown on the relation between man and God ; and this we must briefly trace out.

1. THE PROBLEM INTENSIFIED BY PROPHETIC TEACHING

An earlier age might have thought of the distribution of good and of ill as due to the divine whim, irrespective of the character of the recipient. But from the day when Amos first proclaimed the double doctrine of the righteousness of Yahweh and His supremacy, such a view became impossible. The pre-exilic prophets thought of Yahweh as one who was perfectly just, and at the same time ruled the universe alike of nature and of man. It would seem to follow from these premises that goodness would always be rewarded with earthly prosperity, and that sin must be punished with material disaster.

Men are slow to realize the results of their own thinking. A century and a half after the days of Amos, Habakkuk asked the age-long question : " Thou that art of purer eyes than to behold evil, and that canst not look on

perverseness, wherefore lookest thou upon them that deal
treacherously, and holdest thy peace when the wicked
swalloweth up the man that is more righteous than
he ? " (Hab. i. 13). Such a question could not have
arisen save on the basis of the teaching of the eighth
century prophets. The fact of the inequalities of life
was always obvious ; the problem arose when the fact
had to be reconciled with the doctrine of divine justice.
So that when once that doctrine had been accepted
Habakkuk's question became inevitable.

In so far as he himself attempted a solution, it was
expressed in the obscure phrase : " The just shall live
in his faithfulness " (see the R.V. marg. of Hab. ii. 4).
The prophet's meaning cannot be said to be clear ; most
probably it suggests that virtue is its own reward, and
that a man who really is faithful can have no higher gift
or benefit bestowed on him. Goodness is so good that it
cannot be recompensed save by itself ; sin is so terrible
that no punishment can be adequate. But even if this
be the prophet's meaning, which is by no means certain,
it is not an answer which will satisfy everyone.

Jeremiah was faced with the same question, but he
found no answer at all.

It was, naturally enough, in exilic and post-exilic
times that the pressure of the question became most
severe. It was handled by such writers as the author of
Ps. xxxvii., who reached the conclusion that the adversity
of the righteous and the prosperity of the wicked are
alike evanescent, and that before death each will reap
the due reward of his deeds. This became, in fact, the
orthodox view of post-exilic Judaism, in spite of numerous apparent exceptions. Where it did not fit the obvious
facts, it was assumed that the sufferer who seemed to be
righteous was in reality guilty of some terrible secret sin
for which he was being punished by Yahweh, and thus
to disaster was added the cruel and doubtless often
unjustified suspicion of wickedness.

2. The " Servant Songs "

A real advance in the thought about this problem was
contributed by the thinker and writer to whom we owe

the so-called " Servant Songs " embedded in Isa. xl.–lv.
In the best known of these, lii. 13–liii. 12, we have a
picture of the final calamities which overwhelm the
faithful " slave of Yahweh." This is no place to discuss
the authorship or the original application of this and its
companion passages. It would seem, however, that no
one individual sat for the ideal portrait, but that the
writer draws on the experiences of at least two different
men.[1] The Servant is one who suffers from physical
pain, " a man of pains, and known unto sickness."
For this or for some other reason his face is veiled, " as
one who hid his face from us, he was despised." [2] In
the terrible word " stricken " the truth is brought home ;
the man is a leper. But in some strange way his sufferings
are redemptive for others, and bring to those who survive
him forgiveness and peace. They, however, do not
understand until it is too late, and the servant has to
endure persecution, a false charge, a tyrannical sentence,
and a criminal's death and burial. It is a dark picture,
yet there are moments of vision when he realizes the
meaning of his own agony : " away out of the agony of
his soul shall he look, and shall be satisfied by his knowledge." [3]

It is here that we have light on the problem immediately
before us. For a man who has fully and perfectly
surrendered himself to the will of his Master, Yahweh,
for a man who knows to the uttermost the meaning of
self-denial, it is enough to understand that his own
suffering will win something of incalculable value for
others,—he is " satisfied by his knowledge." He who
has really " poured out his soul unto death " will not seek
or demand reward for himself, for in the knowledge that
others are blessed through his pain he finds his heart's
desire.

Such a solution may be satisfactory for the sufferer

[1] The difference of view taken by my collaborator in Chapter V and
my own here does not affect the teaching of the Song, which is our
main present concern. It will be well to compare what is said there
with what is written here ; for taking our respective views as a whole
they are complementary rather than opposed (T. H. R.).

[2] This rendering involves a very slight change in the vocalization
of the Hebrew, the omission of a single dot, reading *mastir* for *mastēr*.

[3] So, probably, liii. 11a should be rendered.

himself, if he be fully surrendered, but to the more contemplative mind it fails to justify God. The man himself may have no complaint to make, but is it fair that Yahweh should make the agony of one person the indispensable condition of the happiness of another ? Abstract justice would seem to require that pain and pleasure should at least balance one another in the experience of one and the same individual ; absolute equity might conceivably accept an atonement vicariously offered, but it could hardly demand it, still less assume that this was to be the normal means whereby the sinner should be restored.

3. The Book of Job

It is in the book of *Job* that we find the most thorough, frank, and honest discussion which the subject has ever received. This is not the place in which to enlarge upon the qualities of a book which may reasonably claim to be the finest piece of literature that the world has yet seen. Its central problem is the question which we now have under consideration, the problem of suffering in relation to the goodness and the omnipotence of God.

The poet had before him an old story, told in prose, of the sufferings which befell Job, of his patience under his afflictions, of his conversation with his friends, and of his final restoration. The beginning and end of this he has taken for his own purposes, accepting as the basis of his discussion the account of the successive misfortunes which fell on the hero, and accepting, too, the view that in the first instance they were due to the jealous zeal of Satan, the official Accuser-General attached to the divine court. But instead of retaining the central portion of the narrative he has inserted his own poem, placing himself in the position of Job, and speaking through his mouth.

The poem is a record of the conflict between the old orthodoxy and the relentless quest for truth. The former is represented by the three friends, the latter by Job. Eliphaz, Bildad, and Zophar all accept the current view, which we have noted as being that of Ps. xxxvii., namely, that all suffering is punishment for sin, and that a man's misfortunes prove that he must have done wrong in the sight of God. They therefore urge Job to confess and repent, and promise him that if he does so, he will be restored to his former prosperity. While the three friends are skilfully differentiated, they all present the same general point of view ; and when this has once been stated in the first speech of Eliphaz, no further advance whatever is made by any of them. Each speaks in turn, and there are three series of speeches. In our present text there are only two speeches in the third series, Zophar remaining silent ; but it is probable that this is due to textual corruption, and that part, at any rate, of Zophar's third speech is now included in one of Job's.

Job opens the debate, and speaks after each of his friends, appealing in the last speech to God to appear and justify His actions. A fifth character is introduced, Elihu by name, but there are good reasons for believing that his speeches, which are neither answered nor noticed by Job, are the insertion of a later poet, who was not satisfied with the book as it stood. Finally, in answer to Job's appeal, God appears, and by His words reduces Job to humble submission to the divine will.

The heart of the book lies in the progress of Job's thought as he struggles for a solution of his difficulties. He has two problems, distinct, yet closely interrelated. The first is that of God's own attitude towards himself, and he has to find out for himself whether God is his friend or his enemy, for him or against him. The second is the wider, more general question of the justice to be found in the divine government of the universe as a whole, and of human life in particular. The answer to the first will be a personal faith, the solution of the second will be a theodicy. The consummate art of the poet is nowhere better illustrated than in the fact that while the friends never make the slightest movement from the position they have originally taken up, the advance Job makes is from time to time based on remarks that have fallen from them.

Job's first speech in chapter iii. is simply a cry of pain. Would that he had never been born ! If he must be born, would that he had perished at once and never reached years of self-consciousness ! If he must live his life and suffer, would that he could die now and end his pain ! In all this there is no *problem* ; there is intense suffering, but no real question as to his relation with God. Eliphaz replies, however, that God must be punishing him for some secret sin, and that if he will but humble himself and repent, all will yet be well. The effect on Job is to raise the problem of his relations with God. He knows that he has not sinned in such measure as to deserve what he endures, and he will not confess to crimes which he has not committed. It must be an arbitrary love of fortune, or hatred of the victim, which rouses God to inflict such agony on His creature. Can God not leave Job alone for a moment ? He is doomed to die, but— and here we have the first faint glimmering of a ray of light—God will realize His mistake, and will seek for His servant, only to find that it is too late : Job will have passed out of God's reach into *She'ol*.

Bildad reminds Job that God is righteous, and raises a new train of thought. " Righteous " is a term with more than one meaning. It may imply moral justice, or it may be used in its primitive sense of a man who wins his case in a court of law. In the second sense, Job says, God is " righteous," for no power can overcome Him, no argument can prove Him wrong. If a man were to come into conflict with Him, He would be at once accuser, jury, judge, and executioner. Yet he toys with the idea of a meeting in which he might lay his whole case before God. But he puts it from him for the time ; there seems no hope that way. It is God who tortures him, behaving to him like an omnipotent demon. He is God's creature, and God has absolute power over him. Were they to meet, the infinitesimal could only be crushed utterly by the Infinite. After all, the best for which he can hope and plead is that God will leave him alone till nature and disease bring him to the grave.

Zophar has nothing to add to his predecessors, but his speech is a more pointed personal attack than theirs, and Job is aroused to a more direct complaint of the " comfort " which they all have to offer him.

Eliphaz speaks yet more strongly than before ; he is convinced that Job is one of the worst of sinners. Job sees the futility of hoping for any help from his friends ; the tension becomes stronger ; his anguish of spirit becomes more poignant ; he must have a refuge ; and he turns to God. He appeals from the God of conventional theology to God as He really must be :

> O earth, cover not my blood,
> And let my cry have no resting place.
> Even now, behold, my witness is in heaven,
> And he that voucheth for me is on high.
> My friends scorn me ;
> But mine eye poureth out tears unto God ;
> That he would maintain the right of a man with God,
> And of a son of man with his neighbour (Job xvi. 18–21).

So nearly has he found a rock on which to plant his feet. But the wave of despair returns, and sweeps him back with it ; he is doomed, and must die. What hope is there then, he asks, that even God will justify him ?

Again Bildad speaks, more sharply than ever rebuking the sinner before him ; and once more Job is convinced that he has nothing to look for from his friends. In frantic distress he turns now to them, now to God, until, at the very last gasp, he makes the great leap of faith and finds that he has passed that barrier of threatening death against which he had hitherto beaten himself in vain. The text of xix. 25–7 is obscure and almost certainly corrupt in parts, but on this we may rely :

> But I know that my redeemer liveth,
> And that he shall stand up at last upon the earth,
> . . . . . .
> Yet without my flesh shall I see God,
> Whom I shall see for myself,
> And mine eyes shall behold, and not another.

There is no general or formulated doctrine of the resurrection of the dead here. Yet there is the conviction that, for Job at least, death is not the end ; there will still be possible some kind of valid relationship between himself and his God. There is no thought of eternal life, no suggestion of heaven, but there is an assurance which will inevitably lead to these doctrines.

This, of course, does not solve the problem for Job ;

but it does enable him to approach it in a calmer spirit. He knows now that God is on his side, and he dare with greater freedom claim to enter the divine presence and utter his complaint. But his difficulty is that he does not know where he may find Him, for though the evidence of his power is everywhere, He Himself remains concealed. Finally, Job stakes all on one great challenge to God, and appeals to Him to reveal Himself. And God answers. And then there follows an exposition of the greatness of God in the works of creation. True, Job's questions are not answered, but for him it is enough, for in the presence of God they are forgotten. It is, after all, here that the final message of the book lies. Questions may agitate the mind of man, problems may torture his spirit, but when once he has seen God, when once he has stood before Him, and begun to know Him, the questions and the problems vanish. There is something deeper than reason, more convincing than logical argument, and in the light of experience others may cry with Job :

> I have heard of thee with the hearing of the ear,
> But now mine eye seeth thee,
> Therefore I abhor myself and repent
> In dust and ashes (Job xlii. 6).

That the writer here implicitly expresses his belief in life after death can hardly be doubted. But as this subject is dealt with in Chapter XIII, we say nothing further about it here.

The problem of suffering was not solved ; but this whole-hearted grappling with it brought to the minds of the writers of this book the realization of some vital truths. Suffering may be a mystery, but the true believer in God will not be alienated from his faith thereby ; it may test the faith of the pious, but it will show that his *piety is disinterested* : " Though he slay me, yet will I wait for him " (Job xiii. 15). Suffering may be a bitter, painful experience ; but when the sufferer has passed through the fire of affliction he will come to the realization that *suffering has strengthened his character* :

> He delivereth the afflicted by his affliction,
> And openeth the ear by adversity (Job xxxvi. 15).

The suffering of the righteous may raise the question of the justice of God's government of the world ; but the contemplation of the divine creative work brings man *to a deeper apprehension of God,* and he comes to see that God is concerned with something more than the mere punishing and rewarding of men ; and thus there is generated a clearer *sense of the proportion of things.* The psalmist's words compress much that finds expression in the book :

> When I consider thy heavens, the work of thy fingers,
> The moon and the stars which thou hast ordained,
> What is man that thou art mindful of him ?
> And the son of man, that thou visitest him ? "
> (Ps. viii. 3, 4 [4, 5 in Hebrew] ; cp. Job vii. 17, 18.)

CHAPTER XIII

THE DOCTRINE OF IMMORTALITY [1]

1. Some Preliminary Considerations

The doctrine of Immortality among the Hebrews cannot be rightly envisaged without taking into account certain other beliefs, which reach back into a remote past, but which, as we have seen in the earlier part of this work, either left their marks, or continued as living beliefs, during much later periods. [2]

We have seen that the remnants of Totemism are to be clearly discerned in the Old Testament, so that at one time it must have been actively in vogue among the forbears of the Hebrews. Now from the point of view of the present enquiry the facts of primary importance in Totemism are not only the solidarity of the members of the clan, not only the belief in kinship between the members of the clan and the Totem-animal, but, above all, the belief in kinship with the Totem-ancestor of the clan or tribe. This Totem-ancestor was obviously believed to have lived on earth long ago ; and he is conceived of as still living : *where* he carries on his existence is not of primary importance ; the main things are the fact of his existence, and the belief that as the ancestor of the clan he is interested in its members, and can help them. What did men in an early state of culture deduce from this fact of the continued existence of their ancestor with whom they felt themselves indissolubly bound by kinship ? The answer is that they deduced nothing at all from the fact. Uncultured man takes a good many things for granted which he cannot understand, which he cannot account for, and which he has

---

[1] In order to treat this subject as a whole both the earlier and more developed beliefs are dealt with here.

[2] Part I, Chapter I, § 4 ; Chapter V, 1.

not the slightest desire to account for. But it is not difficult to realize that when, in the course of ages, the beginnings of speculations arose as to what happened to the dead hereafter, this accepted fact of a belief in the continued existence of a clan, as embodied in its ancestor, would be a factor in those speculations.

Further, we have seen that the Old Testament contains distinct traces of Ancestor-worship ; it does not need insisting upon that if men worship their ancestors it is not merely a memory that they are worshipping, but beings who are firmly believed to be in existence somewhere. Here again, it is not asked where they are, for the simple reason that it does not matter ; the point is that they are powerful for good and evil, and must therefore be propitiated ; hence sacrifices to the dead.[1] But if, according to this very ancient custom, men were worshipped who had once lived on earth, their worshippers must have thought of them as still living somehow and somewhere. So that here again, though men did not deduce from this anything regarding themselves, when the time came for speculations to arise, this belief and custom which had been gradually preparing their minds would have had their influence in the development of thought ; and in comparatively early times we can see how the belief in the continued existence of life after death was held not only with regard to eponyms but in the case of others too ; hence the practice of placing food in the tombs beside corpses.[2] That in such cases it was not a question of offerings *to* the dead is proved by the fact that instances are on record of the dead man's hand being placed in the dish of food by his side ; in another case, in a tomb in Greece, the dish is placed by the mouth of the corpse, the head being turned towards it.[3]

Once more, the whole subject of Necromancy,[4] with its belief in the power of invoking the dead, points to

---

[1] Sacrifices *for* the dead do not belong to this stage of belief.

[2] As S. A. Cook pointedly remarks : " A people accustomed to the annual death and revival of nature might easily formulate theories of the survival of the dead, and care is accordingly taken to provide for the needs of the deceased " (*The Religion of Ancient Palestine*, p. 56).

[3] Gressmann, *Altorientalische Bilder zum alten Testament*, No. 227 (1927).　　　　　　　　　　　　[4] See Part I, Chapter VII.

the conviction that beyond the grave departed spirits
exercised an influence on the affairs of men ; in other
words, that the former were very much alive, though
where they were was not enquired into.   We get, however,
one indication of this in the case of the Witch of Endor
calling Samuel up, i.e. he was thought of as coming from
the depths of the earth.

Then, further, there are some old-world Hebrew
expressions which must be briefly alluded to.   Why
should so much importance have been attached to a
man " being gathered to his fathers " (Judges ii. 10),
or " sleeping with his fathers " (2 Sam. vii. 12 ; 1 Kings
i. 21), or " being laid in the sepulchre with his fathers "
(2 Kings ix. 28), or " going to the fathers " (Gen. xv.
15) ?   Such expressions are meaningless unless they
witness to the belief that in some vague and undefined,
but none the less real, way a man did join his ancestors
either in or near the tomb ; but this must mean something
more than that one dead body was laid beside others ;
we should not find expressions like those mentioned
occurring so often if they suggested nothing more than
this.   The fact is that we have here the old clan-solidarity
idea persisting, only it has become somewhat more
individual, and is, in so far, a development of belief.
It was not asked how, though the where had become more
definite, but men did believe that the family circle was
joined after death, and therefore a definite belief in
immortality must have existed in comparatively very
early times.

A different and somewhat quaint expression is that
of being " bound up in the bundle [better " bag "] of
life " ; in 1 Sam. xxv. 29 Abigail says to David : " And
though man be risen up to pursue thee, and to seek thy
soul, yet the soul of my lord shall be bound up in the
bundle [" bag "] of life with Yahweh thy God ; and the
souls of thine enemies, them shall he sling out, as from
the hollow of a sling."   These words witness as clearly
as possible to the belief, widespread among semi-cultured
peoples, that the soul can be detached from the body [1] ;

---

[1] See also Isa. xiv. 20 ; Ezek. xiii. 17–23.   The expression is used, but
in a purely metaphorical sense, in the Hebrew of *Ecclus.* vi. 16.

the belief was doubtless vague in so far as concerned such questions as to how the soul detached itself from the body, the nature of the bundle, or bag, in which Yahweh kept men's souls, and of the relationship between body and soul during the absence of the latter ; but this did not affect the main point of the independent existence of the soul, however materialistic the conception. Once given this, one can see that belief in the existence of life after death, though not defined, becomes inevitable ; because if the soul (*nephesh*, whatever may have been the ancient Hebrew conception regarding this) is detachable from the body and can be kept by Yahweh during the lifetime of a man, why not after his lifetime ? Sooner or later that question would have suggested itself.

Lastly, one other point is worth mention, though we cannot enlarge upon it here.[1] In early Hebrew thought death was conceived of as so abnormal that its origin had to be accounted for. Man was originally intended to be immortal,[2] and the Babylonian story, upon which the *Genesis* Garden of Eden story is based, was originally told in order to account for the existence of death. Whether behind both forms of the story a common Semitic tradition existed need not trouble us ; the point of importance is that in early Hebrew thought death was thought of as unnatural, something that ought never to have entered into man's experience ; and it is clear that the background of such a conception must have had a share in the later development of the belief in immortality. It is, then, with the recognition of these facts that we must consider next what became the normal belief regarding the Hereafter among the Hebrews, according to the Old Testament.

2. She'ol the Abode of the Departed

In contrast to the form of belief regarding the Hereafter adumbrated above, a belief which was ingrained in the

[1] See *Immortality and the Unseen World*, pp. 193–199.

[2] On the other hand, my collaborator, with others, believes that man was held to be mortal from the first, and that the punishment for disobedience was to be immediate death. Cp. *The Abingdon Commentary* on Gen. ii.–iii., especially p. 221, col. *b* (1929) (W.O.E.O.).

bulk of the Hebrew people, there was what came to be the orthodox and official belief as embodied in the *She'ol* conception. We are, at the outset, confronted here with one or two difficult questions ; and we are not sure whether a satisfactory answer can be given in each case, though the attempt will be made. The first is : Why was it that the religious leaders sought to displace the older belief in favour of the *She'ol* conception ? In essence, the older belief, in spite of superstitions, was the more natural, and we may even say the more rational, and so far as its essence was concerned, viz. the reality and fullness of life hereafter, it ultimately gained the day. There must, however, have been strong reasons for seeking to abolish it. The second question is : When did the process of eradicating the traditional belief in favour of the *She'ol* conception begin ? Here again we shall attempt to give an answer, though we realize that, in view of the exiguous *data*, the answer can only be tentative.

We must begin, however, by stating first what the Babylonian belief concerning the Hereafter was, and then the nature of the Hebrew *She'ol* conception, for it is difficult to believe that the latter was not dependent upon the former.

(i) *The Babylonian Belief concerning the Hereafter.*— It has already been pointed out that Totemism, Ancestor-worship, and Necromancy [1] played a great part both in general Semitic and in Babylonian religion ; it must therefore be obvious that ideas regarding the Hereafter, as affected by these, were similar to the parallel ideas among the Hebrews, as outlined above ; it is unnecessary to go over these details again. But as among the Hebrews, so among the Babylonians, a different form of belief arose which, as we shall see, was very closely parallel among each. Why and when the later form of belief arose among the Babylonians cannot be said : we can only record the fact that among them, as among the Hebrews, two quite distinct stages regarding belief in a future life existed—the earlier and more primitive one, and a later one. It is also the fact that among

[1] See Part I, Chapters V, § 1, VII, and the literature there referred to.

both Babylonians and Hebrews these stages of belief overlapped and continued side by side. An interesting sidelight is thrown on the subject by some words in an inscription of the Assyrian king, Ashurbanipal (he died in 626 B.C.); he says: "The rules for making offerings to the dead and libations to the ghosts of the kings my ancestors, which had not been practised, I reintroduced. I did well unto god and man, to dead and living." [1]

The later form of belief centred in an underworld which was the abode of the departed. It was thought of sometimes as a great hollow mountain; at other times, and more usually, as an immense city which could not be measured for size, and it lay beyond the waters that are under the earth. The city of the dead is enclosed with seven walls, and there are seven gates with bolts and bars. It is in total darkness, and dust lies over everything. The shades of men glide about in silence, or if there is any sound it is that of the moaning of the sorrowful inhabitants. They live on the dust that surrounds them, and they drink of murky water. They have neither hope nor affections, but lead a joyless existence. It is spoken of as "the land without return," "the abode which whosoever enters never leaves again"; the path to it is one "from which there is no return."

It is quite uncertain whether the term *Shu-'alu*, be its meaning "place of enquiry," or "hollow place," is ever used in reference to the abode of the departed; experts differ on the subject.

There are signs of a more developed Babylonian belief regarding the Hereafter to which we shall refer later.

(ii) *The Hebrew She'ol Conception.*—That this conception corresponds with that of the Babylonian abode of the departed will be seen from the following:

In Isa. xiv. 9 occur the words: "*She'ol* from beneath is moved . . ."; in Gen. xxxvii. 35 it is said: "I will go down to *She'ol*" (see also Job. xi. 8, xvii. 16, xxvi. 6; Prov. xv. 24; Jonah ii. 6 [7 in Hebrew]). In these

[1] Quoted by Mr. Sidney Smith in *The Cambridge Ancient History*, iii. 127 (1925).

and other passages it is clear that *She'ol* is thought of
as situated under the earth.

In Isa. xxxviii. 10 Hezekiah says : "I shall go into the
gates of *She'ol* "; in Job xvii. 16 "the bars of *She'ol* " are
spoken of (cp. xxxviii. 17; Ps. ix. 13, cvii. 18); "gates "
and "bars " thus represent it as a city.

In Job x. 22 *She'ol* is spoken of as "the land of darkness," and in Ps. cxliii. 3 it is said of an enemy that he
"hath made me dwell in dark places, as those that have
been long dead " (see also lxxxviii. 6, 12, and Job x. 21,
22). In Ps. cxv. 17 it is said : "The dead praise not
thee, Yahweh, neither they that go down into silence "
(cp. xciv. 17). In Ps. xxx. 9 it is asked : "Shall the dust
praise thee ? Shall it declare thy truth ? " (cp. xxii.
15; Job xxi. 26).

In Job x. 21 it is said in reference to *She'ol* : "Before I
go whence I shall not return."

We have thus a number of Hebrew and Babylonian
ideas about *She'ol* which are absolutely identical.

There are, further, a few other things regarding the
Hebrew belief. *She'ol* is thought of as a place where
all things are forgotten ; thus, in Ps. lxxxviii. 12 (13 in
Hebrew), it is said : "Shall thy wonders be known in
the dark ? And thy righteousness in the land of forget-
fulness ? "[1] An indication of a somewhat developed
belief is the fact that *She'ol* is sometimes personified ; in
Isa. v. 14, for example, it is thought of as an all-devouring
monster : "Therefore *She'ol* hath enlarged her desire,
and opened her mouth without measure . . . " (cp.
Ps. cxli. 7), and more striking is Isa. xxviii. 18 : "And
your covenant with Death shall be disannulled, and your
agreement with *She'ol* shall not stand." In this last
passage it will be seen that Death is synonymous with
She'ol; the same is seen in Job xvii. 13, xxi. 13; Ps. xviii.
4, 5 (5, 6 in Hebrew), xlix. 14 (15 in Hebrew), cxvi. 3, and
elsewhere.

Another mark of development is to be observed in
the use of three other expressions in close association
with *She'ol*. In Isa. xiv. 15 it is said : "Yet thou shalt

---

[1] Isa. xiv. 9 ff. represents a later development (see Duhm, *Das Buch
Jesaia, in loc.* [1914]).

be brought down to *She'ol* to the uttermost parts of the
Pit (*Bôr*)'' (cp. also Ps. xxviii. 1, xxx. 3 (4 in Hebrew),
lxxxviii. 4 (5 in Hebrew), cxliii. 7). The '' Pit '' is
generally used as synonymous with *She'ol*, but from such
passages as Ezek. xxxii. 23, 25, 28–30, one gains the impression that it was some place in *She'ol* reserved for the
worst enemies of Yahweh. Another synonym for *She'ol*
is *Shachath*, '' corruption,'' or '' destruction,'' so in Job
xvii. 13–16 (see also Isa. xxxviii. 17, li. 14 ; Ps. xxx. 9
(10 in Hebrew); Ezek. xxviii. 8 ; Jonah ii. 6 [7 in Hebrew]).
The idea of total annihilation suggested by the word
Shachath points to a development. And lastly there is
the word *'Abaddon*, from the root meaning '' to perish,''
or '' to destroy,'' so that it connotes a somewhat similar
idea to that of *Shachath* ; it is also used as a parallel to
She'ol (see Job xxvi. 6, xxviii. 22 ; Ps. lxxxviii. 11
(12 in Hebrew) ; otherwise it occurs only in Prov. xv. 11,
xxvii. 20).

We have reserved one most important matter about
the Hebrew *She'ol* conception until now because it
stands in contrast to what must be regarded as a developed
form (see below) of the Babylonian conception of the
underworld. According to the Hebrew belief Yahweh
is wholly unconcerned with the shades of the departed
in *She'ol* ; this is brought out, e.g., in Isa. xxxviii. 18, 19 :

For *She'ol* doth not give thee thanks, Death doth not praise thee ;
They that go down to the Pit hope not for thy faithfulness ;
He that liveth, he that liveth, he (it is) that praiseth thee, as I do this
    day.

It is in the *Psalms* that this teaching receives special
emphasis ; thus in Ps. vi. 5 (6 in Hebrew) it is said :

For in death there is no remembrance of thee,
In *She'ol* who shall give thee thanks ?

So, too, in Ps. xxx. 9 (10 in Hebrew) :

What profit is there in my blood when I go down to the Pit ?
Shall the dust praise thee, shall it declare thy faithfulness ?
                        (Cp. xxviii. 1, cxliii. 7.)

A definite assertion to the effect that Yahweh Himself

has no interest in the shades of men in *She'ol* is contained in Ps. lxxxviii. 4, 5, (5, 6 in Hebrew) :

I am counted among them that go down into the Pit;
I am become as a man without help [perhaps we should read : " without God "] ;
Cast off among the dead,
Like the slain that lie in the grave,
Whom thou rememberest no more,
For they are cut off from thy hand.

The whole psalm should be read ; it illustrates the belief that Yahweh plays no part in the world of the Hereafter, and naturally so, because the shades of the departed would not be capable of response.

In contrast to this there is the Babylonian belief in the presence of divine beings in the underworld. These were subordinate to the higher gods of the Babylonian pantheon, but still they were powerful deities. The goddess Erishkigal was called " the mistress of the great place " ; she was known also as Allatu, " the mighty one," and her husband was Nergal, called " Lord of the great land." [1] They were the rulers of the underworld. This is clearly a development of the earlier Babylonian conception regarding the underworld ; and—it may be mentioned, though it does not directly concern us here— there is a further development in that we meet with a distinct adumbration of a doctrine of resurrection, repre- sented by the term " awakeners of the dead." This term is applied to various Babylonian deities ; originally the " awakening " had reference to the " resurrection " of nature, but it is also applied to man ; thus it is said of the sun-god Shamash : " It is in thy power to wake the dead alive, and to release those who are bound." The god Nebo is praised as being one " who can lengthen the days of life, and who can awaken the dead." Of Marduk it is said that he is " the merciful one, who loves to awaken the dead " ; and similar power is ascribed to Gula, his spouse, " the mistress, the awakener of the dead." [2]

This, however, is by the way. To come back to the

---

[1] Jeremias, *Hölle* . . ., pp. 16, 17 ; *Das alte Testament* . . ., pp. 10, 46.

[2] Jeremias, *Hölle* . . ., pp. 22, 23.

Hebrew *She'ol* belief ; it is pertinent to enquire when the process began whereby the Hebrew religious leaders sought to substitute the *She'ol* belief in place of the older one, and why was it felt necessary to do this ? In seeking to give an answer to these questions it is of importance to realize that the *She'ol* belief is never mentioned in pre-prophetic times ; it occurs in 1 Kings ii. 6, 9, but it is recognized by the great mass of scholars that 1 Kings ii. 1–11 is a Deuteronomic addition. In 1 Sam. ii. 6 *She'ol* is mentioned ; but, again, the Song of Hannah in which this occurs is the insertion of a later scribe ; that, too, is generally recognized both because of its contents and because it disturbs the course of the narrative. In 2 Sam. xii. 23 David says in reference to his dead child : " I shall go to him, but he shall not return to me " ; but this does not necessarily represent the *She'ol* belief, rather the contrary, because this is not the way in which *She'ol* would be thought of ; the shades of the departed in *She'ol* were emotionless. What is reflected in this passage is the older belief according to which the family gathered in the ancestral tomb, the sleeping with the fathers, as in 2 Sam. vii. 12.

The earliest mention of *She'ol* is in literature belonging to the eighth century B.C. ; before that time we have practically no reference to the departed excepting the narrative in 1 Sam. xxviii. 3–25 (the calling up of Samuel from the underworld), which clearly reflects the early traditional belief. Another significant fact is that, as we have seen, *She'ol* is conceived of as a great city with gates and bars ; such a conception would not be possible to nomads. It seems fairly evident, then, that the *She'ol* conception among the Hebrews cannot have arisen until city-life had become familiar, and this can scarcely have been the case in any real sense until the time of David ; and even so it must have taken time for the new teaching to gain acceptance.

We are thus led to believe that the Hebrews came into contact for the first time with the *She'ol* conception after the settlement in Canaan, but that for a long time it meant nothing to them. Then, when the champions of Yahweh-worship were at last able to assert themselves

under the leadership of Elijah, it became more and more
realized that the practices and superstitions of the older
belief, connected as it was with Ancestor-worship and
Necromancy, was incompatible with Yahweh-worship.
The polemic against the older belief continued to gain
force until the rise of the great prophets of the eighth
century, when it became definitely a mark of disloyalty
to Yahweh, and the *She'ol* conception became firmly
established as the official belief. That it took a long time
before it was generally accepted is evident from the legal
enactments which we find in later times against Necromancy. That is therefore the answer to the questions
as to when and why the *She'ol* conception arose among
the Hebrews.

Knowing what we do about the Babylonian belief
regarding the underworld, it can hardly be doubted that
the Canaanite belief which the Hebrews learned and
ultimately adopted came from Babylonia ; but it came
to the Hebrews directly from the Canaanites, so that the
She'ol conception was the one thing that was adopted
and permanently conserved from the religion of Canaan,
anyhow until the second century B.C.

3. The Development of Belief

Whether or not belief in Immortality in advance of the
official *She'ol* doctrine was held before the Greek period
among the Jews is a question upon which opinions differ.
In Chapter V the conviction is expressed that Deutero-
Isaiah, or whoever it was who wrote the fourth " Servant
song," believed in a life hereafter in the fuller sense.
We recognize that many scholars do not hold this view.
In Chapter XII, also, when dealing with Job xix. 25–27, we
pointed out that while no formulated doctrine of the
resurrection of the dead was expressed, yet there was the
conviction in the mind of the writer that death was not
the end. In this case, too, we realize that other interpre-
tations of this passage are given. But there are a few
other passages in regard to which although there may not
be entire unanimity it is probable that the preponderance
of opinion is in favour of seeing in them a definite belief
in a fuller life hereafter.

The doctrine of a life after death was, however, by
no means confined to the Jewish faith ; it had also been
developed by Greek thinkers.　But there was a characteristic difference in the form which the doctrine took in
the two types of minds.　To the Greek, man was essentially a spirit temporarily imprisoned in a body, and it
was natural that when the body decayed, the liberated
soul should still continue to exist and to pursue its course.
The Hebrew, on the other hand, thought of a man as a
body animated by a spirit, and when he developed a
doctrine of immortality, it naturally took the form of
a resurrection of the body, reanimated by the same or
by another spirit.　This is the form in which the belief
appears in practically all Jewish and Jewish-Christian
Apocalypse.

There are, however, a few instances in which it seems
as if the thought of a Hebrew writer approached more
nearly to that of the Greek than to that of the normal
Jewish conception.　This certainly seems to be true of
the writer of Ps. lxxiii., who was led to a consideration
of the problem by the stress of the inequalities in the distribution of prosperity and adversity.　The case has
seldom been stated more clearly than in the opening
section of this psalm ; the writer's first impulse is to
take refuge in the theory that disaster will some day overtake the wicked.　But he feels the danger that lies in
the temptation to delight in the coming vengeance, and
turns to that positive assurance which he, and others
like him, felt :

Nevertheless, I am continually with thee ;
Thou hast holden my right hand ;
Thou guidest me by thy counsel,
And afterward thou wilt take me to glory.
Whom have I in heaven (but thee) ?
And having thee [lit. " being with thee "], I desire nought else on earth.
My flesh and my heart faileth,
But God is the strength of my heart and my portion for ever.

                                                (Ps. lxxiii. 23–26.)

These verses suggest something closely approximating
to that conception which we have learned to associate with
the Greek philosopher.　The Psalmist does contemplate
decay and destruction and dissolution of the physical

frame, but knows that this will not affect his relations with the God whom he has loved and served. And here alone we have a valid doctrine of immortality ; it is this realization of the relationship with God hereafter that is specifically Jewish when once the fuller belief has been attained. Herein lies the most important difference between the Greek and the Jewish doctrines, i.e. the former is primarily philosophical, the latter is essentially religious. The Greek based his speculations on his metaphysic, his anthropology, and his psychology, and reached his conclusions from his study of man. It is true that Socrates, if we may thus far trust Plato's picture of him, spoke of meeting the gods, but association with them is a single incident, almost an accident. The Jew, on the other hand, attained to his faith through his theology. Starting with the belief that God was righteous and all-powerful, he was led by slow stages to the conviction that the moral inequalities of this world could be adjusted only in a life after death. He came to believe in the resurrection of the dead, as we shall see, and this not so much because he had studied man, but because he knew God. Worshippers of a God who dealt with individuals would never be satisfied with the suggestion that a man's life was completed in that of his posterity, and that the reward of his actions would be reaped by those who came after him ; no, they must themselves find the seal set on their life.

A definite belief in the resurrection of the body is expressed in Isa. xxvi. 19 ; the chapter belongs, according to the opinion of most authorities, to the Greek period, perhaps early in this period ; some, however, place it later. This verse is a difficult one, and the text of it has evidently undergone some revision ; but it may be rendered : " Thy dead men [i.e. of Israel] shall arise ; the inhabitants of the dust shall awake, and shout for joy ; for a dew of lights is thy dew, and the earth shall bring to life the shades." This abrupt assertion of the resurrection, without any explanatory words, shows that the belief was generally accepted when this was written ; and it is for this reason that some commentators would date the passage as late as the second century B.C. ; this is, of course, possible ; but if, as we have attempted to show (see above, pp. 269 f.), the beginnings of a belief in immortality are to be discerned soon after, or conceivably even during, the Exile, there is no need to postulate so late a date. The words imply that just as the dew at nights comes down to fructify the vegetation of the soil, so a heavenly dew will descend to reanimate the bodies of the dead lying in the earth ; it is a " dew of lights " because it comes from the heavenly sphere illumined by the stars.

The only other passage in the Old Testament in which belief in the resurrection of the body is definitely expressed is Dan. xii. 2, belonging approximately to the middle of the second century B.C. : " And many of them that sleep in the dust of the earth shall awake, some to everlasting life, and some to shame and everlasting contempt." The general resurrection of both the good and the evil with a definite differentiation between their respective states in the next world marks a developed stage of belief ; but we begin to enter here into the domain of Apocalyptic, and with this we shall be more particularly concerned in Chapter XV.

It is necessary at this point to draw attention to a very important fact in the development of Hebrew religion, a fact by no means always recognized, a fact which at first sight seems disconcerting, yet one which the evolution of religious belief rendered inevitable ; namely this, that one vital element in the prophetic religion had of necessity to be discarded ultimately by post-exilic Judaism. The prophets, it is true, gave to the world, for the first time, something which the world dare never ignore without gravest detriment ; we mean, the truth of the indissoluble union between Religion and Ethics ; and, of course, all that tended to monotheistic belief in the prophetic teaching was cherished and developed in the post-exilic period. Nevertheless, apart from this, something that was fundamental in the teaching of the prophets became impossible of acceptance by the Jews of this period. The reason of this will be understood as soon as stated.

It was a constant theme of the prophets that the sins

of the nation would inevitably bring about its downfall.
Post-exilic prophets too taught that the Exile was the
just punishment for the sins of the nation.   That thought,
that teaching, was due to the parallel doctrines that all
misfortune was the manifestation of divine wrath for sin,
and that retribution was confined to the present world.
We have seen (Chapter XII, § 3) how vehemently the
former was protested against in the book of Job, and how
in his anguish Job is made to blaspheme God to His face,
and how very nearly, but not quite, he discerned the way
of a solution of his doubts.   It all described the struggle
of the nation as reflected by its thinkers ; for the inner
consciousness of the nation, as well as the facts of life,
necessitated a repudiation of that doctrine.   At the
worst, Israel was no worse than other nations, and had
neither merited the Exile nor its degradation as a subject-
race ever since ; indeed, it was better than other nations,
for it alone of all the nations acknowledged the One and
Only God.   Misfortune therefore was not the result of
sin.   Thus the nation could not do otherwise than
repudiate that doctrine of retribution as taught by the
prophets ; yet that repudiation involved so much.   We
have but few hints regarding the process whereby this
repudiation was gradually developed [1] ; but the proof of
its existence is, as we have seen, in the adoption of a
new doctrine of retribution, namely, that which extended
the scope of retribution to the future life, which to the
Jews postulated belief in a resurrection.

The doctrine of immortality seems to have been
accepted by the bulk of the people but slowly in Israel ;
and even down to the time of the destruction of the
Temple it was denied in the prominent and powerful
Sadducæan circles from which the priestly leaders of
the people were mainly drawn.   One characteristic piece
of this period of literature from this school survives in
what we call the book of *Ecclesiastes*.   This is a very
extraordinary work, and its inclusion in the Canon of
the Jewish Scriptures can only be explained by the
tradition which ascribed it to Solomon ;   even so its

---

[1] Is it possible that the extraordinary *tirade* against Prophetism in
Zech. xiii. 3–6 is an echo of this ?

canonicity was disputed to the very eve of the Christian
era, and possibly still later. Its prevailing note is that
of disillusionment. The writer has looked at and studied
human life from many points of view, and all he finds in
the end is " vanity." He knows that men think of God
as rewarding goodness and punishing wickedness, yet
he does not see that there is any practical difference
between them in the end (cp. Eccles. viii. 10, ix. 1–3).
All paths lead to one end—the grave, and there men share
the same lot, and have no memory of what their life has
been. The writer is aware of the doctrine of human
immortality, but he cannot accept it ; there is no proof of
it : " Who knoweth the spirit of man whether it goeth
upward, or the spirit of the beast whether it goeth downward into the earth ? " (Eccles. iii. 21.)

Again, in the *Wisdom of Ben-Sira* (*Ecclesiasticus*),
which contains indications of having issued from Sadducæan circles, and belongs approximately to 200 B.C.,
there are similarly no signs of a fuller belief in immortality,
the standpoint being the traditional *She'ol* doctrine.

The Sadducæan position, however, failed to maintain
its hold on the mass of the people, and, as a serious
element in Jewish thought, did not survive the destruction
of the Temple in A.D. 70. It was always more closely
bound up with the priestly caste, and so connected with
the religion of the Temple. The popular creed, on the
other hand, of the Scribes and Pharisees was that most
common in the synagogues ; and it is interesting to note
that in one of the pre-Christian elements of the Jewish
synagogal Liturgy, the prayer called *Shemoneh 'Esreh*
(the " Eighteen Benedictions "), belief in the resurrection finds explicit utterance : " Blessed art thou, O
Lord, that quickenest the dead." It was this side of
Judaism that survived, therefore, and which has continued up to the present day.

CHAPTER XIV

WISDOM AND ITS DEVELOPMENTS

1. The Semitic Mind

It is commonly said that the Semitic races have no gift for philosophy, and that for a thorough discussion of metaphysical questions it is necessary to turn to the Indo-European mind. It is pointed out that the Semite feels very strongly, but is not given to abstract speculation. He is intensely sensitive to personal appeals, sees quickly and clearly in pictures—so quickly and clearly as to pass from one metaphor to another with a speed which bewilders the pedestrian Aryan mind. But he does not reason consecutively or follow a complicated train of thought. The forms of literature most characteristic of the Hebrew genius are the lyric and the short prophetic oracle, instinct with life, throbbing with emotion, but rarely the product of deep and conscious reflexion. Among such a people we must not look for any elaborate or deeply conceived metaphysic, unless and until they come into contact with some other race to whom philosophical speculation is more natural. We may then find a combination of the old and the new, the native and the foreign, especially when the Semitic people has a deep respect for the intelligence of its new acquaintance.

There is, furthermore, a fundamental difference in outlook between the Semitic and the Indo-European mind. The latter, in that quest for unity which is the mainspring of all metaphysic, has invariably tended to become pantheistic, reducing all the objects of experience to a single whole, and assuming that every appearance of separate identity, whether of person or of thing, is illusory or transient.[1] The Semitic mind, on the other

[1] An apparent exception is presented by Zoroastrianism, though there are indications which suggest that this faith would have had a history similar to that of Indian religion if it had been able to develop without interference.

333

hand, laid intense stress on personality. Its exponents would not have used the expression; it was so fundamental to all their thinking that it never occurred to them to formulate it in so many words, and we may doubt whether they even had a term corresponding to our word. Yet their conception of the universe was based on what we call personality, and though in religion they thought of the community as the human unit, that community was commonly described in terms which suggest that it was personified in their thought. To the Jew men were persons, and God was a person; no explanation of their thought can be valid unless it is based on this fundamental presupposition.

2. The Māshāl

The aim of all science and philosophy is the unification of experience, the reduction of all phenomena to a single rule, the discovery of a single fact or principle with which all the varied manifestations of the universe can be brought into accord. Its earliest effort at expression is normally in the epigram or proverb, a short saying in which a number of different facts are brought together, a generalization which shall include the results of a number of different observations. The wise man is he who has so observed life and the inter-relations of man and man, of man and nature, or of man and God, that he is able to group them, or many of them, under a single general "law." Such a law may be either descriptive of experience in the material world, when it will be an elementary form of natural science, or it may be normative of conduct, when it will be a moral precept, or it may go deeper into the nature of reality, when it will be classed as metaphysical.

We find this tendency showing itself in the thought of Greece, especially at that comparatively early stage which is represented to us in the older Ionian philosophy, and remained to some extent the popular conception. We are all familiar with the old story of how the seven sages came together to formulate the world's wisdom in a series of short, pithy sentences.[1] The famous "Know

[1] It is perhaps unnecessary to remark that this story has no historical value whatever; the sages concerned were not contemporaries. But it does illustrate the love of early Greek thinking for this type of generalized statement.

thyself," and " Nothing too much," are ethical generalizations by which their authors sought to reduce to a
common law all rules for conduct.   " All things are in a
state of flux " is primarily an attempt to state the laws
of the physical universe, but is capable of being extended
into a metaphysical generalization. These efforts after
unification of experience are genuinely scientific and
philosophical, though the science and the philosophy
are still on a very elementary plane.

Such statements of life are common to practically all
nations and types of mind at a particular stage of their
development, and it is impossible not to feel that even
to-day the epigram is a far more powerful instrument of
conviction than logic. Millions who know nothing of
meteorology will quote and believe :

> A red sky at night
> Is the shepherd's delight ;
> A red sky in the morning
> Is the shepherd's warning.

Many peoples, on reaching a stage at which literature
becomes possible, have formed collections of these
sayings : Martin Tupper has a long pedigree. We find
these collections in Egypt in such works as the well-
known *Teaching of Amen-em-ope* and other books, and
in Mesopotamia in the *Sayings of Ahikar*, of which
a fifth century copy in Aramaic has recently come
to light.[1] In Hebrew and Jewish literature they are
chiefly concentrated in three books, *Proverbs*, *Ecclesiastes*,
and the *Wisdom of Ben-Sira* (*Ecclesiasticus*). All three
were originally written in Hebrew, and the Hebrew
text of the two former survives complete, but the
third is best known to us in the Greek translation,
though some portions of the original Hebrew text have
been recovered among Egyptian papyri. Though this
last is the latest of the three, it has much closer affinities
with *Proverbs* than with *Ecclesiastes*, and it will be
convenient to glance at the books in this order.

The Hebrew title of the book of *Proverbs* is *Mishlê*.
The singular of this word, *māshāl*, is used in a wide variety

[1] See especially Oesterley, *Commentary on Proverbs*, pp. xxxiii–lv
(1929).

of meanings. Its root signification seems to have been " comparison," and the analogous root is used in Arabic to this day almost in the sense of the preposition " like." But it is used of such different pieces as the oracles of Balaam (Num. xxiii., xxiv.), the great taunt-song over the fall of the tyrant in Isa. xiv. 4–21, and the short epigram in Ezek. xviii. 2. It is clear that it is in the same sense as in the last-mentioned passage that the word is used in the title of the book of *Proverbs*. For that book is, in the main, a collection of these generalizations, short and memorable, on life and conduct. In form each is usually a distich, or line in two well-divided parts, manifesting that parallelism which is the outstanding feature of Hebrew and of some other early poetry. The book professedly contains several collections, and tradition ascribed the earliest work of collection to Solomon, and certainly one aspect of his renowned wisdom was supposed to lie in his ability to produce such sayings.

Many subjects are covered by these *Meshalim*. Some of them deal with human relationships, some are simple comparisons or metaphors, some are concerned with religious matters. It is now fairly clear that the collection drew on similar documents found in other literatures, and not a few of the utterances can be paralleled in many parts of the world. It is impossible to assign any specific date to them : some may be very ancient, and others comparatively modern. The collections, as collections, are hardly likely to have been any earlier than the middle monarchy, though there is no reason to doubt the tradition which links them with Solomon. He may quite well be responsible for the form which some of them take. The book in its final form is almost certainly post-exilic, and throughout breathes a high moral tone. At the same time we miss, inevitably, some of the features which make the religion of the prophets so valuable. The moral precepts enjoined are reinforced, not by an appeal to the will of God, nor to an absolute standard of ethics, but by purely material and prudential considerations. " Be good because you will be happy if you are ; refrain from sin because you will suffer if you commit it " is the usual burden of the speakers.

Ben-Sira presents us with much the same quality, but is more ambitious, and the book includes several well-known passages, particularly the great panegyric on the heroes of Israel. But both are marked with one feature which strikes every reader who compares the Hebrew wisdom with that of Egypt. While the resemblance between the two is at times so close as to make an independent origin impossible, the whole of the Egyptian thought is oriented to a doctrine of a future life. This has no place whatever either in *Proverbs* or in *Ben-Sira*, and both contemplate the life of man on this earth and consider nothing further. This is readily comprehensible in the book of *Proverbs*, which probably reached its present form before the development of the doctrine of the resurrection, but we are compelled to regard *Ben-Sira* as a typically Sadducæan work.

Ecclesiastes has already been mentioned, and attention has been drawn to its categorical rejection of a belief in life after death. In other respects it resembles to some extent the collections of the *Meshalim*. It is, however, the work of one author. He is a man who has studied human life through many years, and in old age finds himself disillusioned. All is hollow, empty, vain. His first sentence, " Vanity of vanities, saith the preacher, all is vanity," is his thesis, and he proceeds to develop it by reference alike to the world of nature and to that of human life. Here is a generalization which is necessarily philosophical, though pessimistic. Yet, paradoxically enough, his is a much more deeply religious mind than that of the *Meshalim* composers. They deal throughout with human life and with that alone—or almost alone. *Ecclesiastes*, on the other hand, always has God in the background of his thinking, and it is striking testimony to the intense hold that religion had on the Jewish mind that even so hopeless a writer can still retain his personal faith in God. God cannot do much for him, it is true, but God is there, and must not be neglected.

3. Wisdom and its Fuller Meaning

Hebrew philosophy could not and did not stop short with the construction of epigrams. It was compelled

22

to look further into reality and to attempt a deeper analysis of experience. There was never any inclination to doubt the being of God, or of trying to explain Him as an Indo-European philosopher might have done. But there were two main problems which needed to be discussed, two outstanding questions to which an answer was slowly evolved. These we may call the problems of creation and of revelation ; the questions : " How did God make the world ? " and " How can and does God communicate with man ? "

Neither problem presented any real difficulty to the rather more primitive Hebrew of pre-exilic days. His conception of God was anthropomorphic, and he thought of Yahweh as possessing a physical body, not unlike that of man, though with much greater powers. The creation of the world, then, was accomplished just as a human artificer would construct a work of art. The story told in Gen. ii. assumes the existence of the world, and offers no speculation as to how matter came into being. It tells of Yahweh modelling the moistened clay to make, first man, then the animals, and speaks of His planting the garden in which His man is placed. The heavens are the work of His fingers, and His hands have fashioned the earth.

A more sophisticated age could not be content with such a position, and as the conception of Yahweh grew more spiritual and less material, it became necessary to look for some other explanation of the Universe. The outlook of the first centuries after the Exile is represented in Gen. i.[1] The contrast with the older narrative is very striking. All the anthropomorphism has vanished, and in its place we have a stately, scientific, almost evolutionary process. There is no longer any suggestion of a human frame or of mechanical measures for the construction of the Universe ; God speaks, and it is done. If we had been able to cross-examine the writer we should probably have learnt that when he used the phrase " God said," he was not thinking of actual utterance. Hebrew

---

[1] In its present form this passage dates from the fifth century, though it is almost certainly a modification or an adaptation of a far older narrative.

has a very limited and a very concrete vocabulary, and the thought of the passage would be more faithfully represented by saying " God *willed*." But the metaphor of speech is there, and was destined to have an important effect on the development of Jewish theology.

Men looked farther. In all the arrangement, the adjustments, the regularity of the world and its working they recognized the expression of a mind, immeasurably greater than their own but like it in nature. It seemed to them that, just as a piece of man-made machinery could be adduced as evidence of a mind which had planned and produced it, so the Universe betrayed at every moment the activity of a supreme Intelligence, and they spoke of " Him that by wisdom made the heavens." Thus wisdom became the highest of all personal qualities, and began to receive especial attention, and the Wisdom of God became almost an object of adoration. In Job xxviii. we have a passage which is hardly original in that book, but which is of great importance for the development of Jewish thought, inasmuch as it confines true wisdom to God ; men may search for it where they will, but God alone knows where it is and how it may be found. And in such a passage as Prov. viii. we have a personification of Wisdom which may have been poetical in origin, but is on the verge of becoming a philosophical doctrine.

The problem of communion has a similar history. In pre-exilic days it was held that Yahweh could and did appear to men in human form. Often they did not recognize their visitor until some superhuman act betrayed His divinity. As time passed, this simple theophany gave place to other theories. Men sought to discover communications from God in mechanical ways such as the casting of the sacred lot, or through other methods by which He could be put to the test and so declare His will. Should He desire to enter spontaneously into men's lives, He took possession of some man or woman, " breathed " into them, and through them uttered His message. The medium of communication was thus the breath or " spirit " of God. But in post-exilic years this source of knowledge failed, and men were compelled to look for less startling modes of revelation. Again the divine intelligence made its appeal to men, and they recognized in all human thinking the impact of the divine mind. So here also men were led to the same conclusion as in seeking an answer to the question. In Prov. viii. the personified Wisdom is the vehicle of the divine message to men, and the two problems find a single solution in later Jewish thought.

The doctrine is stated more completely than elsewhere in the book which passes under the name of the *Wisdom of Solomon*, and it is here that we have its fullest development on purely Jewish soil. The great passage vii. 22–viii. 1 may be regarded as the kernel of the book for our present purposes. Wisdom is personified even more completely than in Prov. viii., and the personification has risen beyond a poetical metaphor to a philosophical doctrine. She is the agent of creation, the artificer of all things. It is she who brings man into contact with God : " In all ages entering into holy souls, she maketh them friends of God, and prophets "—note the identification of Wisdom with the prophetic spirit of old time. So much we might have deduced from earlier Jewish thinking, but in one point a striking advance is made. This is in the conception of Wisdom in her relation to God Himself. " She is the breath of the power of God, and a pure effluence flowing from the glory of the Almighty . . . the brightness of the everlasting light, the unspotted mirror of the power of God, and the image of His goodness " (*Wisd.* vii. 25, 26).

Here we have the elements of a philosophical theology, a speculation on the very being of God. Wisdom is at once a quality of God and a Person within the divine personality—in technical theological language, a hypostasis.

It seems hardly possible that this doctrine should be wholly independent of Greek thought. But the evidence of Hellenic influence is most in evidence when we study the work of Philo of Alexandria. This is no place to discuss the history of Greek philosophy ; suffice it to say that there the same problems had exercised men's minds, and that by the beginning of the Christian era men had come to believe in the " Logos "—" Word " or " Reason "—as the ultimate principle that lay behind all the universe. Needless to say, in the Greek thinkers this philosophical conception had little room for religion, and could not rank as theology. But in Philo we have a Jew who was also a Greek philosopher. Few, if any, have ever understood or expounded Plato better, and yet his primary interest was to expound Moses. He identified the Wisdom of Jewish theology with the Logos of Greek philosophy, and, like the writer of the book of *Wisdom*, held her to be a divine hypostasis. To him the *Logos* (this is the term he prefers) is the divine agent alike in creation and in communion, that through which alone God comes into contact with man and makes and sustains the universe. Yet the influence of Greek thinking has had one interesting effect on Philo. He does not seem to be quite sure whether the *Logos* is really personal or not. We are left uncertain as to whether we are considering one so completely individual as the Wisdom of the Jewish philosopher or an abstraction like that of the Stoic. Nevertheless, it is in Philo that we have the confluence of the two great streams of thought, Hebrew and Greek ; and in a very real sense both find, not only their union, but also their highest point, in him.

One further step remained. The *Logos*-Wisdom, however firmly believed in, was a philosophical conception, the produce of metaphysical speculation. Men reached the idea by argument, and must inevitably be left with some uncertainty on the whole subject. At any point men might break away and evolve a new theory altogether. Certainty could be attained only by experience, and this was not to be had within the bounds either of Judaism proper or of Greek thought. The climax, the final certification, was only reached outside the borders of the Jewish faith when the evangelist, summing up the result of all that was best and truest in the thought of the two civilizations, placed the coping-stone on men's philosophy with the words, " The Logos became flesh and dwelt among us, and we beheld his glory, glory as of the only-begotten of the Father, full of grace and truth."

CHAPTER XV

ESCHATOLOGY AND APOCALYPTIC

1. JEWISH ESCHATOLOGY

ESCHATOLOGICAL, with its frequently accompanying apocalyptic, thought among the Hebrews goes back to an early period. It centred in the popular idea that a "Day of Yahweh" would come, a day on which the national God would show His might by overcoming the enemies of His people and inaugurate a time of well-being and prosperity for them. This expectation was shattered by Amos (v. 18–20), who brought in an ethical element hitherto absent in eschatological thought. But the way in which Amos refers to the "Day of Yahweh" shows that already in his time the people of Israel were familiar with the idea [1]; indeed, there is much in the prophetical books and elsewhere which makes it clear that the circle of ideas connected with the eschatological outlook goes back to far more ancient times.[2] With the earlier phases of eschatological thought we cannot deal here; but we must recall briefly the main themes of Hebrew eschatology, for it is our purpose to show that Jewish eschatological and apocalyptic ideas as we find them during and after the Persian period have been *added* to by elements taken from the eschatology of Persia. True, this latter is largely the product of earlier pre-Zoroastrian times, too; but Jewish eschatology in its later phases is nevertheless indebted to Persia; and to examine in what directions this was the case is our present task.

[1] See Part II, Chapter VIII, ii (*d*).
[2] The classical works on the subject generally are: Gunkel, *Schöpfung und Chaos in Urzeit und Endzeit* (1895); Gressmann, *Der Ursprung der israelitisch-jüdischen Eschatologie* (1905); A. von Gall, Βασιλεία τοῦ θεοῦ (1926); Bousset, *Die Religion des Judentums*, pp. 202–301 (1926); and see further, Volz, *Jüdische Eschatologie von Daniel bis Akiba* (1903).

Jewish Eschatology as it came down from earlier times comprised (among others to be considered presently) the following themes : The belief that in the " Day of Yahweh " God would intervene in favour of His chosen people, and would overthrow the enemies of Israel. There was next the hope of the establishment of a new kingdom ruled over by a Messianic king belonging to the House of David. Further, there was to be the ingathering of the scattered members of the race in their own land, and the conversion of the Gentiles to the belief in Yahweh. These beliefs and hopes had existed in one form or another since the Exile and before ; and they were intensified and came to fuller expression whenever the times became dark and perplexing.

Now if the eschatological beliefs of Judaism had had to do with these alone we should not necessarily have grounds for thinking that extraneous influences had been at work. But alongside of these beliefs we find that there are thoughts and expectations of a rather different kind. Thus, it is not for Israel exclusively that the bright future is anticipated. Although in the foreground it is the chosen people who appear, the purview is widened, and the whole world is embraced within this hope. Then, too, there is the expectation of the annihilation of the world in order that the new world of the future may take its place. Again, as regards the present world-order, it is seen to be divided up into different periods, the precise length of each of which is accurately calculated, and at the right time God will intervene in the world's history and bring about this annihilation and the creation of the new world. Further, the judgement upon Israel's enemies becomes the final judgement of the whole world. And finally, in connexion with the end of this world and the new one to come, there appears the belief in the resurrection of the dead, and a world-wide kingdom of God.

We find therefore that with the earlier national Messianic hope there are now combined expectations which are *cosmological* and *universal*. And these new thoughts do not develop organically from the old Messianic prophecies ; rather, they are superimposed upon, or else run parallel with, the traditional beliefs. The time-honoured Messianic hopes are not discarded; they continue alongside of these new ideas. It is this mingling of new and old which is one of the causes of the confused and ill-balanced character of the picture of the future presented in Jewish Apocalyptic, wherein we find, for example, hopes concerning this world indiscriminately mixed up with those about the world to come. There are good grounds for believing that the superimposed ideas referred to were not indigenous to Israel, but that they were absorbed by Jewish apocalyptic thinkers, from extraneous sources. One of these extraneous sources, and so far as the present subject is concerned the most important, is to be sought in the religion of ancient Persia, Iranian religion. It was pointed out above, p. 273, that the antecedents of the religion of Persia go back many centuries before the time of Zoroaster; it is necessary to bear this in mind, as it applies to much that we meet with in Iranian apocalyptic belief.

2. Persian Eschatology and Apocalyptic

It is not our purpose to deal with all the marks of Iranian influence on Jewish Apocalyptic, but we shall concentrate on those points which are of importance. As a preliminary, however, we must give in very brief outline a general *résumé* of Iranian Apocalyptic.

At the base of this lies the dualistic conception of the irreconcileable antagonism between the highest god, Ahura-Mazda, who is all-good, and Angra-Mainyu, the great spirit of evil. They are in constant conflict for the possession of the world and of mankind. The existence of the world is to last for a period of 12,000 years. The first six thousand years' period is unimportant for our purpose; it is sufficient to say that it consisted of two eras of three thousand years each, during the first of which all things were invisible. We get a reference to this in the *Secrets of Enoch* xxiv. 4, where God says to Enoch: "For before all were visible I alone used to go about in the invisible things." During the second of these two eras Ahura-Mazda created the material, good world, and the first man.

The second six thousand years are also divided into two eras ; and it is during both of these that the conflict between Ahura-Mazda and Angra-Mainyu takes place. The first three thousand years of this second great division of the world's history is the time of the complete ascendancy of Angra-Mainyu, the evil spirit. But at the end of these first three thousand years there appears the figure of Zarathustra, and with him arises the hope of better things, though the conflict between the powers of good and evil continues. Then, at a certain time, occurs the miraculous birth of Saoshyant, of the seed of Zarathustra and the virgin Hvôv : he is to be the saviour of the world, for his work is to be the gradual improving of mankind until it reaches perfection, when the end of the world will begin to take place. Then the dead will be raised and will be judged. Fire will come down from heaven and will burn up the earth. All men will have to pass through that fire ; but some will pass through it easily, and unharmed, " as though through a milky warmth " ; while others will suffer fearful torments from it ; for the fire will burn up all the dross of iniquity which still clings to them. But ultimately all will be saved. And then Ahura-Mazda will come forth with his angelic hosts for the final conflict against Angra-Mainyu and his legions of evil spirits. Ahura-Mazda will gain the victory, and the powers of evil will be annihilated. After that there will be inaugurated a life of happiness in a new world, wherein evil and sorrow and pain will find no place.

That is a very brief outline of Iranian Eschatology and Apocalyptic ; many details have not been touched on, but what has been indicated includes all that is really fundamental.

We must now compare this with Jewish Apocalyptic ; and here we shall restrict ourselves to four subjects, which will, however, be seen to be those of main importance, viz. (i) Dualism; (ii) World-Epochs ; (iii) the Judgement, and the Destruction of the world by fire ; (iv) the Resurrection of the dead. And then, finally, we shall refer to one or two other points of interest.

(i) *Dualism.*—Throughout Iranian Eschatology and

Apocalyptic there lies, as we have seen, the fundamental thought of the contrast and conflict between Ahura-Mazda and Angra-Mainyu. The entire history of mankind is conditioned by, and is the result of, this perpetual and varying struggle ; and the end of the world, with the final judgement, coincides with the triumph of the Lord of good over the powers of evil.

Dualism is foreign to Judaism, so that when dualistic conceptions occur in Jewish apocalyptic writings it is to Persian influence that we must ascribe their presence there. Thus, in a late apocalyptic passage in the book of *Isaiah* we have these mystical words : " And it shall come to pass in that day, that Yahweh shall punish the host of the high ones on high, and the kings of the earth upon the earth. And they shall be gathered together as prisoners into a pit, and shall be shut up in a dungeon, and after many days they shall be punished. Then the moon shall be confounded, and the sun shall be put to shame ; for Yahweh Zebaoth shall reign in mount Zion and in Jerusalem, and before his ancients there shall be glory " (xxiv. 21–23). What is here referred to is seen in a number of passages in the *Book of Enoch*, of which one of two must be given. In x. 11 ff. it is said : " And the Lord said unto Michael, Go, bind Semjaza and his associates . . . bind them fast for seventy generations in the valleys of the earth, till the day of their judgement and of their consummation, till the judgement that is for ever and ever is consummated. . . . Destroy all wrong from the face of the earth, and let every evil work come to an end." Again in xci. 15 we read : " There shall be the great eternal judgement, in which he will execute vengeance amongst the angels." Similarly in various other passages of this book, as well as in the *Book of Jubilees*, the *Testaments of the Twelve Patriarchs*, the *Secrets of Enoch* and the *Assumption of Moses*, books which contain the floating apocalyptic material of earlier centuries. In all such passages that which lies behind the ideas of punishment, vengeance, judgement, etc., is the victory of the Lord of good over the powers of evil, at the head of which stands Satan or the Devil (see especially *Test. xii. Patr.*, Naphthali 8, Issachar 7,

Benjamin 5) ; in other words, we have the same dualistic conception which, as we have seen, is specifically Iranian. Particularly noticeable is the fact that the contending forces are *spiritual* powers.

Now, nobody would for a moment assert that dualistic conceptions had ever formed part of the prophetic or official Hebrew religious thought ; and it is certain that orthodox Judaism would have repudiated them ; so that when we find that after the Persian period they have entered into the circle of ideas in Jewish Eschatology, and that they correspond with what is fundamental in Iranian belief, the conclusion is irresistible that the former was influenced here by the latter.[1]

(ii) *World-epochs.*—This subject, it is true, is not of much interest, but it is worth a passing notice because it belongs so closely to Iranian thought and has so clearly left its mark on Jewish Apocalyptic. In this latter the idea of world-epochs occurs, for example, in the calculation that the present world-order is to last for six thousand years : this number is strongly reminiscent of Iranian reckoning, and it would easily have lent itself to Jewish adaptation, since here it could be based on the number of days of the Creation, and according to Ps. xc. 4, a thousand years are as one day with God. Another reckoning of the duration of the world was seven thousand years, while in the *Book of Enoch* the time of the world's existence is divided into different periods quite in the Persian style (see xci. 12–17 and xciii.).

This idea of world-epochs, again, is not indigenous to Jewish thought ; it came from outside into Jewish Apocalyptic, and it would be difficult to say where it could have come from if not from Iranian Apocalyptic.

(iii) *The Judgement, and the Destruction of the World by Fire.*—Here we come to a subject of greater interest. The two ideas of Judgement and of World-conflagration belong together. To be sure, prophecies of a coming

---

[1] It is also worth pointing out that Persian dualism was influenced by the earlier Babylonian Dragon (*Tiamat*)-myth, as one would naturally expect ; but although this myth appears every now and again throughout the Old Testament, and must therefore have been quite familiar to Israel, there is never any hint that Hebrew religion was affected by it, as the Persian belief was.

judgement run through the whole of Old Testament prophetic literature ; and the special idea of a *World*-judgement, not only that of Israel and its enemies, but of all flesh, the living and the dead, and also of angels, is to be discerned in some of the later writings of the Old Testament (see the book of *Joel*, Isa. xxiv.–xxvii, and *Daniel*). It is therefore not in the thought of a World-judgement, as such, that there is necessarily any connexion between Iranian and Jewish Apocalyptic. The mark of the influence of the former on the latter is, however, to be seen in the consummation of the Judgement, in the idea of the destruction of the world by *fire*. Reference was made above to the fire, which, according to Iranian belief, was to come down from heaven and burn up the earth ; the account of this occurs in the *Bundehesh*[1] xxx., where it tells of a fiery stream of molten metal coming down from above and melting mountains and hills ; all men, good and bad, have to pass through it. There are indications of the same conception in the earlier *Gathas*,[2] which contain the oldest tradition. This is a conception which is peculiar to Iranian Apocalyptic, so that when we find it appearing in the later phases of Jewish Apocalyptic, it is only natural to ascribe its presence here to Iranian influence. One or two illustrations may be given. It is first adumbrated in Zeph. i. 14–18, iii. 8. Other passages are, for example, the following ; in the fourth book of the *Sibylline Oracles*, 173 ff., occur these words : " Then fire shall come upon the whole world . . . the whole world shall hear a rumbling and a mighty roar. And he (i.e. God) shall burn the whole earth, and consume the whole race of men, and all the cities and rivers, and the sea. He shall burn everything out, and there shall be sooty dust. . . ." A similar thought lies at the back of Dan. vii. 10 : " A fiery stream issued and came forth from before him, thousand thousands ministered unto him, and ten thousand times ten thousand stood before him ; the judgement was set, and the books were opened."

[1] This work belongs to the later Pahlavi literature ; it contains the eschatology of the Parsis, much of which comes from more ancient sources.

[2] The earliest part of the *Avesta*, the Zoroastrian Bible.

The conjunction of the fiery stream with the judgement here is significant. The judgement coming *after* the fiery stream, the point of which is the destruction of all flesh, strikes one as strange ; but in the context of the passage from the *Sibylline Oracles* just quoted, it says that " God will clothe the bones and ashes again in human shape, and re-make men as they were before " ; so that we are evidently meant to understand that the resurrection intervened between the World-conflagration and the Judgement.

Again, in the extraordinary account of the end of the present world-order and of the Judgement given in the *Assumption of Moses*, x. 1–10, it is clearly as a result of the World-conflagration that it is said that " the fountains of waters shall fail, and the rivers shall dry up." Then also, in the many speculative ideas contained in *Enoch* i.–xxxvi. there is one which conceives of this fire as being kept in a certain place whither Enoch journeys ; for he tells of how he was taken " to the fire of the west, which receives every setting of the sun " ; he comes also " to a river of fire in which the fire flows like water, and discharges itself into the great sea towards the west " (xvii. 4, 5). And once more, in an eschatological passage in the *Psalms of Solomon* xv., the thought of the World-conflagration appears in the words of vers. 6, 7 : " The flame of fire and the wrath against the unrighteous shall not touch him, when it goeth forth from the face of the Lord against sinners."

These passages—and a number of similar ones could be given—all refer to the same event, directly or indirectly. And many authorities, though not all, are agreed that the content of such bear on them the impress of Iranian influence. And, indeed, so far as this particular subject is concerned, the conception occurs nowhere but in Iranian and in the later Jewish Apocalyptic ; so that the only alternative to Iranian influence is to suppose that it arose independently in the minds of the Jewish Apocalyptists ; this is intrinsically improbable, for according to the traditional Jewish eschatological scheme, the earth was to be the place where the Messianic kingdom would be set up.

This subject has a further interest from the fact that

the idea of a World-conflagration was taken over into Christian Apocalyptic ; among other passages in early Christian literature showing this there is the well-known one in 2 Pet. iii. 10 : " . . . The heavenly bodies shall be dissolved with fervent heat, and the earth and the works that are therein shall be burned up." [1]

(iv) *The Resurrection.*—Here we come to the most important point of the whole subject, as it is also the most debateable. We have already expressed our conviction that the thought of resurrection was, at any rate, adumbrated in Isa. liii. 12, which we believe to have belonged to the exilic period (see above, p. 269) ; it would therefore seem at first sight to be incongruous to suppose that Jewish belief was indebted to Persia ; but it must be remembered that there are good grounds for the contention that Persian influences were at work for a considerable time before the Babylonian empire came to an end.[2]

In any case, however, we are dealing here with the more developed forms of Jewish Apocalyptic, and it will be seen that there is every reason for believing in the influence of Persian thought here.

In both Iranian and Jewish Apocalyptic the Resurrection is closely connected with the World-conflagration and the Judgement, and the conjunction of these themes is to be found in Iranian and Jewish Eschatology alone. And further, as Bousset [3] has pointed out, in Jewish Eschatology we have two incongruous ideas side by side ; there is, *in addition* to the Judgement and the general Resurrection of the dead at the last day, retribution on the individual immediately after death, and therefore before the Resurrection. The idea of a twofold retribu-

---

[1] Granting that κατακαήσεται is not the best reading (אBKP Syr_p have εὑρεθήσεται), its occurrence in AL and in one of the Syriac Versions is sufficient witness to the existence of the thought in early Christian circles. It is also worth pointing out that 2 *Clem.* xvi. 3, which is based on this passage, has : καὶ πᾶσα ἡ γῆ ὡς μόλυβδος ἐπὶ πυρὶ τηκόμενος (" . . . melted as lead in fire "). Dr. E. Bevan reminds us (in a private letter) that the Stoics believed in a destruction, or rather absorption, of the *Kosmos* by fire ; in his opinion this is the more probable source of the Christian belief.

[2] Opinions differ as to Zoroaster's date, but he lived during the earlier rather than during the later part of the 1 mill. B.C.

[3] *Die Religion des Judentums,* pp. 511 f. (1926).

tion in the Hereafter occurs nowhere else but in Iranian
Eschatology. The two facts mentioned should be
sufficient to prove the indebtedness of Jewish Apocalyptists to Persia. To go further into the question would
take us too far afield, and would involve giving a number
of quotations from the Apocalyptic literature.[1] We
must content ourselves with a reference to Bousset's
book (pp. 469–524), and to Böklen's work (to be mentioned below), where the whole subject is most carefully
dealt with.

So far, then, we have, in the briefest possible way,
drawn attention to four subjects in Jewish Eschatology
in which, it is maintained, Persian influence is to be
discerned. With the exception of World-epochs these
subjects are of far-reaching importance on account of
later developments both in Jewish and Christian thought.

3. Some Further Marks of Persian Influence

The subjects dealt with are far from exhausting the
marks of Persian influence ; a few others, of less importance, it is true, but not without interest, are worth drawing attention to, as they offer further arguments in favour
of our thesis.[2]

(i) In various passages in the *Bundehesh* and in the
Gathas there are indications that it is the part of Shaoshyant,[3] the great benefactor of the human race, to take
a leading part in the Resurrection of the dead. In
Jewish Eschatology it is, as a rule, the Almighty Himself
who does this ; but there are exceptions, which are in
all probability due to Persian influence. Thus, in *Enoch*
li. 1 ff., in a passage dealing with the Resurrection, the
central position is taken by the Messiah, the Elect One :
" And in those days shall the earth also give back that
which hath been entrusted to it, and *She'ol* shall give
back that which it hath received, and Hell shall give
back that which it owes. For in those days the Elect One

---

[1] A few of these will be found below.

[2] For a full presentation of the case for Persian influence one could
hardly do better than consult Böklen's *Die Verwandschaft der jüdisch-
christlichen mit der parsischen Eschatologie* (1902).

[3] He is the last (and most important) of other *Shaoshyants* who
appeared at earlier periods.

shall arise, and he shall choose the righteous and holy from among them ; for the day hath drawn nigh that they should be saved. And the Elect One shall in those days sit upon my throne, and his mouth shall pour forth all the secrets of wisdom and counsel ; for the Lord of Spirits hath given them to him, and hath glorified him." It is clear here that the Elect One (i.e. the Messiah) is thought of as the central figure at the Resurrection ; and this is entirely parallel to that of Shaoshyant in Persian Eschatology.

(ii) Another, somewhat curious, illustration of Persian influence is connected with some rather naïve ideas concerning the nature of the risen body. In *Bundehesh* xxx. 6 it is said that the risen body will be composed of the same elements as those comprised in the formation of man's original, earthly body :

> Bones from the spirit of the earth,
> Blood from water,
> Hairs from the plants,
> Life's vigour from fire.

It must surely be ultimately from this that the fuller description of man's component parts, though not, it is true, in reference to his risen body, given in the *Secrets of Enoch* xxx. 8, was taken :

> His flesh from the earth,
> His blood from the dew,
> His eyes from the sun,
> His bones from stone,
> His intelligence from the swiftness of angels and from cloud,
> His veins and his hair from the grass of the earth,
> His soul from my breath and from the wind.

(iii) And to give but one other illustration : there was the strange idea that the possession of immortality would be retained by partaking of certain food which men will enjoy after the Resurrection. This food, it is said in *Bundehesh* xxx. 25, is the white Haoma, and the fat of the ox Hadhayaos. This idea of food for the immortals seems to have been taken over in Jewish Apocalyptic, though the nature of the food differed. In the difficult passage, Isa. xxvi. 19, one thing, at any rate, seems clear, and that is that the dead bodies which shall rise will partake of the dew of light. It is a far more exalted conception than the Persian one, but the thought of food for the risen is the same. According to *Enoch* xxv. 4, 5, there is in the abode of the risen a tree which has " a fragrance beyond all fragrance, and its leaves and blooms and wood wither not for ever ; and its fruit is beautiful, and resembles the dates of a palm." Similarly, in the *Test. of the xii. Patr.*, Levi xviii. 10, 11, it is said that the Most High will open the gates of Paradise, and " shall give to the saints to eat from the tree of life " ; and in the *Secrets of Enoch* viii. 2 ff., the same thought occurs and is elaborated : " Every tree sweet-flowering, every fruit ripe, all manner of food perpetually bubbling with all pleasant perfumes . . . and the tree of life is at that place " (see also Rev. xxii. 2, 17). These illustrations will suffice, though there are others which could be given.

What has been said is sufficient to show that Persian influences have left their mark on Jewish Eschatology.

4. THE JEWISH APOCALYPTISTS AND THEIR LITERATURE

We have emphasized the fact of Persian influence in Jewish Apocalyptic because, while it is what might be expected from the nature of the case, it is by no means always recognized, and indeed is altogether denied by some writers, though on insufficient grounds.

But to recognize Persian influence in this sphere is not to deny that there is plenty of individuality and independence of thought among the Jewish Apocalyptists.

The period to which the Jewish Apocalyptic Movement belongs is roughly from B.C. 200 to A.D. 100, but its roots and its extraneous engrafted growths go back, as we have seen, to earlier times.

The nameless teachers and writers of Jewish Apocalyptic occupied in some respects the position of the prophets of old ; and this mainly in their denunciation of the godless, with prophecies of punishment, and in their words of comfort and encouragement to those seeking to do what was right, but suffering at the hands of oppressors ;

for these, too, prophecies were uttered, and of a nature
that was calculated to hearten them.

As an illustration of the former the following may be
quoted :

> And when sin and unrighteousness and blasphemy
> And violence in all kinds of deeds increase,
> And apostasy and transgression and uncleanness abound,
> Then shall a great chastisement from heaven come upon all these.
> And the holy Lord will come forth with wrath and chastisement,
> To execute judgement upon the earth.
> In those days violence shall be cut off from its roots,
> And the roots of unrighteousness together with deceit,
> And they shall be destroyed from under heaven.
>
> *(Enoch* xcii. 7, 8.)

On the other side we have words such as these :

> But with the righteous he will make peace,
> And will protect the elect,
> And mercy shall be upon them.
> And they shall belong to God,
> And they shall be prospered,
> And they shall all be blessed.
> And he will help them all,
> And light shall appear unto them,
> And he will make peace with them.
>
> *(Enoch* i. 8.)

The sense of passages like these occurs very often ; and
thus the main concern of the Apocalyptists was with the
future, with the age that was to come, when all the
inequalities and incongruities of the present age would be
put right.   In their pictures of the destruction of the
present world-order the Apocalyptists are fond of lurid
painting, and a supernatural element looms largely.
The frequent occurrence of this theme of world-destruction,
adapted, as we have seen, from Iranian Eschatology,
arises from the fact that the Jewish Apocalyptists regarded
this world, with the majority of mankind, as hopelessly
corrupt ;   in their despair of amelioration they became
pessimists ;   there was nothing for it but utter annihilation in order that a fresh start might be made, and in a
new world, i.e. the Messianic times.[1]

[1] In the later Jewish literature the woes which are to precede the
Messianic Age are called " the birth-pangs of the Messiah " (*Cheble
ha-Mashiach*) (cp. Mark xiii.).

This leads us to say something of the Messiah as portrayed by the Apocalyptic writers. And here it is especially necessary to bear in mind that extraneous elements have been absorbed, and that the varying views of different writers preclude the possibility of a uniform picture. Therefore it need not cause surprise if at one time we find the Messiah spoken of as an ordinary man, at another as of superhuman nature. Thus, in the *Test. xii. Patr.* Judah xxiv. 5, it is said : " Then shall the sceptre of my kingdom shine forth, and from your root shall arise a stem " ; the words are purported to have been uttered by Judah to his sons ; the Messiah is therefore thought of as belonging to the tribe of Judah. On the other hand, in Dan. vii. 13 the Messiah is clearly conceived of as superhuman, as appearing on " the clouds of heaven." The belief in the Messiah's *pre-existence* obviously assumes his transcendental character ; it is said, e.g. in the *Apocalypse of Ezra* xiii. 52 : " Just as one has not the power to search out and to find or to know what is in the depths of the sea, so can none of those who are upon the earth see my Son or them that are with him except in that time in his day " ; here pre-existence is clearly implied (cp. ver. 26, xiv. 9) ; so, too, in *Enoch* lxii. 7 :

> For from the beginning the Son of Man was hidden,
> And the Most High preserved him in the presence of his might,
> And revealed him to the elect.

Passages presenting each conception could be greatly multiplied. When the Messiah appears he will, of course, come as King (*Psalms of Solomon* [1] xvii. 21, 42 ; cp. *Enoch* lii. 4). But he will also come as Judge to punish sinners and destroy the enemies of Israel (*Test. xii. Patr.* Judah xxiv. 6 ; *Psalms of Solomon* xvii. 22 ff.) ; on the other hand, he will come as the Saviour of those who " have hated and despised this world of unrighteousness " (*Enoch* xlviii. 7).

A great deal more is, of course, said about the Messiah,

---

[1] Not to be confused with the *Odes of Solomon*, which are Christian, and belong to about A.D. 200 or a little earlier ; the *Psalms of Solomon* are Pharisaic, and were written about 50 B.C.

of his close relation to God, of his character, and of his
work ; but to deal with all this would take up too much
space.

Though the Apocalyptists were dreamers and seers of
visions they were fully alive to the claims of practical
religion ; and therefore they were loyal to the Law,
though not in the rigid way of the strictly orthodox,
laying stress rather on the spirit of its observance than in
carrying out legal precepts in the letter ; herein prophetic
influence is plainly discernible.

Reference has been made above to World-epochs
as a sign of Persian influence on Jewish Eschatology ;
in connexion with this mention must be made of the
doctrine of Determinism, which is characteristic of this
literature. All things that happen in the world, both as
regards its physical changes, as well as the history of
nations, has been predetermined by God ; thus it is
said in the *Apocalypse of Ezra* iv. 36, 37 :

> For he hath weighed the age in the balance,
> And by number hath he numbered the seasons;
> Neither will he move nor stir things,
> Till the measure appointed be fulfilled.

But all these things were secrets which could only be
made known to certain God-fearing men who possessed
the faculty, divinely accorded, of being able to peer into
the hidden things of God ; the Apocalyptists believed
themselves therefore to be commissioned by God to
reveal these secrets to their fellow-creatures. Thus, both
as receivers of revelations, and as revealers of them to
others, they are appropriately called Apocalyptists.

A further mark of prophetic influence may perhaps be
seen in the generally speaking universalistic attitude of
the Apocalyptists ; passages from their works in a
contrary sense could be given, but it is true to say that
they are inclined to a universalistic rather than to a
national particularistic outlook (*Enoch* xlviii. 4 ; *Test.
xii. Patr.* Levi xviii. 4, 5, 9 ; Judah xxiv. 6 ; *Apocalypse
of Ezra,* xiii. 26, and many other passages). In the
main, they embrace the Gentiles equally with those of
their own nation in the divine scheme of salvation which

they put forth ; and the wicked, who are excluded from happiness hereafter, are not restricted to the Gentiles ; the Jews equally with them will suffer punishment according to their deserts.

This leads us, finally, to say a word about the developed ideas concerning the state of the departed.   It can hardly occasion surprise to find that the Apocalyptists have differing views as to the sequence of events hereafter ; sometimes it is resurrection, judgement, punishment ; at other times the resurrection comes last ; sometimes it is taught that all will rise, the evil as well as the good ; at other times only the good are thought of as partaking of the resurrection.   Then there is also the idea of an intermediate state after death and before the resurrection : the good go to paradise, the evil to a place of torment ; after the allotted time comes the Judgement, followed by eternal bliss or eternal punishment.

It is possible that extraneous influences, Persian and Greek, may have been at work here ; but it does not seem necessarily to have been the case ; for, after all, speculations of this kind would logically have forced themselves upon the mind ; and though there is a good deal to be said in favour of non-Jewish influences here, it is wisest not to dogmatize upon the subject.

There is much else which might be dealt with ; but the more outstanding matters have, we hope, been mentioned.

CHAPTER XVI

THE LAW AND ITS DEVELOPMENTS

THIS subject can find a place within the Greek period, for although the process of development began before and continued after it, there can be no doubt that the development was proceeding during this period. Attention has already been drawn to the fact that the beginnings of what came to be the religion of the Law must be sought during the Exile and the period following upon the Return. By 400 B.C., or soon after, the written Law was completed ; but even before this time the nature of the Law was such that developments must have begun to arise. By developments we mean, firstly, such things as the addition of new legal precepts necessitated by change of circumstances, the demand for new decisions, directions for cases not contemplated in the written Law, etc. ; in a word, all that would be included under the term " Oral Law," which, in course of time, became equally binding with the written Law ; secondly, the prominence and central position of the Law, and insistence on the observance of legal *minutiæ* ; thirdly, the glorification of the Law ; and fourthly, the merit acquired by its observance.

It must be acknowledged that the steps in the process of development cannot be traced. But we can see from various later sources that these developments did take place ; and these sources we must briefly examine. They are four in number : (1) some books in the Apocrypha ; (2) some events in the history of the Maccabæan rising ; (3) the New Testament, more particularly the Synoptic Gospels, and some of the Pauline Epistles ; (4) the Mishnah.

1. SOME BOOKS OF THE APOCRYPHA

The two books which come into consideration here are the *Wisdom of Ben-Sira* (*Ecclesiasticus*) and the *Book of*

Tobit, both pre-Maccabæan, belonging approximately to 200 B.C., or a little later. To deal with the subject exhaustively is out of the question here ; we shall therefore give just a few illustrations, taking in order the points of development mentioned above.

It seems probable that Ben-Sira has the Oral Law, to which as representing the " Sadducæan " attitude he would object, in mind when in xxxii. 17 he says :

The man of violence concealeth instruction [so the Syriac Version]
And forceth the Law to suit his necessity.

But more significant is xlv. 5, for here the two terms *Mitzwah* (lit. " commandment ") and *Torah* (" Law ") occur together ; the former, used in the plural, is used of the details of the Law, and in Rabbinical literature very often connotes the Oral Law ; so that there are grounds for the belief that the two terms found together here refer to the Oral and the Written Law (*Torah*) respectively.[1] This is not contradicted by what was said just now about Ben-Sira being opposed to the Oral Law ; for the " Sadducæan " point of view recognized an Oral Law, but it was of a less rigorous kind than that of the " Pharisaic " point of view.[2]

Again, in viii. 9 Ben-Sira says :

Reject not the tradition of the aged,
Which they heard from their fathers ;
For thou wilt receive instruction from this,
And (be able to) answer in time of perplexity.

The reference to the oral tradition, " the tradition of the fathers," or Oral Law, but in the Sadducæan sense, is obvious here. Another important illustration, too long to quote, will be found in xxxix. 1 ff., where the activities of the Scribe are enumerated.

We have thus ample evidence that the development

[1] See the quotation from Maimonides given below, on p. 366.
[2] We use the names " Sadducæan " and " Pharisaic " for convenience' sake ; as definite parties the Sadducees and Pharisees did not arise until after the Maccabæan rising ; but the respective points of view represented by either existed long before.

represented by the Oral Law had begun to take place before 200 B.C.

The prominent position occupied by the Law as the centre of religion, and insistence on its observance, together with its glorification, may be illustrated by the way in which it is identified with Wisdom ; here again Ben-Sira is instructive, e.g. in xix. 20 :

> All wisdom is the fear of the Lord,
> And all wisdom is the fulfilling of the Law.

More pointed still is the passage in which, when speaking of the things concerning Wisdom, he says : " All these things are the book of the covenant of God Most High, the Law which Moses commanded as an heritage for the assemblies of Jacob " (xxiv. 23 ; cp. also xv. 1).

The prominence of the Law is also emphasized in *Tobit*, e.g. in xii. 8, where prayer, almsgiving, and fasting, especially the second, are strongly insisted upon. The laws of tithe (i. 7, v. 13), marriage (vi. 12, vii. 13, 14), honouring parents (iv. 3), keeping the feasts (i. 6, ii. 1), purifying oneself (ii. 5), as well as others, are all inculcated. All this shows the very important position in the life of the people which the Law held by this time, and, of course, prior to this time, for such a position could not have been gained quickly.

In some interesting passages we see that already by this time the doctrine of merit was recognized ; thus in *Ecclus*. iii. 30 it is said :

> A flaming fire doth water quench,
> So doth almsgiving atone for sin (see also xxix. 12).

A rather striking passage occurs in *Tobit* iv. 8–10 : " . . . If thou have little, be not afraid to give alms according to that little ; for thou layest up a good treasure for thyself against the day of necessity ; because alms delivereth from death, and suffereth not to come into darkness." So, too, in xii. 9 : " Alms doth deliver from death, and it shall purge away all sin."

While words such as these do not directly claim merit and reward for the works of the Law, they point in the direction of this ; and, as we shall see, in course of time, this idea became fully developed.

2. Some Events in the History of the Maccabæan Rising

The very fact of the Maccabæan rising is eloquent testimony of the paramount importance attached to the Law ; but there are some events connected with the rising which illustrate this somewhat pointedly.

A piece of indirect evidence is afforded by the strong opposition offered by the orthodox party among the Jews to the Hellenizers among their own people. Stress must be laid upon this, for it was an outcome of the Maccabæan rising and its causes that a great development of Legalism, in a " Pharisaic " direction, took place. What is not always sufficiently grasped is that the causes which ultimately led up to the Maccabæan rising are to be sought prior to the time of Antiochus Epiphanes ; his action in trying to stamp out Judaism in 168 B.C. (i.e. seven years after he came to the throne) was probably due as much to encouragement from Hellenistic Jews as to a personal desire to champion Hellenism. This is not the place to go into any detail regarding the question ; but it cannot be too strongly emphasized that the antagonism aroused by the Hellenistic Jews among the more orthodox had as much to do with the development of Legalism as anything that Antiochus Epiphanes did.

We must begin by quoting again (see p. 305 above) the well-known words from 1 *Macc.* i. 11–15, and then by drawing attention to one or two significant points in the passage :

" In those days came there forth out of Israel transgressors of the Law, and persuaded many, saying, Let us go and make a covenant with the Gentiles that are round about us ; for since we were parted from them many evils have befallen us. And the saying was good in their eyes. And certain of the people were forward herein and went to the king [the advent of Antiochus Epiphanes to the Syrian throne is mentioned in the preceding verse], and he gave them licence to do after the ordinances of the Gentiles. And they built a place of exercise in Jerusalem according to the laws of the Gentiles ; and they made themselves uncircumcized, and forsook the holy covenant, and joined themselves to the Gentiles, and sold themselves to do evil." [1]

The first point to be noted here is that unfaithfulness to Judaism is described as transgression of the Law, so that the Law is practically synonymous with the religion of the Jews. Then, the words " since we parted from them," which refer to the fact that the observance of the Law had been set up as a barrier between the Jews and the Gentiles, illustrates again the central position assigned to the Law. And, lastly, it will be noticed that the initiative in this movement against the Law is taken by the Jews ; no outside pressure is brought to bear.

It was seven years after this that Antiochus Epiphanes, as an act of vengeance because the orthodox party refused to recognize his nominee to the high-priesthood, ordered a massacre in Jerusalem, which was carried out " by the chief collector of the tribute " (1 *Macc.* i. 30–32). In the citadel, the narrative goes on to say : " They put a sinful nation, transgressors of the Law, and they strengthened themselves therein " (ver. 34) ; obviously, the reference here is to the Hellenistic Jews. The verses which follow must be quoted in full in order to see what the real position of affairs was : it is said in reference to these " transgressors of the Law " that " they stored up arms and victuals, and gathering together the spoils of Jerusalem, they laid them up there ; and they became a sore snare ; and it became a place to lie in wait against the sanctuary, and an evil adversary to Israel continually. And they shed innocent blood on every side of the sanctuary, and defiled the sanctuary. And the inhabitants of Jerusalem fled because of them ; and she became a habitation of strangers, and she became strange to them that were born in her, and her children forsook her. Her sanctuary was laid waste like a wilderness, her feasts were turned into mourning, her Sabbaths into reproach, her honour into contempt." This passage makes it clear that it was these " transgressors of the Law," the Hellenistic Jews, who took the initiative in the anti-Jewish movement ; small wonder that Antiochus

[1] Cp. Dan. ix. 11 ; the book of *Daniel* was written about 166 B.C.

Epiphanes with such encouragement should have been eager to take his part.

But what we wish particularly to emphasize is that the Jews, in defence of their Law, had as their primary antagonists men of their own race. It is easy to understand how this would intensify zeal for the Law on the part of the orthodox.

To this indirect evidence for the prominence of the Law some of a more direct character may be added. In 1 *Macc.* ii. 32 ff. it is told of how a number of the loyal Jews were attacked on the Sabbath; but refusing to break the Sabbath by fighting, they willingly submitted to massacre, both they, their wives, and their children. A similar episode is recounted on the occasion of the capture of Jerusalem by Ptolemy I Soter, in 321 B.C., though not so tragic; being a Sabbath the orthodox Jews made no resistance, and were carried away captive to Egypt.[1]

A more vigorous championship of the Law is recorded in 1 *Macc.* ii. 42 ff. : " Then were gathered unto them a company of the Chassidim, mighty men of Israel, everyone that offered himself willingly for the Law. . . . And Mattathias and his friends went round about, and pulled down the altars ; and they circumcized by force the children that were uncircumcized, as many as they found in the coasts of Israel. . . . And they rescued the Law out of the hand of the Gentiles. . . ."

This will suffice to show the position which the Law had come to hold towards the middle of the second century B.C.

3. THE NEW TESTAMENT

Religious freedom and political independence were the final results of the Maccabæan struggle. Religious freedom meant the unrestricted sway of the Law. The foremost champions of the Law during this struggle had been the *Chassidim* (1 *Macc.* ii. 42–8) ; when religious

---

[1] Edwyn Bevan, *The Ptolemaic Dynasty*, p. 24 (1927) ; see also Reinach, *Textes d'auteurs grecs et romains relatifs au Judaisme*, p. 43 (1895).

freedom had been gained they withdrew from further participation in the struggle, for they were indifferent to the question of political independence (1 *Macc.* vii. 10 ff.). Therefore we hear nothing more of them until the struggle is over. When next they appear, under the high-priesthood of John Hyrcanus (135–104 B.C.), it is with the name of Pharisees ; and they are now no longer supporters of the Maccabæan or Hasmonæan [1] dynasty ; for the High-priest had become much more a political than a religious leader, and consequently lax regarding the Law ; whereas the Pharisees, in conformity with their tradition, made the Law the centre of all their activity. It is, thus, at this time that the Pharisees first appear as a distinct party ; and they are opposed to the High-priestly or Sadducæan party, so-called from the claim of the High-priest to be descended from Zadok the priest (1 Kings i. 26 ff.) ; this was the ruling, and therefore the aristocratic, party. To the Pharisaic party belonged the Scribes,[2] as was natural enough, for upon them had long devolved the duty of both copying out the Law and explaining it, and from their explanations of the Written Law grew the Oral Law.

The Pharisees had the bulk of the people on their side, and exercised a great influence upon them ; Josephus tells us further that, "they delivered to the people a great many observances by succession from their fathers, which are not written in the laws of Moses."

Some of the results of this influence and of the development of the Law, here clearly pointed to by Josephus, are dealt with in the New Testament ; to this we must now devote a little attention.

The main tendency in this development was that the observance of legal precepts came to be looked upon as meritorious. The merit acquired by observing the details of the Law's requirements justified a man in the sight of God, and thus constituted a claim for reward.

---

[1] Asmonæus, or Hasmonæus, was the name of the ancestor of the family.

[2] "Scribes of the Sadducees" are, however, not unknown entirely, e.g. Josephus, *Antiq.* XIII. x. 6 ; and the Scribes and High-priests are coupled together both in *Mark* and *Luke* several times, which would seem to point to Sadducæan scribes.

It followed logically that the attainment of salvation was a matter of purely human effort. Belief in divine grace was, of course, not absent ; but the sense of justification felt by a zealous observer of the Law had the effect of obscuring the fact of the initial divine guidance ; and in practice the fulfilment of works of the Law came to be looked upon as the means of salvation.

Much of the teaching of Christ, as well as of St. Paul, is directed against this false estimate of the Law. A few examples must be offered.

The harm done to spiritual religion by observing precepts of the Law for the sake of gaining glory from men (Matt. vi. 1–18) was serious enough ; but the claim of reward from God because of the fulfilment of works of the Law was clearly a more subtle danger ; and the evidence afforded in the New Testament of this development is overwhelming. No more illuminating illustration of the way in which our Lord sought to counteract it could be given than the parable of the Labourers in the Vineyard (Matt. xx. 1–16). The immediate cause of its utterance was St. Peter's words : " Lo, we have left all, and followed thee ; what then shall we have ? " (Matt. xix. 27). The mental attitude which prompted this was precisely the same as that of the legalist who, having acquired merit by carrying out the precepts of the Law, believed himself entitled to claim a reward from God. Without going into the details of the parable, the significance of its teaching may be briefly pointed out :

The householder is entirely independent as regards each individual labourer, and therefore the fact of his seeking them to work in his vineyard is an act of grace on his part. In order to emphasize that it *is* an act of grace he goes out at various hours of the day to offer the advantage of employment to other labourers who would otherwise have nothing to do. " Why stand ye here all the day idle ? They say unto him, Because no man hath hired us." When the time for payment comes and some of the labourers claim more because of their longer hours of work, the householder shows them that their claim is not justified in the words : " Is it not lawful for me to do what I will with mine own ? " The reference is not so much to the amount of wages paid, as to the fact of paying any wages at all, i.e. of taking them into his service ; for it was that which constituted an act of grace on the part of the householder.   The claim for more implied a right on account of work done, whereas the possibility of doing any work at all was the result of an act of grace ; and the same applied to all ; hence, " the last shall be first, and the first last."

The same teaching underlies the parable of the Pharisee and the Publican (Luke xviii. 9–14), and is contained in the words, " When ye shall have done all the things that are commanded you, say, we are unprofitable servants ; we have done that which it was our duty to do " (Luke xvii. 10).   Further illustrations could, of course, be given.

Similarly St. Paul combats again and again the doctrine of justification by the works of the Law and what this implied ; e.g. : " By the works of the Law shall no flesh be justified in his sight " (Rom. iii. 20) ; " . . . A man is not justified by the works of the Law " (Gal. ii. 16) ; " Not of works, that no man should glory " (Eph. ii. 9) ; and elsewhere.

No doubt this development had begun to take place long previously, but we do not get such pointed evidence both of the development and of its effects as is given in the New Testament.

4. THE MISHNAH

It will be worth giving here a quotation from the great mediæval Jewish teacher Maimonides (he died in A.D. 1204), for his words represent the Jewish belief regarding the Oral Law from, at the least, the second century B.C.   It is taken from the Preface to his work called *Yad ha-chazakah* (" The Strong Hand ") :

" All the commandments which were given to Moses on Sinai were given with their interpretation ; for it is said (Exod. xxiv. 12), ' And I will give thee the tables of stone, and the *Torah* (Law), and the *Mitzwah* (Commandment) ; *Torah :* that is, the Written Law ; *Mitzwah :* that is, its interpretation.   He commanded us to observe the *Torah* in accordance with the *Mitzwah*.   And this *Mitzwah* is called the ' Oral Law.'   Moses our teacher wrote down the whole Law with his own hand before he died . . . the *Mitzwah*, that is, the interpretation of the Law, he did not write down, but he commanded it to the Elders, and to Joshua, and to the rest of Israel ; for it is written, ' All the words which I have commanded you, these shall ye observe and do " (Deut. xii. 28). And therefore this is called the ' Oral Law.' "

This is based in the first instance on the opening words of the Mishnah tractate, *Pirqe Abóth* (" the Sections, or ' Sayings,' of the Fathers "), viz. : " Moses received (the) *Torah* from Sinai, and he delivered it to Joshua ; and Joshua (delivered it) to the Elders ; and the Elders (delivered it) to the Prophets ; and the Prophets delivered it to the men of the Great Synagogue." Here *Torah* (" Law)," written without the definite article, includes the entire body of divine laws, both written and oral, i.e. the Pentateuch and what is described, e.g. in Mark vii. 3, as " the tradition of the Elders." The Great Synagogue was, according to Jewish tradition, founded by Ezra ; the basis of the tradition is in all probability the assembly spoken of in Neh. viii.–x. It is mentioned here for the first time ; and as neither Philo nor Josephus makes any allusion to it, one must regard it as extremely doubtful whether this Great Synagogue ever existed.

The Mishnah is a Hebrew word which comes from the root meaning " to repeat " ; then it is extended to mean " to learn " or " to teach " by repetition ; thus " Mishnah " came to have the sense of teaching by (oral) repetition.

In its present form the Mishnah embraces earlier compilations ; it is due to the work of Rabbi Judah ha-Nasi, " the Prince," the date being approximately A.D. 200. In it we are enabled to see the full development of the Law, though even this great collection of traditional legal material does not profess to be exhaustive ; for, as Schechter says, it was compiled " not with the purpose of providing the nation with a legal code, but with the intention of furnishing them with a sort of thesaurus, incorporating such portions of the traditional lore as he [i.e. Rabbi Judah] considered most important." [1]

---

[1] In Hastings' *Dictionary of the Bible*, v. 61*b*.

To give a real insight into the way in which the developments of the Law as here presented would be out of place and beyond the scope of the present volume ; for this we must refer our readers to some of the tractates translated into English and published by the S.P.C.K.[1]

This brief survey shows, then, that the Law became the most important element in Judaism. As compared with that zenith of Hebrew Religion presented by the teaching of Deutero-Isaiah this supremacy of the Law cannot but strike one as having been a religious evolutionary process in a less exalted direction. But while we feel this to be the case, justice demands that we should recognize what was the underlying motive-power in that exaltation of the Law. It was always taught that it was by means of the Law that God revealed Himself to His people ; in it the Divine mind was believed to be reflected, in it the Divine will was believed to be stated ; therefore the Law was inseparable from God. This conviction is illustrated by the following beautiful little parable :

"It is as though a king had an only daughter ; and one of the kings comes and marries her. He [the latter] then wants to return to his own country and to take his wife back with him. Then the king says to him : ' She whom I have given to thee is my only daughter ; I cannot bear to be separated from her ; yet I cannot say, Take her not, for she is thy wife. But show me this kindness,—wherever thou goest prepare me a chamber that I may dwell with you, for I cannot bear to be separated from my daughter.' Thus spake the Holy One to Israel : ' I gave you the *Torah* ; I cannot separate myself from it ; yet I cannot say to you, Take it not. But whithersoever ye journey make me a house wherein I may dwell.' For it is said : *And let them make me a sanctuary that I may dwell among them* " (Exod. xxv. 8).[2]

---

[1] *Translations of Early Documents*, Series III, Rabbinic Texts.
[2] *Shemoth Rabba* 33, quoted by Weber, *Jüdische Theologie*, p. 17 (1897).

INDEX OF SUBJECTS

INDEX OF SCRIPTURE PASSAGES

[The order of the books is that of the Hebrew Bible.]

389

Made and Printed in Great Britain
by Hazell, Watson & Viney Ltd.
London and Aylesbury